DONALD P. ELY and BARBARA B. MINOR,
Editors

EDUCATIONAL MEDIA AND TECHNOLOGY YEARBOOK

1992

VOLUME 18

Published in Cooperation with the
ERIC® Clearinghouse on Information Resources
and the
Association for Educational Communications
and Technology

1992

Libraries Unlimited, Inc. • Englewood, Colorado

LIBRARIES UNLIMITED, INC.
P.O. Box 6633
Englewood, CO 80155-6633

Library of Congress Cataloging-in-Publication Data

Suggested Cataloging:

Educational media and technology yearbook,
    1992 volume 18 / Donald P. Ely and Barbara B. Minor, editors. —
    Englewood, Colo.: Libraries Unlimited, 1992.
    xi, 369 p. 17x25 cm.
    Includes bibliographical references and index.
    ISBN 1-56308-015-X (1992 edition)
    ISSN 8755-2094
    Published in cooperation with the ERIC Clearinghouse on Information
Resources and the Association for Educational Communications and
Technology.
    1. Educational technology—yearbooks. 2. Instructional materials
centers—yearbooks. I. ERIC Clearinghouse on Information Resources.
II. Association for Educational Communications and Technology.
III. Ely, Donald P. IV. Minor, Barbara B.
LB 1028.3.E372   1992   370.778

EDUCATIONAL MEDIA AND TECHNOLOGY YEARBOOK

Contents

Part Three
CURRENT DEVELOPMENTS

Part Four
THE PROFESSIONAL LITERATURE

Part Five
LEADERSHIP PROFILES

Part Six
ORGANIZATIONS AND ASSOCIATIONS
IN NORTH AMERICA

Part Seven
GRADUATE PROGRAMS

Part Eight
MEDIAGRAPHY: PRINT AND NONPRINT RESOURCES

Preface

The day had finally come. The shelves were full and, if room were to be made for new, up-to-date acquisitions, some books would have to go. And there they were, past volumes of the *Educational Media and Technology Yearbook* (and its predecessor title, the *Educational Media Yearbook*). Seventeen years of history; organizations come and gone; new and defunct master's and doctoral programs and articles on the hot topics of the year. These were contemporary histories of people and movements that spanned almost two decades. Now what would be the decision? Save precious shelf space for outdated books, or preserve snippets of the field's history? Our decision was to *save* them because there is no other systematic effort to document the developments in the field of educational technology from year to year.

These volumes are a tribute to Dr. James W. Brown, the first editor, and the others who followed him: Dr. Elwood Miller, Dr. Brenda Branyan-Broadbent, and Dr. Kent Wood. The original vision came from Brown, whose name is quickly associated with the classic textbook, *AV Instruction: Technology, Media and Methods* by Brown, Lewis, and Harcleroad. Six editions from 1964 to 1983 made it the most frequently used textbook of the time. Brown was a past president of the Association for Educational Communications and Technology (AECT) when it was called the Department of Audiovisual Instruction (DAVI) of the National Education Association, and for many years was associated with the very fine academic program in the field at San Jose State University. His efforts led to this annual publication that is a chronicle of the field's growth from 1974 on. That concept continues in this edition. It is fitting that AECT is a co-sponsor of the *Yearbook* and maintains a prominent position in contributing to its content.

The tradition established by Jim Brown continues with the new editors. We will document current developments in the field of educational media and technology in North America and provide a current listing and background information about the organizations, agencies, colleges, and universities that are serving the field in a variety of ways. We will also include, in each edition, an up-to-date "mediagraphy"—a term coined by Jim Brown that never quite caught on. (It has not found a place in the *Thesaurus of ERIC Descriptors!*) The concept here was that this listing of current resources should provide comprehensive coverage of new information, regardless of the medium in which it was stored. We have tried to maintain the basic intent, but seem to find much more in print than in other formats. Perhaps this coverage will change over time.

In the 18th edition, we begin with a content analysis of the 1991 literature of the field that yields a series of trends. The article, written by one of the editors, also lists some longer term trends that draw on the literature of the past four years. The trend articles will continue in the future to help trace the strands of new developments in the field. Richard Clark reconsiders some of his positions on the role of media in teaching and learning. He has not changed his basic position that it is the *context* of use rather than the medium that determines its effectiveness, but he has mellowed in his interpretations. Fred Saba reviews some of the new developments in telecommunications that directly influence instructional design and delivery. A new doctoral program in instructional technology at the University of Northern Colorado is described by Ed Caffarella, the architect of the program. It reflects a cutting-edge approach to the way people are trained at advanced levels for service in the field. Michael Molenda delves into the school restructuring movement to articulate his impressions regarding the place of educational technology in these new developments that promise some drastic changes in education. When *The Evolution of American Educational Technology* appeared last year, a roomful of professionals appeared at the AECT session where the book was reviewed by Robert Reiser and Gerald Torkelson. Paul Saettler reacted to their critiques and fielded questions from the multitude. The reviews by Reiser and Torkelson and the rebuttal by Saettler are included in this volume.

In an attempt to highlight the contributions of leaders in the field, this edition features articles on Charles F. Schuller, written by Kent L. Gustafson; Robert Gagné, written by Robert Morgan; and Robert Heinich, written by Michael Molenda. The history of any field is a story of people and these people have made significant contributions to educational media and technology. Recognition of these contributions is in order.

The editors are eager to know what you think of this edition. Is it useful? Is it unique? Does it read well? We are open to your suggestions (and, where appropriate, corrections of inaccurate information). Let us hear from you. This is your *Yearbook*. When you look at your previous editions on the shelf and ask whether they should remain, we hope that your decision, like ours, will be to keep them as a living history of our field.

Donald P. Ely
Barbara B. Minor

Contributors to the
Educational Media and Technology Yearbook 1992

Edward P. Caffarella
Educational Technology
Division of Research, Evaluation and
    Development
University of Northern Colorado
Greeley, CO 80639

Richard E. Clark
University of Southern California
Room 801, WPH
University Park
Los Angeles, CA 90089

Lydia Doty
200 East 43rd Street
Austin, TX 78751

Kent L. Gustafson, Professor
University of Georgia
College of Education
Department of Instructional Technology
607 Alderhold Hall
Athens, GA 30602

Bobbie L. Kamil, Executive Director
Cable in the Classroom
1900 North Beauregard Street,
    Suite 108
Alexandria, VA 22311

Michael H. Molenda, Associate Professor
Instructional Systems Technology
Indiana University
School of Education
W. W. Wright Education Building
3rd and Jordan
Bloomington, IN 47405

Robert M. Morgan, Director
Learning Systems Institute
Florida State University
206 Dodd Hall
Tallahassee, FL 32306

Nancy Preston, User Services Coordinator
ERIC Clearinghouse on Information
    Resources
030 Huntington Hall
Syracuse University
Syracuse, NY 13244-2340

Farhad Saba
Department of Educational Technology
College of Education
San Diego State University
San Diego, CA 92182-0311

Howard Troutner
ADCIS Conference Manager
Suite 199
1121 Worthington Woods Boulevard
Worthington, OH 43085

Part One
Trends and Issues

Trends in Educational Technology 1991

Donald P. Ely
Professor
Instructional Design, Development, and Evaluation;
Associate Director
ERIC Clearinghouse on Information Resources
School of Education
Syracuse University
Syracuse, New York

with
Anne Foley
Wendy Freeman
Nancy Scheel
Graduate Students
Instructional Design, Development, and Evaluation
Syracuse University

INTRODUCTION

There are many ways in which trends could be identified: expert opinion, panels of specialists, or informed observation. This study chose content analysis as the primary vehicle for determining trends, based on earlier works of Naisbitt (1982) and his model (Janowitz 1976). The basic premise of these works is that current trends can best be determined by what people are saying publicly, through newspapers and magazines. Naisbitt used actual counts of linear inches in key periodicals to determine trends. This study, and the two that preceded it, used the same basic procedure: the identification of emerging topics in key publications over a period of one year. The rationale seems sound; it is possible to determine trends by considering what people are saying publicly about matters within the field. There may be other trends that can be determined by such methods as counting sales of products or discovering where professionals are being placed and analyzing what they are doing. We chose to use the literature of the field as the best comprehensive coverage of current thinking and events in the field. We carefully reviewed a selected body of literature using a team of educational technology specialists to help determine the status of the field today and, perhaps, to indicate where it might be headed in the future.

A consistent methodology has been used from year to year. Basically, it has followed the general principles of content analysis, using a group of trained coders who made independent judgments about the literature being reviewed. Group discussion about findings had to reach a high interrater reliability for each item before it was placed in an agreed-upon category. The recording units remained constant (for the most part) each year. Some additional subcategories were required to reach a higher level of specificity.

While reading this study, one must be careful not to extrapolate the trends too far into the future. It is often tempting to use trends as predictors of future developments. Actually, they are more like indicators that foreshadow the future. They are statements of current happenings in the field and, as such, must be considered tentative movements that will bear watching as time goes on. They are useful because they represent current public statements of many professionals that have been systematically analyzed and reported.

LITERATURE SOURCES

To maintain consistency from year to year, the same sources of information were used as in the 1988 and 1989 studies, with a few exceptions. To aid in the selection of sources, the Moore and Braden (1988) report, "Prestige and Influence in the Field of Educational Technology," was used. This source reported the people, publications, and institutions of "high prestige" that were identified by a survey of personnel in the field. The highest ranking journals and the dissertations produced by the universities that ranked the highest served as two major sources of literature. Additional sources of data were the papers given at major national and international conferences and the input to the ERIC database in the field of educational technology. Conferences are one of the most visible ways of presenting new ideas and findings to colleagues and therefore contribute to the trends. The ERIC system solicits unpublished materials such as reports, evaluations, studies, and papers for review and, following evaluative criteria, selects the best for inclusion in the database. The Clearinghouse on Information Resources is responsible for the field of educational technology; therefore, documents selected from that source are likely to represent current developments in the field. The sources are presented in Figure 1.

Journals

British Journal of Educational Technology (United Kingdom)
Education and Training Technology International (United Kingdom)
    [Note: a replacement for the *Journal of Instructional Develop-
    ment*, which ceased publication in 1989]
Educational Technology
Educational Technology Research and Development
    [Note: a merger of the *Journal of Instructional Development*
    and *Educational Communication and Technology Journal*, both
    of which were analyzed separately in 1988]
TechTrends

Dissertation Sources

Arizona State University
Florida State University
Indiana University
Syracuse University
University of Southern California

(Figure 1 continues on page 3.)

Conferences

Association for Educational Communications and Technology
Educational Technology International Conference (United Kingdom)
National Society for Performance and Instruction

ERIC Input

All documents in the field of Educational Technology entered into the
ERIC system

Figure 1. Content Sources

The journal *Education and Training Technology International* was chosen to replace
the *Journal of Instructional Development* and to provide a greater international perspective on the literature. All journals were published between October 1990 and September
1991. The conferences were held in 1991. The ERIC documents were entered into the
system between October 1, 1990, and September 30, 1991.

LEADING TOPICS

From the reviews of four coders, who discussed more than 1,300 items, came a list of
"topics" that were most frequently presented in the literature. That list, together with the
1988 and 1989 numbers, is presented as Table 1.

Table 1.

Rank Order of Content Analysis Categories

	1991	1989	1988
Instructional processes	1	1	1
Management	2	3	4
Technological developments	3	2	3
Research/theory	4	8	8
The field	5	4	5
Services	6	5	6
Society and culture	7	7	7
Personnel	8	6	2

Each of the categories has a series of subtopics (or recording units) that attempt to identify content more specifically. These subcategories help develop the themes that eventually get translated into trends. Table 2 shows the top 13 recording units, with subcategories as appropriate.

Table 2.

Rank Order of Top 13 Recording Units

	1991	1989	1988
Design and development (includes message design, product development, individual differences)	203	259	448
Implementation	146	98	24
Evaluation (includes process evaluation, product evaluation, cost/benefit)	144	99	97
Research/theory	91	38	51
Distance education	88	81	61
Status	80	95	61
Computer-related	65	90	82
Telecommunications	59	71	14
Curriculum support	51	79	25
Society and culture	45	71	72
Interactive learning	41	83	29
Artificial intelligence/expert systems	35	46	31
Logistics	3	32	43
Others	265	387	228
TOTAL	1,316	1,514	1,338

The recording units offered a first indicator of trends. Further analysis of each category and subcategory revealed sharper distinctions. At this point the key literature was added to the mix. *Key literature* included policy papers, reports, and statistical data for each topic area that were published during the time period of the study. This literature came from professional associations representing large numbers of people within and outside the field of educational technology, state and national governmental agencies that speak with some authority, organizations of policymakers, and business/industry sources. This information, together with the content of the literature reviewed, was studied by the author of this article, who, using personal observations (probably with some personal biases), drafted the trends and sent them for further discussion to the individuals who reviewed and categorized the literature. A copy of the draft was sent for review to a recognized professional in the field and to a reviewer in the Office of Educational Research and Improvement of the U.S. Department of Education. Changes were made when compelling arguments were presented.

CONCERNS ABOUT PREVIOUS STUDIES

As past editions of the *Trends and Issues* publications have been read and critiqued, four concerns have been expressed. These were addressed before the 1991 version was prepared. The first whether content analysis is effective for large bodies of text; the second, the validity and reliability of coding; the third, the selection of the documents reviewed; and the fourth, the translation of quantitative content data into descriptive trends. Each of these concerns is addressed here.

Content Analysis of Large Bodies of Data

Conventional content analysis looks at words and phrases in an effort to "tease out" substantive meanings. The approach followed here uses complete journal articles, doctoral dissertation abstracts, conference program descriptions, and ERIC document input. Weber, in a new monograph on content analysis, says:

> Large portions of text, such as paragraphs and complete texts, usually are more difficult to code as a unit than smaller portions, such as words and phrases, because large units typically contain more information and a greater diversity of topics. Hence they are more likely to present coders with conflicting cues (Weber 1990, 16).

In following the "large portions of text" approach, the findings of this study must be tempered by Weber's caution. He also points out that "[t]here is no simple *right* way to do content analysis. Instead, investigators must judge what methods are most appropriate for their substantive problems" (1990, 13). If there is some flaw in the approach used here, it has been consistent from year to year. Analyzing the periodical and document literature for a specified period of time still seems to be a useful procedure to identify the general trends or emphases that come from the literature of that period. Much of the value comes from the consistency of recording thematic units that have been used over the past four years.

The Validity and Reliability of Coding

The concern here is the stability, reproducibility, and accuracy of the coding process (Krippendorff 1980, 130-54). Weber (1990, 15) says: "Classification by multiple human coders permits the quantitative assessment of achieved reliability." Each year graduate students in educational technology are trained as coders. Definitions of categories are given together with practice items for each document type. The author provides consistency in reviewing by serving as an additional coder each year. The criteria level for intercoder reliability in 1991 was .75; that is, three of the four coders had to agree upon a category for placement of each item.

Content Selection

Journals, conference programs, doctoral dissertations, and ERIC documents constitute a broad range of the literature generated by the field each year. There seems to be no stronger argument than that the content appearing during any given year is what professionals in the field are saying; hence, content units that can be counted provide a reasonable representation of the topics or themes that are emerging. One must be careful not to use these topics as *projections*, since they represent what *has* already happened.

In selecting the journals, conferences, and universities, questions may arise such as, "Why these and not others?" The decision was based on the survey by Moore and Braden (1988) that reported the most prestigious journals and university programs. Beyond this criterion was another that eliminated journals or conferences devoted to a specific medium, such as computers in education. If articles about computing were found in the general literature, they were counted. However, a journal or conference devoted entirely to a subfield within educational technology would skew the findings toward one medium.

Translation of Data into Trends

This is a subjective step and probably the most difficult to defend, as it ultimately relies on the judgment of one person. The numbers of articles, conference papers, dissertations, and ERIC documents report the volume of information about specific topics by category. These numbers are then the basis for identification of the most frequent topics. The topics are the basis for selecting confirming topics in the policy literature. *Policy literature* includes statements, reports, "white" papers, and other official publications of professional organizations, government agencies, and influential bodies such as foundations and think tanks. For each of the leading trends, the policy literature is searched for supporting statements to support the dominant trends. For example, in the past the study team has used publications of the Office of Technology Assessment of the U.S. Congress, the National Governors' Association publications about education, publications of the U.S. Department of Education's Office of Educational Research and Improvement (OERI), and publications of the various educational laboratories and research and development centers funded by OERI. Public statements and reports of the National Education Association and the American Federation of Teachers are used, as are the publications of the Association for Educational Communications and Technology. Quantitative data from Quality Education Data and Market Data Retrieval provide consistent, reliable trend information on hardware and software. When the dominant themes from the primary literature sources are verified by policy statements from responsible organizations, trends are confirmed and provide a reasonable rationale.

Summary

Trends do not flow fully developed from the literature. Using a content analysis procedure that goes beyond the conventional word-and-phrase approach, the magnitudes of general themes in the annual literature of educational technology are identified, counted, and verified by the policy literature. The translation from quantitative summaries to qualitative trend statements is mostly subjective in nature.

CONTEXT

This publication should answer the question, "Where is educational technology headed?" Technology does not move alone, apart from the society in which it exists. Information and communication technologies are being used in the home and workplace at all levels — local, state, regional, national, and international. To separate them from the context is to highlight the products rather than their uses and impact. Therefore, much of the discussion in this article involves the total fabric of technology in society rather than technology as an entity in itself. Technology is often referred to as a "tool" that incorporates the "media" of communication. The hardware and systems that carry information are often the primary focus, with little attention paid to the audience, purpose, and consequences of their use. Design, development, evaluation, and diffusion are lost by the overpowering influence of hardware and software.

It is clear that educational technology is frequently used in the local school and, increasingly, in the home. Within the school, college, or university, the individual teacher or professor is the single most important factor leading to appropriate implementation of media and technology for learning. That key individual is usually part of a system which, in turn, is connected to a larger unit — a state department of education or a university. National programs and initiatives are somewhat remote. International efforts seem even more distant.

Since the last study of *Trends and Issues*, there have been major national and international efforts to explore and promote the use of educational technology in the schools. In the United States, *America 2000* has been launched to focus attention on educational goals for the nation's schools. The New American Schools Development Corporation has been established as a further effort to build schools in visible locations where citizens can see educational restructuring, much of it enhanced by technology. The National Governors' Association continues to monitor programs in all the states, with technology in the schools as one major focus.

A report of the International Association for the Evaluation of Educational Achievement, *The Use of Computers in Education Worldwide* (Pelgrum and Plomp 1991), contains findings from a major survey of 19 countries worldwide. The ministers of education from 27 European states met to discuss *Education and the Information Society: A Challenge for European Policy* (Eraut 1991). This meeting was "the response of European education systems to the development of an 'information society' " (p. ix). The World Conference on Distance Education, held in Caracas, Venezuela, in October 1990, attracted the largest number of participants ever. Much of distance education is dependent upon educational technology applications. Educational technology has become more global than ever before.

One of the major outcomes of these efforts is linkage, between the schools and other entities, that has not been evident in previous times. *Networking* is being used as the code word for the many connections that are being made, most of them new. Networking by definition is the linkage made between and among people held together by a common theme or connection. The means for networking use both new and existing systems that permit real-time, live interaction between individuals and groups: telephone, Fax, E-mail, computers, and cable and satellite television, as well as face-to-face and traditional correspondence approaches. Other systems store information for use at a chosen time: videotape recordings, videodiscs, CD-ROM discs, floppy discs, and audiocassettes. It is easy to be enthusiastic about these new media (and they dominate the literature), but voices of concern about cost, equity of access, skills required, and purpose still are heard and will have to be heeded.

Networks exist within a school; within a school system; within a region; within a state; and among the states. Networks exist between schools and business; schools and government agencies (state and federal); schools and universities; schools and public libraries; schools and professional associations; schools and broadcasting sources; and schools and homes. There appears to be a movement to create networks where none exist and to connect networks that already exist. Passage of the High Performance Computing Act of 1991, which authorizes the creation of the National Research and Education Network (NREN), is a significant move in this direction.

With all these contexts impinging upon educational technology, it must be remembered that the trends discussed in this article are more internal to the field than external to the settings in which they happen to reside. The literature reviewed is authored by people inside the field and the intended audience is mostly people inside the field. These are often practitioner-advocates who have agendas to promote educational technology and use publications and conferences to do so.

At the same time, there appear to be stronger calls for technology in education by groups outside education, such as state governors, business and industry executives, and newspaper education writers. The target of both the educational technologists and the influential critics seems to be mainline schools—the "establishment" that tends to perpetuate the status quo. Until there is openness to using technology among educators in general, the calls for technology in the schools will be unheeded or accepted only in marginal ways.

This study focuses primarily on the K-12 schools in the United States, although some information addresses higher and adult education. Information from other technologically advanced nations is used when appropriate. Attempts are made, whenever possible, to relate the trends to the educational goals set by the president and the nation's governors.

It should be noted that many trends in the field of educational technology are found outside the educational settings that are featured in this study. New professionals graduating from the many graduate programs in the field are being placed in business and industrial training environments. There is another body of literature, not covered in this study, that reflects the many new developments in non-school settings. That fact is, in itself, a trend.

TRENDS 1991

Using a content analysis of the 1991 educational technology literature, the following trends have emerged.

Trend 1

The creation of technology-based teaching/learning products is based largely upon instructional design and development principles.

There appears to be more evidence that materials developed for the purpose of teaching and learning use design principles that have their roots in cognitive psychology and instructional science. More than 15 percent of the items reviewed for this year's study were devoted to design and development. Major subheadings included message design, product development, individual differences, and course development. Less prominent were needs assessment and task analysis. Further, models and theories in support of specific design and development approaches are being proposed and hold a substantial place in the literature.

The term *constructivism* appears with increasing frequency. At least two major sessions at the 1991 conference of the American Educational Research Association were devoted to the topic, and two special issues of *Educational Technology* focused on constructivism. The concept of constructionism (now called constructivism) was first proposed by Bruner in the mid-1960s and builds on earlier ideas of Piaget. Basically, it holds that the learner rather than the teacher develops (or "constructs") knowledge and that opportunities created for such "construction" are more important than instruction that originates from the teacher. This line of reasoning supports the work of Papert and other Logo advocates. It is fully explained in a new work, *Constructionism*, edited by Idit Harel and Seymour Papert (1991). The debate, which focuses on constructivism and educational technology, is thoroughly discussed in the special issue of *Educational Technology*, which was edited by Tom Duffy and David Jonassen (1991). The authors take sides for or against constructivism; those who are more negative toward the concept seem to emphasize the design element of instruction as a more appropriate position. Some authors would like to choose sides based on specific goals rather than on firmly held positions regarding constructivism or instructionism.

As more research on screen design is reported, designers and developers are beginning to incorporate findings into teaching/learning products. The traditional concepts of message design, which follow earlier research in perception psychology, are being enhanced by new efforts aimed at the individual learner using a display surface, usually a computer monitor (visual display unit).

Trend 2

Evaluation has taken on greater importance as the concept of performance technology has been further developed.

More than 10 percent of the 1991 literature was concerned with some aspect of evaluation: process evaluation, product evaluation, cost-effectiveness assessments, and formative evaluation. *Performance technology* is appearing more frequently in the literature as a descriptor for instructional design and delivery that works. It is being used more in business-industry-government settings than in school and college environments. It is based on the conviction that training does not necessarily solve all performance problems in an organization. Rather, personnel selection, assignment, motivation, and environmental characteristics are as likely to be critical factors, as is a need for more information.

Other contributions from the 1991 educational technology literature that feature evaluation seem to stress outcomes for decision making rather than for information alone — the evaluation versus research question. Topics that once would have been studied using a research approach are now being evaluated. Evaluation is becoming a more important aspect of educational technology than ever before.

Another dimension of evaluation is *product evaluation*, the assessment of instructional materials that have been recently produced and have some potential use in other settings. As more software for microcomputers has been created, evaluations have been published in journals and by organizations that recommend instructional resources to schools, such as the Educational Products Information Exchange (EPIE). *Only the Best: The Annual Guide to Highest-Rated Education Software, Preschool-Grade 12* (Neill and Neill 1990) uses 37 "respected" education evaluation services in the United States and Canada and requires software to receive two "excellent" grades or one "excellent" and three "good/favorable" grades to be published in this annual sourcebook.

Typically, evaluation has been an add-on or afterthought in the field of educational technology. As more emphasis is placed on instructional design, it is becoming an integral part of the process and, as such, is often an ongoing part of the larger process.

Trend 3

> The number of educational technology case studies is growing and provides
> general guidance for potential users.

More than 11 percent of the literature reported on specific use of media and technology in teaching/learning settings. Almost all the case studies were "successful" and many could serve as models for potential users. Very few reported failure or negative outcomes. About one-half of all the case studies related to computer use in teaching and learning. Less than one-half reported on the use of telecommunications. There were almost no cases of traditional media use or instructional procedures that have been proven in the past.

In making the content analysis, the key words were *diffusion* and *implementation*. Almost all the case studies in this category emphasized implementation. Implementation not only means that educational technology ideas have been diffused and accepted, but that there has been actual use of new media or technology in an educational setting.

The results of case studies are not always fully documented. Most of them are not experimental in nature. Therefore, it is difficult to generalize about the outcomes, because they vary in substance and in presentation. However, a closer analysis of these items could create some general principles for others in similar circumstances to follow.

Trend 4

> Distance education is evident at almost every educational level in almost every
> sector.

Distance education (or distance learning) has become a major instructional force in American education. A recent estimate is that 25 to 50 percent of the nation's students are reached by distance learning technology ("Wade right in" 1991). The National Governors' Association reported that "virtually all states" use distance learning (National Governors' Association 1991). Distance education provides systematic instruction to individual learners who are physically separated from teachers. The delivery of instruction is usually by telecommunications and computer hardware and software, although not always. Learners sometimes work independently and sometimes in small groups.

A database of distance learning projects compiled by the U.S. Department of Education (Garnette and Withrow 1990) reveals more than 100 projects that involve "live, real-time interactivity between student(s) and their teacher ... in elementary and secondary school." The authors state that "specific projects were noted in 37 states [and] there appear[s] to be distance learning activities under way in every state with the exception of three states" (p. 520). Over 1,500 school districts are participating in some form of distance education, with some states sparsely represented and others including virtually every district. Specific numbers from the database help to illustrate the extent of impact.

- Technologies used:

Satellite	56	Coaxial cable	21
Audiographics	15	Computer-based	13
Microwave	17	Fiber optics	11

- Of those projects that offer courses for students, half offer foreign languages, one-third of the projects offer advanced mathematics, and a quarter offer at least one science course.

- Half the projects offer teacher training or staff development as one component of the project.

- Less than 25 percent of the projects have had any kind of formal evaluation.

- 40 percent of the projects were initially funded by the states.

- 20 percent of the projects involved collaboration between the school district and an outside agency such as the local telephone or cable company.

- 60 percent of the projects have been in operation since 1986.

A final note regarding the breadth and variety of projects helps to confirm the magnitude of distance education efforts. The range of participation is "from one school producing and developing its own courses using telecommunications to the 780 sites in 32 states served by the Texas Interactive Instructional Network (TI-IN)" (Garnette and Withrow 1990, 517).

State policies regarding distance education are evolving. Of particular note are the state programs in Kentucky, Oklahoma, Michigan, Minnesota, Texas, and Virginia. Also, Iowa is investing $50 million in statewide telecommunications infrastructure. Missouri is taxing videotape rentals to subsidize distance learning. Minnesota has about 30 distance learning networks with over 150 schools participating. About 40 percent of the state's low enrollment courses share the networks ("Distance learning" 1990). The University of Texas at Austin is using two-way audio communication as a cost-effective delivery system for rural school districts. Telelearning classes are "live," as teachers and students talk with each other via telephone equipment that uses multiple source input and reception, connecting all participants in a manner similar to a telephone conference call. The cost of the courses ranges from $200 to $400 per student per semester.

Many distance learning programs are couse-based; that is, they offer complete courses with the teacher in a remote location. However, some users of distance learning are using this approach as a supplement to classroom instruction to enrich learning. The Northwest Regional Educational Laboratory's *Enhancing Instruction through Telecommunications* (1991) describes federal resources in telecommunications (such as NASA's Spacelink bulletin board and satellite teleconferences); news by telecommunications (such as CNN Newsroom); and student/teacher connections by telecommunications (such as the AT&T Learning Network). Course-based distance education dominates higher education efforts.

There is probably no other single trend that encompasses the theory and practice of educational technology better than distance education. Its frequency in the literature confirms this observation.

Trend 5

> *The field of educational technology has more and better information about*
> *itself than ever before.*

Eighty surveys about various aspects of the field were reported during the timeframe of this study. For example, studies of the most frequently published textbook authors, a list of current dissertations, the extent of microcomputer penetration in the schools, and other such reports help to paint a quantitative picture of the profession. They are found most frequently in documents entered into the ERIC system, but also in journals and in conference presentations. Only one dissertation in 1991 was devoted to status.

These are reports of studies in which professionals are looking at themselves and the activities or facilities they administer. They tend to count things, people, and activities. They survey the state of the art in reference to a specific topic, as in Gustafson's *Survey of Instructional Development Models* (1991).

This trend also includes special publications about the field itself, usually by organizations with specialized interest in development and advancement of the field. Paul Saettler's *Evolution of American Educational Technology* (1991) is one such publication. This volume is the most comprehensive history of the field ever written. It goes beyond the events of the past and looks into the 1990s and beyond. The final chapter in this nearly 600-page volume covers state-of-the-art sections on instructional television, computer-assisted instruction (CAI), CAI software, instructional theory and design, interactive multimedia systems, and intelligent tutoring systems, and offers future prospects for the field. The International Society for Technology in Education (ISTE) published *Vision:TEST (Technologically Enriched Schools of Tomorrow)* (Braun 1990) as a set of recommendations to the profession and to other professional educators regarding the future of education in America and the potential role of technology in that future. The staff for the study consulted some 200 experts and visited 45 schools nationwide to find examples of teachers producing dramatic educational improvements through technology. The *Educational Media and Technology Yearbook* (Branyan-Broadbent and Wood 1991), published in cooperation with the Association for Educational Communications and Technology (AECT), reviews events of the year, reports on educational technology activities in the states, lists organizations and associations in the field within North America, and provides an updated list of graduate programs in the field.

Even with all the information published in 1991, there is still some uncertainty about the definition of the field of educational technology—what is included and what is not—and what constitute appropriate roles for personnel serving in the field. The Definition and Terminology Committee of the Association for Educational Communications and Technology will issue a report in 1992. Perhaps some of these questions will be answered at that time.

Trend 6

> *Computers are pervasive in the schools. Virtually every school in the United*
> *States has microcomputers.*

Computer applications permeated the literature of educational technology in 1991. Purposely omitted from the analysis of trends and issues were 14 journals associated with computer-assisted instruction and conferences that focused on the computer as an instructional medium. Inclusion of such works would have skewed the data sufficiently to overshadow all the other trends. Even with this omission, computers frequently emerged in the general literature, dissertations, conference programs, and ERIC input. Sometimes the items were directly focused on the use of computers in the classroom for direct subject-matter instruction, but most referred to learning about the computer as a tool. Many items discussed the resistance or "roadblocks" to the use of computers in schools.

Two organizations surveyed the schools in 1990 and 1991 to determine the quantitative state of computers (and other technologies) in the schools. Quality Education Data, Inc., Denver, Colorado, has conducted annual surveys since 1981 and includes in its most recent report (Quality Education Data 1991b) results from 83,283 elementary and secondary public schools in the United States. Market Data Retrieval's first-ever examination of emerging technologies in the education market used responses from 40,000 schools representing nearly 50 percent of the total K-12 enrollment in U.S. public schools (Market Data Retrieval 1991). The findings are not always comparable and often vary significantly. Therefore, in reporting the findings here, basic numbers, rather than percentages, are used. Since Quality Education Data (QED) reports annually and comprehensively on computers in schools, their data are used.

Microcomputer density (students per computer) has been reduced from 125:1 in 1983-1984 to 20:1 in 1990-1991. The range is from 8,858 schools with less than 9 students per computer to 7,082 schools with more than 90 students per computer. The percentage of schools with microcomputers in the United States has steadily increased for the past 10 years until it reached 98 percent in 1990-1991. QED also reports "market share" for each company: Apple (including Macintosh)—65.7 percent; IBM—14.1 percent; other MS-DOS—4.5 percent; Radio Shack—6.2 percent; Commodore—5.4 percent; other—4.2 percent. Of the 81,203 schools that have microcomputers, 34,662 have 21 or more units.

In 1991, the National Education Association embarked upon a campaign to make microcomputers available to its members (Merina 1991). The NEA EdStar computer was jointly developed by NEA and IBM. It is a special-edition IBM PS/1 with a VGA color monitor, a 30-megabyte hard disc preloaded with a computer-based grade book, a desktop publishing program, Microsoft Works, and IBM Linkway. A modem and printer are also part of the package. To make the computer package attractive to potential users, a price under $2,000 was established, with the possibility of financing for under $50 a month with no down payment. The director of NEA's Center for Innovation said, "We're not going to have computer-using teachers until teachers become computer-using people" (Merina 1991).

Universities have also been studied. The National Survey of Desktop Computing conducted by the Center for Scholarly Technology at the University of Southern California determined "that the *placement* of computers, rather than the total number, is perhaps the key variable in defining access and assessing the deployment of institutional computing resources" (Green and Eastman 1991). Access, or microcomputer density, in higher education institutions in general averages about 47:1 across all types of institutions.

A major comparative study, *The Use of Computers in Education Worldwide*, was published in 1991 by the International Association for the Evaluation of Educational Achievement (IEA). It summarizes the results of a survey of computer use in education in 19 countries (Pelgrum and Plomp 1991). Major topics in the report, too complex to present here, involve the availability of computer hardware and software, the purposes for which computers are used, staff development, attitudes of principals and teachers toward computers, and gender equity in relation to computers.

The U.S. Department of Commerce, Bureau of the Census, studied computer use in the United States in 1989 and published its report in 1991 (Kominski 1991). From the highlights of the findings, it is reported that 15 percent of all U.S. households had a computer, an increase from 8.2 percent in 1984. Among children 3 to 17 years of age, 46 percent used a computer at home or at school (or both), a rise from 30 percent in 1982. Of over 115 million employed adults, 36.8 percent said that they use a computer at work, compared with 24.6 percent in 1984. By the fall of 1989, about a third of the U.S. population (74,884,000 people) used a computer in some way (Kominski 1991).

All the surveys and statistics do not point to the *purpose* of computer use. In a preliminary paper for the IEA study, Plomp and Pelgrum (1990) discovered that the types of software programs most commonly used by teachers in the United States were: (1) word processing (93 percent); (2) drill and practice (92 percent); (3) educational games (91 percent); and (4) tutorial programs (81 percent). A study of computer-using teachers who have integrated computers into classroom practice discovered that software was used in the following manner: (1) text processing tools (95 percent); (2) instructional software (89 percent); (3) analytic and information tools (87 percent); (4) programming and operating systems (84 percent); (5) games and simulations (81 percent); and (6) graphics and operating tools (81 percent) (Sheingold and Hadley 1990).

As these data are considered, it would be well to recall the four major reasons for computer use in schools proposed by Hawkridge, Jaworski, and McMahon (1990):

1. *The social rationale*. Policymakers want to be sure that all children are "aware and unafraid of how computers work." Because "computers are pervading industrial societies and are likely to be important in all countries," learners should be prepared to understand computers and be aware of their role in society.

2. *The vocational rationale*. Learning to operate computers is an important competency. There will be employment opportunities for individuals who have the proper computer skills.

3. *The pedagogic rationale*. Students can learn from computers: "computers can teach." There are advantages over other traditional methods in using computers to learn.

4. *The catalytic rationale*. "Schools can be changed for the better by the introduction of computers." Computers facilitate change. They are symbols of progress. They encourage learning. "Computers are seen as catalysts, enabling desired change in education to occur."

One of the next steps in studying the role of the computer in education is to discover the extent and role of computers in the teaching and learning process according to the social, vocational, and pedagogic rationales. There is still very little evidence in the literature to support computer contributions to learning.

Trend 7

Telecommunications is the link that is connecting education to the world.

Telecommunications is an overarching term that describes electronic point-to-point connections between individuals and groups. Translated into electronic delivery terms, telecommunications technology includes connections that utilize existing telephone lines, dedicated lines, and cable and satellite transmission. Some messages are intended to be *interactive*, such as electronic mail (E-mail), computer conferences, and two-way audio and video conferences. Some are intended to be *one-way*, such as television directed to classrooms through cable and satellite systems. Usually broadcast radio and television are not included in the term, nor are prerecorded audio- and videotapes distributed through nonbroadcast channels.

It is clear from the 1991 literature that the term *interactive* is rapidly becoming popular, especially in relation to telecommunications. Much of the interest stems from distance education applications when computers are used to establish networks between an instructor and students or satellite television beamed to schools in a widely dispersed area. (Interactive video, another rapidly growing area, is usually not considered to be within the ambit of telecommunications, since it is usually delivered by self-standing, independent equipment. This trend is discussed in the next section.)

The dominant trend within telecommunications is *networking*, the electronic connection of individuals who have common interests. Basically, networking is conducted by electronic mail (E-mail) between one person with a computer terminal and another person with a computer terminal. Both individuals are participants in the same electronic mail system. Ehrmann (1990) describes four conversational models for networking: (1) direct instruction; (2) real-time conversation; (3) time-delayed conversation; and (4) learning by doing. Kurshaw and Harrington (1991) summarize the state of networks today:

> Technological innovations have paved the way for new communities and collaborations to develop. While the modes of conversation have remained the same, the means by which these modes of conversation are carried out have not. Today, electronically networked communities employ all of these modes of conversation with varying technological sophistication (p. 5).

Kurshaw and Harrington (1991) also list the varied purposes for networking:

- Professional collaboration

- Student collaborative investigations

- Access to experts

- Information access

- Access to resources

- Collaborative development (electronic publishing)

- Teacher enhancement

- Online courses

- Networked community support.

All these applications are visible in the current literature. Each one is usually tied to a specific network. Some use commercial information utilities, such as Compuserve and Prodigy. Others are part of education-specific networks such as AT&T Learning Network and the National Geographic Society (NGS) Kids Network. Bulletin board systems, such as FrEdMail and FIDOnet, offer message-sending and receiving capabilities at little or no cost for participation. State networks in New York (NYSERNET), Texas (TENET), and Virginia (VA.PEN) are further indicators of the rapid spread of networking within education.

At the federal level, congressional passage and presidential approval of the High-Performance Computing Act of 1991 authorizes the creation of a National Research and Education Network (NREN). The network, which has been designated America's "information superhighway," is expected to provide access to electronic information resources maintained by libraries, research facilities, publishers, schools, universities, and affiliated organizations. The intent is to improve the information, computing, and communications infrastructure for the country's researchers and educators.

The other principal dimension of telecommunications is the use of television for teaching in a variety of settings. Whether the television image in the classroom comes from a cable outlet, a satellite dish, or a videotape recording, the quality of the program is the ultimate value for teaching and learning. Much of the literature speaks of the delivery systems that are being put in place and the applications of these systems for such uses as distance education. One must remember that it is possible to record on videotape any program that comes into the school, taking into account copyright restrictions and permissions. The recording provides flexibility in use and the possibility of reuse. Most of the 1991 literature was more concerned with getting the signal to the school than with its ultimate use.

Teachers are using television. In a study by Mann (1991), 96 percent of teachers in grades 6 to 12 expressed enthusiasm for television in instruction and three out of four plan to use it more next year. About 60 percent of the schools had access to cable television, but about 45 percent of the teachers said that they had trouble getting equipment to use in the classroom. Some 56 percent of the teachers in the survey listed PBS as their prime source of programming, but there was also considerable use of CNN Newsroom (12 percent use—the most frequently used cable program), followed by A&E Classroom, Assignment Discovery, and C-Span. The subject-matter area ranked first in use was current affairs (56 percent), followed by literature (38 percent), performing arts (37 percent), and history (33 percent). One surprising finding was that one out of eight classrooms did not have an electrical outlet!

Cable and satellite delivery systems reached new heights in 1991. The cable industry established Cable in the Classroom as a national project aimed at providing all junior and senior high schools with free cable service and at least one VCR and one monitor. Through cable access, many programs are entering the classroom. A&E Classroom is a one-hour block of programming airing Monday to Friday from 7 to 8 a.m. EST. The program is divided into subject areas focusing on history, drama and novels, performing arts, biographies, and anthropology and archaeology. Assignment Discovery is delivered through the Discovery Channel from 9 to 10 a.m. every day. They report use by 438,000 teachers and viewing by over 8 million students. CNN Newsroom is a daily 15-minute news program specifically designed for school use. The Learning Channel, a 24-hour television service, offers more than 20 programs for in-school use by teachers.

Channel One remains a controversial cable service because of the commercials that accompany the daily program. In 1991, the network reached over 10,000 schools (Skelly 1991). Whittle Communications, the sponsoring organization, provides a satellite dish, two VCRs, and television monitors for each classroom. The news program is 12 minutes daily and includes 2 minutes of commercials. Various states have taken legal action to prohibit schools from signing on to the service. New York passed a law prohibiting use of Channel One in the schools. North Carolina judges ruled that the programs are supplementary and that local schools boards do have the authority to accept the program. California tried, but failed twice, "to impose an overall statewide ban on 'electronic advertising' " ("Free to Watch TV" 1991).

The Monitor Channel produces Monitor World Classroom in English and Spanish, Monday through Friday, and airs it at 4 a.m. for recording. Printed support materials for classes in geography, social studies, global issues, and international affairs are available along with complimentary copies of *The Christian Science Monitor*.

Satellite transmission is a vital link in telecommunications. A recent study of satellite dish uses in public schools (Quality Education Data 1992) reported that 33 percent of the schools in the United States have satellite dishes (27,582 out of 83,281 schools). Hawaii, Kentucky, and the District of Columbia report that all schools have satellite dishes. More than 20 states have joined the Satellite Educational Resource Consortium (SERC). The purpose of SERC is to provide credit courses that would otherwise be unavailable via satellite, microwave, or cable technology. SERC also offers inservice and graduate courses for teachers.

States seem to be the organizing units for the delivery of telecommunications technology. For example, the Massachusetts Corporation for Educational Telecommunications (MCET) operates the Mass LearnPike, a satellite and computer-based network dedicated to improving the quality of learning in the state. The Kentucky Educational Network is linked by satellite to all of its 1,300 public elementary, middle, and high schools. One person in the United States is monitoring state policy issues for telecommunications. Richard Hezel, author of two previous reports on state coordination of telecommunications for the Annenberg/CPB Project, outlines current issues in part of an excellent 1991 publication, *Education Policy and Communication Technologies* (Sheekey 1991).

Programming for telecommunications was enhanced by this year's announcement of a $60 million grant by the Annenberg Foundation to the Corporation for Public Broadcasting for a new national project designed to improve mathematics and science instruction at the elementary and secondary school levels. The project includes an array of technology-based media: computers, interactive video, laser discs, and electronic networks.

The present trends study emphasizes the use of technology in elementary and secondary education. Higher education is also active in its application of technology to education. PBS Adult Learning Service indicates that 59 percent of all colleges and universities in the United States are using telecourses. Much of the activity is based in the two-year, postsecondary institutions. The International Telecommunications Consortium, an affiliate of the American Association of Community and Junior Colleges, represents more than 400 educational institutions from the United States and Canada and sponsors professional development meetings, supports telecommunications research, and provides a forum for its members to share expertise and materials.

The many telecommunications subtrends will have to be followed individually to keep up to date with the rapidly changing technologies. The technological developments outstrip the schools' readiness to adopt them. But, as this year's report shows, much progress is being made. In light of the restructuring movement that is inherent in the *America 2000* plan, it is likely that technology will have an active role to play.

Trend 8

The teacher's role in the teaching and learning process is changing as new technologies are introduced into the classroom.

"Teachers cannot be replaced by machines!" The cry has been heard since the invention of the printing press. The implicit threat of technology overtaking the teaching function has been ever-present in the generally conservative education community. However, there have been several indicators that the tone of the protest has calmed. One major factor is the growth of distance education programs in the schools and in higher education. In many distance education programs, instruction is delivered by a medium—a teacher surrogate—that is responsible for the major portion of information presentation. Through videotapes, audiotapes, computer programs, programmed textbooks, and combinations of media, subject matter is systematically presented to the learner. Even when the teacher is remote, as in "live" telecourses, the local teacher has been replaced by the teacher at the end of the line, wherever that may be. In reality, teachers are not replaced in the literal sense; they change their role from that of a presenter of information to a coordinator of learning resources. Such a role frees the teacher to work more independently with individuals and small groups while leaving the formal presentations to another medium. When materials are designed for distance learners, the teacher subject-matter specialist is the source of the information and often the designer of the presentation.

The dream of many technologists, and those who would change the role of the teacher, has been *integrated learning systems* (ILS). Known by such trade names as Computer Curriculum Corporation and Jostens and Wicat Systems, ILSs offer comprehensive coverage in terms of lesson plans and integration of electronic media. They generally make fewer demands on the teacher than do individual programs that treat small sections of the curriculum. According to *Inventing Tomorrow's Schools*, a newsletter published by the Mecklenburger Group: "ILSs are the fastest growing segment of the educational software industry.... There are more ILS vendors now than a few years ago—and most are financially healthy—to the point that they are an 'industry' that is among the formidable forces that will shape the future of education" (Sherry 1991).

The Educational Products Information Exchange (EPIE Institute 1990) has compiled a detailed report on ILSs that includes information on vendors, program descriptions, courseware evaluation, and visits to implementing sites. Market Data Retrieval (1991) reports that ILSs are in use at more than 4,200 schools, 11 percent of the respondents in their 1991 study.

Much of the value stemming from the ILS and other technologically based learning resources is not possible until teachers are thoroughly prepared to use the new systems. Sherry (1991) ends his ILS report by saying, "ILSs have a bright future, especially as vendors and schools alike pay the necessary attention to pre-service and in-service teacher training that encourages the full use of these ever-more-sophisticated resources." Some of the same issues are addressed by the Southwest Educational Development Laboratory in its newsletter, *New Things Considered*. In the August 1990 issue, pertinent questions and concerns are raised about the new requirements for teachers. For example:

- How do we prepare teachers if the traditional capabilities and applications will no longer be necessary, and we do not know which types of knowledge will be needed instead?

- The changes have happened so fast that relatively few teachers and teacher educators have had an opportunity to become comfortable with using computers, much less other technologies. Consequently, there are few effective staff development programs to help teachers create ways to integrate technology into the curriculum ("What curriculum" 1990).

The need for teacher involvement in technology is being recognized by one of the largest teacher unions in the United States, the National Education Association. Among its adopted resolutions for 1991-1992 was a key resolution related to educational technology.

Technology in the Educational Process

The National Education Association recognizes the advancement and application of instructional technology and high-technology devices and materials that provide new opportunities for developing skills, furthering research, and expanding knowledge in our society.

The Association believes that —

a. All education employees must be afforded the opportunity to explore the potential of emerging technology.

b. Education employees should have access to necessary technology for managing and advancing instruction. Further, they should be provided encouragement, time, and resources to experiment with and to research applications of technology in order to integrate technology into the curriculum.

c. Teachers must be involved in all aspects of technology utilization including planning, implementation and evaluation.

d. Teacher preparation in instructional technology must begin in college and university programs and extend through continuing opportunities for professional development.

e. Students must become aware of the social and economic impact of technology and must be provided with access to and instruction in the use of such technology. Further, technological education programs must provide equity in training, funding, and participation for all students, regardless of age, race, gender, socioeconomic level or geographic location.

f. All students and staff should have an understanding of copyright law and the responsible use of technological materials.

g. Effective use of technology requires a licensed teacher in every classroom. Instructional technology should be used to support instruction, but not to supplant education employees (NEA 1991).

Voices from diverse sources are calling for more active roles in the use of technology in the classroom. Terrel H. Bell, Secretary of Education from 1981 to 1985, in a 1991 book, *How to Shape Up Our Nation's Schools*, makes an urgent appeal for technology in schools, according to *Washington Post* writer Brent Mitchell. He says in a September 24, 1991, article about the book: "Schools are often the only places that children do not deal with phones, computers and video players, and the book suggests these innovations could occupy one-third of a student's day and free the teacher to give other children more individualized attention." Quoting Bell, "Look at the supermarket and high tech behind the checker today.... Now look at what we are providing teachers." Such a call naturally leads to the next trend.

Trend 9

> *There is increasing pressure for the schools to consider the adoption of technology while, at the same time, concern is expressed for the impact of technology on children in the society at large.*

This trend is a two-edged sword. Pleas for the use of technology in the schools, such as those of Dr. Bell, are increasing in frequency. Simultaneously, there are cries of concern over the impact of technology, especially television, on children and youth. Each matter must be considered separately.

Continued monitoring of the National Governors' Association project, *Results in Education*, reflects progress on one of the seven major themes: technology. The 1990 report shows very little progress in the implementation of technology to bring about major changes in the schools.

> Despite the gains, technology's potential to transform and customize American classrooms remains largely unrealized. Most school districts still do not turn to technology to expand and diversify; nor has technology been integrated into the instructional practices of most classrooms. In short, little progress has been made toward the central recommendation of the task force—to use state powers to help schools reorganize, using technology and other means, so that they become more efficient and effective (p. 35).

With the numerical growth of computer and video-based technology in the schools, this observation may seem contradictory. The discrepancy is probably focused on the use of the technologies in ways that bring about dramatic and visible transformations in the schools. Use of media and technology as supplementary aids for enrichment does not improve efficiency and may have minimal impact on effectiveness.

The International Society for Technology in Education (ISTE) received a substantial grant to carry out a study of the potential that technology offers to education. One of the key purposes of the study was "to help educational decision makers identify steps they must take to create educational change in response to the charge given to them by the President and the governors" (Braun 1990, 5). The complete report, which involved more than 150 educators from all levels of education, is called *Vision:TEST (Technologically Enriched Schools of Tomorrow)*. It spells out five major recommendations, global in nature, that involve the use of technology:

1. As a nation, the United States must recognize the need for improvement in its educational system and seize the opportunities offered by technology.

2. As a nation, the United States must provide every student with the opportunity to become what each is capable of becoming. It must provide each student with an environment that is conducive to learning.

3. As a nation, the United States must empower all teachers to provide the best education for every student in their classes.

4. As a nation, the United States must redesign its school systems to prepare its students for the twenty-first century.

5. As a nation, the United States must ensure that schools are managed effectively (Braun 1990).

Another perspective, removed from the K-12 focus of this study of trends, is the use of technology for adults. Nell Eurich's book, *The Learning Society: Education for Adult Workers*, is based largely upon the use of technology to train and retrain adult workers. It reports a variety of current activities in which technology is used to make learning more efficient and effective with this special audience. She concludes that "about one-third of the work force is getting trained. That leaves the majority of workers still to be reached, but at least many adults are learning under their employers' auspices" (p. 18). In a case-study-based chapter, Eurich provides rich rationale for the use of media and technology, concluding that "the potential gain could be enormous *if* we supply content of quality for the media and select the technological means wisely for the goal" (p. 38). It is curious that technology has made more impressive gains in business and industry than in the schools.

The National Engineering Consortium released the findings of a study on the usage, value, and needs of technology in education in *Educational Technology in Kindergarten through Twelfth Grades* (Janowiak 1990). This highly media-specific study found that videodisc and interactive multimedia systems were the most promising new technologies, while more "traditional" technologies like microcomputers and video recorders had growth potential. An emerging trend seemed to be integrated multimedia systems combining video, data, and sound to provide information on demand.

Turning to the impact of technology on children, continuing concerns have been expressed about the influence of television on children's behavior. One direct outcome of this concern was the passage of the Children's Television Act of 1990. The new legislation limits advertising on children's programs to 10½ minutes an hour on weekends and 12 minutes per hour on weekdays. The Federal Communications Commission is instructed to carefully review the practices of each station up for license renewal to determine compliance and whether its overall programming "has served the educational and informational needs of children." The Act also establishes the National Endowment for Children's Educational Television, which is intended to stimulate the creation and production of educational programs for children. There continues to be an undercurrent of dissatisfaction about the nature and quality of many commercial television programs, even though many studies do not support the notion of gross negative influence of television on children.

To review the comprehensive research conducted by behavioral scientists over the last 40 years on the influence of television on the lives of American children and adolescents, George Comstock (1991) wrote *Television and the American Child*. The book identifies major topics that have been investigated and focuses on recent research that confirms or rejects the conventional wisdom about the effect of television on youth. There continues to be ambiguity in the findings of dozens of studies, but Comstock is able to put the findings into a perspective that permits the reader to apply the conclusions to specific conditions with specific types of young people.

Trend 10

Professional education of educational technologists has stabilized in size and scope.

There may not be much uniformity in the titles of academic programs that prepare individuals to serve in the field of educational technology (instructional technology, educational systems, instructional design, etc.), and the academic "homes" are not consistent from university to university but, in general, the field is holding its own. Programs tend to include similar content, are primarily offered at the graduate level, and prepare students for similar positions.

Educational Media and Technology Yearbook 1991 (Branyan-Broadbent and Wood 1991) lists 63 doctoral programs in the United States. No new doctoral programs were instituted in 1991, but the East Texas State University program was eliminated because of economic cutbacks and the University of Northern Colorado program was substantially revised. The *EMTY 1991* lists 195 master's and six-year degree programs, some of which are located at the institutions offering doctoral degrees. Programs were eliminated (or combined with other programs) at four universities in 1991. A third listing in the *EMTY 1991* includes 82 programs in educational computing, 32 more programs than in 1986 when the listing first appeared. Like the master's degrees in educational technology, some of the master's degrees in education and computing are also located at institutions offering doctoral degrees.

New and revised programs reflect emerging trends in the field at large. At Northwestern University, a Ph.D. program in the Learning Sciences has as its purpose, "to advance the research and development of innovative educational structures and technologies." At the University of New Mexico, the Department of Training and Learning Technologies incorporates the areas of training and development, adult learning, and instructional technologies. The revised doctoral curriculum at the University of Northern Colorado is future-oriented, with emphasis areas in instructional design/development, interactive technologies, and technology integration.

More professional conferences, conventions, and workshops feature specific media and technology applications to education and training. The largest is Commtex, which was held in Orlando, Florida, in February 1991 and attracted the largest number of participants in recent years. Other meetings tended to feature computer and telecommunications applications.

BEYOND THE TRENDS 1988-1991 – THE LONGER VIEW

With baseline data from 1988 and 1989, it is possible, using data from 1991, to begin to consider the trends over time. Five or ten years would be a better timespan, but analysis can begin at this point and be adjusted in the years to come. A starting point is with the frequency of items in the literature, dissertations, conference programs, and ERIC input. Tables 1 and 2 (see pages 3 and 4) reveal a relative consistency of content categories and recording units used in this study. Although there are several aberrations from year to year, they do not seem to alter the trends significantly. For all intents and purposes, the sequence of 10 trends uncovered this year is as viable as the 1988 and 1989 lists. Therefore, this longer range view should go beyond the data and attempt to identify the more subtle trends that do not reveal themselves after following the replicable methodology that has been used in the three editions of this report.

This analysis of trends comes from the more personal views of the author, who has lived with this process over the past four years. It includes subjective data gathered while serving as Director (and later, Associate Director) of the ERIC Clearinghouse on Information Resources. As a participant in the document selection process for *Resources in Education* and journal article selection for the *Current Index to Journals in Education* (CIJE), hundred of items pass his eyes each year and a substantive judgment must be made about each one. As professor and chair of an academic department that prepares professionals for the field of educational technology, he also discusses many substantive issues about new developments in the field with faculty and students. Opportunities to serve as a consultant in other states and other parts of the world generate information about developments in the field that would not ordinarily come through the literature. In 1990, the author was a Visiting Professor for three months at the University of Twente in The Netherlands, and a consultant for the Open University in Indonesia for two months in 1991. Also in 1991, the role of facilitator for the California Educational Technology Summit (Cradler 1991) provided an opportunity to verify some of the trends that were being held as tentative.

Other signals also add to the mix of inputs that help to articulate the longer view of trends. As the team reviewed the literature of 1991, using the same recording units as past efforts, it was clear that many new concepts were emerging that could not comfortably fit the existing categories. When some of these concepts, now translated into specific terms, continued to emerge, it became apparent that new categories would have to be created. In part, identification of new concepts may reflect a limitation in the old schema, but the fact that so many new terms were independently assigned to items in the literature seemed to indicate that there were emerging ideas that had not been accounted for in the previous rounds. Likewise, some existing terms in the recording units were hardly used at all. They had fallen into disuse, even though they had appeared more frequently in earlier efforts. For example, the following terms grew out of this year's review:

Integrated Learning Systems	Gender
Multimedia	Authoring Systems
Presentation	Constructivism
Cross-cultural	Diversity
Cognitive Science	Instructional Strategies
Program Evaluation	Impact
Educational Technology Competencies for Teacher Education	Networking
	Hypermedia

Other indicators of movement within the field come from placement records. Where are educational technology graduates going? What are they doing on the job? What is the demand for such people? Currently there is no systematic collection of data to answer those questions, but if someone is engaged in the process of helping master's and doctoral graduates find positions, it is likely that some feeling for employer needs is gained. Thus, another ingredient is added to the mixture.

Recognizing these idiosyncratic sources, and the admission of subjectivity by the author, a list of trends that takes a longer view than the year-to-year reports is presented for the reader's consideration. These personal opinions may serve as a basis for further discussion among colleagues in the educational technology community.

- *Educational technology is being shaped more by external forces than by the internal influence of its own professionals.*

Calls for using technology to solve some of the problems facing schools come more from the business and industry community than from the schools themselves. The National Governors' Association has been advocating and monitoring the use of technology in education for the past five years. The New American Schools Development Corporation expects technology to lead the way in creating "break-the-mold" schools. A relatively small number of professionals within the schools and universities try to reach the vast number of teachers and professors in attempts to encourage the reluctant ones to try technology. There has been little impact. Some partnership ventures between computer companies and schools and cable companies and schools have led the way to greater infusion of technology. Most of these events are isolated in local settings and do not have the impact that technology advocates claim. The potential for contributions to teaching and learning through technology are still waiting for breakthroughs that will reach each teacher in each school in the country.

- *The use of traditional media resources has become routine in most elementary and secondary classrooms.*

Not many classrooms lack permanent overhead projectors available at all times. They have become as ubiquitous as the chalkboards that they often replace. Audiocassette recorders are easily available to most teachers, whether to introduce a story to preschoolers or to practice foreign language skills. Ninety-four percent of the nation's elementary and secondary schools have videotape recorders (Quality Education Data 1991b) and that means there are television monitors available as well, for incoming programs on cable or from broadcast sources. Availability of equipment does not seem to be a major problem in most schools. Schools have gradually built up a reservoir of equipment over the past 30 years. Its use is probably uneven, just as the quality of teaching is uneven in the more than 80,000 schools in the land. It appears that teachers could use help in using even the basic hardware that is already available to them.

- *There is little evidence to show that the computer has made major contributions to learning in the classroom other than to help learners know how to use it.*

The novelty wears off. What starts as a new, exciting teaching/learning medium gradually becomes commonplace and, unless new software is acquired, the extent of computer use seems to be computer literacy and word processing. The studies of computer use in the schools continues, but there is very little solid evidence that computers in the classroom make a difference in learning. Perhaps this is still the era of introduction, when teachers and students are fascinated with the novelty and really do not learn much more than how to use the machine. It may be a function of software quality. Much has been written about the poor quality of software for teaching and learning, although it seems to be getting better. Some commercial organizations are known for having higher quality software than others. There is also some doubt as to where the computers belong in the school. Some classrooms have several units, but rarely enough for the entire class. Some schools have computer classrooms: an entire class comes to one room where two students can work together on one machine. Still other schools use the school library media center as the place where computers can be used or borrowed by teachers to take to the classroom. There appear to be no patterns regarding locale of use. There appears to be little integration of computer-based instruction with regular curricular efforts. It may be too early to demonstrate contributions of the computer to learning, but researchers are still trying and the findings may be near.

- *The self-contained classroom is the greatest single barrier to use of educational technology principles and practices.*

The self-contained classroom, where most students follow their course of study, is usually the basic unit in most schools. One of the most popular statistics for most schools is the teacher:student ratio, usually expressed as 25:1 or 30:1 or some such figure. The understanding is that one teacher is responsible for a certain number of students. It is the teacher's responsibility to engage the students in learning activities during a specified period of time, perhaps 35 to 45 minutes as most periods are defined. The teacher is autonomous – alone with a syllabus and, hopefully, a repertoire of teaching techniques that will attract and hold attention so that learning will occur. Audiovisual media have been used for the past 40 years as one technique to attract and hold attention. Most media are group-paced; that is, when something is shown, the entire class is involved. If a teacher wants to help an individual learner, or a small group, other activities must be created to engage the rest of the class. Very often such variations on the entire-class theme are a logistical nightmare. Educational technology, properly used, can help to engage students individually or in small groups. Use of teacher aides or teaching teams can open new possibilities beyond the self-contained classroom. Until differentiated staffing arrangements are put in place and resource stations are installed and monitored, educational technology will not make the contributions that its advocates claim. Change begins in the individual classroom with the teacher.

- *The field is shifting from the use of media and technology for enrichment to technology for replacement.*

Ever since the post-World War II era, the use of media has been encouraged by contemporary educational change agents. The first term to be used was *audiovisual aids* – media for enrichment. The motto "Bring the world to the classroom" indicates the role of media during the early days. Some teachers used media to fill time, while others tried to integrate the use of media with the curriculum. In almost every case, the medium was used for *enrichment*, to improve the quality of teaching. Although this approach was admirable, it did not necessarily guarantee learning. Faint whispers of "replacing the teacher" were heard as each new medium was introduced: radio, motion pictures, and television. However, there were no documented cases of any teacher being replaced by any medium.

In recent times, the distance education movement has in fact replaced teachers. The replacement is actually a television or radio program, a computer disc, printed material, a laboratory kit, or a combination of several media. Teachers have put themselves and their ideas in a medium that replaces the face-to-face instruction that historically characterized most education. For example, when rural schools cannot find a teacher to teach a specialized subject, they can turn to one of the distance education organizations delivering television courses by satellite. When postsecondary students want to pursue a college degree, but most also maintain a full-time job, they seek open university courses offered at a distance. Teachers in their traditional roles in front of a class are replaced by teachers on tape, on film, or in written materials. This is truly an appropriate role for technology in education.

- *Instructional development is being practiced more in nonschool settings than in schools.*

Instructional development is the process of systematically designing materials and procedures for learning, using a variety of media for delivery. The process is an outgrowth of earlier efforts to create replicable learning packages or modules that guaranteed results. One of its earliest examples is programmed instruction. As business, industry, government, military, and medical communities discovered the cost-effective results of instructional development, they moved to create training packages and programs for their employees. Principles from the field of educational technology worked well in these training environments and soon many nonschool organizations were deeply involved in using these principles. However, schools and universities continued to be reluctant clients and users of media for enrichment, if they used media at all. The graduates of professional graduate programs in educational technology currently obtain employment more in the business and industry sector than in education. This trend began over a decade ago, and there are prospects of it not only continuing but growing, despite the pleas of both educational technology professionals and advocates from business (Bowsher 1989).

- *Distance education has become an operational analog of educational technology.*

Distance education and educational technology are congruent concepts. Distance education encompasses virtually every aspect of educational technology. From a basic concern for the individual learner to a complete treatment of instructional design and development procedures, educational technology is apparent. The use of multimedia delivery systems in a variety of dispersed settings requires replicable materials that will ensure attainment of learning objectives by every learner. Evaluation is central, as is feedback to the student. The entire system must be managed well to facilitate learning and to ensure proper recordkeeping.

- *Cognitive science provides the best source of theoretical principles that underlie instructional design.*

There is a trend toward the use of cognitive science as a basic underpinning for the process of instructional design and development. Even though the remnants of behavioral psychology still dot the landscape, especially in training programs, cognitive psychology seems to be the theoretical direction in which the field is moving. There is some controversy regarding its application among the constructivists and non-constructivists. The concepts and empirical findings are helping to guide instructional design toward new understandings of how people learn and how to design instruction for optimal results.

- *Evaluation is valued but infrequently used.*

Almost every instructional development model includes evaluation, yet there is not much evidence that it is widely used in practice. Evaluations of products, such as computer software, are published regularly, but evaluations of the instructional development process seem to get lost in the rush to implement a newly developed course. It seems that the "trouble" of evaluation provides an excuse for moving ahead without much data regarding the products and processes developed. Most professional education programs preparing educational technologists do not offer a separate course in evaluation. The concept and procedures are incorporated into other courses, but they tend to have a minor place in the entire professional education curriculum.

- *Educational technology continues to be perceived as a field concerned more with hardware and software than with its applications for teaching and learning.*

No matter how much is written about the process of instructional design, development, and evaluation, people working within the field of educational technology are perceived to be primarily concerned with the hardware and software used to deliver instruction. References are made to "the technology" when describing hardware/software systems. Most people who use the term, including many in the profession itself, do not fully understand the comprehensive meaning of the word *technology*. Technology is the application of scientific principles to solve practical problems. It is a process; it deals with problem solving. It is *not* machines; it is *not* software. It is a systematic blend of people, materials, methods, and machines to solve problems.

The profession has tried to explain itself. The Association for Educational Communications and Technology (AECT), the national professional association for the field, published *The Definition of Educational Technology* in 1977. It was widely distributed. The Association finds it necessary to create an entirely new volume in 1992 based on reinterpretations of the field and its definition. Perhaps the field will have to continue to explain itself through its actions rather than through its publications.

REFERENCES

Association for Educational Communications and Technology. (1977). *The definition of educational technology*. Washington, D.C.: Author.

Bell, T. H., and Elmquist, D. L. (1991). *How to shape up our nation's schools: Three critical steps*. Salt Lake City, Utah: Terrel Bell & Associates.

Bowsher, J. E. (1989). *Educating America: Lessons learned in the nation's corporations*. New York: John Wiley & Sons.

Branyan-Broadbent, B., and Wood, K. (1991). *Educational media and technology yearbook*. Englewood, Colo.: Libraries Unlimited, Inc.

Braun, L. (1990). *Vision:TEST (Technologically Enriched Schools of Tomorrow)*. Eugene, Or.: International Society for Technology in Education. ED 327 173.

Comstock, G., with Paik, H. (1991). *Television and the American child*. San Diego, Cal.: Academic Press, Inc.

Cradler, J. (1991). *California Educational Technology Summit Proceedings*. Sacramento, Cal.: California Planning Commission for Educational Technology. ED 338 215.

Distance learning usage climbs in Minnesota. (1990, July). *The Heller Report* 1(10): 8-9.

Duffy, T. M., and Jonassen, D. H., eds. (1991, September). Continuing the dialogue on the implications of constructivism for educational technology. [Theme issue]. *Educational Technology* 31(9).

Education and the information society: A challenge for European policy. (1991).

Ehrmann, Stephen C. (1990). Reaching students, reaching resources: Using technologies to open the college. Washington, D.C.: Annenberg/CPB Project. ED 327 171. Also: (1990, April). *Academic Computing* 4(7): 10-14, 32-34.

Eisenberg, M. B. (1991). *Trends and issues in library and information science*. Syracuse, N.Y.: ERIC Clearinghouse on Information Resources. ED 335 061.

Ely, D. P. (1989). *Trends and issues in educational technology 1988*. Syracuse, N.Y.: ERIC Clearinghouse on Information Resources. ED 308 859.

Ely, D. P. (1990). *Trends and issues in educational technology 1989*. Syracuse, N.Y.: ERIC Clearinghouse on Information Resources. ED 326 212.

EPIE Institute. (1990, February). *The integrated instructional systems report*. Hampton Bays, N.Y.: Author.

Eraut, Michael (ed.). (1991). *Education and the information society*. London: Cassell PLC.

Eurich, N. (1990). *The learning society: Education for adult workers*. Lawrenceville, N.J.: Princeton University Press.

Free to watch TV. (1991, November 20). [Editorial]. *Washington Post*.

Garnette, C. P., and Withrow, F. B. (1990). Analysis of the U.S. Department of Education's database of distance learning projects. *Journal of Educational Computing Research* 6(4): 515-522.

Green, K. C., and Eastman, S. (1991, Summer). Access to computing: How many computers and where do we put them? *EDUCOM Review*, 59-61.

Gustafson, K. (1991). *A survey of instructional development models*, 2d ed. Syracuse, N.Y.: ERIC Clearinghouse on Information Resources. ED 335 027.

Harel, I., and Papert, S., eds. (1991). *Constructionism*. Norwood, N.J.: Ablex Publishing.

Hawkridge, D., Jaworski, J., and McMahon, H. (1990). *Computers in third world schools*. London: Macmillan Press.

High-Performance Computing Act of 1991 (P.L. 102-194, 9 December, 1991).

Janowiak, R. M. (1990). *Educational technology in kindergarten through twelfth grades.* Chicago: National Engineering Consortium.

Janowitz, M. (1976). Content analysis and the study of sociopolitical change. *Journal of Communication* 26(4): 20-21.

Kominski, R. (1991). *Computer use in the United States: 1989.* Current Population Reports, Special Studies, Series P-23, No. 171. Washington, D.C.: U.S. Department of Commerce. ED 338 210.

Krippendorff, K. (1980). *Content analysis: An introduction to its methodology.* Beverly Hills, Cal.: Sage Publications.

Kurshaw, D., and Harrington, M. (1991). *Creating communities: An educator's guide to electronic networks.* Washington, D.C.: National Science Foundation.

Mann, D. (1991). *How teachers and media specialists grade cable TV.* New York: Teachers College, Columbia University.

Market Data Retrieval. (1991). *Education and technology.* Shelton, Conn.: Author.

Merina, A. (1991, February). Introducing NEA EdStar. *NEA Today* 9(6): 25.

Mitchell, Brent. (1991, September 24). Educator urges speed in revitalizing schools; Standardized tests, high technology backed. *Washington Post.*

Moore, D. M., and Braden, R. A. (1988, March). Prestige and influence in the field of educational technology. *Performance & Instruction* 21(2): 15-23.

Naisbitt, J. (1982). *Megatrends.* New York: Warner Books.

National Education Association. (1991, September). The 1991-92 resolutions of the National Education Association. *NEA Today* 10(1): 15-25.

National Governors' Association. (1990). *Results in education: 1990. The governors' 1991 report on education.* Washington, D.C.: Author. ED 327 969.

Neill, S. B., and Neill, G. W. (1990). *Only the best, 1991. The annual guide to highest rated educational software, Preschool-Grade 12.* New York: R. R. Bowker.

Northwest Regional Educational Laboratory. (1991). *Enhancing instruction through telecommunications.* Portland, Or.: Author.

Pelgrum, W. J., and Plomp, T. (1991). *The use of computers in education worldwide.* Oxford: Pergamon Press. Also: Pelgrum, W. J., and Plomp, T. (1991, April). *The use of computers in education worldwide.* Paper presented at the 1991 annual conference of the American Educational Research Association, Chicago. ED 337 157.

Plomp, T., and Pelgrum, W. J. (1990). Introduction of computers in education: State of the art in eight countries. Paper presented at EURIT (Herning, Denmark, April 1990).

Quality Education Data, Inc. (1991a). *Satellite dish usage public school districts 1990-91 school year*. Denver, Colo.: Author.

Quality Education Data, Inc. (1991b). *Technology in schools 1990-91 school year*. Denver, Colo.: Author.

Saettler, P. (1991). *The evolution of American educational technology*. Englewood, Colo.: Libraries Unlimited.

Sheekey, A. D. (1991). *Education policy and telecommunications technologies*. Washington, D.C.: U.S. Department of Education, Office of Educational Research and Improvement.

Sheingold, K., and Hadley, M. (1990). *Accomplished teachers: Integrating computers into classroom practice*. New York: Center for Technology in Education, Bank Street College of Education.

Sherry, M. (1991, November). The future of integrated learning systems. *Inventing Tomorrow's Schools*, 1(1), 6.

Skelly, M. S. (1991, August). Classroom television: Should schools tune in? *School and College* 22-27.

"Wade right in," manager tells educators. (1991, November). *School Technology News* 8(9): 1.

Weber, R. P. (1990). *Basic content analysis*, 2d ed. Beverly Hills, Cal.: Sage Publications.

"What curriculum for the 21st century?" (1990, August). *New Things Considered*, 6, 1.

The White House Conference on Library and Information Services
Implications for Educational Media and Technology

Donald P. Ely

Although the White House Conference on Library and Information Services was primarily directed toward the nation's libraries, the fact that the operation of and delivery of services by American libraries are largely based on technology means that the field of educational media and technology is part of this movement. The 1991 conference did not focus on media and technology, but many of the 95 recommendations coming out of the Conference have direct implications for educational media and technology. Others have indirect relationships. This article provides a brief summary of the conference and highlights the recommendations that have relevance for professionals in educational media and technology.

THE CONFERENCE: FIVE DAYS IN JULY

The most important fact about the White House Conference (WHCLIS) is that it happened. More than 100,000 people participated in 61 preconferences and related events. Over 1,100 resolutions developed during the preconferences were reduced to the 95 recommendations that were passed by the 700 official delegates from all 50 states, 7 U.S. territories, the District of Columbia, Native Americans, and the federal library community. Legislative mandate and the White House imprimatur brought about the level of recognition that the conference enjoyed and national awareness of library and information services was significantly increased.

From the three conference themes — literacy, productivity, and democracy — came nine subthemes that served as the organizing structure for discussions and the recommendations that eventually emerged. These subthemes were:

1. Availability and Access to Information

2. National Information Policies

3. Information Networks through Technology

4. Structure and Governance

5. Services for Diverse Needs

6. Training to Reach End Users

7. Personnel and Staff Development

8. Preservation of Information

9. Marketing to Communities.

Using the 1,100 recommendations stemming from the preconferences, discussion groups wrestled with a variety of issues surrounding each topic. The final recommendations from each group were presented to all the voting delegates for action during the final days of the conference. The result was 95 recommendations that were forwarded to the President of the United States on November 21, 1991, and soon thereafter to the Congress. As a side note, the first White House Conference, held in 1979, presented 64 recommendations to the President, 55 of which have been implemented in part or whole at the federal, state, and local levels. The summary report of the 1991 Conference is presented in *Information 2000: Library and Information Services for the 21st Century.* The recommendations discussed here come from that report.

WHCLIS RECOMMENDATIONS

Many of the recommendations made at the Conference have direct implications for people working in the field of educational media and technology. It is in the area of *information technology* that the interests of the two communities intersect. The highlights that pertain to educational media and technology are excerpts from the complete list of recommendations. It should be noted that *all* the recommendations have significance for all citizens and that the items listed here are selected for their special relevance for a specific audience. The complete list should be reviewed to understand the comprehensive nature of the recommendations.

The delegates voted to earmark a group of recommendations for priority action. The remainder of the recommendations were considered after the priority items had been voted upon. The priority list has been scanned first and those parts that appear to be of direct concern to media and technology are highlighted.

PRIORITY RECOMMENDATIONS WITH IMPLICATIONS FOR EDUCATIONAL MEDIA AND TECHNOLOGY

1. *Adopt Omnibus Children and Youth Literacy Initiative.* This recommendation calls for a four-pronged initiative to invigorate library and information services for student learning and literacy through legislation. The first component stresses funding for resource-based instructional activities that would serve as demonstration centers. Also requested are grants for information technology to school media centers and for adequate professional staffing of these centers.

2. *Share Information via Network "Superhighway."* The National Research and Education Network (NREN) is the emphasis here. The recommendation calls for "an information 'superhighway,' allowing educational institutions, including libraries, to capitalize on the advantages of technology for resource sharing and the creation and exchange of information." Also included is a statement about "education at all levels" as an important area of service. (During the Conference, the House of Representatives passed H.R. 656, the High-Performance Computing Act of 1991, which included NREN.)

3. *Amend Copyright Statutes for New Technologies.* Key elements of this recommendation are: "Provid[ing] the right to use information technology to explore and create information without infringing on the legitimate rights of authorship and ownership" and "[e]nsur[ing] that all library and information service users have access to all forms and formats of information and library materials." Also noted is the need for preferential fair-use status for libraries that would be equivalent to educational institutions.

4. *Designate Libraries as Educational Agencies.* In an attempt to help libraries become more active participants in the *America 2000* program, this recommendation calls for "a school library media officer [in the U.S. Department of Education] to oversee research, planning, and adoption of the goals of *Information Power: Guidelines for School Library Media Programs*. Also requested was categorical funding for school library media programs.

OTHER RECOMMENDATIONS

From the theme of Availability and Access to Information comes a request to *dedicate funding to strengthen school library media centers*. Collection development funds are requested "to strengthen out-dated, deteriorating, and inadequate collections, encouraging these media centers to share resources." Another recommendation— *legislate preferential library telecommunications rates* —focuses on the need for affordable telecommunications rates that are regulated by states as well as the federal government.

In regard to National Information Policies, a request to *ensure equal and timely access and delivery* asks Congress to reduce current postal rates for library and educational materials and increase appropriations for revenues lost. In the same category, recommendations to *implement and extend transmission networks* and to *create nationwide information structure*, offer implications for media and technology. These are requests to "adopt the policy that a fiber-optic transmission network ... be extended to all homes and businesses ... to create a nationwide information infrastructure."

The Information Networks through Technology theme calls for a comprehensive program for networking and electronic sharing of resources to make more information available to more people. In general, this recommendation calls for leadership from the President and the Congress to develop a networking plan with the support and collaboration of all community levels and cooperation of volunteers.

Of special note is the statement, *ensure statutory support for role in America 2000*. "Every *America 2000* New American School should be networked to share information, resources, and ideas using a technologically advanced library media center as its information technology hub." Also of interest is the call to *develop policies, procedures for information in all formats*. This recommendation seeks public-private partnerships to develop uniform standards for access to government information in all media formats, both print and electronic.

Many of the recommendations in the Training to Reach End Users category have direct implications for media and technology professionals. Most pertinent are *expand support for lifelong education, extend user-friendly technology to all citizens*, and *provide grants for innovative model training projects*. These recommendations speak to professionals who are in instructional design and development, urging them to assist in the training of people to use the technologies that are available (or should be available) to them.

OUTCOMES

Action on the recommendations will occur in the months and years to come. The fact that they were generated by a national, representative body and that they are addressed to the President and Congress of the United States by legislative mandate gives them special status on the national agenda. Delegates to the conference held a national teleconference on December 11, 1991, at 272 sites in 44 states, with over 20,000 people participating.

National professional organizations are poised to press for legislation at the federal level and state groups are working at the state level. The movement is evident; the results will be observed in the future.

Professionals in the field of educational media and technology should be alert to local and state activities that attempt to implement the recommendations. As partners with professionals in the library and information service professions, educational technologists have much to gain. There are many areas that overlap, especially with information technology. Together, much can be accomplished; alone, it is the status quo or less.

Part Two
The Profession

Introduction

One of the purposes of the *Yearbook* is to present an annual report on the state of the profession. Each year there are articles and studies that speak to new developments related to such topics as professional education, salaries, certification, and continuing education. This year, professional associations and a new academic program are featured.

There are many professional associations in the field of educational media and technology. The seven that are included in this edition are considered to be the major organizations in North America. Their inclusion is based on longevity, number of members, professional journals published, and visibility. Other professional associations are listed in part six, Organizations and Associations in North America.

Associations are indicators of professional status and growth. People in a field organize themselves to improve communications among a group of people with common interests and objectives. They advance the profession by establishing performance standards and usually adopt a code of ethics. Each of the associations featured in this section have achieved recognition for their contributions to the advancement of educational media and technology. In some cases, the scope of interest of one organization overlaps that of another. Some professionals realize that their interests are not contained only within one association and, therefore, join others that are compatible with their interests, values, and goals.

The appearance of a new doctoral program is worthy of mention in the *Yearbook*. In a time of reductions in higher education, a new program is a vote of confidence in the future of the field. The doctoral level is also noteworthy because it is the highest degree offered and is not the most common degree: the master's degree is.

The University of Northern Colorado is not new to the preparation of educational technology personnel. Forty years ago the Colorado State Teachers College at Greeley boasted a comprehensive media program. James D. Finn, one of the pioneers in the field, was a faculty member there. Now, as the University of Northern Colorado, the program has appeared again in what promises to be a dynamic contemporary doctoral program. It is described in detail beginning on page 52 by Edward Caffarella.

It is the intention of the editors to continue this section in each *Yearbook* as an annual status report to the profession.

– THE YEAR IN REVIEW –

ADCIS

Association for the Development of
Computer-Based Instructional Systems

Howard Troutner
Conference Manager
Association for the Development of
Computer-based Instructional Systems

ADCIS is an international association with a worldwide membership of professionals who are actively involved in the development and use of computer-based instructional technologies. Members work in a wide variety of settings, including business and industry; elementary and secondary schools; junior colleges, colleges, and universities; vocational and specialized schools; and the military and the government.

ADCIS brings together people of many different perspectives and careers, who share the common goal of excellence in instruction through the effective use of computer technology. Their interests range from the most basic concepts of computer literacy to the most advanced concepts in interactive video and artificial intelligence. Information shared is based on the highest quality research available.

The Association provides an international forum for:

- Intellectual leadership in the field

- Professional growth opportunities

- The integration of theory and practice.

THE ADCIS MISSION AND MEMBERSHIP

The mission of ADCIS is to promote human learning and performance through the use of computer-based technologies. All ADCIS members receive a free subscription to the *Journal of Computer-Based Instruction (JCBI)*, a quarterly periodical that is highly respected as one of the most scholarly publications in the field of computer-based instruction.

ADCIS members also receive reduced registration fees to the annual ADCIS International Conference and Trade Show. This conference attracts over 750 conferees from around the world. During the four-day meeting, more than 300 presentations are made in the 15 interest areas covered by the special interest groups. These presentations are selected from juried papers and bound in a 400-plus page *Proceedings*, which is received by all conferees. The International Conference is normally held the second week of November. The 34th International Conference will be held in Norfolk, VA, November 8-11, 1992.

The ADCIS membership divides itself into four divisions and 15 special interest groups (SIGs). Members receive one free membership in a SIG of their choice; additional SIGs may be joined for $5 each. The 15 SIGs are listed by division:

Computers in Training Division

- SIGCBT   Computer-Based Training
- MISIG   Management Issues

Multimedia, Authoring, and Delivery Systems Division

- HYPERSIG   Hypermedia
- SIGIVA   Interactive Video/Audio
- SIGPILOT   PILOT User's Group
- PUG   Plato User's Group
- SIGTELE   Telecommunications

Technologies Division

- ETSIG   Emerging Technologies
- SIGTAR   Theory and Research

Computers in Education Division

- ELSECJC   Elementary/Secondary/Junior College
- HESIG   Health Education
- HOMEC   Home Economics
- SIGAC   Academic Computing
- MUSIC   Association for Technology in Music
- SIGHAN   Educators of the Handicapped

NEWSLETTERS

ADCIS members receive the *ADCIS News*, an association newsletter that keeps members up-to-date on important developments in the field of computer-based technologies. Each SIG also publishes a newsletter for its members.

NETWORKING AND JOB OPPORTUNITIES

Contacts with professionals who have similar interests or who are working on similar projects or problems are coordinated through the ADCIS headquarters office and through the SIG structure. Members stay in touch with each other through electronic mail. A membership directory is provided to facilitate communication among members.

The ADCIS headquarters office serves as a clearinghouse, posting job openings within the profession that are listed with the ADCIS Job Opening Service.

CURRENT OFFICERS/BOARD MEMBERS

Lloyd Rieber, President; Tim Spannaus, Vice President; Janet Azbell, Immediate Past President; Donna Larson, Immediate Past Vice President; Cynthia Leshin, Program Chair; John A. Merrill, Immediate Past Program Chair; Sue Leslie, SIG Council Chair; Jim Hutton, Celia Kraatz, and Tom Downey, SIG Council Representatives; Howard Troutner, Conference Manager; and Carol Norris, Account Manager.

ACCESSING ADCIS SERVICES

Individuals interested in joining ADCIS, subscribing to the *Journal of Computer-Based Instruction*, or receiving registration information for the International Conference should contact ADCIS International Headquarters, 1601 West Fifth Ave., Suite 111, Columbus, OH 43212. (614) 488-1863. Carol Norris, contact person.

AECT

Association for Educational Communications and Technology

Established in 1923, the Association for Educational Communications and Technology is an international professional association dedicated to the improvement of instruction through the utilization of media and technology. The mission of the association is to provide leadership in educational communications and technology by linking professionals holding a common interest in the use of educational technology and its applications to the learning process. In the past few years, convention topics have focused on hypermedia, teleconferencing, and converging technologies, and AECT co-sponsored the teleconference, "Teaching and Technology: A Critical Link," which addressed issues on the restructuring of public schools and the role of technology. AECT also honors outstanding individuals or groups making significant contributions to the field of educational communications and technology or to the association. (See the separate listing in part 6 for full information on these awards.)

MEMBERSHIP

AECT members include instructional technologists; media or library specialists; university professors and researchers; industrial/business training specialists; religious educators; government media personnel; school, school district, and state department of education media program administrators and specialists; educational/training media producers; and numerous others whose professional work requires improvement of media and technology in education and training. AECT members also work in the armed forces, in public libraries, in museums, and in other information agencies of many different kinds, including those related to the emerging fields of computer technology.

MEMBERSHIP SERVICES

AECT serves as a central clearinghouse and communications center for its members. The association maintains TechCentral, a national electronic mail network and bulletin board service. Through its various committees and task forces, it compiles data and prepares recommendations to form the basis of guidelines, standards, research, and information summaries on numerous topics and problems of interest to the membership. AECT professional staff members report on government activities of concern to the membership and provide current data on laws and pending legislation relating to the educational media/technology field. AECT also maintains the ECT Foundation, through which it offers a limited number of financial grants to further the association's work. Archives are maintained at the University of Maryland.

CONFERENCES

The Annual Conference features the nation's largest instructional media exposition, InfoCOMM International Exposition, which is held jointly with the International Communications Industries Association (ICIA). The next convention will be held January 13-17, 1993, in New Orleans, Louisiana; the theme will be "Gateway to Learning."

PUBLICATIONS

AECT maintains an active publication program which includes *TechTrends* (6/yr., free with membership); *Report to Members* (6/yr., newsletter); *Educational Technology Research and Development* (4/yr.); various division publications; and a number of books and videotapes, including the following recent titles: *Copyright and Instructional Technologies: A Guide to Fair Use and Permissions Procedures* (2d ed. 1989); *Doctoral Research in Instructional/Design and Technology: A Directory of Dissertations* (1989, 1992); *Information Power: Guidelines for School Library Media Programs* (with the American Association of School Librarians, 1988); *Information Power Discussion Guide* (1988); *Masters Curricula in Educational Communications and Technology: A Descriptive Directory* (4th ed. 1992); *Mediatoons* (1989); *Safety in the Library Media Program: A Handbook* (1987); *Standards for College and University Learning Resources Programs: Technology in Instruction* (2d ed. 1989); *The Information Power Video* (videotape, 1988); *Introduction to HyperCard* (videotape, 1989); *Interactive Learning with HyperCard-Apple MacIntosh Computers* (videotape, 1989); and *Interactive Video Demonstration Tapes-Video Archive*, vols. 1-3.

AFFILIATED ORGANIZATIONS

Because of similarity of interests, a number of organizations have chosen to affiliate with AECT. These include the Association for Multi-Image (AMI); Association for Special Education Technology (ASET); Community College Association for Instruction and Technology (CCAIT); Consortium of University Film Centers (CUFC); Federal Educational Technology Association (FETA); Health Science Communications Association (HeSCA); International Association for Learning Laboratories (IALL); International Visual Literacy Association (IVLA); Minorities in Media (MIMS); National Association of Regional Media Centers (NARMC); National Instructional Television Fixed Service Association (NIA/ITFS); New England Educational Media Association; Northwest College and University Council for the Management of Educational Technology; Southeastern Regional Media Leadership Council (SRMLC); and State University of New York Educational Communications Center.

Two additional organizations are also related to the Association for Educational Communications and Technology: the AECT Archives and the AECT ECT Foundation.

AECT DIVISIONS

AECT has nine divisions: Division of Educational Media Managment (DEMM); Division of Interactive Systems and Computers (DISC); Division of Instructional Development (DID); Division of School Media Specialists (DSMS); Division of Telecommunications (DOT); Industrial Training and Education Division (ITED); International Division (INTL); Media Design and Production Division (MDPD); and Research and Theory Division (RTD).

CURRENT OFFICERS/MEMBERS OF THE AECT
BOARD OF DIRECTORS

Stanley D. Zenor, Executive Director; Larry Kitchens, President; Roger Tipling, Past President; Patricia J. Fewell, Secretary-Treasurer; and Kay Bland, Roberts S. Braden, Janis H. Bruwelheide, William J. Burns, Marvin Davis, Franz Frederick, Michael Obrenovich, and Rusty Russell, Board Members.

Further information is available from AECT, 1025 Vermont Ave. NW, Suite 820, Washington, DC 20005. (202) 347-7834. Fax (202) 347-7839.

AMTEC

Association for Media and Technology
in Education in Canada
L'Association des Media et de la Technologie
en Education au Canada

PURPOSE

As Canada's national association for educational media and technology professionals, AMTEC is a forum concerned with the impact of media and technology on teaching, learning, and society. As an organization, AMTEC provides national leadership through annual conferences, publications, workshops, media festivals awards, and ongoing reaction to media and technology issues at the international, national, provincial, and local levels, and linkages with other organizations with similar interests.

MEMBERSHIP

AMTEC's membership is geographically dispersed and professionally diversified. Membership stretches from St. John's, Newfoundland, to Victoria, British Columbia, and from Inuvik, Northwest Territories, to Niagara Falls, Ontario. Members include teachers, consultants, broadcasters, media managers, photographers, librarians/information specialists, educational technology specialists, instructional designers/trainers, technology specialists, artists, and producers/distributors. They represent all sectors of the educational media and technology fields: elementary and secondary schools, colleges, institutes of technology, universities, provincial governments, school boards, military services, health services libraries, and private corporations.

ACTIVITIES

Workshops. AMTEC offers workshops in cooperation with other agencies and associations based on AMTEC members' needs, in addition to the in-depth workshops at the AMTEC annual conference.

Annual Conference. The AMTEC annual conference provides opportunities to meet delegates from across the nation and to attend sessions on the latest issues and developments in such areas as copyright law, instructional design, distance education, library standards, media production, broadcasting and educational technology, media utilization, and visual literacy. AMTEC 92 was held June 13-17, 1992, in Vancouver, B.C., and AMTEC 93, June 12-16, 1993, in Windsor, Ontario.

Awards. AMTEC annually recognizes outstanding individual achievement and leadership in the field through the EMPDAC (Educational Media Producers and Distributors Association of Canada) Achievement Award and the AMTEC Leadership Award. In addition, AMTEC acts as the correspondent for the Commonwealth Relations Trust Bursary for educational broadcasters. This annual bursary provides a three-month study tour of educational broadcasting in the United Kingdom.

Reaction to Issues. AMTEC provides opportunities for members to contribute to educational media and technology issues and their solutions. The association frequently communicates with other associations and levels of government to resolve issues of concern to the membership.

Publications. Publications include:

- *The Canadian Journal of Educational Communications (CJEC)*, a quarterly covering the latest in research, application, and periodical literature. It also publishes reviews on significant books, films, and critiques on computer programs.

- *Media News*, a quarterly newsletter covering the news in the field, including helpful tips, future conferences, comments on current projects, and information about AMTEC members and the AMTEC Board.

- *Membership Directory*, which expands the professional network of AMTEC members.

In addition, occasional publications are produced to assist members in keeping abreast in the field. These include directories, guidelines, and monographs.

Current Officers. The AMTEC Board of Directors includes the association's President, David A. Mappin; Past President, Bruce MacLean; President-Elect, Barbara Martin; Secretary/Treasurer, Allen LeBlanc; and three Directors, John Godfreyson, Dan Malone, and Eslo Marzotto.

Additional information may be obtained from AMTEC, 3-1750 The Queensway, Suite 1818, Etobicoke, Ontario, Canada M9C 5H5.

ISTE
International Society for Technology
in Education

PURPOSE

The International Society for Technology in Education is a nonprofit professional society of educators. Its goals include the improvement of education through the appropriate use of computer-related technology and the fostering of active partnerships between businesses and educators involved in this field. The majority of ISTE's efforts are aimed at precollege education and teacher preparation.

MEMBERSHIP

ISTE members are teachers, administrators, computer coordinators, curriculum coordinators, teacher educators, information resource managers, and educational technology specialists. Approximately 85 percent of the 7,000-person membership is in the United States, 10 percent is in Canada, and the remainder is scattered throughout nearly 100 other countries.

ACTIVITIES

ISTE works to achieve its mission through its publication program, which includes 12 periodicals as well as a wide range of books and courseware; co-sponsorship or sponsorship of a variety of conferences and workshops; its extensive network of regional affiliates, a Private Sector Council; a distance education program; and membership in NCATE (National Council for the Accreditation of Teacher Education).

PUBLICATIONS

Periodical publications include membership periodicals: *The Computing Teacher* (8/yr.); *Journal of Research on Computing in Education* (q.); and *ISTE Update: People, Events, and News in Education Technology* (newsletter, 8/yr.). Quarterly periodicals for special interest groups (SIGs) include: *Logo Exchange*, for the Logo SIG; *Journal of Computing in Teacher Education*, for the Teacher Educators SIG; *HyperNEXUS*, for the Hyper/Multi-Media SIG; *Journal of Computer Science Education*, for the Computer Science SIG; *T.I.E. News*, for the Telecommunications SIG; and *SIGTC Connections*, for the Technology Coordinator SIG. Other periodicals include *Education Information Resource Manager Quarterly; Microsoft Works in Education*, a quarterly for users of Microsoft Works; and *CAELL Journal* (Computer Assisted English Language Learning Journal), a quarterly for teachers of English, foreign languages, and adult literacy.

ISTE also publishes a variety of books and courseware.

CONFERENCES

ISTE is the financial sponsor of the National Educational Computing Conference, which was held June 15-17, 1992, in Dallas, Texas. ISTE will be running another national conference October 1-4, 1992, in Denver, Colorado.

CURRENT OFFICERS

The current ISTE Board includes Bonnie Marks, President; Sally Sloan, President-Elect; Gary Bitter; Ruthie Blankenbaker; Cyndy Everst-Bouch; Sheila Cory; Susan Friel; Margaret Kelly; Don Knezek; Jenelle Leonard; Marco Murray-Lasso; Paul O'Driscoll; and David Walker.

Further information is available from ISTE, 1787 Agate St., Eugene, OR 97403-1923. (503) 346-4414. Fax (503) 346-5890.

IVLA
International Visual Literacy Association

PURPOSE

IVLA, Inc., a nonprofit international association, was established in 1968 to provide a multidisciplinary forum for the exploration, presentation, and discussion of all aspects of visual communication and their applications through visual images, visual literacy, and literacies in general. The association serves as the organizational bond for professionals from many diverse disciplines who are creating and sustaining the study of the nature of visual experiences and literacies and their cognitive and affective bases, and who are developing new means for the evaluation of learning through visual methods. It also encourages the funding of creative visual literacy projects, programs, and research and promotes and evaluates projects intended to increase the use of visuals in education and communications.

MEMBERSHIP

IVLA members represent a diverse group of disciplines, including fine and graphic artists, photographers, researchers, scientists, filmmakers, television producers, graphic and computer-graphic designers, phototherapists, business communication professionals, school administrators, classroom teachers, visual studies theorists and practitioners, educational technologists, photojournalists, print and electronic journalists, and visual anthropologists.

MEMBER SERVICES

Members of IVLA benefit from opportunities to interact with other professionals whose ideas may be challenging or reinforcing. Such opportunities are provided by the annual conference, information exchanges, research programs, workshops, seminars, presentation opportunities as an affiliate of the Association for Educational Communications and Technology (AECT), and access to the Visual Literacy Collection located in the Center for Visual Literacy at Arizona State University.

PUBLICATIONS

IVLA publishes two periodicals: *Journal of Visual Literacy* (2/yr.) and *Review*, a visual literacy newsletter. It also publishes an annual book of conference readings.

CONFERENCES

The 24th annual conference will be held in Pittsburgh, Pennsylvania, September 30 to October 4, 1992. The conference theme will be "Imagery in Science and the Arts."

CURRENT OFFICERS

Rhonda S. Robinson, President; Roberts A. Braden, President-Elect; and Alice D. Walker, Membership Chair.

Further information may be obtained from IVLA, Educational Technologies-LRS, Old Security Building, Blacksburg, VA 24061-0232.

NSPI
National Society for Performance
and Instruction

NSPI is an international association dedicated to increasing productivity in the workplace through the application of performance and instructional technologies. Founded in 1962, the society promotes the improvement of human performance among governmental, legislative, business, corporate, and educational leaders, and through the national media.

MEMBERSHIP

The 5,000 members of NSPI are located throughout the United States, Canada, and 30 other countries. Members include performance technologists, training directors, human resource managers, instructional technologists, change agents, human factors practitioners, and organizational development consultants. They work in a variety of settings, including business, industry, universities, governmental agencies, health services, banks, and the armed forces.

SERVICES TO NSPI MEMBERS

NSPI offers its members opportunities to grow professionally and personally, to meet and know leaders in the field and learn about new things before they are published for the world at large, to make themselves known in the field, and to pick up new ideas on how to deal with their own political and technical challenges on the job. Membership benefits include subscriptions to *Performance & Instruction* and *News & Notes*; the *Annual Membership Directory*; participation in the annual conference and exposition; access to a variety of resources and individuals to help them improve their professional skills and marketability; a variety of insurance programs at group rates; leadership opportunities through participation in special projects, 12 major committees, and task forces, or serving as national or chapter officers; an executive referral service; and discounts on publications, advertising, conference registration and recordings, and other society services.

ACTIVITIES

The NSPI Endowment sponsors the Young Academic Program, an awards program for recent recipients of a doctoral degree currently working in academic positions. Designed to promote excellence in the field, the award is given for research on topics related to performance and instructional technology, including literature reviews and/or meta-analyses with implications for performance-enhancing interventions. The recipient of the award of $500 is required to prepare and make a presentation at the annual conference and submit a potentially publishable manuscript.

CONFERENCES

Annual Conference and Expo, Miami Beach, Florida, April 13-17, 1992; Chicago, Illinois, March 22-26, 1993.

PUBLICATIONS

NSPI publications include *Performance & Instruction Journal* (10/yr.); *Performance Improvement Quarterly; News & Notes* (10/yr.); and the *Annual Membership Directory*.

CURRENT OFFICERS

Esther Safir, President; Roger Addison, President-Elect; Deborah Lee Stone, Vice President — Technology Applications; H. Rosalind Cowie, Vice President — Chapters and Membership; Carol Robinson, Vice President — Finance; Maurice Coleman, Vice President — Research Development; Paul Tremper, Executive Director.

Further information is available from NSPI, 1300 L Street NW, Suite 1250, Washington, DC 20005. (202) 408-7969.

SALT
Society for Applied Learning Technology

PURPOSE

The Society for Applied Learning Technology (SALT) is a nonprofit professional membership organization that was founded in 1972. Membership in the society is oriented to professionals whose work requires knowledge and communication in the field of instructional technology. The society provides members a means to enhance their knowledge and job performance by participation in society-sponsored meetings, through subscriptions to society-sponsored publications, by association with other professionals at conferences sponsored by the society, and through membership in special interest groups and special society-sponsored initiatives/projects.

The society sponsors conferences that are educational in nature and cover a wide range of application areas, such as interactive videodisc in education and training, development of interactive instructional materials, CD-ROM applications in education and training, interactive instruction delivery, and learning technology in the health care sciences. These conferences provide attendees with an opportunity to become familiar with the latest technical information on application possibilities, on technologies, and on methodologies for implementation. In addition, they provide an opportunity for interaction with other professional and managerial individuals in the field.

In addition, the society offers members discounts on society-sponsored journals, conference registration fees, and publications.

PUBLICATIONS

SALT's publications include:

- *Journal of Interactive Instruction Development*. This established quarterly journal meets the needs of instructional systems developers and designers by providing important perspectives on emerging technologies and design technologies.

- *Journal of Medical Education Technologies*. Now in its second year of publication, this exciting new journal helps keep readers abreast of developments utilizing technology-based learning systems to train health care professionals and educate students involved in the various health care disciplines.

- *Journal of Educational Technology Systems*. This quarterly publication deals with systems in which technology and education interface and is designed to inform educators who are interested in making optimum use of technology.

- *Instruction Delivery Systems*. Society members are eligible to have a free subscription to this bi-monthly magazine, which covers interactive multimedia applications and happenings. With up-to-date application descriptions and valuable reference editions, it is devoted to enhancing productivity through appropriate applications of technology in education, training, and job performance.

UPCOMING CONFERENCES

Conferences in 1992 were held February 26-28 in Orlando, Florida, and August 26-28 in Washington, DC. Conferences for 1993 will be held February 24-26 in Orlando, Florida, and August 25-27 in Washington, DC.

CURRENT OFFICERS

Dr. Nathaniel Macon, Chairman; Raymond G. Fox, President; Dr. Stanley Winkler, Vice President; and Dr. Carl R. Vest, Secretary/Treasurer.

Further information is available from the Society for Applied Learning Technology, 50 Culpeper St., Warrenton, VA 22186. (703) 347-0055. Fax (703) 349-3169.

Current Developments in Educational Technology Programs

The Ph.D. Program in Educational Technology at the University of Northern Colorado

Edward P. Caffarella
University of Northern Colorado

The field of educational technology is continually changing, based upon new learning theories, additional research, more powerful software, and new hardware developments. This continual change presents a challenge for the training of the leaders in the field. The faculty at the University of Northern Colorado (UNC) met this challenge by implementing a new Ph.D. program in educational technology. The program is future-oriented, with emphasis areas in: (1) Instructional Development/Design, (2) Interactive Technologies, and (3) Technology Integration. The Instructional Development/Design emphasis area deals with the systematic development and design of instructional systems. The Interactive Technologies emphasis area concentrates on two specific interactive technologies: computer-based instruction and distance education. The Technology Integration emphasis area looks at how technology is implemented in educational and training situations based upon innovation theory and change research.

The University of Northern Colorado doctoral program in educational technology focuses on the convergence of three major communication and information industries into a single industry. Negroponte (Brand 1987) believes that the broadcasting and motion picture industry, the print and publishing industry, and computer industry, although historically distinct, are undergoing a metamorphosis and will be one large industry by the year 2000. Negroponte has a vision that

> All communication technologies are suffering a joint metamorphosis, which can only be understood properly if treated as a single subject, and only advanced properly if treated as a single craft. The way to figure out what needs to be done is through exploring the human sensory and cognitive system and the ways that humans most naturally interact. Join this and you grasp the future (p. 11).

This vision has major implications for doctoral programs in educational technology. Within each of the three industry groups identified by Negroponte there is an educational subindustry. These subindustry groups have been and will continue to be major components in the field of educational technology. As the larger industry groups undergo a metamorphosis, so will the respective education-related subindustry groups.

Educational technology professionals must be prepared to function within the converged industries rather than in only one of the historically distinct industries. The University of Northern Colorado doctoral program in educational technology prepares graduates who will be leaders after the metamorphosis. By taking this approach, the UNC program is unique among educational technology doctoral programs. Other programs focus on separate aspects, such as computer-based instruction or media production, but rarely do other programs focus on the convergence of communication and information.

This doctoral program uses a community-of-scholars model of interaction among students and faculty members. The students are viewed as developing colleagues with progressively higher levels of responsibility as they move through the program. Cooperative research and other scholarly projects are encouraged between faculty members and students. The doctoral program in educational technology provides the students with a broad base of knowledge in the use of technology in educational and training settings.

Courses in each of the major educational technology areas extend the student's level of specialization in instructional design, curriculum development, computer-based education delivery systems, hardware and software systems interface, designing instructional telecommunications programs, educational research, educational accountability procedures, technology systems evaluation, and educational technology hardware/software design. The doctoral program provides in-depth coverage of the major elements involved in educational technology as well as expanding individual opportunities for students to discover extensive specialized fields of interest for research and development purposes.

PROGRAM OBJECTIVES

The doctoral program is specifically designed to increase the levels of competence achieved in the master's degree program. Students entering the doctoral program must have a master's degree in educational technology or a related field. Students in the educational technology program master a set of common program objectives and a set of objectives specific to an emphasis area in either instructional development/design, interactive technologies, or technology integration. Graduates of the doctoral program in educational technology are proficient in the common core courses and at least one of the three emphasis areas.

Common Core for All Students

- Historical basis for current research in educational technology

- Prescription of treatments to maximize learning/performance outcomes in a variety of contexts

- Evaluation of instructional systems

- Synthesis and evaluation of empirical research on educational technology processes and products

- Generation of sound data collection/analysis procedures

- Procedures for conducting basic and applied research

- Management and supervision of large-scale research projects

- Conduct of empirical research; students are expected to contribute to the knowledge base of educational technology and to disseminate the results at professional meetings and in scholarly journals.

Instructional Development/Design Emphasis

- Utilization of selected assessment and analysis methodologies

- Use of instructional system design for applications in educational and training situations

- Implementation of instructional development models and theories

- Design and execution of both formative and summative evaluation plans

- Application of instructional theories to the design of instruction

- Design and integration of instruction to maximize performance outcomes, regardless of context.

Interactive Technologies Emphasis

- Development and implementation of computer-based courseware in education and training contexts

- Use of software development environments such as authoring systems, authoring languages, and general-purpose languages

- Convergence of computer technology, presentation technology, recording technology, and telecommunications technology into interactive technology

- Integration of interactive technology into education, training, and management environments

- Evaluation of interactive solutions, such as instructional software or telecommunications

- Design and development of teaching materials appropriate for distant delivery of instruction

- Selection and coordination of various telecommunications configurations for instructional applications

- Design of research on interactive technologies according to theoretical bases within the field of educational technology.

Technology Integration Emphasis

- Development of diffusion plans for the integration of technology

- Specification of technological systems for educational and training applications

- Administration and management of educational technology and technology systems

- Provision of leadership for the integration of technology.

FIELD OF STUDY

Educational technology is a systematic process that uses scientific principles to solve instructional problems for the improvement of instruction and the enhancement of learning. Percival and Ellington (1984) define *educational technology* as "a systematic approach to a problem, together with the application of appropriate scientific research both from 'hard' sciences such as physics and electronics and from social sciences such as psychology and sociology" (p. 14). Another classic definition states that educational technology is "a complex integrated process involving people, procedures, ideas, devices, and organizations, for analyzing problems, and devising, implementing, evaluating, and managing solutions to those problems, involved in all aspects of human learning" (Association for Educational Communications and Technology 1977, 130).

Educational technology is simultaneously focused on three major factors: the instructional design process, the software, and the hardware systems. By appropriately balancing each of these factors with the other two, the educational technologist can design effective instruction. The effective educational technologist must understand the advantages and limitations of all three aspects. The solution to a problem is not embedded in any one factor, but emerges in the orchestration of all three.

The knowledge base for educational technology is drawn from a wide variety of fields. Richey (1986) identifies four major theoretical bases for educational technology: (1) general systems theory, (2) learning theories, (3) communication theories, and (4) conceptual models of instruction. The first three are clearly recognized as theories. Richey indicates that "the fourth theoretical base at this point has probably not progressed developmentally to the status of theory. However, there are well-formed conceptual models of instruction which exert considerable influence on instructional design activities" (p. 23).

Educational technology is built upon a multidisciplinary foundation that uses constructs from the fields of cognitive psychology, communications theory, mass communications, ergonomics, human resource development, organizational management, curriculum development, computer science, system theory, educational media, and instructional computing. Educational technologists learn to apply these constructs to improve performance outcomes within educational, instructional, and training contexts, regardless of the specific discipline or setting within which they are applied.

Educational technologists also learn that performance improvement strategies must be embedded at the teacher/sender end of instruction as well as at the student/receiver end of instruction. By taking a holistic, multidisciplinary approach, based upon principles of instructional system analysis, design, and evaluation, the educational technologist can make the teaching/learning process more efficient for all involved.

Educational technology programs focus upon both product issues and process issues. *Products* tend to be tangible in nature and are the primary means through which instructional messages are transmitted. Examples of products include computer-assisted instruction authoring systems, slide/tape materials, instructional videotapes, job aids, written instructional procedures, and even textbooks. Another, somewhat less tangible, class of products includes instructional and/or training programs designed to develop comprehensive instructional delivery systems. Educational technology *processes* consist of the analytical, design, and evaluative activities that enable the systematic planning of instruction and/or training. Process concerns include conducting needs analyses, performing task descriptions, preparing objectives statements, selecting appropriate means of instructional delivery, and evaluating instructional efficiency. The relationships among products and processes are both dynamically interactive and interdependent. They constitute a conceptual system that allows an educational technologist to develop instruction or training within replicable parameters (Wagner 1986).

The major functional areas for individuals in educational technology include: (1) research-theory, (2) design, (3) production, (4) evaluation-selection, (5) logistics, (6) utilization, (7) utilization-dissemination, (8) organizational management, and (9) personnel management (Association for Educational Communications and Technology 1989). Within educational technology there are three major specialty areas: (1) instructional program development, (2) media product development, and (3) media management. The role of the educational technologist can be defined by applying the nine functions to the three specialty areas. Some functions are more important to a particular specialty than others. Prigge (1977) identified the specific functions that are important to each specialty area and, for each function within a specialty area, identified numerous specific competencies.

The doctoral program at the University of Northern Colorado is directed mainly at what Prigge calls the instructional program development and the media management specialties. At UNC these are reflected respectively in the instructional development/design and technology integration emphasis areas. Within the media product development specialty, the UNC program prepares individuals only in the area of interactive technologies.

ADMISSION REQUIREMENTS

The prospective student must have a minimum combined verbal, quantitative, and analytical score of 1,650 on the Graduate Record Examination taken within the last five years. The individual verbal, quantitative, and analytical scores must be above 500. The prospective student must have a grade-point average of 3.2 on the most recent 60 semester hours of course work. Other requirements include a two-page statement of career goals, an interview with the faculty, and three letters of recommendation from individuals familiar with the professional and subject area competence of the prospective student. The letters should address the potential growth of the individual as a designer, producer, implementer, teacher, scholar, evaluator, and researcher in educational technology. The program is designed to be rigorous but practical, encouraging the serious, mature, motivated, and competent student to apply for admission.

PROGRAM AND GRADUATION REQUIREMENTS

A minimum of 67 semester hours beyond the master's degree is required for the doctorate in educational technology. The student must complete a minimum of two consecutive semesters as a full-time student (nine semester hours) and be registered for resident credit offered on-campus and applicable to the doctoral degree. Students admitted to a program must maintain a satisfactory grade-point average of 3.2.

At the end of the doctoral student's first semester in residence, or 15 semester hours in the program and at the end of the student's second semester, or 30 semester hours, the educational technology program notifies the student in writing that the student is: (1) encouraged to continue in the program, (2) discouraged from continuing in the program, or (3) placed on review for one semester. Students who are placed on review are reviewed again at the end of the next semester. At that time, the student is either encouraged to continue in the program or is asked to terminate the program.

Each doctoral student must pass a written comprehensive examination for the degree. This examination cannot be taken until the student has completed the residency requirement and at least 36 semester hours beyond the master's degree. The student must also have received two letters of support from the educational technology program faculty before taking the written comprehensive examination. The comprehensive examinations are designed, administered, and evaluated by the faculty in educational technology. The written part of the examination can address all aspects of the student's doctoral program. Two unsuccessful performances on the written examination result in dismissal from the program. Successful performance on the written comprehensive examination is a prerequisite to the oral examination. The oral examination may include questions from any part of the student's program and is designed to test the student's understanding of the field of educational technology. Two unsuccessful performances on the oral examination result in dismissal from the program. Successful performance on both the written and oral examinations is a prerequisite to doctoral candidacy and the dissertation.

The dissertation research advisor and the research committee for the dissertation are appointed after the student has passed the written and oral comprehensive examinations. The dissertation research advisor is identified as early in the student's program as possible, particularly for students with a well-defined dissertation topic. For these students, the probable dissertation research advisor is appointed as the doctoral program advisor. The dissertation proposal and dissertation are completed under the supervision of the research advisor and research committee. The actual decision on the proposal is made during a closed meeting of the research committee. Once the dissertation proposal has been accepted by the research committee and by the graduate school, the student's name is submitted to the graduate school for admission to doctoral candidacy. In addition to passing the written and oral comprehensive examinations, candidacy requires the student to have earned at least 39 semester hours beyond the master's degree. The doctoral dissertation is examined by members of the research committee in an oral defense that is publicized and open to the general public. The research committee then makes the determination of the acceptability of the dissertation in a closed meeting.

PROGRAM CURRICULUM

The educational technology program offers a doctoral degree with emphasis areas in instructional design/development, interactive technology, and technology integration. Because the program of study builds upon the requirements for the master's degree in educational technology, students must have taken comparable course work to satisfy the core and emphasis area requirements of the master's degree in educational technology, or must take these courses as electives in the doctoral program. Doctoral students must complete both the common educational technology core and the research core, and specialize in one of the three emphasis areas. Students entering the doctoral program with a master's degree from an accredited institution are required to take a minimum of 67 semester hours of graduate credit.

COURSE REQUIREMENTS

Educational Technology Core

ET	524	Design of Computer-Assisted Instruction	3
ET	602	Instructional Analysis and Design	3
ET	610	Production of Instructional Materials	3
ET	784	Doctoral Seminar in Educational Technology	3
ET	797	Doctoral Proposal Seminar	4
EPRE	682	Cognition and Instruction	3
		Subtotal	19

Research Methodology Core

EPRE	602	Elements of Statistics	3
EPRE	603	Analysis of Variance	3
EPRE	610	Statistical Packages in Educational Research or	
EPRE	680	Qualitative Research Methods	3
EPRE	700	Advanced Research Methods	3
		Subtotal	12

Each student also completes 12 semester hours of course work in one of the three emphasis areas. Three of these hours must be in an internship or practicum.

Emphasis Area: Instructional Development/Design

ET	650	Corporate Course Design	3
ET	692	Internship: Instructional Development/Design or	
ET	693	Practicum: Instructional Development/Design	3
ET	702	Instructional Design Theory	3
ET	782	Research in Instructional Development/Design	3
		Minimum Subtotal	12

Emphasis Area: Interactive Technologies

ET	613	Instructional Telecommunications	3
ET	615	Distance Education: Theories and Practice	3
ET	627	Computer-Assisted Instruction Authoring Systems	3
ET	628	Interactive Video Technologies	3
ET	692	Internship: Interactive Technologies	
		or	
ET	693	Practicum: Interactive Technologies	3
ET	725	Programming Languages for Educational Applications	3
		Minimum Subtotal	12

Emphasis Area: Technology Integration

ET	680	Integration of Technology into Curricula	3
ET	692	Internship: Technology Integration	
		or	
ET	693	Practicum: Technology Integration	3
ET	735	Design of Complex Technology Systems	3
ET	780	Diffusion of Technological Innovations	3
		Minimum Subtotal	12

Electives

(Selected in consultation with the advisor)

General Electives	6
Electives from outside Educational Technology and program required courses	6
Subtotal	12

Dissertation

ET	799	Doctoral Dissertation	12
		Subtotal	12
		Minimum Total	67

Research Tools

Doctoral students in educational technology must demonstrate competency in two out of the four following research tools: (1) Research Design/Applied Statistics/Quantitative Methods, (2) Computer Applications, (3) Evaluation, and (4) Foreign Language.

COURSE DESCRIPTIONS

ET 500 *Introduction to Performance Technology* (3). Human performance improvement systems (including technology, learning, management, communication, human factors, and media) and their impact upon the process of education and training are described.

ET 502 *Instructional Development* (3). Covers development procedures and analysis systems/techniques for determining instructional content. Determining instructional efficiency at the systems, curriculum, course, and lesson levels.

ET 503 *Computers in Education* (3). A survey course of computer systems, operating languages, and educational applications. Includes types of classroom programs and software applications.

ET 504 *Instructional Materials Design* (3). Procedures for designing and developing instructional materials. Includes scripting and production specifications for graphic, audio, slide/tape, and/or video formats.

ET 524 *Design of Computer-Assisted Instruction* (3). Prerequisite: ET 503. A study of the authoring systems/languages used for computer-based delivery on micro- , mini- , and mainframe systems. Provides experience in using learning system protocols and creating sample lessons/tests.

ET 530 *Media Cataloging and Classification* (3). Study the purpose, theory, and principles of cataloging and classifying media. Includes Dewey Decimal, Library of Congress, and other systems, as well as online cataloging.

ET 533 *Reference and Information Management* (3). Discusses suitable materials for elementary, secondary, and postsecondary resource centers, as well as databases and research indexes for students, instructors, and administrators.

ET 535 *Administration of Instructional Resources* (3). The essentials of organizing and administering instructional resource centers at elementary, secondary, and postsecondary levels. Includes budget preparation and personnel management.

ET 536 *Media Selection, Utilization, and Evaluation* (3). Prerequisites: ET 401, ET 504, and consent of instructor. Selection principles, utilization strategies, and evaluative criteria for print and nonprint media for individuals, groups, and different ages and cultural groups. Includes CAI/CMI evaluation.

ET 602 *Instructional Analysis and Design* (3). Application of contemporary theories of learning and instruction to systematic instructional development. Includes research foundations and current issues and trends of instructional analysis, design, and evaluation.

ET 610 *Production of Instructional Materials* (3). Prerequisite: ET 504. Techniques of desktop publishing and other modes of media production are emphasized.

ET 613 *Instructional Telecommunications* (3). Prerequisite: Consent of instructor. Conceptual issues and production techniques for developing instructional telecommunications systems and programs.

ET   615   *Distance Education: Theories and Practice* (3). Includes an overview of distance education foundations, design issues, systems development, and applications across curricula.

ET   627   *Computer-Assisted Instruction Authoring Systems* (3). Prerequisite: ET 524. The generation and validation of computerized courseware. Involves management components for teachers and trainers and instructional components for students.

ET   628   *Interactive Video Technologies* (3). Investigation of the theory, implementation, practice, and research on interactive, computer-based instructional systems. Systems include interactive videodisc, interactive videotape, digital video interactive, CD-ROM, rewrite optical, and image-capture technologies applied in instructional or performance interventions.

ET   650   *Corporate Course Design* (3). Prerequisite: Consent of instructor. Reviews issues related to corporate course design. RFP preparation, human factors, incentive systems, pluralism, and resource management are also featured.

ET   680   *Integration of Technology into Curricula* (3). Prerequisite: ET 503 or consent of instructor. Deals with issues and methodologies for integrating technology into existing K-12 curricula. Specific approaches and problems with current models are investigated and directions for research are discussed.

ET   684   *Seminar in Educational Technology* (3). Prerequisite: Consent of instructor. For students wishing to develop advanced competency in educational technology. Periodically, seminar may focus on a topic reflecting the instructor's interest area or on developing a student's inquiry.

ET   692   *Internship: Subtitle* (3). Needs advisor's recommendation and permission of program director. Individual field experience in educational technology. Field experience and summative report format must be approved by instructor.

ET   693   *Practicum: Subtitle* (1-3). Supervised professional activity requiring a minimum of 10 hours per week. Develop project, product, or technological device unique to the field. An approved end-of-semester project report is required. May be repeated with different subtitles.

ET   702   *Instructional Design Theory* (3). Prerequisite: ET 602. In-depth examination of theories underlying instructional design methods. Multidisciplinary influences upon instruction theory development are examined. Both macro and micro design theories are featured.

ET   725   *Programming Languages for Educational Application* (3). Study of structured programming languages applied to educational practice, design, development, and research. Exploration of Object-Oriented Programming and Design as it applies to educational programming. Includes work with high-level languages such as Smalltalk/V and C++.

ET 735 *Design of Complex Technology Systems* (3). Exploration of the design, organization, and administration of large and complex technology systems. Investigation of the essential elements necessary for successful operation of large, complex systems.

ET 780 *Diffusion of Technological Innovations* (3). Investigation of the literature and research base in the diffusion of innovations. Application of theoretical and research findings to the diffusion of technological innovations.

ET 782 *Research in Instructional Development/Design* (3). Prerequisite: Consent of instructor. Review and critique of basic and applied research investigating instructional design and development applications in a variety of contexts.

ET 784 *Doctoral Seminar in Educational Technology* (3). Investigation of the development of the field of educational technology, including the theoretical and research bases for the field. Exploration of current research problems and directions for future research in educational technology.

ET 797 *Doctoral Proposal Seminar* (1-4). Design of research proposals and conduct of pilot studies to examine feasibility of proposed hypothesis. Summarize existing research, identify problems, develop hypotheses, and justify selection of design components.

ET 799 *Doctoral Dissertation* (1-12). Required of all doctoral candidates. Student must earn 12 hours of credit for the dissertation as partial fulfillment of requirements for all doctoral degrees.

INSTITUTIONAL FACILITIES

A number of units within the university support the efforts of the educational technology program. The *Interdisciplinary Center for Educational Technology* (ICET) provides media support, computing support, and instructional design assistance for students, faculty, and staff at the University of Northern Colorado. ICET houses a Macintosh lab, an Apple IIE lab, and a Phoenix system for computer-assisted instruction. ICET is also responsible for an IBM microcomputer laboratory. The *Western Institute for Distance Education (WIDE)* is dedicated to research and development in distance education. Services include instructional design, faculty development, and training in distance delivery systems. The *Educational Materials Services (EMS)*, a faculty support service, assists in the acquisition and use of educational media materials and equipment for classroom instruction. The *UNC Laboratory School* provides opportunities for graduate students and faculty to conduct research in areas of emphasis within the educational technology program with K-12 students. The *University Computer Center* supports the instructional, research, and administrative programs of the university.

STUDENT FINANCIAL SUPPORT

A variety of types of financial support are available to graduate students pursuing degrees in educational technology, including a number of teaching and graduate research assistantships. During the 1991-92 academic year, all educational technology doctoral students desiring financial support were provided with support. Teaching assistants also receive a full tuition waiver per semester as part of their compensation.

The various University of Northern Colorado initiatives in educational technology (such as ICET and WIDE) represent a ready source of financial support for doctoral students in educational technology. Financial assistance is also available on a need basis. Merit-based awards are available through the graduate school and the Colorado Fellowship Program.

PROGRAM SIZE

The Ph.D. program admits nine new students each year, with an expected graduation rate of six students each year. The numbers are kept relatively small to insure the quality of the program and the ability of faculty to do individual work with students. The projected graduation numbers parallel the numbers of graduates at other educational technology doctoral programs with similar numbers of faculty members. Doctoral programs in educational technology, with three exceptions, tend to be rather small and highly selective (Caffarella and Sachs 1990). Other than the three largest programs (Indiana University, University of Southern California, and Boston University), the typical number of graduates at the major programs averages slightly more than three per year. The University of Northern Colorado is currently the 24th largest program in terms of graduates. With the projected numbers of graduates in the Ph.D. program, UNC will become the seventh largest educational technology program in the United States. (The six largest programs include the schools previously listed and Syracuse University, the University of Pittsburgh, and Florida State University.)

REFERENCES

Association for Educational Communications and Technology. (1977). *Educational technology: Definition and glossary of terms: Volume 1*. Washington, DC: Author.

Association for Educational Communications and Technology. (1989). *Guidelines for accreditation of programs in educational communication and information technologies*. Washington, DC: Author.

Brand, S. (1987). *The Media Lab: Inventing the future at MIT*. New York: Viking.

Caffarella, E. P., and Sachs, S. G. (1990). Doctoral dissertations in instructional design and technology, 1977 through 1988. *Educational Technology: Research and Development*, 38(3): 39-42.

Percival, F., and Ellington, H. (1984). *A handbook of educational technology*. London: Kogan Page.

Prigge, W. C. (1977). Accreditation and certification: A frame of reference. In *Guidelines for certification of media specialists*, ed. M. Galey & W. Grady. Washington, DC: Association for Educational Communications and Technology.

Richey, R. (1986). *The theoretical and conceptual bases of instructional design*. New York: Nichols.

Wagner, E. (1986). Educational technology process systems: The methodology of instructional development. *Educational Technology*, 26(5): 36-39.

Part Three
Current Developments

Introduction

One obligation of an annual review such as the *Educational Media and Technology Yearbook* is to present up-to-date information on new developments in the field. This book represents a growing field with new products, innovative ideas, and exciting new applications of media and technology to the processes of teaching and learning. This part offers a smorgasbord of information that should be useful to every educational media and technology professional. Although it would be impossible to capture all of the new developments, there is some order and rationale for the articles that follow.

The categories used in the design of this part facilitated the solicitation of the specific articles contained here. It is the intention of the editors to continue these categories in future editions of the *Yearbook* so that there will be a regular chronicle of developments in the field over the years. There has not been any such documentation, except for what appears on a random basis in professional journals. The categories and the author for each article are

Research	Richard E. Clark
School Restructuring	Michael Molenda
Networking	Ann P. Bishop
Information Technology	Gary Marchionini
	Eileen Schroeder
Telecommunications	Bobbie L. Kamil
	Farhad Saba
Contemporary Social Issues	Delia Newman
	Lydia Hajnosz Doty

Individuals may read articles in this part selectively. Each article is self-contained; there is no overall theme. Each article offers state-of-the-art information that speaks to contemporary issues and each author is a specialist in his or her respective area.

Six Definitions of Media
in Search of a Theory

Richard E. Clark
University of Southern California

In this article, both European and North American research on media and learning are reviewed. The conditions under which media can be made to optimally influence learning are being explored from at least six perspectives: (1) media as technology or machines; (2) media as teachers or tutors; (3) media as socializers; (4) media as motivators; (5) media as mental tools for thinking; and (6) multimedia and interactive video. A key point that distinguishes these six areas from one another are six or more different definitions of *media*. This article attempts to provide the most representative definition of media and a brief review of the results of research in each of the six areas. The point is made that in only one of the six areas (media as mental tools) is there any serious attempt to generate a coherent theory that would explain why we might expect any learning benefits from media.

A TECHNOCENTRIC DEFINITION OF MEDIA

For many years it has been common for educational researchers to define a medium in technocentric ways, that is: "the mechanical and electronic aspects that determine its function and, to some extent, its shape and other physical features. These are the characteristics that are commonly used to classify a medium such as a television, a radio, and so on" (Kozma 1991, 180). For decades, researchers have used this technocratic definition to study whether one medium produced more learning than another medium, or whether one medium was better than another for certain curriculum content or types of students. These studies were generally not guided by any theoretical explanation for why we would expect the technology of one medium to produce more learning than the technology of another. During the 1980s, after many hundreds of these atheoretical comparison studies, it became obvious that learning from media had little to do with media's technological or mechanical aspects. This view is gradually being accepted (for reviews of the research and related issues see, for example, Clark and Salomon 1986; Hannifin 1985; Hooper and Hannifin 1991; Kozma 1991; Ross and Morrison 1990; Salomon and Gardner 1986). An often-quoted conclusion from reviews of this technocentric research is that media, defined as technology or machines, "are mere vehicles that deliver instruction but do not influence student achievement any more than the truck that delivers our groceries causes changes in our nutrition" (Clark 1983, 457). The point of the grocery truck analogy is that when media are defined only by their form or machines (and not by the content they deliver or the context in which they operate), then we can expect no learning benefit from them.

The Educational Implications of Technocentric Research

It seems obvious that when machines alone define media, we could expect no learning benefits from them, but school and government policy often reflects a different view. Money allocated for the purchase of school media, such as television or computers, is often rationalized by the expectation that instruction and learning will improve as a result (Clark and Salomon 1986). Technocentric research strongly suggests that public policymakers must turn their attention to the content of the media being used for instruction and the way they are utilized in schools.

MEDIA AS TEACHERS

Another familiar application of media is as a substitute for, or an augmentation of, the classroom teacher (Cuban 1988). In this approach, *media* is defined as communication equipment and forms plus the instructional content delivered by the equipment and the context in which it is provided. In this tradition, we study media very much like those who do research on teaching. The goal of technology as teacher or tutor is to provide additional teaching resources to schools limited by large class size; or to locations that are limited by budgets that are too inadequate to provide a rich curriculum; or to students who are isolated or who have individual tutoring requirements because of special needs. Occasionally, when media is used as a teacher, it is intended to supply teaching resources and skills that the local classroom teachers either do not possess or are too busy to provide.

Research in this area tends to take the form of large-scale surveys in which systematic counts are made of factors such as: the number of units of different kinds of media technology in use over time; the types of subject matter being taught by different media; the funds spent on technology and instructional programs and the source of those funds; the variety and cost of instructional packages or courseware purchased or developed by schools and currently in use at different levels of schooling; and the training of teachers to integrate computers into classroom activities and school curricula. Because of the scope and logistical problems with descriptive studies, they tend to be specific to one technology. Recently, the computer has been the focus of many surveys.

Surveys of Computer Use

In two of the best and most recent examples of survey research in media, Sugrue (1991) compares European and North American computer applications and Becker (1986) provides in-depth analysis of computer use in American elementary and secondary schools. Sugrue draws on surveys conducted in Europe and the United States to report that some of the similarities between the different geographic areas are that:

1. Local funds for the purchase and use of computers in schools are at least as important as state or national funding.

2. Teacher training for the use of computers across the school curriculum is minimal, with a few notable exceptions.

3. Elementary schools lag behind secondary schools in the use of computers for instruction, though the difference between the two levels is greater in Europe than it is in North America.

4. Secondary schools have tended to use the computer to teach about the computer rather than using the medium as an instructional device.

Sugrue mentions three main differences between European and North American computer use. First, European educational software for the computer tends to be developed within the education sector, most often supported by central government or European Community grants. U.S. educational software tends to be developed more by private and business initiatives and evaluation is conducted by schools and universities (if at all). Second, North American schools appear to have about twice as many computers per student when compared with only the largest European states. Third, there is a much greater diversity of computer hardware and software in European schools than in North America.

Becker's (1986) analysis of large-scale studies of computer use in the United States describes plans to make much more use of computers in the area of word processing (using the computer to write), mathematics education, and English language training. He reports that American schools consider their most serious problems with computers to be that teachers' knowledge of computers is too weak and that computer instruction is too difficult to fit into the existing curriculum and classroom activities.

Learning to Write with Computers

Other "media as teacher" studies provide experimental and evaluation data related to specific types of media-based instructional packages. For example, Cochran-Smith (1991) provides a thorough review of the research on using computers to teach word processing and writing in elementary school and the problems teachers encounter integrating media with the existing curriculum and teaching activities. She suggests a number of "propositions" based on the existing research, including:

1. Successful teachers have clear writing goals and tend to organize students into collaborative and coached writing arrangements to make use of computer text-editing programs.

2. When compared with paper-and-pencil writing classes, computer word processing seems to affect the surface characteristics of student papers (for example, the number of revisions increase, texts are longer, and grammar errors decrease somewhat), but meaning-level changes are not frequent.

3. Students who are better writers before using computers benefit from existing programs more than those who are poor writers.

4. Students of all ages and backgrounds seem able both to master the computer and to have a generally positive attitude toward using the computer to learn writing.

It must be noted that few of these studies actually measure the amount of learning that takes place that is directly attributable to any specific type of media program. The concern in this "media as teacher" area of research is to make accurate surveys and report on evaluations of aspects of media use that are thought to be related to increased school effectiveness.

MEDIA AS SOCIALIZERS

The longest tradition in media research is to be found in studies of the educational and social effects of so-called "mass media." Here *media* is defined as the contents or programs presented by commercial and entertainment-based mass communication efforts directed at people in their homes or in out-of-school locations. Examples of the media examined in these studies are broadcast television and radio programs, newspapers, magazines, and movies. In recent years, the focus of most of these studies has been on the effects of broadcast television programs on the behavior, attitudes, and school performance of children. Strittmatter (1990), in a review of European (largely German) and American mass media studies, notes the criticism that in both Europe and the United States "there is a lamentable deficit in the theoretical groundwork for the research activities" (p. 489).

In the United States, a great deal of research effort has been targeted on questions about whether mass media encourage violent attitudes and behavior and/or detract from children's school work. Other questions are concerned with the influence of entertainment media on children's learning of values related to areas such as sex roles, work, and equity issues. General results indicate that some aspects of violent behavior and the development of values and behavior can be found in entertainment media use and that the effect is greater for some children than for others. It is important to note that the origin of these effects is to be found in the *contents* of the programs that are broadcast or delivered in magazines or newspapers, *not* in the technology of the media.

Television Viewing and School Performance

One of the most enduring issues confronting researchers in this area is the concern voiced by many parents about possible negative effects of the time children spend watching television. Studies report either no effect or relatively small negative correlations between the number of hours children spend watching entertainment television and their school performance (Vooijs and Van Der Voort 1990). However, the effect of entertainment may be greater for some children than for others. Among U.S. children entering school, the average amount of time spent watching television is about two hours each evening and this amount increases as children get older. It is estimated that by the time most American children leave school, they have spent more time watching television than being taught by a teacher (Dorr 1986). Yet, there are very large individual differences between children in hours spent in front of the television. Approximately one-third of all children watch television constantly, whereas 10 percent do not watch at all. These individual differences in viewing time stay very stable over the years during childhood (Dorr 1986). What accounts for these large individual differences? Plomin et al. (1990) presented interesting evidence that genetic factors unrelated to either children's intelligence or their temperament influence the amount of television viewing. They argue that because the genetic factor that influences television viewing is unrelated to aptitudes that have been found to influence achievement in school, television viewing will most likely not be found to detract from school performance. Yet children do learn both positive and negative attitudes and behaviors from entertainment media. Thus, another area of research asks whether it is possible to influence children's learning in positive directions and help to insulate them against the negative influences.

Critical Television Viewing Curricula

Vooijs and Van Der Voort (1990) summarized the results of existing European and American studies of curricula designed to teach children how to watch television in a way that eliminates its negative effects. They report that "there is little evidence that television curricula are capable of changing television's impact on children's attitudes and behavior" (p. 550). However, they stress that existing studies may not give the best impression of what future curricula *might* be able to accomplish. They suggest more theory-based studies of longer duration that focus on the home behavior (as opposed to school-based behavior) of children who are most "at risk" of negative effects.

MEDIA AS MOTIVATORS

Some measure of the enthusiasm of researchers and policymakers for newer media is due to the expectation that students will be more motivated to learn. The interest in cognitive theories of motivation has stimulated recent research on the motivating qualities of students' values, beliefs, and attributions in relation to different media (see Salomon 1984). In this motivation research, *media* is variously defined as technology, as tutors, and as socializing agents. The results of these studies are complex and somewhat counterintuitive. A brief sample of some of the many interesting results from various reviews of this research would include novelty effects, benefits for special students, individual differences in preferences for different media, and the quality of effort invested in media programs.

Novelty Effects

While there is an initial increase in motivation (and therefore an effort to learn) with the introduction of a new instructional medium, motivation tends to decrease over time in elementary and secondary school students until it reaches pre-introduction levels. In computer or visual instruction studies, for example, the novelty benefit of the computer or television disappears in most studies lasting longer than eight weeks (Clark and Salomon 1986). This novelty effect is not as common in studies of media use in universities.

Benefits to Special Students

Motivation benefits may be important for minority and special students. For example, Clark and Salomon (1986) review studies in which students were consistently motivated by media that they perceived as less prejudiced and more reliable and fair than their teachers.

Individual Differences in Preferences for Media

Salomon (1984) provided a very interesting model for the study of media motivation based on an integration of cognitive motivation theory. He notes large individual and cultural differences in students' beliefs and attributions about different media. Clark and Sugrue (1989a) noted that individual differences in motivation for one or another medium may be unstable and might change over a relatively short period of instruction.

Mindless Effort from Some Media

Clark (1982) reviewed aptitude-treatment interaction studies in which students chose instructional media programs that they liked but which were consistently found to produce significantly less achievement than media programs they had rejected. Salomon (1984) provides evidence that students like media which they perceive as "easier" and suggest that children give only "mindless" effort to easy media. On the other hand, media that are perceived as a bit more challenging might be liked a bit less, but students are more "mindful" when they learn.

Based on past research, caution should be exercised when deciding to adopt instructional media on the expectation that it will increase student motivation to learn over time.

MEDIA AS MENTAL TOOLS FOR THINKING AND PROBLEM SOLVING

The most recent research effort is directed towards exploring ways that newer media, such as computers and videodiscs, might present instruction that teaches students to think *in terms* of the tools presented (Salomon 1988; Kozma 1991). These new instructional programs might, for example, simulate expert reasoning about writing and grammar in a symbolic form that is particularly suited to the way that students mentally represent such information. The student is expected not only to learn various rules of grammar, but also to incorporate the reasoning heuristics of the expert and to be able, in the future, to think in more expert terms about writing. Salomon calls this process the "internalization" of cognitive tools, and he provides both research evidence and theoretical support for the approach (1988).

Kozma (1991, 181) notes that the definition of media is expanded considerably in the mental tool approach to include not only the technology of a medium but also

> the symbol systems it can employ and the processes that can be performed with it. For example, a computer with a graphics board or a speech synthesis board can use different symbols in its presentations than those without those features. Computers with enough memory to run expert systems can process information in different ways than those without such a memory. These additional symbol systems and processes are likely to account for the cognitive effects of these systems, rather than the technology, per se.

Experiments have demonstrated that it is possible, for example, to improve children's ability to notice parts of paintings and other visual displays through exposure to repeated operations of a zoom lens on a film or television camera. Changes have been found in cognitive style measures after children watched animation sequences where three-dimensional objects were "unwrapped" into two dimensions and different visual perspectives on a single event were examined (Clark and Sugrue 1989b; Salomon 1988). These experiments provide compelling evidence that the children who participated actually internalized the symbolic representation of mental processes that increased their ability to attend to cues and change their visual perspective. Kozma (1991) expanded the experimental examples of the mental tool approach to include some of the tools that are made possible by various forms of the information capabilities of books, computers, and multimedia technologies. Winn (1990) presented an interesting theoretical and empirical extension of the tool approach to learning from graphic displays, including computer graphics.

Disputes about the Mental Tool Approach

It is important to note that, as with any new area, there are disputes about the mental tool approach. One argument is that the tool research may ignore the "cognitive impenetrability" of some thinking processes (see, for example, Winn 1990). Another argument is about whether the technology of media plays any necessary role in the cultivation of the cognitive skills that are the object of this research. Clark and Sugrue (1989b) suggested that no media technology provides a unique symbol system or process that is necessary to learn any particular thinking or problem-solving skill. They acknowledge that treatments such as visual zooming and unwrapping can, under the conditions noted by Salomon (1988), cultivate mental skills. But they provide evidence that very different experimental treatments (taken from different symbol systems and processes) can produce the same or similar thinking skills (for a discussion of these issues, see, for example, Clark and Sugrue 1989b, 26-30). Critics contend that if different media, symbols, and processes produce similar cognitive skills, then the independent variables in learning research are not media-based symbols or processes. Instead, it is claimed that some symbol systems or processes may be more *efficient* for some students and that it is learning efficiency (for example, speed and cost) that is being influenced by symbols and processes, rather than learning per se (Clark and Sugrue 1989b; Hooper and Hannifin 1991; Hannifin 1985; Ross and Morrison 1990). Since few studies provide measures of learning efficiency or comparisons of efficiency between different treatments, the critics claim that we may not be realizing the potential benefit of this new approach.

MULTIMEDIA AND INTERACTIVE VIDEO RESEARCH

It is more difficult to pin down a specific definition of media in this very new area of research. Generally, *media* are defined as a *set* of different technologies and contents, often controlled by a computer. Implicit in the multimedia and interactive video research assumption is the expectation that media in combination may produce learning benefits that are not possible from any single or separate medium. This is a reasonable assumption, since it is common in science to find interactive benefits when single variables do not produce results. When separate variables are combined, they sometimes *interact* to produce strong and important effects. This is, for example, the basis for the entire area of "aptitude-treatment interaction" research (refer to Clark 1982). Thus, multimedia researchers examine the possibility that multiple media combinations may be more than the sum of their separate media. While there are many failed studies that compare the learning advantage of one medium versus another medium, few studies have compared the *multiplicative* effects of many media in combination versus any of the combined media used alone to teach the same subject matter.

Interactive Videodisc Studies as Examples of Multiplicative Research

The best current example of multiplicative media studies is to be found in the experiments that have been conducted on interactive videodisc (computer control of videodisc access) compared with either computers alone or other single medium. Bosco (1986) reviewed 28 of these comparison studies and found results similar to those reported by Clark (1983; 1985) for single-media comparison studies. When learning was assessed as an outcome, results were mixed. Some studies showed advantages for the multimedia interactive video, some for the single-media comparison (most often computers or television), and some comparisons resulted in "no significant differences." One suspects the familiar lack of control of instructional method and curriculum content (Clark 1983) between the different media. A similar conclusion was reached by Hannifin (1985) in his reviews of a number of studies of computer-controlled interactive video. He suggests that learning is influenced by the cognitive effects of instructional methods, not by the choice of media. He implies that the same teaching method can be used in a number of "specific instructional technologies" (media). He states:

> While interactive video technology itself may offer interesting potential, it seems unlikely that interactive video differs from allied technology from either learning or cognitive perspectives. Technologically-independent research in learning and processing provides empirically-based techniques and methods likely to facilitate learning. Similarly, studies designed to examine the ways in which the mental activities of the learner are supported to improve learning offer insights into effective lesson design and activity independent of specific instructional technologies. It seems improbable that these principles will be redefined as a consequence of interactive video technology (p. 236).

Also similar to the results reported in the single-media comparisons, the interactive video studies show "attitude" and training time advantages under some conditions. Subjects seem to report liking the interactive video better than the single-media comparison conditions. However, this attitude advantage might be an example of the novelty effect described by Clark (1983; 1985), since most of these studies represent a relatively brief exposure to the multimedia condition.

Another problem with these studies tends to be a lack of control of the informational content of the lessons presented in the different treatments (Clark 1985). What sometimes happens is that the research team attempts to duplicate an existing, single-medium instructional program on a multimedia system. During the duplication process, information required by the test and available in the original lesson is, by accident or oversight, not transferred to the multimedia version. In this case, we would expect to find evidence that the more complete, single-medium version results in greater learning. Examples of studies in which this control problem can be found are described by Clark (1985) and Clark and Salomon (1986).

Conclusions about the Learning Benefits of
Multiple versus Single Media

Available research does *not* support the claim that when two or more media are combined, their learning benefits are not greater than when they are used alone. While there are relatively fewer studies in this area, their results seem to follow the same pattern as the single-media comparison studies.

Why have the media comparison studies resulted in such negative and ambiguous results? The primary difficulty with the studies may stem from a lack of control of the instructional method or technique used to teach the tested learning content. So, for example, in a study on the use of interactive videodisc versus a noninteractive televised presentation of the lesson, the superior learning from videodisc will be attributed to its "multiple" media capacity. Yet, it would be difficult to rule out the strong possibility that the variable that produced a learning gain was not media, but the method variable many of us refer to as "interactivity."

Interactivity: A Medium or a Method Variable?

Interactivity is variously defined (refer to Hannifin 1985), but common to most definitions are the qualities of providing corrective and informational feedback based on student responses during instruction. Floyd defines *interactivity* as an instructional context where "the sequence and selection of messages are determined by the user's response to the material" (1982, 2). Although practitioners might argue that these qualities are the inherent features of the interactive videodisc technology, it is possible to provide interactivity in other media. For example, all these instructional variables could be presented by computer-based instruction and by live instructors. Hannifin (1985) describes experiments in which interactivity was successfully presented to learners by various single media. These experiments provide evidence for the claim that instructional methods such as interactivity can be provided with a variety of single and multiple media to produce similar learning benefits.

When studies that do not control instructional methods are reported, they tend to show evidence in favor of the multimedia treatment when the results are actually due to powerful instructional methods that are used *only* in the multimedia condition. This is most likely the case with the recent, large-scale meta-analysis of 47 North American interactive videodisc studies reported by Fletcher (1990). In the introduction to the report, Fletcher acknowledges the validity of Clark's (1983) argument in a statement that media such as videodisc "do not guarantee [learning] impact, but the functionalities they support and their applications do" (p. II-1). Functionalities is a construct similar to instructional methods. Interactivity is a "functionality" of instruction with videodisc *and* other media, including human beings. Nevertheless, Fletcher, in his summary of the review, permits the reader to slip back into the strong media argument when he concludes that, "Interactive videodisc instruction was more effective than conventional approaches to instruction ... and ... computer-based instruction ... but there was little in the reviewed studies to indicate how interactive videodisc instruction achieves its success" (pp. IV-1, 4). Since meta-analytic reviews seldom examine experimental control for methods or functionalities, the conclusions they reach tend to be as confounded as the studies they review. Well-designed studies that control for methods by having the same method available in all media treatments generally show no significant differences on learning outcomes (Clark and Salomon 1986).

Conclusions about Interactivity and Other Methods

Although it is impossible to reach a definitive conclusion, the best evidence seems to support the claim that various instructional methods (such as interactivity) are responsible for the measured achievement gains when multiple-media treatments are compared with more "conventional" single-media treatments. This result has been found with each successive wave of new media and technology for at least the past seven decades of educational research. Why then do we continue to repeat the same conceptual and design error? It is likely that part of the problem is our tendency to base research questions on problems that have financial or popular support but no theoretical justification.

CONCLUSION

If judged by the sheer number of studies, media inquiry continues to be one of the most active areas in educational research. Yet, until recently it has proceeded largely without the benefit of any theory that directs experiments. Perhaps because of the lack of theory, hundreds of very similar studies have come to the same unproductive end. This most obvious dead end is to be found in the technocentric research, which provides gross comparisons of, for example, the relative learning results obtained from teachers or television lessons. A number of the conceptual difficulties that plague the technocentric research are also to be found in the media as tutor, media as socializing agent, and multimedia and interactive video studies. The lack of theory in those areas has resulted in a body of experiments that are both difficult to interpret and to apply in our schools and communities (Clark 1985 and Hannifin 1985; Salomon 1984; Ross and Morrison 1990; Salomon and Gardner 1986). Much of the research on media motivation is now guided by the very healthy developments in cognitive motivation theory (Salomon 1984). Because the recent results of experiments in that area are very counterintuitive, they have even greater potential importance when applied to practice. Finally, the development of theory in the mental tool research is proceeding quickly and in an environment of healthy debate and discussion (see Clark and Sugrue 1989a; Salomon 1988; Kozma 1991). Most observers believe that some of the most vital and interesting research in the next decade will be found in the development of mental tools.

REFERENCES

Becker, H. J. (1986). *Instructional uses of school computers: Reports from the 1985 national survey* (Issues 1-6). Baltimore, Md.: Johns Hopkins Univ., Center for Social Organization of Schools.

Bosco, J. (1986). An analysis of the evaluations of interactive video. *Educational Technology*, 26(5): 7-17.

Clark, R. E. (1982). Antagonism between achievement and enjoyment in ATI studies. *Educational Psychologist*, 53(4): 91-101.

Clark, R. E. (1983). Reconsidering research on learning from media. *Review of Educational Research*, 53(4): 445-59.

Clark, R. E. (1985). Confounding in educational computing research. *Journal of Educational Computing Research*, 1(2): 28-42.

Clark, R. E., and Salomon, G. (1986). Media in teaching. In *Handbook of Research on Teaching* (3d ed.), ed. M. Wittrock. New York: Macmillan.

Clark, R. E., and Sugrue, B. M. (1989a). North American disputes about research on learning from media. *International Journal of Educational Research*, 14(6): 507-20.

Clark, R. E., and Sugrue, B. M. (1989b). Research on instructional media, 1978-1988. In *Educational Media Yearbook 1988*, ed. D. Ely. Littleton, Colo.: Libraries Unlimited.

Cochran-Smith, M. (1991). Word processing and writing in elementary classrooms: A critical review of related literature. *Review of Educational Research*, 61(1): 107-55.

Cuban, L. (1988). *Teachers and machines: The classroom uses of technology since 1920*. New York: Teachers College Press.

Dorr, A. (1986). *Television and children: A special medium for a special audience*. Beverly Hills, Cal.: Sage.

Fletcher, J. D. (1990). Effectiveness and cost of interactive videodisc instruction in defense training and education. Alexandria, Va.: Institute for Defense Analyses. (Report No. 81-1502).

Floyd, S. (1982). Thinking interactively. In *Handbook of interactive video*, ed. S. Floyd and B. Floyd. White Plains, N.Y.: Knowledge Industry Publications.

Hannifin, M. J. (1985). Empirical issues in the study of computer-assisted interactive video. *Educational Communications and Technology Journal*, 33(4): 235-47.

Hooper, S., and Hannifin, M. J. (1991). Psychological perspectives on emerging instructional technologies: A critical analysis. *Educational Psychologist*, 26(1): 69-95.

Kozma, R. B. (1991). Learning with media. *Review of Educational Research*, 61(2): 179-211.

Plomin, R., Corley, R., DeFries, J. C., and Fulker, D. W. (1990). Individual differences in television viewing in early childhood: Nature as well as nurture. *Psychological Science*, 1(6): 371-77.

Ross, S. M., and Morrison, G. R. (1990). In search of a happy medium in instructional technology research: Issues concerning external validity, media replications and learner control. *Educational Technology Research and Development*, 37(1): 19-33.

Salomon, G. (1984). Television is "easy" and print is "tough": The differential investment of mental effort in learning as a function of perceptions and attributions. *Journal of Educational Psychology*, 76(4): 647-58.

Salomon, G. (1988). AI in reverse: Computer tools that turn cognitive. *Journal of Educational Computing Research*, 4(2): 123-34.

Salomon, G., and Gardner, H. (1986). The computer as educator: Lessons from television research. *Educational Researcher*, 13-19.

Strittmatter, P. (1990). European research on media and technology in education: Current status and future directions. *International Journal of Educational Research*, 14(6): 489-505.

Sugrue, B. M. (1991). A comparative review of European and American approaches to computer-based instruction in schools. In *Problems and promises of computer-based training*, ed. T. M. Shlechter. Norwood, N.J.: Ablex.

Vooijs, M. W., and Van Der Voort, T. H. A. (1990). Teaching television: The effects of critical television viewing curricula. *International Journal of Educational Research*, 14(6): 489-505.

Winn, W. D. (1990). A theoretical framework for research on learning from graphics. *International Journal of Educational Research*, 14(6): 553-64.

Technology and School Restructuring
Some Clarifying Propositions

Michael Molenda
Associate Professor
Instructional Systems Technology
Indiana University

Since *A Nation at Risk* was issued in 1983, a plethora of national reports have called for changes in the American educational system. Many proclaim the need for "reform of our educational system in fundamental ways," as did the original National Commission on Excellence in Education. However, the diagnoses rendered in that report and others like it do not ring true. Ultimately, they propose piecemeal remedies, each focusing attention on different issues at different levels within the system. Some focus on curriculum; others on teacher training, selection, or reward; others on management of the school or the district; and still others on supposedly fundamental school funding mechanisms. Surely there is room for improvement in all these elements, but which are necessary or sufficient to attain the ultimate goal of building a system appropriate for our national aspirations? Might a more systemic vision help us find our way through the complexity?

The purpose of this article is to examine the problem and some possible solutions by means of a series of propositions, each of which can be seen as a hypothesis amenable to logical or empirical analysis. If successful, these propositions will clarify the argument and permit a more fruitful dialogue about resolution.

THE PROBLEM AND ITS CONSEQUENCES

1. *The public education system, designed in the 19th century and modified throughout the 20th century, no longer adequately serves the current or future educational needs of the nation (the* effectiveness *issue).*

This proposition is accepted by most of the critics, although they may disagree as to the precise nature of the shortcoming; some criticize the curriculum, some the methods, some the organizational structure, some the funding mechanisms, and so on. For the moment, it is enough to agree that the *results* of the current system — the sum total of the abilities of its graduates — do not meet the nation's requirements. Reigeluth[1] and Goodlad,[2] among others, convincingly demonstrate the gap between modern societal needs and the capabilities of the old industrial model school.

Not only economic life has made the school of the 19th century obsolete; social and demographic factors are also at work. Schools no longer primarily serve the white, middle-class, agricultural, two-parent household for which they were designed. Demographic projections tell us clearly that the trend toward diversity will accelerate in the future.

We need not take sides in the debate over whether public schools are getting better or worse. The position here is that they do not serve our societal learning needs adequately (on the average) and that they are not getting better fast enough (on the average) to cope with rapidly evolving demands.

2. *The success of a nation's education system has profound consequences for its economic prosperity, its domestic tranquility, and even its security.*

Again, most critics accept this proposition. Perhaps the case is made best by Reich in his analysis of global economics.[3] He points out that "the standard of living of a nation's people increasingly depends on what they contribute to the world's economy — on the value of their skills and insights." That is, the crucial national resource for the coming era is "human capital."

3. *The cost of operating the public education system is too high in relation to benefits (the* efficiency *issue).*

American education, based as it is on the primitive factory model of the turn of the century, suffers from many of the same inefficiencies as the old smokestack industries: dependence on labor-intensive methods, hierarchical layers of bureaucracy, inappropriate division of labor, and failure to achieve economies of scale. In an era of unparalleled prosperity and limited global competition, as prevailed in America at midcentury, these inefficiencies were tolerable in both business and education. They have long since ceased to be tolerable in business; they have become intolerable in education as well. Education news these days is dominated by stories of school district bankruptcy and crippling budget deficits, leading to cutbacks in programs (especially in "marginal" areas such as music, art, and athletics), increases in class size, and even teacher layoffs.

ANALYSIS OF THE PROBLEM

If the first three propositions are accepted, we acknowledge that there is a problem and that it is serious enough to warrant attention. Now we attempt to locate the heart of the problem.

4. *Learning achievement is the crucial product of the educational system.*

Schools obviously attempt to perform many functions in American society, including socialization of youth into the community. However, the primary and *unique* requirement expected of the schools is the attainment of the knowledge, skills, and attitudes specified by state and local boards of education. Not only is that what is *legally* expected of schools, it is what Reich[4] and others insist is the *vital* element for economic survival.

5. *Research indicates that learning achievement is directly affected by several causative factors, which can be summarized as aptitude, effort, and instruction.*

Walberg has been sifting prior educational research as well as conducting his own studies in his quest for a theory of educational productivity. His team of investigators conducted quantitative syntheses of nearly 3,000 investigations of productive factors and they probed the significance of these factors in large sets of national data on learning achievement (such as the National Assessment of Educational Progress). In 1984 he reported a major synthesis of this research in *Educational Leadership*.[5] His overall conclusion: "The major causal influences flow from aptitudes, instruction, and the psychological environment to learning." He identified nine specific factors that appear causally linked with educational productivity:

Aptitude

1. Ability or prior achievement, as measured by the usual standardized tests;

2. Development, as indexed by chronological age or stage of maturation;

Motivation

3. Motivation, as indicated by personality tests or the student's willingness to persevere intensively on learning tasks;

Instruction

4. Amount of time students engage in learning;

5. Quality of the instructional experience, including psychological and curricular aspects;

Environment

6. Home, including school-parent cooperation, graded homework, and family socioeconomic status;

7. Classroom social setting — morale, cohesiveness, goal direction, and other classroom climate factors;

8. Peer group outside school;

9. Use of out-of-school time, particularly television viewing.

To display the interrelationships among these and other factors, they have been combined in a visual model (see figure 1).

This visual model can be used to analyze many of the criticisms made of educational practices and various of the claims made for proposed reforms. It demonstrates graphically that only three factors have a *direct* effect on school learning achievement: aptitude, effort, and instruction. Interventions made elsewhere in the system can have an impact on learning *only to the extent that they influence aptitude, effort, or instruction.* For example:

- Class size (an element of Classroom Environment) affects learning indirectly, in that large class size contributes to a depersonalized climate, depressing motivation, which decreases *effort,* and it biases the selection of *instructional methods* towards those that are large-group-based.

- Self-contained classrooms (an element of School Organizational Structure) influence learning indirectly by biasing the selection of *instructional methods* toward those that are passive and large-group-based.

- Norm-referenced standardized tests (an element of School Organizational Structure) influence learning indirectly by depressing aspirations of low-scoring students, thus inhibiting *effort;* they also bias *instructional methods and content* toward lower-level cognitive skills.

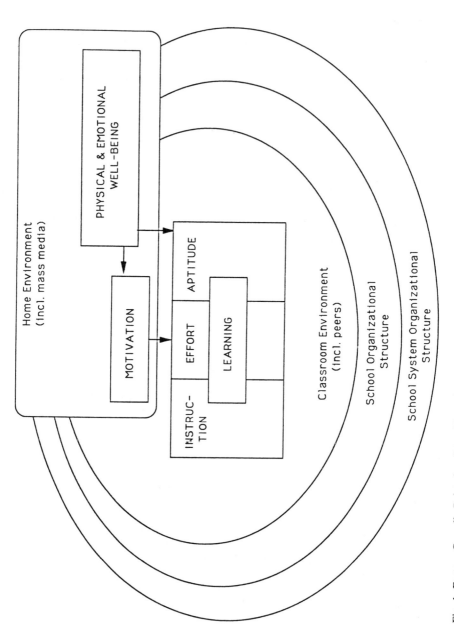

Fig. 1. Factors Causally Related to School Learning Achievement

- School System Organizational Structure reforms, such as site-based management or parental choice of schools, can only influence achievement to the extent that they change school structures in a way that improves the classroom environment and influences *instruction* and *effort*. That is, site-based management itself does *not* improve student achievement; it may be a useful reform if and when it creates better motivational and/or instructional conditions.

6. *Some of the factors that influence learning are largely beyond the control of the school.*

First, the factor most strongly correlated with school learning achievement is aptitude. Aptitude is highly dependent on genetic endowment and prenatal and early childhood care. These determinants are largely beyond the control of schools. However, schools can provide classroom environments and can work with parents to create home environments characterized by physical and emotional well-being that encourage students to activate and use the aptitude they possess.

Similarly, motivation to invest effort in learning and having a positive self-concept are shaped more by home and out-of-school peer environments than by in-school influences. Schools can, however, complement and supplement out-of-school influences through provision of motivating classroom environments and use of instructional methods that promote interest.

Other influential factors over which the school has little control are family socio-economic status, out-of-school peer group, and use of out-of-school time, particularly television viewing.

7. *Schools have complete control over one factor that directly affects school learning achievement — instruction.*

If schools are to improve their educational productivity, they must focus their efforts on *instructional* factors, their best hope for improvement of student performance. This means, at least, increasing the amount of time spent on tasks and exposing learners to more relevant curricular content through more powerful methods.

8. *Schools have partial control over a factor that directly affects school learning achievement — effort.*

The home environment and out-of-school peer environment have a great deal of influence on motivation to expend effort, but schools can reduce some of the demoralizing influences promoted by current practices. For example, norm-referenced testing has demoralizing consequences for many students, immediately in terms of self-concept, later in terms of willingness to invest effort, and ultimately in terms of dropping out of school. Also, the depersonalized institutional climate characteristic of large schools engenders anomie in both students and staff.

9. *Instructional processes flow out of and are constrained by the organizational structure of the classroom, school, and school system.*

Heinich's work amply demonstrates how the base of the educational system — the certified teacher and the Carnegie unit — determines the superstructure — self-contained, grade-level classrooms — that has evolved to support the base, which in turn biases the instructional methods employed.[6]

Many other analysts, including mainstream educational researchers, have begun to acknowledge the correctness of Heinich's diagnosis. For example, Linda Darling-Hammond, commenting on recent federal proposals to establish "national goals," wrote:

> Essentially, this line of thinking assumes that problems exist either because educators don't have precise enough targets to aim for, because they aren't trying hard enough, or both.... However, mounting evidence indicates that the assumptions underlying such thinking are flawed. The problem is not that schoolpeople lack direction and will, but ... that they work within a dysfunctional organizational structure that has made inadequate investments in the knowledge and tools they need to address students' needs.[7]

Schlechty, a school administrator, comments along the same line: "The problem is that the concept of the graded class and the Carnegie unit have both become so enshrined in law, policy, custom, and regulation that the structures which support these conventions are almost impossible to change."[8]

SPECIFICATIONS FOR RESOLVING THE PROBLEM

If the preceeding propositions related to the nature of the problem are correct, what features should be sought in an improved educational system?

The Effectiveness Problem

10. *Student motivation and teacher morale can be enhanced by adopting a wholesome school organizational structure.*

People perform more effectively when their work encompasses whole tasks, they have meaningful control over the means of achieving their goals, they have input into organizational issues, they see concrete results of their work, and when successful, high-quality performance is recognized and rewarded. Both for the sake of individual development and of societal well-being, learning should take place in a humane environment. Humaneness is learned through example and practice; respect for oneself and others grows out of a process in which learners are treated humanely.

11. *The content of the curriculum should both reflect socially valuable skills and enhance the full range of intrinsic capabilities of humans.*

Reich[9] argues that the economic fates of Americans are beginning to diverge and that those who will prosper in the future global economy are those with "symbolic analyst" skills. This is consistent with many other voices within the education community who advocate higher-level thinking skills as the paramount objectives for schools. The subskills of the "symbolic analyst" include abstraction, systems thinking, experimentation, and collaboration.[10] A curriculum to develop these subskills would be the opposite of the narrow, technical, subject-matter-mastery emphases of the "back to the basics" movement.

Looking at the fulfillment of human potential as a guide to the curriculum, Howard Gardner's theory of multiple intelligences would push us toward schooling experiences that promote the development of logical-mathematical, linguistic, musical, spatial, bodily-kinesthetic, interpersonal, and intrapersonal skills[11] rather than the current curriculum, which is heavily skewed toward linguistic, mathematical, and logical skills.

12. *The process of learning should be an active one in which learners have the chance to construct meanings from encounters with whole, realistic problems set in a social context.*

The cognitive revolution has led to a new consensus among educational psychologists as to the nature of the learner and the learning process. According to this view, the dominant theory enshrined in school practice—the transmission theory that emphasizes well-structured presentations of materials through lecture, demonstration, and recitation—is deeply misguided. "Instead," according to Pea and Soloway, "we now see that new learning is *constructed* in terms of prior knowledge by an active learner in a social context, that knowledge is best acquired in functional contexts."[12]

The pedagogical processes appropriate to this new view include immersing learners in realistic problems and guiding them through collaborative problem solving using such techniques as small-group cooperative learning, peer tutoring, and apprenticeship learning.

13. *Since assessment tends to drive curriculum and methods, assessment should be both criterion-referenced and based on demonstrated proficiency on authentic tasks.*

Criterion-referenced assessment attempts to judge learner performance against a prespecified standard or criterion rather than comparing the learner with other learners. Since different standards may be invoked for learners with differing abilities and interests, this view allows "every kid to be a winner," with the concomitant payoffs in self-concept and motivation for continued exertion of effort.

There is widespread consensus that, rather than paper-and-pencil tests, better indicators of mastery of higher-order skills are direct observations of performances such as story telling, drawing, constructing, and problem solving. Evidence gathered through such observations would be collected in a portfolio. Issues of validity, reliability, and feasibility remain unresolved at this time, however.

14. *Instructional methods and organizational structures based on* individualization *are critical for major improvement in effectiveness.*

Branson[13] has presented a convincing case for the "upper limits hypothesis," which holds that the existing school model has reached the upper limits of its perfectability as indicated by the consistent findings of no significant difference when new methods are attempted. That is, schooling based on large-group instruction has been improved as far as it practically can be. To attain greater effectiveness will require abandoning the current design philosophy.

The futility of treating a group of 30 children as though all were alike in abilities, needs, interests, and responsiveness to a particular instructional modality is manifest when one considers the generally accepted rule of thumb that the range of student abilities in a given grade increases with each step up in grade; that is, if there is about one year of range at grade one, by grade eight there is an ability range of about eight years.

Demographic projections based simply on the numbers of children already born tell us that American schools in the coming years will be serving an increasingly diverse population in terms of ethnic and linguistic differences. Without a system better able to accommodate such differences, one can only predict higher and higher failure rates.

Interestingly, one group of public school children is already legally entitled to individualized treatment—those who fit special education criteria. Teachers have found ways to prepare (and presumably deliver) individualized educational plans for handicapped children, thanks to federal legal strictures. Parents of nonspecial students are now beginning to ask why their children do not merit individualized attention.

Individualization, of course, is not to be equated with independent study. Individualized plans that respond to the range of curricular objectives, including social, attitudinal, and interpersonal ones, would necessarily provide a varied menu of independent study, tutoring, small-group interaction, and probably some large-group activities.

What would the organizational structure look like for a school committed to individualization? There is no shortage of models to choose from, either from the drawing boards of dreamers or from real-life prototypes: the Dalton Plan and Winnetka Plan of the past, Montessori schools, Waldorf schools, Dewey's University of Chicago Laboratory School, Goodlad's Nongraded Elementary School,[14] right up to today's Saturn School in Minnesota. Key features are multi-age, nongraded units staffed by teams of both professional teachers and nonprofessionals. Students move in and out of a variety of modes of instruction, some teacher-centered, some resource-based; individual progress is tracked and order maintained with computerized management tools.

John Goodlad's current vision,[15] for example, recommends small primary schools comprised of four "vertical" units of 100 students each. Each nongraded unit would contain 100 students with a four-year age span, with these students and a team of teachers staying together through that four-year phase. With the *equivalent* of four teachers available, a differentiated staff of one head teacher, one support teacher, and several aides and interns is possible.

The Efficiency Problem

15. *Reducing labor costs through differentiated staffing is the most promising source of cost efficiencies.*

Public education has been strikingly backward, compared to other sectors of the economy, in increasing its productivity. The key to the productivity gridlock lies in the labor-intensive character of elementary and secondary schooling. Indeed, labor costs consume up to 90 percent of the budget in many instances. A large chunk of the labor is devoted to staffing the enormous, multilayered bureaucracies necessitated by the factory system. An even larger portion of the labor budget goes to support one certified teacher for each egg-crate classroom.

The temptation of budget cutters is to preserve the current system but make it cheaper by putting more students in each compartment, raising the pupil:teacher ratio. Teachers, protective of their own workload, lobby to reduce the pupil:teacher ratio. Neither side can conclusively prove that raising or lowering the ratio increases or reduces the quality of learning (as discussed earlier, class size itself has no direct effect on learning achievement). The result is stalemate, with budget cutters winning in lean times and teachers winning in fat times, but no one questioning the basic assumptions of the system and its structure. However, many experiments in differentiated staffing have demonstrated that when students are redistributed in a nongraded system staffed by teams of professionals, paraprofessionals, nonprofessionals, interns, and volunteers, overall labor costs are held constant or reduced while educational results remain equivalent or improve.[16]

To probe further into means of increasing cost efficiency, we must consider the possibilities of technology, the next major section of this analysis.

THE ROLE OF TECHNOLOGY IN INCREASING EFFECTIVENESS AND EFFICIENCY

Instructional technologists have long embraced Galbraith's notion of technology as "the systematic application of scientific or other organized knowledge to practical tasks." This view focuses on technology as a *process*—a way of thinking. However, most other educators think of technology only as *products*, the "things of learning"—computers, satellites, audiovisual equipment, and the like. Recently, the product/process distinction has been highlighted by using the terms *hard technology* (products) and *soft technology* (processes). The roles of both hard and soft technologies will be elaborated here.

Effectiveness Tools

16. *Soft technologies of instruction based on the behaviorist learning model (e.g., programmed instruction, programmed tutoring, mastery learning, Direct Instruction, and Personalized System of Instruction) have a well-documented track record of success in terms of conventional measures of achievement.*

There is a large volume of research literature composed of comparison studies in which various behaviorist-based treatments are compared with "conventional instruction" in terms of scores on end-of-term achievement tests. The results of meta-analyses of these bodies of research heavily favor the experimental treatments. An example is Ellson's meta-analysis of comparison studies, in which an experimental treatment was more than *twice* as productive as the control treatment, that is, learning an equivalent amount in half the time or at half the expense.[17] Among the 125 studies that met this criterion, Ellson found that about 70 percent constituted some variation on programmed instruction, programmed tutoring, or direct instruction.

Other examples:

Structured tutoring. Meta-analyses have found various forms of programmed or structured tutoring to be among the most effective and cost-effective innovations, with tutees scoring from the 70th to the 79th percentiles, compared to the 50th percentile for conventional instruction.[18]

Mastery learning. Mastery learning courses, generally in the form of Bloom's Learning for Mastery (LFM) or Keller's Personalized System of Instruction (PSI), "have positive effects on student achievement. On the average, such programs raise final examination scores ... from the 50th to the 70th percentile, in colleges, high schools, and the upper grades of elementary schools."[19]

Personalized System of Instruction (PSI). In the first decade after Keller's invention of PSI, some 75 comparison studies had been published. A review of these studies reported that the typical PSI student scored at the 75th percentile on a standardized test, compared with the 50th percentile for the control treatment.[20] A later review of PSI research found that student preferences also strongly favored PSI courses over conventional ones: "Students rate PSI classes as more enjoyable, more demanding, and higher in overall quality and contribution to student learning than conventional classes."[21]

17. *Soft technologies of instruction based on the cognitive and social-psychological learning models (e.g., simulation/games, cooperative learning, computer hypermedia modules) have demonstrated effectiveness both in terms of conventional measures of achievement and for higher-order thinking skills.*

Techniques derived from cognitive and social-psychological views of learning typically aim for understanding or problem-solving capabilities rather than ability merely to perform successfully on paper-and-pencil tests. Consequently, the evidence for their success tends to be more anecdotal than quantitative. In any event, there is considerable evidence to support the effectiveness of these teaching-learning patterns. Some examples:

Simulation/games. Szczurek carried out a meta-analysis of 58 experiments comparing instructional simulation games with conventional instruction with regard to cognitive learning. He found that an average simulation game student scored at the 63rd percentile, compared to the 50th percentile for conventional instruction.[22] More qualitative evaluations are discussed by Megarry.[23]

Cooperative learning. Slavin developed a number of instructional frameworks for cooperative learning, including Student Teams-Achievement Division (STAD), Team Accelerated Instruction (TAI), and Cooperative Integrated Reading and Comprehension (CIRC). He reports that 33 of 38 comparison studies show significantly greater achievement for the cooperative learning mode. Further, "positive effects have been found on such higher-order objectives as creative writing, reading comprehension, and mathematics problem solving, as well as on such basic skills objectives as language mechanics, math computation, and spelling."[24]

Computer hypermedia modules. Available only since the late 1980s, hypertext computer software provides a means for structuring information in a way that parallels the nonlinear, associative nature of human thinking. Hypertext programs allow a learner to explore a database by establishing links among ideas to form webs or conceptual maps that are meaningful to the particular user. These are referred to as *hypermedia programs* when text fragments, graphics, and video clips are all available to be perused, organized, revised, edited, saved, and shared among users.

Judgments about effectiveness are currently based on evaluative observations, but research and development to date show this to be a technology of great promise for constructivist learning, the sort promoted by the advocates of the cognitive revolution in psychology.[25]

Efficiency Tools

18. *Telecommunication systems (e.g., radio, television, teleconferencing) can effect cost savings by sharing instruction among multiple sites.*

In recent years it has become advantageous to use telecommunications to share teachers among multiple school sites through interactive television. The impetus came from schools that were not able to support teachers in specialty areas but needed courses in those areas to retain accreditation. Services such as TI-IN Network sprang up in Texas, but now reach high school students in dozens of states. Other regional consortia have been supported by the Star Schools program initiated by the U.S. Department of Education. Taken together, these one-way video, two-way audio television courses reach over 100,000 students in 45 states.

In poorer countries, radio serves a similar function, sharing a master teacher among dozens of schools. In Nicaragua, Kenya, Honduras, Papua New Guinea, and other countries, a pseudo-interactive format is used, in which the broadcast radio lessons include embedded questions and prerecorded feedback to the learners' responses. Evaluations indicate that children respond enthusiastically to these programs and that they learn: children in the radio treatment score at the 69th percentile, compared to the 50th percentile in the control treatment.[26]

In all these cases, the mediated course is used unabashedly in place of a live teacher. The investment in hardware and program development is justified on the basis of savings derived from not hiring additional personnel.

19. *Resource-based delivery systems (e.g., integrated learning systems, self-instructional modules) can effect cost savings by substituting for human-based delivery.*

Integrated learning system (ILS) refers to computer-based courseware packages that contain multiyear curriculum sequences. Wicat Systems, Computer Curriculum Corporation, and Jostens Education Systems Corporation are some of the commercial vendors that are developing and installing computer-based systems to cover entire curricula. Student users receive individualized instruction and can progress at their own pace, with evaluation sometimes based on computer-adaptive testing. Vendors match their ILS lessons to local curriculum objectives, so they may be on a low or high cognitive level depending on local objectives.

Of course, this sort of resource-based instruction was conducted generations ago — all the way back to the first quarter of the 20th century — by means of printed self-instructional modules. The difference is in the degree of interactivity now possible through computer mediation. With the advent of expert systems, it is now even conceivable that ILS lessons could adapt to a wide range of learner styles.

WHY RESTRUCTURING IS REQUIRED

20. *Technology can make major contributions to the effectiveness and efficiency of instruction, but, to make sense economically, the costs of technology must be self-liquidating, as they are for business and all other participants in the market economy.*

21. *To become self-liquidating, technology must replace costly human labor to some extent. This threatens the interests of those now doing the labor.*

To become self-liquidating, technology must be viewed as a productivity enhancer. This means replacing and/or amplifying human labor in some way, shape, or form. As such, as Heinich points out, technologies threaten power relationships within the organization and, "as technology becomes more sophisticated and more pervasive in effect, consideration of its use must be raised to higher and higher levels of decision making."[27] Shrock predicts that:

> We can anticipate that teachers comfortable with their traditional role in the classroom will suppress any technology that threatens that role. Unfortunately, the traditional role preferred by most teachers — teacher centered, large group, expository, text supported teaching — is largely incompatible with the recommendations of instructional technologists (and the results of educational research).[28]

22. *Schools must be thoroughly restructured to use technology wisely and well.*

As Doyle points out, most educators see technology as a costly add-on, similar to a car radio; it does not affect performance or direction, but it makes getting there more pleasant.[29] This proposition brings us back to the earlier proposition (number 9) related to the organizational structure of the classroom, school, and school system. The institution and successful, continued use of technological innovations are contingent upon fundamental changes in the legal and organizational superstructure that supports the entire educational system.

SUMMARY

The main points made in these 22 propositions are that:

1. Public education must become more efficient and effective in achieving its goals.

2. Learning achievement is the crucial goal of schools.

3. Learning achievement can only be affected by instruction, effort, and aptitude; of these, instruction is most fully controllable by the school.

4. Interventions such as site-based management or parental choice of schools contribute toward improvement only to the extent that they affect instructional practices.

5. Both hard and soft technologies can have a major impact on school effectiveness and efficiency.

6. For technology (or other interventions) to have a strong and lasting impact, the system must be thoroughly restructured.

NOTES

1.   Charles M. Reigeluth, "The Search for Meaningful Reform: A Third-Wave Educational System," *Journal of Instructional Development* 10:4 (1987), 3-26.

2.   John I. Goodlad, *A Place Called School: Prospects for the Future* (New York: McGraw-Hill, 1984).

3.   Robert B. Reich, *The Work of Nations* (New York: Alfred A. Knopf, 1991).

4.   Reich, *The Work of Nations.*

5.   Herbert J. Walberg, "Improving the Productivity of America's Schools," *Educational Leadership* 41:8 (May 1984), 19-27.

6.   Robert Heinich, "Restructuring, Technology, and Instructional Productivity," in *Instructional Technology Past, Present, and Future,* ed. Gary Anglin (Englewood, Colo.: Libraries Unlimited, 1991).

7.   Linda Darling-Hammond, "Achieving Our Goals: Superficial or Structural Reforms?," *Phi Delta Kappan* (December 1990), 286-95.

8.   Phillip C. Schlechty, *Schools for the Twenty-First Century* (San Francisco: Jossey-Bass, 1990), 65.

9.   Reich, *The Work of Nations,* 196.

10.   Ibid. 229.

11. Howard Gardner and Thomas Hatch, "Multiple Intelligences Go to School," *Educational Researcher* (November 1989), 4-10.

12. Roy D. Pea and Elliot Soloway, "Mechanisms for Facilitating a Vital and Dynamic Education System," *Educational Media and Technology Yearbook 1990* (Englewood, Colo.: Libraries Unlimited, 1990), 36.

13. Robert K. Branson, "Why the Schools Can't Improve: The Upper Limit Hypothesis," *Journal of Instructional Development* 10:4 (1987), 15-26.

14. John I. Goodlad and Robert H. Anderson, *The Nongraded Elementary School* (New York: Teachers College Press, original ed. 1959, rev. ed. 1987).

15. Goodlad, *A Place Called School*, 329.

16. Schlechty, *Schools for the Twenty-First Century*, 68.

17. Douglas G. Ellson, *Improving the Productivity of Teaching: 125 Exhibits* (Bloomington, Ind.: Phi Delta Kappa, 1986).

18. Peter A. Cohen, James A. Kulik, and Chen-Lin C. Kulik, "Educational Outcomes of Tutoring: A Meta-Analysis of Findings," *American Educational Research Journal* 19:2 (Summer 1982), 237-48.

19. Chen-Lin C. Kulik, James A. Kulik, and Robert Bangert-Drowns, "Effectiveness of Mastery Learning Programs: A Meta-Analysis," *Review of Educational Research* 60:2 (Summer 1990), 265-99.

20. James A. Kulik, Chen-Lin Kulik, and Beverly B. Smith, "Research on the Personalized System of Instruction," *Programmed Learning and Educational Technology* (Spring 1976), 13, 23-30.

21. James A. Kulik, Chen-Lin C. Kulik, and Peter A. Cohen, "A Meta-Analysis of Outcome Studies of Keller's Personalized System of Instruction," *American Psychologist* 34:4 (April 1979), 307-18.

22. Mario Szczurek, *Meta-Analysis of Simulation Games' Effectiveness for Cognitive Learning*, unpublished doctoral thesis (Bloomington, Ind.: Indiana Univ., 1982).

23. Jaquetta Megarry, "Simulation and Gaming," in *International Encyclopedia of Educational Technology* (Oxford: Pergamon, 1989).

24. Robert E. Slavin, "Cooperative Learning and the Cooperative School," *Educational Leadership* 45:3 (November 1987), 7-13.

25. A vivid example of the possibilities of hypermedia learning is provided in Theodore W. Frick, *Restructuring Education through Technology* (Bloomington, Ind.: Phi Delta Kappa Educational Foundation, 1991).

26. Maurice Imhoof and Philip Christensen, eds., *Teaching English by Radio* (Washington, D.C.: Academy for Educational Development, 1986).

27.   Robert Heinich, "The Proper Study of Instructional Technology," *Educational Communication and Technology Journal* 32:2 (1984), 67-87.

28.   Sharon A. Shrock, "School Reform and Restructuring: Does Performance Technology Have a Role?," *Performance Improvement Quarterly* 3:4 (1990), 25.

29.   Dennis P. Doyle, "The Challenge, The Opportunity," *Phi Delta Kappan* (March 1992), 512-20.

The National Research and Education Network (NREN)

Promise of a New Information Environment*

Ann P. Bishop

This digest describes proposed legislation for the implementation of the National Research and Education Network. Issues and implications for teachers, students, researchers, and librarians are suggested and the emergence of the electronic network as a general communication and research tool is described.

NREN LEGISLATION

Senator Albert Gore introduced the National High Performance Computing Act of 1990 (S. 1067) in order to create a national network of "information superhighways" designed to transmit billions of bits of data per second. The network would allow researchers, businesspeople, educators, and students around the country to communicate with each other and to access a broad range of research tools and information resources. Although Gore's bill did not pass by the time the 101st Congress adjourned in October 1990, it will most likely be reintroduced in January 1991. If the next version of the bill resembles its predecessors, we can expect that it will seek to accomplish some or all of the following objectives:

- Establish a Federal High Performance Computing Program in which science agencies and national libraries will fund and conduct research, and develop technologies and resources, appropriate for the NREN.

- Mandate the creation of the NREN—to link over 1,000 federal and industrial laboratories, educational institutions, libraries, and other facilities—over the next five years.

- Promote the development of a number of electronic information resources and services on the NREN, such as directories of users and databases, electronic journals and books, access to computerized research facilities, tools, and databases, access to commercial information resources and services, and user support and training.

- Fund the development of supercomputers and advanced software to help resolve certain "grand challenges" in science and engineering.

*This digest was prepared for the ERIC Clearinghouse on Information Resources by Ann P. Bishop, School of Information Studies, Syracuse University. November 1990. ED-IR-90-4.

ERIC digests are in the public domain and may be freely reproduced and disseminated.

This publication was prepared with funding from the Office of Educational Research and Improvement, U.S. Department of Education, under contract no. RI88062008. The opinions expressed in this report do not necessarily reflect the positions or policies of OERI or ED.

The proposed legislation complements ongoing executive branch activities. The main goals of these federal initiatives are to help the United States maintain its leading edge in high-performance computing and to improve national productivity. Continued research and development in high-performance computing and networking are seen as critical to the country's competitiveness, security, scientific and technological advancement, and, ultimately, to the welfare of its citizens. Although it is clear that the emphasis of the bill is on advanced computing and elite users, it nonetheless has the potential to create widespread changes in today's information environment.

A CHANGING INFORMATION ENVIRONMENT

Since the late 1960s, uses and audiences for electronic communication and computing have grown slowly but steadily in the research, education, and library communities. The Defense Advanced Research Projects Research Agency (DARPA) of the Department of Defense funded the development of the first successful prototype packet-switching network, known as ARPANET, in 1969. This network was used to connect organizations involved in government-sponsored research in computing and networking. ARPANET served both as an object of study and as a means to facilitate research communication and computing.

In 1984, NSF began establishing national supercomputer centers and designing a high-speed telecommunications backbone, known as NSFNET, to provide access to those centers for scientists and engineers in a variety of disciplines. Institutions can link their local networks to NSFNET through state or regional networks. These mid-level networks are independently operated and charge fees for connections and use. NSFNET is currently the nation's largest general-purpose research network and serves as the backbone of the Internet, a collection of networks that use the communications protocol developed for ARPANET, called TCP/IP, for coding and transmitting electronic information. The Internet is currently comprised of over 400 interconnected national, regional, and institutional networks and is probably serving over a million users around the world. Further, gateways exist between the Internet and a variety of other networks.

Perhaps the most important of these is BITNET, a cooperative network founded in 1981 that is widely used in research and education today. BITNET differs from the Internet in several ways: it is not sponsored by the government, is not open to commercial enterprises, aims to serve scholars as well as scientists and engineers, and generally supports only electronic mail and file transfer. BITNET merged its organization with CSNET, a network used by computer science researchers and became the Corporation for Research and Education Networking (CREN) in 1989. It currently connects over 1,300 sites around the world.

Network resources and services have expanded greatly in the 1980s, along with familiarity with the technology. Networking is gradually becoming a more familiar tool in the classroom, laboratory, office, and library. Current available services include:

- Electronic mail for exchanging messages

- File transfer for transmitting papers and data

- Online bulletin boards for posting queries and participating in discussions

- Online newsletters and journals for sharing news and research results.

These services make it easier to provide instruction to remote learners, collaborate with geographically dispersed colleagues, and tap the expertise of a wide range of contacts.

Networks also currently provide online access to a variety of resources and tools, such as:

- Library catalogs and databases

- Commercial, governmental, and not-for-profit information services (e.g., Dialog, OCLC)

- Supercomputers

- Specialized software

- Specialized research instruments (e.g., telescopes), applications (e.g., medial imaging), and databases (e.g., satellite data).

These network services and resources facilitate both traditional and innovative education and research activities. They offer individuals at small or geographically remote institutions a "lifeline" to their colleagues and an opportunity to perform cutting-edge research. The NREN would, hopefully, encourage the further development of electronic services and resources. In addition, the NREN would make them available to an even broader audience, and its speed and capacity would exceed those of existing networks.

ISSUES IN NATIONAL NETWORKING

Government and industry are working to solve technical problems such as increasing speed, capacity, connectivity, reliability, and interfaces of electronic networks. Political and economics problems are also receiving increased attention. But a number of other important issues will need to be resolved before national networking can reach its full potential. Problems include:

- Determining costs and establishing fees

- Guaranteeing universal access

- Providing adequate user support and training

- Determination of network use and management policies

- Overcoming organizational resistance to networking

- Providing directories and maintaining quality control of information resources

- Fitting network services to research and education norms for formal and informal communication.

These problems will be extremely difficult to resolve because a national network will connect a variety of institutions with differing goals, norms of behavior, and needs and because the network will still consist of a collection of smaller, independent networks. The library and educational communities have expertise to lend in these areas, but they need to make both their expertise and their views better known to policy makers.

EMERGENCE OF NEW INITIATIVES

The gradual emergence of national networking has spawned a number of new initiatives for network research, services, and advocacy. The Corporation for National Research Initiatives, with a $15.8 million grant from NSF, is overseeing hardware and software experimentation that will be carried out by a number of corporate, academic, and government institutions. NSF is also sponsoring research on the development of a national "Collaboratory," a collection of electronic research resources that would promote and facilitate collaboration on a national scale. Reference Point, primarily a service organization, hopes to assist the volunteer sector in the development and use of new technologies for accessing, exchanging, and disseminating information. An important new advocacy group is the Coalition for Networked Information (CNI), whose members are academic and corporate information and computing professionals. CNI aims to promote the provision of electronic information services, and is particularly concerned with linking libraries to the network. The Electronic Frontier Foundation has been established to address the impact of electronic communication on society. It will foster public education on social and legal issues and support litigation to protect First Amendment rights in an electronic environment.

What these initiatives share is the desire to shape the future of national networking in such a way that its benefits are made available to a broad spectrum of users. Librarians and educators, in particular, can get involved in such initiatives to assure that the needs and perspectives of their constituencies receive adequate attention from national policy makers and network developers.

REFERENCES

Arms, Caroline R. (1990, September). A new information infrastructure. *Online*, 14(5), 15-22.

Arms, Caroline R. (1990, September). Using the national networks: BITNET and the Internet. *Online*, 14(5), 24-29.

Cline, Nancy. (1990, Summer). Information resources and the national network. *EDUCOM Review*, 25(2), 30-34.

Doty, Philip, Bishop, Ann P., and McClure, Charles R. (1990). The National Research and Education Network (NREN): An empirical study of social and behavioral issues. In Diane Henderson (ed.), *Proceedings of the 53rd Annual Meeting of the American Society for Information Science* (pp. 284-299). Medford, N.J.: Learned Information.

Gore, Albert. (1990, Summer). Remarks on the NREN. *EDUCOM Review*, 25(2), 12-16.

McClure, Charles R., Bishop, Ann P., Doty, Philip, and Rosenbaum, Howard. (1990). Realizing the promise of the NREN: Social and behavioral considerations. In Carol A. Parkhurst (ed.), *Library perspectives on NREN: The National Research and Education Network* (pp. 23-32). Chicago: Library and Information Technology Association.

Panel of Information Technology and the Conduct of Research. (1989). *Information technology and the conduct of research: The user's view*. Washington, D.C.: National Academy of Sciences.

Quarterman, John S. (1990). *The matrix: Computer networks and conferencing systems worldwide*. Bedford, Mass.: Digital Press.

Rogers, Susan M. (1990, Summer). Educational applications of the NREN. *EDUCOM Review*, 25(2), 25-29.

U.S. Congress, Senate Committee on Commerce, Science, and Transportation. (1990). *High-Performance Computing Act of 1990: Report on S. 1067*. 101st Cong., 2d sess. S. Rep. 387. Washington, D.C.: GPO.

The National Research and
Education Network (NREN)
Update 1991*

Ann P. Bishop

This digest reports on the current status of federal policy initiatives related to the National Research and Education Network (NREN) and discusses trends and issues in electronic networking that are of interest to members of the education and library communities. The NREN is envisioned as an expansion and enhancement of the existing U.S. Internet, the collection of interconnected computer networks that is currently used by over one million United States researchers, educators, students from K-12 to postgraduate levels, and others.

STATUS OF FEDERAL NREN INITIATIVES

Legislation authorizing the creation of what has been referred to as an electronic "information superhighway" was first introduced by Senator Albert Gore in 1988. The latest version of the NREN legislation, called the High-Performance Computing Act of 1991 (Pub. L. No. 102-194), finally passed both houses of Congress on November 22, 1991 and was signed into law by the president on December 9, 1991. In addition to establishing the NREN, the Act calls for the implementation of a government research and development program in advanced computing technology and applications. It serves, for the most part, to mandate goals and strategies that are already being pursued in the executive branch under the name of the High Performance Computing and Communications (HPCC) Program. The HPCC Program is outlined in a 1991 report entitled *Grand Challenges: High Performance Computing and Communications*, issued by the Office of Science and Technology Policy.

The intent of both the legislative and executive branch initiatives is to improve the information, computing, and communications infrastructure for the country's researchers and educators, while at the same time promoting the development of new computing and communications technologies. The government hopes that such efforts will enhance national productivity and competitiveness as well as speed scientific and technical advances in a number of fields. Important features of the federal government's plans for funding, creating, and managing the NREN include:

*This digest updates *The National Research and Education Network (NREN): Promise of a New Information Environment*, by Ann P. Bishop. This digest was prepared for the ERIC Clearinghouse on Information Resources by Ann P. Bishop, Assistant Professor, Graduate School of Library and Information Science, University of Illinois at Urbana-Champaign. EDO-IR-91-9.

ERIC Digests are in the public domain and may be freely reproduced and disseminated.

For more information about ERIC or about obtaining ERIC articles and documents, call ACCESS ERIC, 1-800-LET-ERIC.

This digest was prepared with funding from the Office of Educational Research and Improvement, U.S. Department of Education, under contract no. RI88062008. The opinions expressed in this report do not necessarily reflect the positions or policies of OERI or ED.

- Appropriations of at least $1 billion to implement a high-speed network linking educational and research institutions in all 50 states in order to facilitate communication, computation, and access to information resources and research equipment;

- Cooperation with the private sector in developing NREN technologies and providing electronic information products and services;

- Designation of the National Science Foundation as lead agency for providing networking infrastructure support and information on NREN access and use;

- Federal assistance for schools and libraries unable to take advantage of private sector NREN connections;

- Provision of information services related to the NREN — such as directories, user training, and access to commercial information services — and technology designed to support computer-based collaboration;

- Use of the NREN for improving the dissemination of information stored in government databases;

- Development of standards related to networking and of mechanisms for ensuring intellectual property protection, assessing and collecting user fees, guiding the eventual transition to commercial use, and maintaining security and privacy;

- Recognition of the need to educate more students in library and information science, as well as in computing and computational disciplines; and

- Establishment of an advisory committee — to include representatives from industry, network providers, and research, education, and library communities — whose mission is to assess federal initiatives in high-performance computing and communications.

Government plans for the NREN have evolved over the past year or so to include a much greater emphasis on educational and library perspectives. Due in large part to successful lobbying efforts by organizations and coalitions representing these communities, NREN policy statements contain more language on, for example, the importance of providing access for educational institutions of all levels and locations, the need to promote shared access to information resources by linking users to libraries and databases, and the importance of promoting NREN applications such as digital libraries and distance education.

It should be remembered that both legislative and executive policy statements only outline, in broad strokes, government plans and strategies related to the NREN. Within this framework, a number of important controversies remain to be resolved, some of which are suggested by the list of NREN policy features previously presented. Individual agencies and other key players will make specific decisions that will affect the actual use of the NREN. The National Science Foundation, for example, will be issuing new contracts in 1992 for both the management of NSFNET (a high-speed national network that serves as the backbone to the U.S. Internet) and the provision of network information services. In addition, it will be chiefly responsible for deciding how funds for NREN connections will be allocated among individuals, institutions, and various network service providers.

GROWTH OF NETWORK USE IN THE EDUCATION AND LIBRARY COMMUNITIES

It is clear that the education and library communities are continuing to expand their use of electronic networks. Researchers, students, librarians, and educators subscribe to electronic conferences, newsletters, and journals on a wide range of topics of concern to them in their work. They use electronic mail to communicate with remote colleagues; file transfer to acquire a variety of public domain information resources, such as software and full-text files; and remote log-in to access supercomputers. In addition, members of the library and education communities are contributing to the creation of electronic information resources and services. For example, many library catalogs and databases created originally for local use are currently available over the Internet. Further, some librarians and educators are an important source of network training and support for their clientele.

As new users and applications are brought online, the potential of computer networks to dramatically transform the nature of education and scholarship is becoming more apparent. In some cases, computer networks are used to make existing processes more efficient, e.g., putting library card catalogs online and disseminating memos from teachers to students. But in other cases, networking is being used to create new relationships, processes, services, and products. For example, students may use electronic networks to learn another language by engaging in electronic conversations with distant peers who are native speakers, and libraries may create and "publish" electronic information resources over the network to an audience far broader than their traditional patron group. Both individuals and institutions are reexamining their goals, capabilities, roles, and responsibilities in learning and scholarly communication as their experience with the use of computer networks grows. Development of the NREN, obviously, has the potential to expand even further the use of computer networking services and products in schools, universities, and libraries.

CONCLUSIONS

Even with the passage of NREN legislation, the transition to a networked information environment will not be easy. Educational and research institutions, libraries, and publishers are faced with difficult social, economic, legal, ethical, and management issues in their attempts to incorporate the provision and use of network services within existing organizational structures and operations. With networking policies, technologies, and user expectations in seemingly constant flux, these issues become even more difficult to resolve. Important policy changes include the recent Supreme Court decision allowing regional Bell operating companies to begin providing commercial information services. Technology trends that could have a tremendous impact on networking include the proliferation of multimedia applications and the development of standards and user-friendly interfaces for information search and retrieval.

FURTHER READING

Bishop, Ann P. (1990, November). *The National Research and Education Network (NREN): Promise of a new information environment.* Syracuse, N.Y.: ERIC Clearinghouse on Information Resources. (EDO-IR-90-4). ERIC Document number ED 327 219.

EDUCOM Review. (1991). Special double issue. 26(3/4).

Lynch, Clifford A. (1991). The development of electronic publishing and digital library collections on the NREN. *Electronic Networking: Research, Applications, and Policy*, 1(2), 6-22.

Mabrito, Mark. (1990). Annotated bibliography of resources in computer networking. *Computers and Composition*, 7(4), 23-39.

McClure, Charles R., Bishop, Ann P., Doty, Philip, and Rosenbaum, Howard. (1991). *The National Research and Education Network: Research and policy perspectives*. Norwood, N.J.: Ablex.

Okerson, Ann, ed. (1991). *Directory of electronic journals, newsletters, and academic discussion lists*. Washington, D.C.: Association of Research Libraries.

Scientific American. (1991). Special issue: Communications, computers, and networks. 265(3).

Tennant, Roy. (1991). Internet basic training: Teaching networking skills in higher education. *Electronic Networking: Research, Applications, and Policy*, 1(2), 37-46.

U.S. Office of Science and Technology Policy. (1991). *Grand challenges: High performance computing and communications, the FY 1992 U.S. research and development program*. Washington, D.C.: OSTP.

Technology and Equity*

Delia Neuman

INTRODUCTION

Books and news stories regularly focus popular attention on inequities within our educational system. In about one-third of our states, lawsuits have sought or are seeking to remedy funding disparities correlated with lower achievement for students from poor communities. Concerns about our changing school population, the plight of our cities, and the perceived failures of public education have all fueled cries for educational reform that meets the needs of all our children.

Technology is routinely touted as a potentially powerful agent of that reform. For years, the microcomputer was cited as the vehicle for overcoming a wide array of inequities. Today, distance education approaches like teleconferencing, interactive television, electronic mail, and expanded telecommunications networks are promoted as avenues to improved resources for underserved students (Bruder 1989). But despite the promise of emerging technology, it is important to remember that technology and equity are not inevitable partners.

COMPUTERS AND EQUITY

The literature on computer equity reveals that many students—not only minority, disadvantaged, and inner-city but also female, handicapped, and rural—have been hampered by inequitable access to computers and by widespread patterns of inequitable distribution and use of computers within and across schools (Anderson, Welch, & Harris 1984; Ascher 1984; Becker 1986; Hayes 1986; Urban 1986). Problems begin at the "counting" level, with wealthy districts having a 54:1 student-computer ratio and poor ones having a ratio of 73:1 (Hood 1985).

Limited hardware and software can in turn lead to scheduling patterns that limit the numbers and types of students who have access to computers. Becker and Sterling (1987) reported that "better" students use computers more than either average or slower students in elementary, middle, and, especially, high schools. Further, Becker (1987) noted that at all school levels, the most exciting computer opportunities are disproportionately available to students with the highest abilities; low-achieving, high-risk students, particularly in high school, are less likely to be in classes in which these opportunities occur. While these conclusions stem from data collected in 1985, preliminary analysis of data collected in 1989 shows only modest changes in schools' overall patterns of hardware and software use (Becker 1990).

*This digest was prepared for the ERIC Clearinghouse on Information Resources by Delia Neuman, Assistant Professor, College of Library and Information Services, University of Maryland at College Park. December 1991. EDO-IR-91-8.

ERIC Digests are in the public domain and may be freely reproduced and disseminated.

For more information about ERIC or about obtaining ERIC articles and documents, call ACCESS ERIC, 1-800-LET-ERIC.

This digest was prepared with funding from the Office of Educational Research and Improvements, U.S. Department of Education, under contract no. RI88062008. The opinions expressed in this report do not necessarily reflect the positions or policies of OERI or ED.

Factors other than sheer numbers can also limit computer access to selected groups. Locating hardware in labs and classrooms restricted to advanced students and setting unnecessarily difficult prerequisites for computer courses can easily deprive average and slower students of computer opportunities. Handicapped students can be withheld from computer opportunities by lack of adaptive devices, special software, or information about how to adapt regular software.

Finally, software that incorporates stereotypes and uses of technology that reflect subtle biases can create the most pernicious inequities of all. "Drill and kill" programs heighten the "masculinity" of both math and computers, thus reinforcing girls' frequently negative attitudes towards both (Collis 1987). Economically disadvantaged students, who often use the computer for remediation and basic skills, learn to do what the computer tells them, while more affluent students, who use it to learn programming and tool applications, learn to tell the computer what to do (Watt 1982).

Within the literature on computers and equity, authorities often concentrate on problems and solutions for individual categories of students. Gender equity has been the focus of considerable research (see, for example, Linn 1985). *The Neuter Computer* (Sanders & Stone 1986), a resource guide and teaching manual for fostering increased computer competence by female students and adults, is one of the many programs and publications directed at this audience. The Council for Exceptional Children sponsors the Center for Special Education Technology, which focuses on technological equity for students with physical, sensory, and learning handicaps. Both Apple Computer and IBM support units about adaptive technology and special software for students with physical and other disabilities. The Educational Computer Consortium of Ohio has sponsored over 40 projects for minority and disadvantaged students, girls, and disabled students. The results of these projects have been compiled in *Yes, I Can*, a handbook that deals with policy and applications for these groups (Fredman 1990). EQUALS in Computer Technology, a project originally created to enhance gender equity, offers *Off & Running*, a book of precomputer activities designed to prepare all students, particularly girls and minorities, to seek computer time and profit from it (Erickson 1986).

While each category of students embodies equity problems that merit specific attention, many of the concerns and techniques cited within individual segments of the literature apply across categories. The central recommendations—gaining awareness of the scope and complexity of the issues and taking active steps to promote equity for the group in question—are found in the literature for all groups. Creating positive attitudes toward technology so that underserved students understand its relevance to them is a basic theme that runs throughout the literature. Finally, the need for active, committed involvement by equity advocates concerned about the needs of underserved groups is also necessary to ensure equity with and through technology (Neuman 1990). Inequity often results from oversight rather than intent, and sensitivity to the danger of excluding some students from technology's opportunities can prevent many of the problems documented in the extensive literature on this topic. As CD-ROM and online searching enter the curriculum, vigilance will be especially necessary to provide all student groups with the benefits of electronic information resources.

CONCLUSION

Technological equity is a complex issue that encompasses disparities in access to and uses of powerful learning tools because of differences in socioeconomic status, gender, ability level, racial and ethnic identification, geographic location, and handicapping condition. Each of these areas has its own problems, research community, and suggested solutions. What the areas share is a need for unremitting attention. Only when all students are routinely granted access to hardware and to appropriate software, and only when technology is used to help each student achieve his or her own personal best, can we speak of technology and equity as partners.

REFERENCES

Anderson, Ronald E., Welch, Wayne, W., & Harris, Linda J. (1984, Apr.). Inequities in opportunities for computer literacy. *The Computing Teacher*, 11(7), 10-12. ERIC number EJ 297 043.

Ascher, Carol. (1984, Jan.). *Microcomputers: Equity and quality in education for urban disadvantaged students. ERIC/CUE Digest Number 19.* New York, N.Y.: ERIC Clearinghouse on Urban Education. ERIC number ED 242 801.

Becker, Henry J. (1986). *Instructional uses of school computers: Reports from the 1985 national survey, Issue no. 2.* Baltimore, Md.: Johns Hopkins Univ., Center for Social Organization of Schools.

Becker, Henry J. (1987, Feb.). Using computers for instruction. *BYTE*, 12(2), 149-62. ERIC number EJ 349 598.

Becker, Henry J. (1990). *How computers are used in United States schools: Basic data from the 1989 I.E.A. Computers in Education Survey.* Baltimore, Md.: Johns Hopkins Univ., Center for Social Organization of Schools.

Becker, Henry J., & Sterling, Carleton W. (1987). Equity in school computer use: National data and neglected considerations. *Journal of Educational Computing Research*, 3(3), 289-311. ERIC number EJ 358 372.

Bruder, I. (1989, Apr.). Distance learning: What's holding back this boundless delivery system? *Electronic Learning*, 8(6), 30-35. ERIC number EJ 392 390.

Collis, B. (1987, Nov.). Sex differences in the association between secondary school students' attitudes toward mathematics and toward computers. *Journal for Research in Mathematics Education*, 18(5), 394-402. ERIC number EJ 361 605.

Erickson, T. (1986). *Off & running: The computer offline activities book.* Berkeley, Cal.: EQUALS in Computer Technology.

Fredman, Alice, ed. (1990). *Yes, I can: Action projects to resolve equity issues in educational computing.* Eugene, Or.: International Society for Technology in Education. ERIC number ED 323 995.

Hayes, J. (1986). *Microcomputer and VCR usage in schools, 1985-1986.* Denver, Colo.: Quality Education Data.

Hood, John F., et al. (1985, May). *Microcomputers in schools, 1984-85: A comprehensive survey and analysis.* Westport, Conn.: Market Data Retrieval. ERIC number ED 265 822.

Linn, Marcia C. (1985, Jan.-March). Gender equity in computer learning environments. *Computers and the Social Sciences,* 1(1), 19-27. ERIC number EJ 325 508.

Neuman, Delia. (1990, Spring). Beyond the chip: A model for fostering equity. *School Library Media Quarterly,* 18(3), 158-64. ERIC number EJ 410 587.

Sanders, Jo S., & Stone, Antonia. (1986). *The neuter computer: Computers for boys and girls.* New York: Neal-Schuman.

Urban, Cynthia M. (1986). *Inequities in computer education due to gender, race, and socioeconomic status.* Bloomington, Ind.: Indiana Univ. ERIC number ED 279 594.

Watt, Daniel. (1982). Education for citizenship in a computer-based society. In R. Siedel, R. Anderson, & B. Hunter, eds. *Computer literacy.* New York: Academic Press.

ADDITIONAL READING

Apple Computer Office of Special Education. (1988). *Apple Computer resources in special education and rehabilitation.* Allen, Tex.: DLM Teaching Resources.

The Computing Teacher. (1984). Theme issue on equity. 11(8).

IBM National Support Center for Persons with Disabilities. (1990). *Technology for persons with disabilities: An introduction.* Atlanta, Ga.: Author.

Kozol, Jonathan. (1991). *Savage inequalities.* New York: Crown.

U.S. Congress. Office of Technology Assessment. (1988). *Power on! New tools for teaching and learning.* Washington, D.C.: U.S. Government Printing Office. ERIC number ED 295 677.

U.S. Congress. Office of Technology Assessment. (1989). *Linking for learning: A new course for education.* Washington, D.C.: U.S. Government Printing Office. ERIC number ED 310 767.

Psychological Dimensions of User-Computer Interfaces*

Gary Marchionini

INTERFACES AND PSYCHOLOGICAL THEORY

The human-computer interface is a communications channel between the user and the computer. The interface includes both physical and conceptual components. *Physical components* include input devices such as keyboards, mice, touch panels, joysticks, speech recognizers, eye trackers, and data gloves; and output devices such as visual displays and sound or speech synthesizers. *Conceptual components* include selection methods such as command languages, menus, or direct manipulation; and representation schemes such as screen layout and graphic/text mixes.

The field of human-computer interaction (HCI) is concerned with interface design and is highly interdisciplinary in nature. It involves researchers from psychology, computer science, information science, engineering, education, and communications. A central concern of HCI research is to determine the effects of human physical, cognitive, and affective characteristics on the interactions between users and computers for specific tasks. Thus, HCI researchers develop models of human activity and use these models in designing new interfaces.

The *information processing model of cognition* prevalent in cognitive psychology provides a foundation for interface design. This model establishes that: (1) humans have a working memory limited to five to seven "chunks" of information; (2) humans must have their attention refreshed frequently; and (3) *recalling* information requires more cognitive effort than *recognizing* information. Computer interface styles consistent with this model include menus, query-by-example, and direct manipulation. Novices and casual users prefer menus to command languages because recognizing an appropriate option is easier than remembering a command. Direct manipulation interfaces (such as touch panels in information kiosks or input devices and graphic displays in most video games) overcome many psychological limitations because they share the "load" between physical and cognitive activity. In addition, their immediate feedback and easy reversibility invite user exploration.

*This digest was prepared for the ERIC Clearinghouse on Information Resources by Gary Marchionini, Associate Professor, College of Library and Information Services, University of Maryland at College Park. EDO-IR-91-5.

ERIC Digests are in the public domain and may be freely reproduced and disseminated.

This digest was prepared with funding from the Office of Educational Research and Improvement, U.S. Department of Education, under contract no. RI88062008. The opinions expressed in this report do not necessarily reflect the positions or policies of OERI or ED.

The psychological theory of mental models has also been applied to interface design. Humans develop internal representations (mental models) for objects, events, and ideas. These mental models are active, called into play to explain the world and to predict which actions to take. Mental models are incomplete and often inaccurate, but they help people deal with the world on a daily basis. Users develop mental models for computer systems, and HCI researchers believe that the interface is the basis for the mental models that users develop. Designers are thus concerned with ways to assist users in quickly developing accurate and useful mental models for their systems.

A common approach is to define a metaphor that links existing user knowledge to system function. The desktop metaphor is perhaps the best-known example, although more fundamental metaphors such as the screen as a scroll of paper or online interaction as human-to-human dialogue have had earlier and wider impact. Metaphors are useful, but they can also constrain the user's view of the unique aspects of a system. In effect, concern with ease of learning can eventually interfere with skilled use. HCI researchers have proposed a variety of solutions to the learning-using tension, including: minimal manuals, incremental learning through online help, and progressive disclosure of system features and capability. The most general solution is to develop interfaces that adapt to the users' abilities and needs. In addition to the many technical challenges such interfaces offer, there is a philosophical debate over whether the interface should adapt to the user automatically or only through specific user control.

PRINCIPLES FOR INTERFACE DESIGN

Psychological research has led to a number of design principles:

1. The interface should compensate for human physical and cognitive limitations whenever possible. However, the interface should be "transparent," not getting in the way of the user's actions or impeding his or her progress. The interface itself should not overload the user with complexity or unnecessary "bells and whistles" that interfere with or distract from the task at hand.

2. The physical components of the interface should be ergonomically designed, taking into account the comfort and health of the user as well as his or her special needs and characteristics. For example, a touch panel design for a word processing program demands far too much arm movement for lengthy sessions, but serves quite nicely in an information kiosk of a shopping mall when positioned to be touchable by users of various heights.

3. The interface should be consistent. For example, selection methods, positioning of important text and buttons, text fonts and styles, and window layout and management should be consistent in all parts of an interface.

4. Noncommand interaction styles such as direct manipulation and menus are preferable to command languages, although the expert user should be given "type ahead" capability to quickly move through layers of menus.

5. The interface should handle errors by providing simple and concise error messages that assist the user in recovery and future avoidance.

6. The interface should support reversible actions (e.g., the UNDO capability in many systems).

7. The interface should be subjected to usability testing early in the design process and as each iteration of the product evolves.

Perhaps the most basic principle is that the interface should be designed around the needs of the user rather than added on after a system has been completed, thus serving the constraints imposed by the system. This principle is sometimes expressed by the admonition to "know your user!"

TRENDS IN INTERFACE DESIGN

Computer systems are becoming increasingly interactive, and this trend will continue as new interfaces are developed. Interactivity will be supported by new input and output (I/O) devices that take fuller advantage of the many communication channels humans employ. For example, some of the devices that are under active investigation in HCI laboratories include:

- voice I/O

- open-based input devices (handwriting, drawing)

- remote sensing devices that focus on personal transmitters (e.g., on finger rings) or that monitor physiological activity

- personal display monitors a few centimeters square

- three-dimensional displays

- eye tracking devices

- motion detectors

- lip-reading systems.

Perhaps more significant than the many different types of I/O devices is the development of interfaces that support multiple I/O devices in parallel. Interfaces that accept voice and gesture concurrently will give richer control to users who must move about while controlling systems and make possible a variety of virtual reality applications. Likewise, video and sound output together provide a more powerful communication channel for information flow.

In addition to advances in physical interface components, there is active research in conceptual components such as interaction styles. Direct manipulation interfaces will continue to emerge and more robust adaptive systems will be developed that change according to the type of task and user experience level. Intelligent agents are also under development. Agents can be assigned specific tasks by the user and then sent out to execute those tasks. The next metaphor of the computer world may be the theatre or command center, where directors assign roles to software agents and examine the results of their subsequent performances.

REFERENCES

Borgman, C. L. (1986, November). Why are online catalogs hard to use? Lessons from information retrieval studies. *Journal of the American Society for Information Science*, 37(6), 387-400. EJ 345 851.

Card, S., Moran, T., & Newell, A. (1983). *The psychology of human-computer interaction*. Hillsdale, N.J.: Lawrence Erlbaum Associates.

Carroll, J., & Aaronson, A. (1988). Learning by doing with simulated intelligent help. *Communications of the ACM*, 31(9), 1064-79.

Egan, D. E. (1988). Individual differences in human-computer interaction. In M. Helander, ed., *Handbook of human-computer interaction*. Amsterdam: North-Holland, 541-68.

Foley, James D. (1987, October). Interfaces for advanced computing. *Scientific American*, 257(4), 126-35. EJ 359 987.

Marchionini, G. (1989). Making the transition from print to electronic encyclopedias: Adaptation of mental models. *International Journal of Man-Machine Studies*, 30, 591-618.

Norman, D. A., & Draper, S. W., eds. (1986). *User centered design: New perspectives on human-computer interaction*. Hillsdale, N.J.: Lawrence Erlbaum Associates.

Shneiderman, B. (1987). *Designing the user interface: Strategies for effective human-computer interaction*. Reading, Mass.: Addison-Wesley.

Interactive Multimedia Computer Systems*

Eileen E. Schroeder

DEFINITION

The merging of various types of media with the computer has presented the field of education with a hybrid technology called *interactive multimedia*. This technology utilizes new developments in data storage, ever-increasing computer speeds and capabilities, and sophisticated software tools to allow a learner to move through a rich multimedia resource base in a way that fits his/her own learning needs and style.

Interactive multimedia can be defined as "the integration of text, audio, graphics, still image and moving pictures into a single, computer-controlled, multimedia product" (McCarthy 1989, 26). Most current definitions describe a powerful computer connected to a variety of other equipment: videodisc players, compact disc players, scanners, music synthesizers, high-resolution monitors, etc. The workstation of the not-too-distant future will have all the multimedia effects — text, audio, graphics, images, sound, motion footage — digitized or converted into a code that the computer can store and manipulate.

Some equate *hypermedia* with *interactive multimedia*, and here the terms will be used synonymously. *Hypermedia* is the software framework for representing multimedia effects in a nonlinear fashion, allowing user annotation, and providing navigational systems. *Interactive multimedia* refers to the interactive audiovisual aspect of hypermedia systems. The information is stored in *nodes* (concepts) and connected by *links* (associations). Nodes and links are either built into the system or created by the learner as he/she traverses the database. Ambron (1986) sees computer-based multimedia learning stations allowing users to "browse, annotate, link, and elaborate on information in a rich, nonlinear, multimedia data base ... explor[ing] and integrat[ing] vast libraries of text, audio, and video information" (p. 7).

COMPONENTS

Interactive multimedia systems consist of several components: (1) the information or data system; (2) the software for accessing the information; (3) the hardware or technology; and (4) the communications system needed to connect all these parts.

The information or data system (i.e., the contents of the multimedia database) can be any type of text, audio, or visual images. Currently, optical storage methods such as laser videodisc and compact disc are used largely for storage of audio and images (both still and motion), while traditional magnetic storage devices are used for text, graphics, animation,

*This digest was prepared for the ERIC Clearinghouse on Information Resources by Eileen E. Schroeder, doctoral candidate in adult education and instructional systems at the Pennsylvania State University. November 1991. EDO-IR-91-6.

ERIC Digests are in the public domain and may be freely reproduced and disseminated.

For information about ERIC or about obtaining articles and documents, call ACCESS ERIC, 1-800-LET-ERIC.

This publication was prepared with funding from the Office of Educational Research and Improvement, U.S. Department of Education, under contract no. RI88062008. The opinions expressed in this report do not necessarily reflect the positions or policies of OERI or ED.

still images, and audio. With the growing ability to reduce the storage space needed for motion and full color still images, and with the decreasing cost of memory, the trend is toward more storage in optical formats. *Digital video interactive* (DVI) is a developing technology that holds promise in this area. By allowing the compression and decompression of digitized images, it will increase the number of images that can be stored on a compact disc and improve the capacity of that medium to store motion video.

The software component consists of generic programs such as Hypercard, ToolBook, Linkway, Quest, Guide, and Notecards. These programs index, provide access to, and allow navigation through the text, visuals, and audio in the multimedia database. This component usually includes video and audio indexing and control software, an index, a map of everything stored, linkages to navigate through the database, and a way to build new links.

The hardware component currently consists of a variety of discrete pieces of equipment, which may include a CD-ROM player, a videodisc player, a voice synthesizer, an audio digitizer, a video digitizer, and a digital scanner all connected to a single computer system. The communications system consists of local and nonlocal networks connecting the hardware and multimedia databases, which may be stored in one place or scattered across locations.

ADVANTAGES

Hypermedia provides many advantages to the learner, especially through its abilities to adapt to individual differences and to allow the learner to control the path of his/her study. The learner can either be directed or wander through information. The system can provide customized interfaces for each user with varying levels of guidance. Some studies have shown that a learner-controlled environment can be more effective than a program that adapts automatically to learner differences (Allred & Locatis 1988).

By providing information in a variety of modalities, providing a context for the information, and allowing multiple paths through this knowledge, the system allows the learner to select information in the format or formats best suited to his/her learning style, ability level, and information needs through one unified system of access. All of this will increase the learner's engagement with the learning situation as he/she elaborates on current knowledge. A hypermedia system can also be used in cooperative learning or group composition with a group of users contributing to a common database of information.

PROBLEMS

There are also several problems with hypermedia as it is currently conceived. Hypermedia systems can be both confusing and disorienting, especially for the less able student. One major problem is that current user interfaces are not "friendly" enough for the average user and too inconsistent across systems. Disorientation and distraction can be caused by jumping around throughout the database, the sheer quantity of data, and the lack of information on database size and extent. Some systems may be sacrificing depth of learning for breadth.

Finally, there is still a technological lag between the hardware and software currently available and what is needed for efficient, effective systems. Further development is needed in optical and other storage methods and in equipment interaction.

EXAMPLES

Ambron & Hooper (1988; 1990) provide numerous examples of experiments with hypermedia. Most of the projects described in the earlier book are employed in a research context. The later book discusses applications in public schools and higher education. A few of the numerous examples documented elsewhere in the literature include:

Kanji City (Ashworth & Stelovsky 1989): a program for teaching Japanese through trial-and-error exploration of a real-life environment.

Zarabanda Notebook (Underwood 1988): a language program based on a Spanish soap opera.

Palenque (Wilson 1987): a research prototype using DVI that allows learners to explore Mayan ruins in the Yucatan.

Shakespeare Project (Friedlander 1989): a program used to study various productions of Shakespeare plays.

Intermedia (Yankelovich 1986): a hypermedia system with tools for text processing, graphics editing, timeline editing, scanned image viewing, and 3D applications that can be used for a variety of subjects.

THE FUTURE

Numerous design issues need resolving: (1) what authoring principles and methods work; (2) how misconceptions can be corrected and feedback provided; (3) how assignments can be created; (4) how the needed self-regulation can be developed in learners; (5) how both the materials and learning can be evaluated; (6) how links can be created and managed; (7) how assistance can be provided; and (8) how the learner can be prevented from feeling lost (Marchionini 1988). Research and development are needed for more powerful searching techniques, better graphic structure searching, and friendlier user interfaces.

This technology is just beginning to develop. Watch for rapid developments as storage mediums which allow a reduction in the required storage space become more fully implemented; as optical storage formats gain wider acceptance; and as software programs for hypermedia become commonly accepted for accessing databases of visual and audio images. As the technology develops even further, the interactive multimedia computer system will move from a mixture of discrete storage formats utilizing various pieces of equipment to a fully digitized storage format contained on one system.

REFERENCES

Allred, K. F., & Locatis, C. (1988). Research, instructional design, and new technology. *Journal of Instructional Development*, 11(1), 2-5. ERIC number EJ 380 492.

Ambron, S. (1986). New visions of reality: Multimedia and education. *Learning Tomorrow: Journal of the Apple Education Advisory Council*, 3, 5-13. ERIC number ED 302 180.

Ambron, S., & Hooper, K., eds. (1988). *Interactive multimedia: Visions of multimedia for developers, educators, & information providers*. Redmond, Wash.: Microsoft Press.

Ambron, S., & Hooper, K., eds. (1990). *Learning with interactive multimedia: Developing and using multimedia tools in education*. Redmond, Wash.: Microsoft Press.

Ashworth, D., & Stelovsky, J. (1989, June). Kanji City: An exploration of hypermedia applications for CALL. *CALICO Journal*, 6(4), 27-39. ERIC number EJ 392 282.

Friedlander, L. (1989, July). Moving images into the classroom: Multimedia in higher education. *Laserdisk Professional*, 2(4), 33-38. ERIC number EJ 396 860.

Marchionini, G. (1988, Nov.). Hypermedia and learning: Freedom and chaos. *Educational Technology*, 28(11), 8-12. ERIC number EJ 384 406.

McCarthy, R. (1989, June). Multimedia: What the excitement's all about. *Electronic Learning*, 8(3), 26-31. ERIC number EJ 395 537.

Paske, R. (1990). Hypermedia: A brief history and progress report. *T.H.E. Journal*, 18(1), 53-56.

Underwood, J. (1988). Language learning and "hypermedia." *ADFL Bulletin*, 19(3), 13-17. ERIC number EJ 369 045.

Van Horn, R. (1991). *Advanced technology in education*. Pacific Grove, Cal.: Brooks/Cole.

Vandergrift, K. E. (1988, Nov.). Hypermedia: Breaking the tyranny of the text. *School Library Journal*, 35(3), 30-35. ERIC number EJ 384 332.

Wilson, K. S. (1987). *The Palenque optical disc prototype: Design of multimedia experiences for education and entertainment in a nontraditional learning context*. (Technical Report No. 44). New York: Bank Street College of Education, Center for Children and Technology. ERIC number ED 319 377.

Yankelovich, N. (1986). *Intermedia: A system for linking multimedia documents*. (IRIS Technical Report 86-2). Providence, R.I.: Brown Univ., Institute for Research in Information and Scholarship. ERIC number ED 296 735.

Cable in the Classroom
500 Hours of Free Educational Programming
Every Month on Cable Television

Bobbie L. Kamil

Cable in the Classroom is a nonprofit service of the cable television industry. Its members offer educational programming—from news and documentaries to dramatic presentations—as additional tools for teaching. As a national organization, Cable in the Classroom seeks to:

- Build awareness of the cable industry's educational initiative

- Develop materials to support cable companies as they work with educators

- Serve as a clearinghouse for statistical and anecdotal information on cable use in schools.

Major cable companies and national cable programmers created Cable in the Classroom in 1989 because educators came to the industry asking what cable programs they could legally access and use in their classrooms. Working together with the educational community, cable companies made available a wide variety of video resources that keep students interested and involved in learning. Program members offer:

- Over 500 hours of high-quality programs every month, delivered to schools, without commercial interruption, via cable

- Curriculum-based support materials to assist teachers in using the programs in the classroom

- Extended copyright clearances that allow teachers to replay Cable in the Classroom programs on videotape.

The cornerstone of the cable industry's entire effort is that the programming decisions—i.e., whether to use the videotape, how much video to use, whether to hit the VCR's pause, stop, fast-forward, or reverse button—are all in the control of the teachers. They maintain their role as educators and use cable programming as one more valuable tool to complement their teaching styles and methods.

CURRENT USAGE IN SCHOOLS

Cable in the Classroom now reaches over 50 percent of the nation's public junior and senior high school students. Each of these students attends one of the 12,500 public secondary schools that have been connected to cable by the local cable operator. Since Cable in the Classroom began two years ago, member systems have more than doubled the number of public secondary schools receiving cable, from 6,165 schools in 1989 to over 12,500 schools in December 1991.

While the programming is totally free to schools, the cost of this major initiative has been estimated to be worth over $50 million annually. It is underwritten by member cable companies and program networks. Thousands of local cable companies, which together serve over 82 percent of the national cable television audience, provide free installation and free basic service to the public secondary schools passed by cable in their area. Cable in the Classroom members recently agreed to connect state-accredited private and parochial schools passed by cable by September 1994. They are now exploring the possibility of including elementary schools in their mission.

Cable in the Classroom programming may be used when it airs, or videotaped for future use when it fits more appropriately into the classroom curriculum. Teachers can screen a variety of programs, edit the videotapes, and view them with their students on a VCR and monitor when it fits in with their lesson plan. Using a portable VCR and monitor instead of watching a program as it airs allows freedom in scheduling. Research by Quality Educational Data in 1991 shows that, in schools with cable, one VCR is shared by an average of five classrooms.

In addition to the educational programs with liberal copyright clearances, Cable in the Classroom members design support materials and offer training to encourage effective use of these resources in the classrooms. Around the country, educators are working with their local cable companies to conduct inservice training sessions to teach utilization techniques.

The key to using cable programming is knowing ahead of time what will be on and when. A monthly publication, *Cable in the Classroom* magazine (which is distributed to 75,000 educators), lists programs by academic subject area and includes articles written by teachers on how they use the programs. An article might describe how an English or drama teacher uses a program to augment literature. For example, reading Shakespeare or *Our Town* offers students one level of understanding, while seeing it performed as the author intended adds a completely new dimension. Being motivated by a creative teacher to act it out themselves adds an even greater understanding of the power of words.

Cable television allows students to take electronic field trips around the world, with neither economic or geographic constraints. Where else can an educator turn to keep up with our rapidly changing world? Teachers cannot rely solely on the textbooks typically available for grades K-12. The world is changing too rapidly to use even recently published history and government chapters on the Communist bloc, Eastern Europe, and the Middle East.

PROGRAMMING

Twenty nationally delivered cable networks currently provide commercial-free educational programs on their respective channels. Each program begins with a Cable in the Classroom logo and an on-screen advisory stating how long the program may be kept for educational viewing. Copyright clearances allow off-air record rights for at least a year and, in some cases, for perpetuity.

Programming includes news, documentaries, dramatic presentations, performing arts, and curriculum-based programs for math, English, science, social studies, biology, foreign languages, health, and vocational and technical studies. The following networks have regularly scheduled daily programming blocks for educational use.

Arts & Entertainment Network

A&E is one of several networks using the days of the week as a topical programming guide. For instance, Monday is devoted to shows pertaining to history; Tuesday presents drama; Wednesday, performing arts; Thursday, biographies; and Friday, archaeology and anthropology. A&E also offers study guides on its daily programming. Some of these include the Kennedy/Nixon debates, women in jazz, Shakespeare's *Macbeth*, and *Dinosaur*, a four-part series that teaches about prehistoric life.

BRAVO

BRAVO's "Culture in the Classroom" features drama, opera, classical music specials, dance, and award-winning foreign films. BRAVO also has a special weekly series of cultural programs for children in grades K-6. The series includes literary adaptations of classic stories such as *Grimm's Fairy Tales*.

CNN

CNN NEWSROOM is a 15-minute daily news program that draws from CNN's world news coverage to produce a specially designed package for school use. The program is accompanied by a daily classroom guide that offers suggested reading lists and background information; questions, vocabulary words, and ideas for discussion; and related homework activities. These daily guides are available through electronic mail, GTE Education Network, LEARNING LINK, and X*PRESS X*Change, a cable-delivered information service.

CNN NEWSROOM also features a "Special Report" that investigates political, social, national, and economic issues. For example, on Monday the futures desk offers reporting on global issues, developments, and unfolding trends in the news of the week. On Tuesday, the international desk explores selected events around the globe with leading news organizations from other nations. Wednesday, the business desk examines what is happening in business and commerce and its effect on Wall Street and Main Street. Thursday, the science desk identifies scientists' achievements that will shape the future. Friday, the editor's desk covers major weekly events and takes students behind the scenes in the news to help them understand the stories of the week.

C-SPAN

C-SPAN offers 24 hours of programming on the governmental and public policy process. Live gavel-to-gavel coverage of the House of Representatives and Senate floor activity, congressional hearings, press conferences, call-in shows, international legislatures, and other public policy events air unedited and without commentary on C-SPAN. In addition, C-SPAN offers free teaching guides and lesson plans, monthly newsletters, and access to Purdue Archives, an educators' hotline. All C-SPAN programming can be retained indefinitely for classroom use.

The Discovery Channel

"Assignment Discovery," a one-hour educational program that airs every weekday, provides educators with curriculum-driven documentaries in the areas of science and technology on Monday; history and geography on Tuesday; natural science on Wednesday; arts and humanities on Thursday; and world events and contemporary issues on Friday. Each hour consists of two documentary segments that are customized for the classroom in terms of length and content, followed by an educator's Bulletin Board, which provides timely listings of information, resources, and opportunities for educators.

The newest show offered by Discovery is *Teacher TV*, which premiered in November 1991. It is a magazine-style show that highlights educators in their classrooms and communities. Issues such as new trends in education, specific teaching strategies, and new resources open to the education community are discussed.

The Learning Channel

TLC's "Electronic Library" includes two hours of curriculum-based programming every weekday. Monday, "Einstein's Corner" focuses on math and science programs; Tuesday, "The Global Connection" presents foreign-language and cultural programs to the classroom. Wednesday, "Footnotes" brings books to life with "The Classics." Thursday, "Expanding Horizons" supplements social studies curricula. Friday, "Bridges to Knowledge" provides college preparation, career information, and current events programs.

In October 1991, the network launched an innovative programming format focusing on professional development: programs for educators, programs for lifelong learners, and programs that enhance global learning.

Mind Extension University

ME/U, in conjunction with the Library of Congress, offers a series of programs known as the Global Library Project, which are designed to share the treasures and artifacts of world history with America's students. ME/U also offers college-level classes from affiliated colleges and universities in foreign languages, mathematics, political and social science, and the humanities. Most of these courses require that the student obtain the books or materials that coordinate with each class.

Accredited interactive instruction for high school students provides them with access to specialized courses not offered by their districts. With this distance learning channel, students can see and hear the teacher and, using a simple speaker-phone arrangement, can even interact with the teacher to ask or answer questions. Distance learning makes advanced science, math, and language courses a distinct reality in rural and urban areas or any area unable to afford or attract a teacher or trying to maximize dollars spent on education.

Other Programming

Other Cable in the Classroom networks offering weekly, monthly, or special programming include: Black Entertainment Television, CNBC, Courtroom Television, ESPN, The Family Channel, Lifetime, The Monitor Channel, Nickelodeon, PBS, Showtime, VISN Network, The Weather Channel, and X*PRESS.

CONCLUSION

Television is no longer a novelty for young people. It is widely recognized that during a typical child's school-age years, he or she will spend twice as much time in front of the television as in a classroom, which makes it crucial that quality educational programs be developed and that teachers help students become more critical television viewers. Like computers, television has become an integral part of the classroom experience. Cable in the Classroom exists to insure that the educational programming carried on cable serves the needs of educators and students.

Further information on this project of the Cable Alliance for Education is available from Cable in the Classroom, 1900 N. Beauregard St., Suite 108, Alexandria, VA 22311. (703) 845-1400. Fax (703) 845-1409.

Machine Technology
The Social Aspects of Teaching Machines and Computers in Education

Lydia Hajnosz Doty

In *Walden*, Henry David Thoreau's philosophic exploration of the "essential" life, an often-quoted passage describes Thoreau's reaction to a noisy, steam-powered locomotive that ran along the perimeter of Walden woods. Although Thoreau professes irritation that the train breaks into his meditative revelry with nature and frightens the birds, it is obvious that he cannot help but grudgingly admire the efficiency and intellectual ingenuity symbolized by the train. Thoreau's ambivalent response to technological innovation, which paradoxically seems both destructive and beneficial, is still common today. It seems that society is alternatively fascinated and repelled by the idea of science and technology in our lives. For example, in the early 19th century, the industrial revolution was first met by Luddites who smashed the threatening new machines. Their demonstrations were then quickly followed by innovations such as Charles Babbage's plans for a "calculating engine" (circa 1820) and by later public celebrations of technology's beneficence at the Crystal Palace and the Philadelphia Centennial. At the turn of the century, the Arts and Crafts movement blossomed as a reaction against depersonalization, mechanization, and mass production. However, after the world's first horrific experience with mechanized world war, this too gave way to the era of Art Moderne (the 1920s and 1930s) with its love of the streamlined machine and faith in applied science's ability to improve all aspects of daily life. No area seemed untouched by this enthusiasm for science and technology, be it teaching (Pressey's first teaching machine), entertainment (the advent of sound in motion pictures), or art (development of a machine aesthetic governing the design of everything from toasters to skyscrapers). After successfully mobilizing science and industry to fight another world war and to cope with the panic of keeping up with Sputnik in the 1950s, American society in the 1960s and 1970s found its children—"flower children" and hippies—turning against this high-tech world and advocating a return to a "natural," pre-industrial lifestyle. However, despite espousing these ideological stances, á la Thoreau, the youth of this era did not reject scientific and technological advances. In fact, some of them even embraced another Walden, the *Walden Two* of B. F. Skinner. In today's world, technological advances are so deeply ingrained in the fabric of our lives that they seem almost transparent. In an age of advanced computer and telecommunications capabilities, we do not seem particularly surprised by medicine's ability to perform microsurgery, by our military's power to swiftly fight an automated war, or even by the capability of our television broadcasters to show us events happening a world away. We hardly marvel at the microwave ovens on our kitchen counters or contemplate the implications of having programmable VCRs or CD-ROMs in our living rooms. We assume that technology is working in the background of our lives to make them better and more comfortable. Except for a few theorists, most of us seldom think very deeply about what technology actually means or how it really affects us.

In many ways, the use of technology in education mirrors and is influenced by the same cycles of attitudes toward technology that are found in society as a whole. A history of education shows how educators, parents, and policy makers have, in turn, romanticized, feared, and pointedly ignored various new techniques and devices that have been put forth to deal with instruction. Noting how "similarities in claims, media interest, and investment" for a currently favored innovation embarrassingly parallel those of a fallen technology, Cuban (1986) points out that "superficial similarities between periodic gushes in enthusiasm haunt conferences in educational technology like Marley's ghost" (p. 73). Given present-day society's overwhelming interest in, preoccupation with, and dependence on computer-based technologies in all aspects of life, it is not surprising that a computer was chosen as *Time* magazine's "man" of the year for 1982. In the face of this kind of cultural acceptance, it is inevitable that the computer has also become the darling of today's education community. Although, like many technologies, the computer and its direct ancestor, programmed/machine-based teaching* have been alternately heralded, reviled, and ignored in their relatively brief history, a cursory review of current professional and popular literature attests to the keen focus on computers in schools. In keeping with today's society's uncritical optimism that cutting-edge technology makes life better, and encouraged by politicians, commercial interests, and the popular press, the general public has expressed a great demand for computer-aided and computer-based instruction (CAI) and study of the computer itself (computer literacy) in its children's schools. The proliferation in the 1980s of cheap, desktop microcomputers that are far more user-friendly than the machines previously available has accelerated the trend. Although many technologies are important in education, such as television or non-hardware-based instructional techniques, for many people, social emphasis on the computer has made it take on almost iconic significance as a device that has come to represent Technology in Education.

In this flurry of preoccupation with developing ways to use the computer to deliver, support, or manage teaching and learning, there is often only a perfunctory concern with the theoretical, pedagogical, social, and philosophical implications of using the machines in education. Focus on hardware takes on an inordinately high significance in most people's concerns. A review of the CAI or education literatures shows a large number of articles that possess what might be termed a scholarly *Popular Mechanics* mentality. Educational technologists, who are often (unfairly) accused of harking back to their hardware-loving, audiovisual roots, are not the only ones guilty of turning out atheoretical computer-based materials. The nature of CAI authoring tools, the encouragement of software firms, and the fascination of playing with the hardware are such that nonspecialists in the design of educational materials — classroom teachers, subject matter experts, computer programmers and scientists, and human resources personnel — are motivated to try their hands at producing instructional software, much of which is of questionable worth. In light of this frequent lack of attention to essential theoretical issues, it is not surprising that practitioners also pay little heed to CAI's historical roots in the programmed teaching-machine movement. This is particularly disturbing since many CAI designers co-opt (consciously or unconsciously) the methodology of programmed instruction and superimpose it on CAI without particular awareness of the previous method's flaws or strengths, or assessment of its epistemological grounding. By thinking about computers in education without this historic insight or critical stance, we risk

---

*Just a note about terminology. In this article, whenever I refer to computers or teaching machines, I also mean their software and programs, as these elements are inseparable from the device and are essential for their function. For convenience, I also use the shorthand *CAI* (computer-aided instruction) and *PI* (programmed instruction).

misunderstanding, misusing, and underutilizing this technology. By failing to explore the implications of the relationship between CAI and its predecessor, programmed instruction (PI), we lose opportunities to learn more about CAI and prevent this promising technology from suffering the fate of programmed instruction.

Before focusing on PI's contributions to and implications for CAI, it is important to step back and briefly review the definitions and background of the foundation technology. Although the literal meaning of the terms *programmed instruction* (the information presentation, analogous to software in computer technology) and *teaching machine* (the hardware device that presents information) are generally understood, their more precise meaning is not always easy to pin down. For example, devices not commonly thought of as machines, such as punch boards and scrambled textbooks, have on occasion been referred to as teaching machines. Benjamin (1988) offers a definition that catalogs identifying qualities of a teaching machine. He writes that a teaching machine is "an automatic or self-controlling device that (a) presents a unit of information (B. F. Skinner would say that the information must be new), (b) provides some means for the learner to respond to the information, and (c) provides feedback about the correctness of the learner's response" (p. 704). While B. F. Skinner is most closely associated with the concepts of PI and teaching machines, he had a number of predecessors. Based on U.S. patents, many educational technology historians credit Halcyon Skinner (1866) and Herbert Austin Ainkins (1911) with developing some of the first teaching machines that met several criteria of Benjamin's definition. However, the psychologist Sidney Pressey can be thought of as the developer of one of the first significant teaching machines that was based on learning theory. In 1926, he wrote about his development of an automated testing apparatus "which gives and scores tests and informs the subject with regard to the right answers" (p. 41). Pressey anticipated that his "suggestions may very likely provoke some sentimentalists to outcry against 'education by machine,' " so he was very careful to state clearly that his efforts were to free teachers from the drudgeries of clerical work so that they would be "free for [their] most important work, for developing in [their] pupils fine enthusiasms, clear thinking, and high ideals" (p. 40). Although Pressey was the groundbreaker in the field, Skinner's work is the best known, as he brought the teaching machine to the forefront of education in his "technology of teaching" based on his work in operant conditioning. In his "Teaching Machines" (1958), Skinner discussed the way his machine implemented his theory in instructional settings. He was careful to anthropomorphise the machine and its linear program, comparing it to a "private tutor." He writes:

> The comparison holds in several respects: (a) There is a constant interchange between program and student.... (b) the machine insists that a given point be thoroughly understood, either frame by frame or set by set, before the student moves on.... (c) the machine presents just the material for which the student is ready.... (d) the machine helps the student come up with the right answer.... (e) the machine reinforces the student for every correct response, using immediate feedback not only to shape his behavior most efficiently, but to maintain it in a strength and in a manner which the layman would describe as "holding the student's interest" (p. 143).

Skinner's linear programs and their constructed responses (a written response that the learners made to each small unit of content, the "frame") were eventually challenged by N. A. Crowder's branching programs. In the branching program, which grew out of training military personnel to trouble-shoot electrical problems, the learner responded to multiple-choice answers (both correct and incorrect options). Explanations were given for all choices; students who selected incorrect answers were routed through additional presentations of the topic. Crowder's variation on programming gave the program the flexibility to meet the needs of a wider ability group of students; able students would not feel restrained, since material was not broken down into the small units of Skinnerian instruction, while the weaker learners still had the support of additional presentation (Kay, Dodd, and Sime 1968). Crowder's work also gave the learner a kind of control over the program and his or her learning that Skinner's did not. This branching variation has often found its way into many of the better-designed contemporary CAI lessons.

On the whole, the PI movement flourished during the 1960s to early 1970s, until a variety of criticisms caused it to lose favor; reincarnation as CAI came in the 1980s. Although Skinner (1958) acknowledged his debt to Pressey's vision of an "industrial revolution in education" and emphasis on immediate feedback, he saw Pressey's machine as flawed because it was used after learning had taken place, its multiple-choice answers exposed learners to incorrect responses, and learner response was limited to picking rather than constructing a response. Pressey in turn "was not enamored with the single-mindedness" of Skinner's approach, particularly as it changed the nature of reading. Like others, he decried the limited constructed answers Skinner's machine would accept and argued that his multiple-choice method was "superior in human learning" (Benjamin 1988, 708-9). Skinner also attacked Crowder's branching program for its use of multiple choices and explanations, fearing that they would confuse the student and reinforce error. In 1963, Kay speculated about the reason for "how little is said about the actual arrangement of the subject matter [in Pressey's machine and later versions of his work]. This neglect may have arisen because of the original orientation towards testing with a clear-cut question and answer style of presentation" (Kay 1964, 9). Interestingly, working from an Information-Processing paradigm, Lamos notes that Pressey was indeed deeply concerned with structure and content. However, since he was far more attuned to the phenomenological and social aspects of knowledge than Skinner, Pressey believed that "the break-down of a subject-matter into sequential elemental bits destroyed the structure which gives meaning to the material" (Lamos 1984, 171). Pressey's use of multiple-choice response/feedback (and, by extension, Crowder's use of explanations) is vindicated by Lamos, according to a cognitivist reading, because Pressey's technique helped learners clarify their understanding of a subject and integrate it into their schemas in a way that Skinner's more rigid conditioning technique could not.

By the 1970s, the programmed learning/teaching machine movement had all but faded away from general public attention. Interest gradually began to shift to the new computers, unaware that in many ways these machines were streamlined, enhanced versions of the old teaching machines.

After looking at photographs of ugly, complex-looking teaching machines in Lumsdaine and Glaser's famous sourcebooks on programmed instruction, one might easily guess one major reason for general educators' and students' loss of enthusiasm for teaching machines. Besides lacking the slick visual and auditory displays of today's computer presentations, teaching machines in general seemed gimmicky and inconvenient to use. For example, in Pressey's later efforts, to insure that learners did not cheat, students had to operate punchboards or to work with special chemically treated paper and ink to make their responses. Brigg's large, bulky "subject matter" trainer required that the learner stand at the device and work it almost like a pinball machine. In Skinner's linear programs, learners had to write in an answer and manipulate levers to see feedback. Even if operating these machines initially provided novelty that could motivate use, as Skinner always claimed, the monotony or confusion associated with using them on a regular basis eventually led to learner dissatisfaction. Besides the aesthetic and motivational issues that have been shown to be important concerns in learner acceptance of materials, the problems with teacher adoption were probably not inconsequential. In writing about introducing computers to teachers, Cuban (1986) notes a trend that was also significant for the acceptance of teaching machines by teachers. He states that many schools are run like "military units" and that teachers are viewed as "technicians ... who can apply new devices to the classroom swiftly and without complications." He points out that if teachers find a technology inaccessible, confusing, or unreliable, they will be reluctant to adopt it. This reluctance is even more pronounced when implementation is mandated from the top, administrative levels, downward (p. 56).

While technological operations obviously contributed to the downfall of PI, other factors are also significant. Benjamin (1988) catalogs some of the commonly held explanations:

- Fear of dehumanization of the classroom

- Less personal attention from teachers

- Fear that learners could be manipulated by a master programmer

- Success in teaching only fragmented subject matter

- Belief that machines were only expensive page-turners

- Inadequate training of teachers in use of the technology

- Negative impacts on teachers, such as job loss and increase in class size.

Cost-effectiveness issues and philosophic ideas about the nature of knowledge appear on this list, but social themes are the most pronounced. One of the most interesting aspects of CAI and PI/machine-based teaching is the social epistemology that they espouse. Both technologies underestimated the social relationships inherent in teaching and learning. Social, economic, and political values greatly influence the acceptance and use of technology. For example, the failure of Pressey's machine, one that would make education more efficient, has been attributed to social forces. Like many critics, Kay, Dodd, and Sime (1968) point out that Depression-era America had little social or economic utility for Pressey's innovation: "In spite of the American love of gadgets, the economic crisis of the times put teachers on the dole and brought in stringent days for education" (p. 41). Skinner, in contrast, was the beneficiary of greater social acceptance. He offered his technology of instruction to a society that was faced with the crisis of educating its "baby boom" generation and did not have sufficient teachers to meet the demand. Skinner's teaching machines thus did not even *appear* to threaten jobs, as Pressey's might have. In addition, Skinner presented his technology to a country that had just seen its effectiveness in training military personnel for war. Although social relationships affect the use of technology, conversely technology can modify, change, or even destroy these relationships and the human values they exemplify. Technologies like CAI or PI have great social effect, because they

> influence patterns of communication and the structure of knowledge, mediate the individual's sensory relationship with the environment and re-encode the vocabularies of the culture, while at the same time influencing what gets saved and what gets lost in the transmission process (Bowers 1988, 3).

In addition, contrary to the long-held assumptions of the many educators (including educational technologists), scientists, and engineers who asserted that technology is neutral, there are many other theorists who claim that technology has implicit values in itself, especially when it appears in the "symbolic environment of the classroom" as a factor in the "dynamic interplay among culture, language and thought" (Bowers 1988, 4). Although this idea of meaning in a medium itself is easily accepted by writers, artists, semiotics specialists, and linguists (one readily thinks of Baudelaire's 19th-century "Art for art's sake" and McLuhan's 20th-century "the medium is the message"), many in the scientific-technical community echo Admiral Hyman Rickover's sentiment that "technology is action." Its value and morality lies outside itself in how it is used.

Most programmed instructional devices (as CAI lessons are today) were presented as neutral devices, the use of which is monitored by a teacher (of whom the device was characterized as an extension). British researchers Kay, Dodd, and Sime (1968) summarize this typical attitude:

> Like many of our modern inventions, a teaching machine on its own is neither good nor bad. It needs detailed instructions [derived from programming], the art of gathering together many minds ... and from their interaction producing something which will teach and teach well (p. 13).

This statement differs from Skinner's (1958) famous assertion — "The machine itself, of course, does not teach. It simply brings the student into contact with the person who composed the material it presents" (p. 143) — only in that the 1968 statement more boldly emphasizes sentiments which the political climate of Skinner's time made him express with more rhetorical subtlety. Indeed, all the pioneers of teaching machines, from Pressey to Skinner to today's champions of CAI, have paid at least lip service to the idea that the machine is not intended to replace the teacher. The teacher's role, in addition to managing the machinery, is to provide a "personal example," to be an "instrument of inspiration," and to exemplify "the behavior of the educated man" (Kay, Dodd, and Sime 1968, 33). In criticizing educational technology for not boldly following through with the implications of its scientific-technological vision, Heinich (1984) notes that educational technologists make "frequent reassurances ... about not replacing teachers with technology" and feel "unease over [their] presumption that [they] could replace much of what goes on in education" (p. 63). Nevertheless, one wonders about the power of the social values and relationships that make even educational technologists reticent about advocating the complete abolition of the human teacher's presence in the classroom.

Despite these assurances that the teacher has an essential role, it is interesting to read a description of an ideal programmed classroom envisioned by Kay and his associates (1968). In their vision, children work by themselves in "acoustically sheltered" cubicles. In other parts of the room, students work on their own, "although they can see and speak to their neighbor *if they wish*" (emphasis supplied). Other students, while seated as a group, still work alone at individual screens. Their responses are transmitted to a "control room in which there is a computer. It monitors each of the thirty students, all of whom are at different stages in the course. It records not only how well each student is doing, but also how well the lesson materials are teaching." In this classroom, the teacher's role seems to be merely to rewrite portions of the program that do not function as well as expected (pp. 12-13). In a similar idealization of a futuristic high school, Ramo (1957) pictures students who, with the rest of the class, will spend their time viewing special filmed lectures. Later, the students will be asked to respond to questions about the material by pressing buttons at their assigned seats that are attached to a recordkeeping computer. Based on the master computer's tally of the students' responses, the "teaching engineer" will require the students to work at their own pace with another screen/keyboard teaching machine that will present material based on the computerized records of each student's supposed understanding. In this scenario, the role of the teacher is to assess the adequacy of the machine interventions and to improve the automatic techniques. In both of these examples, social interactions between student and teacher and student and student are minimized. Theoretically, the machine is offered as a device that permits the teacher to carry out higher functions. In practice, the teacher only tends the machine.

The PI (and CAI after it) focus on learner-based instruction reinforced what Bowers (1988) calls the myth that the "self [is] an autonomous and self-directing being" instead of a "part of a larger cultural and natural ecology" (p. 77). Although social forces exerted pressures on PI from the outside, social pressures from within undermined it; similar forces also threaten to subvert CAI. Kay, Dodd, and Sime (1968) write that in the course of the group's research into PI's effectiveness, group forces "played a much larger role in experiments than suspected." They report, almost with annoyance, that "pupils do not shed their group role immediately on being given an individual programme." Students insisted on helping each other and working together. Even the pacing of their individual work was influenced by their peers' work (pp. 123-24). The Kay group missed the significance of these social forces; in response to the social factor, they suggested that research should be directed toward developing a teaching machine that a large group could all use together. Unfortunately, the Kay group's proposal suggested a PI format where members of a large group were still essentially isolated in their individual work even though they were physically together in the learning site. In his later writing, even Pressey (1960) came to reconsider some of these social implications of his work, especially as it came to be redefined by Skinner. Pressey came to believe that "effective learning must keep contact with experiential reality," and he questioned the assumption that "automated education may be so adequate that such contacts are not needed" (p. 498). Pressey also recognized that the social element of learning could not be sacrificed even in the pursuit of individualized instruction. Learning in a social context provides motivation, stimulation, guidance, and elucidation from both peers and teachers. Although he continued to see the teaching machine as a way of freeing the teacher from drudgeries, he thought that its best use should be in the context of "shared fun," and intended that it should increase "desirable socialization of school work" (p. 500). The feared loss of social interaction (which also explains resistance to PI) is a current excuse offered by present-day teachers to avoid CAI: "Teachers believe that interpersonal relationships are essential in student learning. The use of technologies that either displace, interrupt, or minimize that relationship between teacher and child is viewed in a negative light" (Cuban 1986, 61). Cuban further points out that, "In the fervent quest for precise rationality and technical efficiency, introducing to each classroom enough computers to tutor and drill children can dry up that emotional life, resulting in withered and uncertain relationships" (p. 89). These problems of capitalizing on social interaction, preserving human need for contact, and still attending to individual differences are ones with which CAI still must grapple, in light of the previous PI experience.

Another problem of PI that has been transferred to CAI is the "panopticon problem." Named after a philosopher, Jeremy Bentham's design for an efficient prison, the *panopticon*, provided optimal surveillance as its method of control. Designers of PI and CAI often took and still do take pride in pointing out how their devices monitor and control student progress. Data become a means of manipulating students and taking choice away from them. Bowers (1988) notes that it is ironic that, while educators at least publicly commit themselves to students' intellectual and moral growth, they often uncritically accept technologies that exert a control which subverts that growth. He decries a "technicist mind set" that values rationality, prediction, control, and efficiency so much that the context and implicit (nonrational) forms of knowledge that make us "effective cultural beings" are devalued (p. 9).

Finally, PI was flawed in its ability to remove the learner from what Pressey termed "experiential reality." One has to carefully deconstruct Skinner's claim that the program puts the learner in touch with the person who wrote it. Certainly one can claim that any text puts the reader in contact with the writer. However, Skinner's implicit claim is that the program is equivalent to the person, a claim that the written text does not make. The philosophical issue of the desirability of mediating reality through materials was a problem that PI did not fully consider. CAI not only takes up this issue of reality insufficiently, but, through its technical power, can magnify it with potentially frightening consequences. The computer has the technical capability not only to simulate what we term *reality*, but also to produce a new kind of state—virtual reality. For example, in our society a child's preference for a virtual reality-based game of Nintendo baseball instead of the actual experience of playing a game of baseball is passed over with little notice or worry. At most, critics might decry violent themes in a game, but they do not question the larger meaning or wonder if a child should even be playing these games. Indeed, Cuffaro speculates on what the "unanticipated lessons" might be that children learn when working with the two-dimensional reality of a microcomputer screen that is divorced from real-life context. (cited in Cuban 1986, 96). Although he does not see PI or the computer as a tutor as threatening, because "frustration and boredom" prevent prolonged use, Sardello (1985) worries that some forms of CAI (the computer as a tutee paradigm) can transform learners into psychopaths (p. 93). Sardello (and many others, including Bowers, Zajonc, Simpson, Davy, and Cuffaro) point to the example of Seymour Papert's Logo as illustrative of educational computing that disastrously separates the learner from reality. Briefly, Papert's controversial thesis is that by programming the computer with Logo (in essence teaching it, reversing the traditional order of PI), a child learns procedural thinking and is exposed to "powerful ideas." In what many see as a gross misreading of his work with Piaget, Papert claims that developmental stages can be accelerated (Davy 1985; Zajonc 1985). In Logo practice, for example, children can program the computer to make a toy turtle move across the floor or to draw figures such as flowers. Many critics worry that the child may come to prefer the computer-mediated reality to actual reality. Davy (1985) likens this to encouraging normal children to behave like autistic children whose disability makes it possible for them to form relationships only with nonhumans instead of being able to make human connections. He also warns that Papert's work is nonneutral in that it has an articulated epistemology with a clearly cut value system. This epistemology of computer learning taken to its ultimate conclusion "is to remove the child from the actual world and to insert him into his own subjective processes where an imitation world is invented" (Sardello 1985, p. 99).

It is easier to see the problems of PI because they are being imported into CAI, where the technical capabilities have magnified them. In addition, the powerful newer technology's technical capabilities extend the teaching machine's ability to teach and drill to the ability to serve as an educational tutor or as a tutee that the learner can teach. Some educators, such as Bowers and Sardello, see the promise of the computer in its tool role, because "technological devices can free the imagination" (Sardello 1985, 53). However, the programmed teaching functions are still of great value. Cuban (1986) finds no problem with "software that gets students to practice skills or remember knowledge—staples of teaching practise" (p. 93). He also points out that "the claims that students acquire basic skills through CAI have been verified over the last two decades. CAI is effective in certain domains under certain conditions" (p. 95). "Classroom computers should be used by teachers to cope with the routine, often tedious, student learning problems that machines can do patiently. Such use is neither sinister nor wasteful, as some computer boosters suggest. Such use meets a teacher-defined problem well" (p. 100).

The lessons of PI are of great value for educators who use computers. The issues that concerned PI critics and users are the same ones that concern us today. The work of predecessors, especially Pressey's and Crowder's visions of PI, which seem more theoretically useful to the design of CAI than the work of Skinner, can offer insight to today's designers. Above all, a consideration of PI's social implications can lead to more acceptable computer-based instruction that could make a long-term, positive impact on teaching and learning in an information age.

REFERENCES

Benjamin, L. T., Jr. (1988). A history of teaching machines. *American Psychologist*, 43: 703-11.

Bowers, C. A. (1988). *The cultural dimensions of educational computing: Understanding the non-neutrality of technology*. New York: Teachers College Press.

Cuban, L. (1986). *Teachers and machines: The classroom use of technology since 1920*. New York: Teachers College Press.

Davy, J. (1985). Mindstorms in the lamplight. In *The computer in education: A critical perspective*, ed. D. Sloan, 11-20. New York: Teachers College Press.

Hefzallah, I. M. (1990). Forerunners to computers in education. *The new learning and telecommunications technologies*, ed. I. M. Hefzallah, 59-69. Springfield, Ill.: Charles Thomas Publishers.

Heinich, R. (1984). The proper study of instructional technology. In *Instructional technology past, present and future*, ed. G. Anglin (1991), 59-81. Englewood, Colo.: Libraries Unlimited.

Kay, H. (1964). General introduction to teaching machine procedures. In *Teaching machines and programming*, ed. K. Austwick, 1-42. New York: Macmillan.

Kay, H., Dodd, B., and Sime, M. (1968). *Teaching machines and programmed instruction*. Middlesex, England: Penguin Books.

Lamos, J. P. (1984). Programmed instruction to computer-based instruction: The evolution of an instructional technology. In *Instructional development: The state of the art, II*, eds. R. K. Bass and C. Dills, 169-76. Dubuque, Ia.: Kendall/Hunt Publishing.

Marx, L. (1972). *The machine in the garden: Technology and the pastoral idea in America*. London: Oxford University Press.

Pressey, S. L. (1926). A simple apparatus which gives tests and scores—and teaches. In *Teaching machines and programmed learning: A source book*, eds. A. A. Lumsdaine and R. Glaser (1966), 35-41. Washington, D.C.: National Educational Association, Department of Audiovisual Instruction.

Pressey, S. L. (1927). A machine for automatic teaching of drill material. In *Teaching machines and programmed learning: A source book*, eds. A. A. Lumsdaine and R. Glaser (1966), 42-46. Washington, D.C.: National Educational Association, Department of Audiovisual Instruction.

Pressey, S. L. (1960). Some perspective and major problems regarding "teaching machines." In *Teaching machines and programmed learning: A source book*, eds. A. A. Lumsdaine and R. Glaser (1966), 497-505. Washington, D.C.: National Educational Association, Department of Audiovisual Instruction.

Ramo, S. (1957). A new technique of education. In *Teaching machines and programmed learning: A source book*, eds. A. A. Lumsdaine and R. Glaser (1966), 367-81. Washington, D.C.: National Educational Association, Department of Audiovisual Instruction.

Roszak, T. (1986). *The cult of information*. New York: Pantheon Books.

Sardello, R. J. (1985). The technological threat to education. In *The computer in education: A critical perspective*, ed. D. Sloan, 93-101. New York: Teachers College Press.

Skinner, B. F. (1954). The science of learning and the art of teaching. In *Teaching machines and programmed learning: A source book*, eds. A. A. Lumsdaine and R. Glaser (1966), 99-113. Washington, D.C.: National Educational Association, Department of Audiovisual Instruction.

Skinner, B. F. (1958). Teaching machines. In *Teaching machines and programmed learning: A source book*, eds. A. A. Lumsdaine and R. Glaser (1966), 137-58. Washington, D.C.: National Educational Association, Department of Audiovisual Instruction.

Zajonc, A. A. (1985). Computer pedagogy? Questions concerning the educational technology. In *The computer in education: A critical perspective*, ed. D. Sloan, 31-39. New York: Teachers College Press.

Digital Media
A Platform for Converging
Educational Technology "*Pre*paradigms"

Farhad Saba
Professor of Educational Technology
San Diego State University

We live in an exciting time in the history of educational media. The analog-to-digital transformation in media technology, which began during the 1980s, has provided the tools for a radical transformation in the way teachers and students communicate. These new tools allow us to

- Access and use almost any information in any mode of representation

- Control the flow and display of instructional information

- Teach and learn anywhere, at any time

- Experiment with new ideas in the field, primarily driven by postmodern developments.

We are establishing new ways in which educators and students can communicate, thereby redefining the field. The analog-to-digital transformation can expand the horizon for educators and students as print did several hundred years ago. For researchers, the new media provide a platform for reflecting on "*pre*paradigms" (Saettler 1990) of educational technology and exploring their points of convergence towards a unified paradigm.

These developments challenge our view of schools, their mission, and how they can be reformed or restructured. The new media have provided us with the potential to transcend current dialogue and activity on restructuring schools and create virtual spaces in which teachers and students can communicate anywhere at any time. In the postmodern society, new forms of *schooling* may emerge that bear little resemblance to the dissemination of a predetermined amount of instructional information by one person to a limited number of students at a specific geographic location.

In the liberal and democratic tradition of American education, new models of education and instructional design may emerge if the full potentials of these new technologies are realized. These new models can be dynamic and systemic. They can be dynamic because, in the new media environment, teachers and learners can form a cybernetic bond. Through this bond, in a "generative process" of learning (Cognitive and Technology Group 1991), needs are defined, goals are set, learning and instructional strategies are decided, appropriate instructional materials are searched and displayed, instructional materials are produced and presented, and learning outcomes are evaluated. This entire process is managed online either in real time or asynchronously.

The new models can be systemic because, in the new media environment, the learner can become involved in the entire educational process. The computer telecommunication nexus provides the means for learners to assess each component of the educational system that affects their learning. Together with teachers and peers, students are allowed to participate in the realization of their potential in meeting specific learning objectives, or exploring and "constructing" new areas of knowledge. In the same environment, they can be guided, advised, and tutored by teachers and peers. They can affect and be affected by almost everything that is critical to their learning.

These new and exciting possibilities are now available because digital media have been designed with certain unique characteristics that were absent from their comparable analog systems. In this article, these characteristics are described and their ramifications for educators analyzed. Although this article concentrates on media technology, it is not a justification for technological determinism. For example, it is conceivable that we could allow learners to participate fully in all aspects of decision making concerning their learning in a conventional school. Our desire to do so, however, accentuates the physical impossibility of personalizing teaching and learning for thousands of students. The new media do not determine our values—they enable us to actualize them. Exploration of their features is necessary if it is to reveal new ways of enabling learners to reach their personal and societal goals. The importance of the new media is that they provide unprecedented power to educators and students to reach educational goals.

We are at the dawn of a new era in educational media. Possibilities discussed here are among many that are within our grasp. The future, however, will be full of new surprises, as thousands of innovative educators and students experiment with these dazzling technologies. Creative use of the new digital technologies depends on the imagination of the educators and students who use them, in a variety of settings, for teaching and learning a variety of subject matters.

CHARACTERISTICS OF DIGITAL MEDIA

At present, it seems that the new educational media have three characteristics that are critical to the development of the field. These are:

- Interactivity

- Multimodality

- Virtuality.

Interactivity

A significant feature of digital instructional media is interactivity. Unlike their analog predecessors, the new media are programmable and provide unprecedented possibilities for motivation, generative learning, knowledge representation, learner control, objective-based learning, exploratory learning, and simulation. In addition, they set the stage for development of a future generation of media that will benefit fully from virtual reality and expert systems.

Interactivity is a multifaceted concept and has been defined from several perspectives. For example, Moore (1989) delineated three types of interactions: (1) learner-instructor, (2) learner-learner, and (3) learner-content. The first two types of interaction via media are relatively new and their implementation has become possible because of the nexus of computers and telecommunications. Learner-content interaction is older; print materials and analog media have provided for it for many years. However, the new digital multimedia platforms make learner-content interactivity more complex, as they provide for various levels of learner control over how information is searched, displayed, and responded to.

Lucas (1992) delineated three types of learner-content interactivity:

1. Reactive, as characterized by drill and practice;

2. Interactive, when the software is "intelligent" and provides differential responses depending on the learner's characteristics; and

3. Proactive, "when the computer is used as an object to think with" (p. 9).

One example of these types of interactivity is the five-level model of control for laser videodiscs (Van Horn 1991). These levels range from level zero, when the videodisc is played linearly, with no provision for branching, to level four, when the designer and user have several videodisc players, run by one or more computers, to provide for complex proactive simulations. Whatever the form or the level of interactivity may be in the digital media environment, educators and learners have access to all modes of representation.

Multimodality

The new media are "translatable" (Brand 1987, 18). Words, images, and sounds can be placed in one document or can be moved from a document to any other document. Information can be presented in text, graphics, animation, natural video, human voice, music, and special effects on the same platform. Moreover, multimedia software provide for linking a segment of information, represented in any mode, to any other chunk of available information. Hypermedia allows for an "omnidirectional" (Marsh and Kumar 1992) search of information, a part of which may be stored on a CD-ROM (compact disc-read only memory) or a laser disc. The microcomputer drives the disc player to search and display the information (Van Horn 1991).

However, computers with advanced microchips and internal optical drives provide an even more powerful tool for designers and producers. "Media computers" (Osborn 1990) provide an integrated hardware/software platform for production and display of instructional information. Digitized audio, video, and text materials can be stored and retrieved for production of new instructional materials on the same system. Using total digital systems, such as DVI (digital video interactive), educators are able to represent information in any mode on demand. Optical scanners and video cameras enable them to transform information from analog to digital form for editing into multimedia documents. Using image-processing software, visuals can be edited, enhanced, and transformed in a matter of seconds. Conducting such procedures in analog photography remains only in the purview of professionals with fully equipped darkrooms. Music Instrument Digital Interface (MIDI) provides the same freedom of expression for music and sound effects. A keyboard puts the composing, interpreting, and performing power of a full symphony orchestra, a jazz quartet, or a single instrument at the fingertips of instructional designers and media producers.

More complex media production procedures, such as video editing, have also become digitized. On digital video editing systems, analog natural video and audio are digitized and mixed with computer-generated visuals, graphics, and overlays. The final product can be viewed in its digital form or converted to an analog form for storage on videotape. Digitizing full-motion natural video in color requires massive storage capacity. Software that connects microcomputer production workstations with mainframe computers can make the tremendous storage and processing capacity of mainframes available on a desktop. An example of this software is PathWorks™, which makes VAX™ computers accessible to Macintoshes™. The technology that will greatly facilitate these multimodel uses of information is high-definition television (HDTV) (Gilder 1990). It has three advantages over the current National Television Standard Committee (NTSC) standard:

1. It has twice as much resolution

2. Its aspect ratio is larger and is similar to that of the standard motion picture screen (16:9)

3. It uses digital technology for imaging, storage, and transmission.

As digital HDTV becomes popular, probably in the next five years, it will greatly enhance the ability of educators to use video and audio in conjunction with computers for display and use of information in any mode of representation.

The convergence of modes of representation on one interactive platform offers the potential of integrating the process of instructional design with the process of instructional media production. Already, software such as HyperCard™ and ToolBook™ has made rapid prototyping possible. In many cases, professionals and students prefer to develop (design and produce) a prototype of a more elaborate interactive multimedia program with these authoring systems, instead of designing a program in an analog storyboard first and then producing it on a computer. As media computers and their related software mature, it is conceivable that the concept of rapid prototyping will be extended to encompass the design and production of instructional materials as an integrated activity instead of two separate processes. A key factor to this integration, however, is the degree to which the designer/producer can use multimedia workstations to interact with the learner for assessing needs, defining objectives, deciding instructional strategies, and carrying out other instructional design, evaluation, and management activities.

Virtuality

Fiber optic lines with almost unlimited bandwidth and new telecommunications protocols, such as Integrated Services Digital Network (ISDN), extend the digital revolution from multimedia representation to multimedia telecommunications (Heldman 1987). Although existing twisted-pair, copper-wire telephone lines can be used to transmit and receive integrated voice and data, the ideal medium for combined video, voice, and data telecommunications is the optical fiber. A multimedia desktop workstation, complemented with an integrated telecommunication system, provides a bi-directional interactive virtual space in which teachers and students can see each other, talk to each other, and share information in any mode. With more advanced workstations, teachers and students can access libraries, databases, and information services located in different parts of the world. Moreover, on such workstations intelligent tutoring programs provide just-in-time help to users.

The fusion of multimedia desktop workstations with integrated telecommunication systems has accentuated the arbitrary distinction between distance education and conventional education. Moore (1983) introduced the concept of "transactional distance," in which distance is defined in terms of the ability of an instructional system to respond to a student's needs, regardless of the physical proximity of the teacher and the learner. Building on Moore's idea, Saba proposed the concept of "virtual contiguity" in distance education (1990). Interaction in virtual space goes beyond the possibilities of so-called face-to-face interaction and can be defined in a dynamic relationship in teacher-learner communication. In this relationship, transactional distance is defined in terms of how much the instructional system allows for *dialogue* and to what extent it is *structured*. Therefore, in dynamic educational systems, distance between the teacher and the learner is defined by the level of structure and dialogue rather than by the physical proximity of the educator to the learners.

This is just one dynamic model among many that may develop in the future. Postmodern concepts of educational media and technology can better be understood with such dynamic and systemic models, as compared to the static and systematic models of instructional design that have dominated the field in the last two decades. These dynamic and systemic models acknowledge the interactive and multimodal characteristics of the digital media while they accommodate various forms of teaching and learning that are gleaned from behaviorism, constructivism, and motivation theory. The new media, in turn, have provided the platform for researching these models.

TOWARD A UNIFIED PARADIGM OF EDUCATIONAL TECHNOLOGY

The analog-to-digital transformation in educational media is taking place at a time of considerable intellectual activity in conceptual development of the field. A substantial number of current developments are driven by

• The growth of cognitive psychology

• The emergence of a constructive concept of learning

• Interest in the implications of postmodernism for the field

• Continued interest in behaviorism, motivation theory, and systems analysis.

Almost a decade ago, Clark (1987) pulled our attention away from the physical features of media technologies and pointed it towards design variables in creating and presenting effective instruction. His point was well received by many professionals, as the analog media had reached the limit of their development. Exploration of their characteristics and features provided no new insights into how instruction could be enhanced. Today, we are witnessing the emergence of a new breed of media technologies that have unprecedented features and unique characteristics. The new media are providing a systemic platform for experimentation.

For example, using SemNet, researchers have explored how semantic and propositional networks are formed and used. These studies have already provided a more coherent view of the nature of knowledge and how learners acquire or "generate" new knowledge. They promise future progress in how knowledge can be organized and represented and how new curricula can be designed. Moreover, programs such as SemNet provide tools for further exploration in the nature of learning as we begin to realize the implications of perceiving knowledge as constructed reality (Allen and Hoffman 1991).

New system software (e.g., QuickTime) that facilitates integration of video with other modes of representation expedites systemic research and development in art forms that have been used for presenting instruction, although their learning effectiveness has not been adequately explored within an appropriate paradigm. For example, drama, music, and animation have always been used in creating and presenting instructional materials. *Sesame Street* perhaps is the best example of the use of these modes of knowledge representation for instructional purposes. However, study of dramatic, aesthetic and musical modes of representation in instructional media has either been ignored or the significance has been explored within a physical science paradigm. As researchers become more interested in the importance of semiotics, drama, music, and aesthetics in instructional design, media computers provide the appropriate platform for research and developments in these areas (Hlynka and Belland 1991).

Authoring systems, such as HyperCard, Director, Authorware, SuperCard, and ToolBook, also provide "intelligent" environments in which data can be collected as the learner interacts with instruction. Such software allows researchers to collect a variety of data directly, without intervention or the use of conventional tests. Other intelligent media environments, such as automated instructional design systems and expert systems, also promise exciting developments, although more work is required to fully develop and integrate these concepts for research in instructional design and educational technology.

The new media also provide unprecedented opportunities for system research and simulation in the field. For example, based on the System Dynamics concept of simulation and modeling, an Apple IIe computer with a simulation program called DYNAMO was used to create the system model of distance education described in this article. A more recent version of the System Dynamics simulation program, called STELLA, uses the graphical interface of the Macintosh computer and provides a more versatile environment for experimentation (Roberts, Andersen, Deal, Garet, and Shaffer 1983).

These are just a few examples to show that the new digital media have ushered in a new era in research and development in instructional media. Exploration of the features of the new media in relation to new concepts of learning and instruction is an absolute necessity if we are to realize their full potential. Failure to do so will limit us to using them as we used their analog counterparts. Exploration of new media in light of the unfolding *pre*paradigms of educational technology will lead us to their creative use in research and development for eventual development of a field theory of educational technology.

REFERENCES

Allen, B. S., and Hoffman, R. P. (1991). *Varied levels of support for constructive activity in hypermedia-based learning environments*. Unpublished manuscript. San Diego, Cal.: San Diego State Univ.

Brand, S. (1987). *The media lab: Inventing the future at MIT*. New York: Viking.

Clark, R. E. (1987). *Which technology for what purpose*. Paper presented at the 1987 Annual Convention of the Association for Educational Communications and Technology, Atlanta, Ga.

Cognitive and Technology Group, Vanderbilt University. (May 1991). Technology and the design of generative learning environments. *Educational Technology*, 31(5): 34-40.

Gilder, G. (1990). *Life after television: The coming transformation of media and American life*. Knoxville, Tenn.: Whittle Direct Books.

Heldman, R. K. (1987). *Telecommunications management planning: ISDN networks, products and services*. Blue Ridge Summit, Pa.: TAB Books.

Hlynka, D., and Belland, J. C. (1991), eds. *Paradigms regained: The uses of illuminative, semiotic and post-modern criticism as modes of inquiry in educational technology—A book of readings*. Englewood Cliffs, N.J.: Educational Technology Publications.

Lucas, L. (1992). Interactivity: What is it and how do you use it? *Journal of Educational Multimedia and Hypermedia*, 1(1): 7-10.

Marsh, E. J., and Kumar, D. D. (1992). Hypermedia: A conceptual framework for science education and review of recent findings. *Journal of Educational Multimedia and Hypermedia*, 1(1): 25-37.

Moore, M. G. (1983). The individual adult learner. In *Adult learning and education*, ed. M. Tight, 153-68. London: Croom Helm.

Moore, M. G. (1989). Three types of interaction. In *Readings in principles of distance education*, eds. M. G. Moore and G. C. Clark. University Park, Pa.: Pennsylvania State Univ.

Osborn, H. (1990). *Media computers, motivation, and informal education: Gutenberg 2000?* In *Learning with interactive multimedia: Developing and using multimedia tools in education*, eds. S. Ambron and K. Hooper, 357-81. University Park, Pa.: Pennsylvania State Univ.

Roberts, N., Andersen, D. (1983). *Introduction to computer simulation: The system dynamics approach*. Reading, Mass.: Addison-Wesley.

Saba, F. (1990). Integrated telecommunication systems and instructional transaction. In *Contemporary issues in American distance education*, ed. M. G. Moore, 344-52. Oxford: Pergamon Press.

Saettler, P. (1990). *The evolution of American educational technology*. Englewood, Colo.: Libraries Unlimited.

Van Horn, R. (1991). *Advanced technology in education*. Pacific Grove, Cal.: Brooks/Cole.

Part Four
The Professional Literature

Introduction

George Santayana was reported to have said that those who have not learned from history are condemned to repeat it. Professionals who have worked in the field of educational technology, under whatever label, often have the *déja vu* feeling when new hardware and software are introduced into the society and implications for education follow from a host of advocates. Each new medium has its champions and its detractors, as Paul Saettler writes in his new volume, *The Evolution of American Educational Technology*. This new volume, an updated and extended edition of his now classic *History of Instructional Technology*, was published in 1991 and is worthy of more than a mere mention.

Publication of the new history was one of the significant events of the year. Its importance was recognized by the Research and Theory Division of the Association for Educational Communications and Technology (AECT) by its inclusion of a major session at the national convention focusing on Saettler's "monumental effort." It was an unusual session, in that book reviews are not common at meetings that feature gigantic displays of new media and technology. But several hundred people crowded into a room to hear the critiques that were prepared for that session and to hear the author respond to the reviews.

Dr. Gerald Torkelson, Professor of Education Emeritus, University of Washington, and a past president of AECT, offered his observations based on a lifetime in the field. Dr. Robert Reiser, Professor of Education at Florida State University and one of the younger generation of professionals, prepared his critique from an author's perspective based on the chapter on history of the field that he wrote for Robert Gagne's book, *The Foundations of Educational Technology*. Both reviews were given and then the author was asked to respond. His comments were spontaneous at the time but later he wrote his reactions and submitted them to the moderator of the session. All three papers appear here for the first time.

There was active participation from the audience during the question-and-answer session. Those questions and answers were not recorded, but a recent review of Saettler's book appeared in the Winter 1992 issue of *Educational Technology Research & Development*. The article by Brockenburgh Allen adds another dimension to the reactions of the professional community about Saettler's work. The best source is the book itself. It should be on every professional's "to read" list. Perhaps the reviews presented here will stimulate interest in discovering the history of the field firsthand by all who read it. Those who do read it may not be condemned to repeat the past.

Perspectives on *The Evolution of American Educational Technology*

Gerald M. Torkelson
Professor Emeritus
University of Washington

In reviewing Paul Saettler's monumental effort, *The Evolution of American Educational Technology*, I was impressed by its scope, its scholarship, and its relevance for those who wish to be knowledgeable about the origins and developments in the field of educational technology.

Paul's book should be required reading for each person who aspires to being called a professional educational technologist. It is exhaustive in detail, replete with people and events which contributed to its history. Its footnotes are an education in themselves, filled with anecdotal and historical information. It is of impressive proportions, over 500 pages. It is organized chronologically into particular movements. It is encyclopedic in its coverage. To give some sense of its contents, let me briefly run down the table of contents: early forerunners of theoretical thought and practice; the beginnings of a science and technology of instruction; the evolution of the educational film; the rise and decline of the visual education movement; educational technology during World War II; educational radio; media research 1918-1950; communication and educational technology; behaviorism; cognitive science 1950-1980; development of instructional design; educational broadcasting; emergence of the information society; bureaucracy and politics in educational R and D, such as regional centers, educational television, programmed instruction research, computer-assisted instruction. In the 1980s, 1990s, and beyond, new information technologies, such as interactive video; teleconferencing; the role of cognitive processes and their applications; the history and trends in professional organizations related to educational technology; the state of the art in television, computer-assisted instruction, CAI software, instructional theory and design, interactive systems, intelligent tutoring systems. And finally, future prospects for educational technology.

Through it all runs a litany of hope for a utopia that each new technological development might achieve. It also documents how the field has matured, changed its directions, shifted emphases of philosophical orientation, delineated new and complicating research conditions. It also confronts the reader with the nature and structure of public education required to realize the fullest applications and promises of a technology of instruction.

In the author's own words, "this work is essentially a history of the *process* of educational technology rather than of products in the form of devices and media." With the exception of the first chapter, which deals with introductory remarks and definitions, two-thirds of the book is an update of *A History of Instructional Technology*, published in 1968. The last third is new material.

This second edition has dropped the name *instructional* and substituted the word *Educational*, reflecting the current broadening of technology. There is an obvious trend toward cognitive processes as a substitute for behavioristic psychology. The fashionable paradigm for research of the past, comparing relative merits of different forms of media, has virtually disappeared.

A newer area of research, cited by Saettler, involves intelligent computer-assisted instruction, which investigates learning processes and approaches or designs most appropriate for different learners. This research focuses on three areas: the nature of the expertise model, the transfer of meaning, and the sequencing of knowledge. The latter deals with problems of access, planning, problem solving, reasoning, pattern recognition, question answering, hypothesis generation, and evaluation.

The crucial shift in this type of research, when compared with the older research using different forms of media, is the recognition of learners as active/creative participants in learning, sometimes known as *learner feedback*. I recall that the Instructional Film Research Program at Penn State in the late 40s and early 50s utilized the so-called film analyzer for feedback where the subject responded to certain characteristics of a film by using a five-position keyboard. Given more sophisticated response mechanisms available today, it should be possible to delve even more closely into brain mechanisms, especially with a growing knowledge in the neurosciences. While the latter promises to be significant, applications to the affairs of education appear still to be in the distant future.

The current acceptance that more productive areas of research are in cognition and metacognition also puts a greater burden on those who design systems for learning. As is obvious in Saettler's book, there is still a significant gap between the goals of systems of instruction and opportunities for significant learner growth, particularly in learning how to learn and at higher levels of the intellect. Part of the problem is that designs of instruction specifying behavioral objects are still expecting that subjecting the learner to specific conditions will result in an observed response consonant with the specified goal. Saettler quotes Mitchell, who says that "the instructional design movement — if not wrong — is incomplete. [We need] feedback controlled selection of instructional materials, ... not a rigid design."

As another example of allowing learner control, I refer to Stewart Brand's book, *The Media Lab, Inventing the Future at MIT*, cited in Saettler's history. The Media Lab has a project in Hennigan School, an inner-city elementary school in Boston, where learners have ready access to computers at least three to four hours a day. The atmosphere is one of exploration in a nonthreatening environment. The distinct difference from standard systems of control in instruction is that the children explore, probe, try things out, and discover ways to learn by themselves. Children work together on their projects in a process which can be aptly described as "adaptive, collaborative problem worrying," a phrase borrowed from the Architectural Machine Group at MIT. While the example cited from the Media Lab has many attributes of an idealized situation, its innovative nature is far from being adopted by schools nationwide. There is some promise, however, in the *Technological Horizons in Education* (Winter 1991), which published the results of a survey of 2,000 randomly selected subscribers. By December 1991, the prediction is that the Education Industry will buy over 2 million more computers, 2 million more peripherals, over 3 million more software packages, millions of accessories, and over half a million video and optical disc products.

On another topic, Saettler calls attention to shifts of emphasis in AECT itself. AECT has growing competition from other organizations, such as the American Society for Training and Development, the National Society for Performance and Instruction, and the International Society for Technology in Education. The latter, for example, publishes four journals for educators, *Computing in Childhood Education, Computers in Mathematics and Science Teaching, Artificial Intelligence in Education*, and *Educational Multimedia and HyperMedia*. The previous two organizations are doing similar kinds of research and instructional design work, but in the context of industry, business, and federal government. Many graduates of instructional technology programs are finding jobs in these areas, working primarily with audiences in training for specific, task-oriented jobs and also creating software packages for schools. Teachers, on the other hand, still face the problems of inadequate equipment, lower salaries, crowded classrooms, and a fractious public to be satisfied. Are the public schools being abandoned by educational technologists because schools cannot afford their expertise? Or are educational technologists hoping to improve public education through avenues of the commercial creators of educational products?

AECT historically has always been associated with education. As Saettler has pointed out, we were organized first as the Division of Visual Education in NEA, then the Department of AudioVisual Instruction, ultimately becoming the Association for Educational Communications and Technology. As Saettler observes,

> The definitive withdrawal and severance of its ties with communications theory and practice was symbolized in 1989 when the title of the professional journal of the field was changed from *Educational Communications and Technology* to *Educational Technology Research and Development*. Whether this vital part of educational technology will ever be recovered and incorporated into theory and practice remains a question for the future.

Back in 1953, Finn observed in the first issue of *Audio Visual Communication Review* that

> the adoption of the term communication by the leadership of the audiovisual movement has had and will have a much more profound effect on the thinking and direction for the field than is yet realized by most practitioners. For the concept of communication or communications, as the case may be, is a seminal, organizing concept in all of the social sciences similar in scope and effect to the concept of field theory that swept through physics and biology into psychology and philosophy.

As Saettler himself said at the time, "Perhaps some term such as Educational Communication will ultimately be required to describe the communication activities, both verbal and non-verbal, which have a particular application to the classroom." In 1963, DAVI defined *audiovisual communications* as "that branch of theory and practice concerned primarily with the design and use of messages which control the learning process."

Considering that all of us might agree that the ultimate goal of an educational system is to promote active involvement of the learner in all educational experiences, it seems reasonable that those elements identified in communications theory which may hinder this interaction are worthy of re-emphasis by AECT and by those who consider themselves its professionals. Lasswell stated in his classical communications model: "Who, Says What, In Which Channel, To Whom, With What Effect." Or to state his model another way, such a study would involve an analysis of control, content, media, audience, and effects. Considering further that schools and relevant agencies comprise a social-political system, it becomes important to discover those factors which inhibit the application of technological innovations to instructional practice. In my judgment, it is short-sighted to invent a learning system which does not take into consideration the politics and fact of teacher control of the classroom, just to name one factor. For example, I recall from my experience working in Part B of the National Defense Education Act in Washington, D.C., that one study which we financed with a Social Science grant, a research group into the uses nationwide of the so-called newer educational media, resulted in a finding that much of the equipment given to schools through the largesse of Title Three sat on shelves unused.

Similar studies across the years reaffirm this finding. In a book published in 1986, *Teachers and Machines: The Classroom Use of Technology Since 1920*, Larry Cuban, the author, has this to say (quoted from Saettler):

> [F]or a teacher, the question of whether she can keep the entire class interested for fifteen minutes in the topic of federal policy toward railroads in the twentieth century is a far more pressing issue to resolve than the problem identified by reformers of whether instructional television will reduce the shortage of qualified teachers. Moreover, teachers will use new instructional tools to the degree that the classroom and the occupational culture finds acceptable. Thus, watching an occasional film or televised lesson is within the norm, but two or three movies a day or television three hours daily would seldom be sanctioned by either administrators or colleagues.

He says further that "radio, film, instructional television met only marginally most problems that teachers defined as important." And, speaking about a growing number of technological devices in schools, Cuban says that such figures seldom bear a strong relationship to use by teachers or students.

David Cohen, in a 1988 book which reports on *Educational Technology and School Organization*, observes that one of the most powerful and appealing features of the new computer technology is that it opens new approaches to inquiry-oriented instructions. However, he says that there is evidence in school and university classrooms that learners prefer rote learning because it is easier, simpler, and less uncertain. Technology does not cause educational change, it only enables it. Mass educational institutions are likely to select those technology applications that fit established practices of teaching and learning. Cohen concludes on a pessimistic note:

> Instructional practice in American Education is therefore removed from major influence by leaders of revisionist thought about learning and instruction. It also swims in a sea of popular traditional practices of teaching and learning. This has meant that teachers who tried to implement inquiry-oriented reforms typically did so without much helpful leadership, and frequently with much unhelpful resistance inside and outside the school. Considered from the perspective of the latest technology, my analysis suggests a paradoxical conclusion: the features that promise the greatest intellectual gains may make the smallest instructional headway.

I think that the conclusions of both Cuban and Cohen must be heeded by AECT and educational technologists. More partnerships of teachers and technologists must be formed both inside public schools and outside with the producers of educational products, with input from teachers and students, as to appropriate forms and climates of instruction. Instructional technologists must also study those factors in school systems which inhibit change. And part of that change, in my judgment, relates to forms of learning which demand more of students and teachers. To accomplish goals which require higher order thinking than does rote learning, demands more time and facilities for individualized instruction than now possible. Teachers also need more time to exercise their unique qualities of synthesizing, encouragement, insight, and questioning.

Expanding education's purposes more broadly, I take a cue from a 1979 publication of the Club of Rome, entitled *No Limits to Learning*. In this book the authors classify learning in two categories, maintenance and anticipatory. *Maintenance learning* is designed to "bolster and develop the skills, information, and knowledge needed to maintain the society, a function indispensible to the stability on which progress was seen to depend." *Anticipatory learning* is characterized as innovative learning where preparation is for identifying and acting on the consequences of what is produced, said, and done. Given the shrinking world through a worldwide information network, given new technologies — some of them with potential disastrous results for humankind if unleashed, such as nuclear energy harnessed for destructive purposes, it is deemed important to prepare the world's population for anticipating the consequences of these developments through its educational systems. This would require higher order thinking and value judgments which may conclude, for example, that some new technologies are best left undeveloped. Here is an obvious role for a partnership of the educational technologist, of school authorities, and of political leaders and the general public in deciding directions.

Gerbner has called broadcast television the third curriculum which grows more pervasive every day, occupying as much or more time than learners spend in school. What are the values that broadcast television inculcate which are beneficial to the survival and growth of a world population which, for survival, must value cooperation and sacrifice for others rather than competition for and aggrandizement of the world's resources? To quote from *No Limits to Learning,*

> Most of the economic and political institutions of society are predicated on the assumptions of plentiful inexpensive energy, an unlimited absorptive capacity of Nature, a supply of cheap labor (which most industrial countries must now import despite domestic unemployment), sufficient low cost capital, and favorable terms of trade. All or most of these assumptions are now invalid.

It is perhaps unfair to expect in Saettler's book a discussion about future directions for the field, since he has limited himself to its history and to the processes of educational technology. But if I may be presumptuous enough to extrapolate from his own expression of concern with the varying implicit and explicit meanings of educational technology and communications, I judge that Saettler would also express himself in terms somewhat similar to what I have said about the goals and future directions for AECT and educational technologists. In my judgment, there is implicit in the scope of communication theories a broader inclusion of factors affecting educational practice than are usually associated with functions of educational technologists. Some of you might disagree with me. However, regardless of ambiguousness in definitions, unless AECT and associated professionals become cognizant of the social and political factors blocking a full promise of educational technologies' potentials, and take actions to incorporate efforts toward changes in the instructional climate of most public schools, we may find our efforts towards more effective education even farther from being realized.

In the last paragraph of his book, Saettler says, "It is the particular futuristic bias of this author that the educational technology of the future can generate humanistic experiences provided some persistent conceptual, methodological, and political problems can be solved within the foreseeable future. There is hope that educational technology A.D. 2001 and beyond will begin to develop into something far more exciting and creative than it is now."

Reflections upon a History of the Field of Educational Technology

Robert A. Reiser
Professor of Education
Florida State University

This story begins about five years ago, when I was preparing to write a book chapter on the history of the field of educational technology (Reiser 1987). Now, since I'm *much* too young to have lived with much of the history of our field, I decided that the best way to learn about that history was to read about it. And did I read! By the time I had written the chapter, I had read and re-read over 200 articles, books, and book chapters. As I examined those sources of information, I found one source to be more informative than all the others. That source was the book entitled *A History of Instructional Technology*, written by Dr. Paul Saettler (1968).

Now, some 22 years after that book was published, Saettler has produced an updated and greatly expanded second edition, entitled *The Evolution of American Educational Technology* (1990). After having read it, I feel confident saying that this edition is even better than the first one. In the remainder of this paper, I will provide a brief overview of the book, describe a number of things I really like about it, and discuss a few things I think could be improved upon.

First, I think it is important to point out, as Saettler does, that this book is primarily a history of educational technology in American public education. Saettler does not spend much time focusing on the history of educational technology in industry, government, the military, or foreign nations. Yet, even given this slightly narrow historical focus, Saettler's book is by far the most detailed and comprehensive account of the history of educational technology in the United States.

The book is divided into four parts. Part 1 provides an overview of the field, part 2 focuses on the foundations of educational technology from ancient times to 1950, part 3 focuses on historical developments from 1950 to 1980, and part 4 looks at what has occurred in our field since 1980 and what is likely to occur in the future. With the exception of part 2, much of the second edition is new.

Now that I have provided a brief overview of the book, I would like to comment upon some of the key points raised in it. Let me start at the beginning, with the first page of the text.

On the first page of his book, Saettler points out that "this work is essentially a history of the *process* of educational technology, rather than of products in the form of devices or media." He continues this theme throughout the book. For example, a little further on he states that "technology ... should be seen as a system of practical knowledge, not necessarily reflected in things or hardware." Saettler goes on to support this point of view quite well. He cites several technological innovations that involved little or no change in tools or machines; for example, the three-field system of crop rotation and the notion of the division of labor. These examples clearly bring home his point that technology is not necessarily reflected in things or hardware.

A bit further on, Saettler states that "educational technology ... emerged out of the early technological tradition ... of knowledge [being] systematically applied to instruction." From my reading, this is about as close as Saettler comes to actually providing his own definition of our field, and the fact that he was not more direct in providing his own definition was slightly disappointing to me.

The definition of our field that I prefer is one which appears in a 1970 report prepared by the Commission on Instructional Technology. In the report, the Commission indicates that instructional technology may be thought of as "a systematic way of designing, carrying out, and evaluating the total process of learning and teaching ... based on research in human learning and communication, and employing a combination of human and non-human resources to bring about more effective instruction."

By the way, it is interesting to note that although the Commission developed this definition, they choose not to adhere to it. They said it might be more applicable in the future, but that back then (in 1970), it was better to think of instructional technology as "the media born of the communications revolution."

After discussing various definitions of the field, Saettler describes four different views of our field, or as he puts it, "four paradigms that have emerged in educational technology." These are the view of educational technology as media, the communications approach to educational technology, the behavioral approach, and the cognitive science approach. Later on in the book, Saettler elaborates upon the history of all four views, and in doing so, touches upon almost all of the underpinnings of our field. However, in his first chapter, Saettler simply provides a brief overview of these four paradigms, and I would like to comment upon a few of the points he makes.

In discussing the media view of the field, Saettler correctly points out that many people in our field, and, I would add, most people outside of it, still equate educational technology with media. I believe this is most unfortunate. As Saettler indicates, it is the process of educational technology, not the products, that we should be most concerned about.

Another interesting comment Saettler makes in his first chapter concerns the cognitive science view of our field. He states that "by the early 1980s the cognitive model of learning began to become predominant within the field of educational technology, particularly among instructional designers." I would venture to say that although cognitive science has had some impact on instructional design practice, the behavioral view of learning still has the greatest impact on the way most people in our field design instruction. And, as we shall see, Saettler seems to come to the same conclusion later in his book.

Saettler concludes his initial discussion of the four views of the field by indicating that none of them are predominant. I would agree that this divergence of opinion exists and is likely to continue to exist for some time to come.

The next portion of Saettler's book is very similar to what appeared in the first edition, and much of it focuses on the growth of the audiovisual movement from 1900 to 1950. Inasmuch as much of this portion did appear in the first edition, I will not discuss it here, other than to say the section is well worth reading; many of the facts and anecdotes Saettler presents in this section are quite fascinating.

In part 3 of the book, Saettler talks about developments in our field from 1950 to 1980, and has separate chapters focusing on events related to each of the four views of the field that he identified. I would like to mention a few interesting points Saettler makes in this section.

First, Saettler states that communication theory had little effect on our field. He states that "the primary reason that educational technology did not incorporate communication within its conceptual framework to any great degree is that behaviorism began to exert its influence in the early 1960s, just about the time that communication was beginning to have some impact." From what I have read elsewhere, I would tend to agree with this conclusion.

Has the behavioral approach been superseded by the cognitive point of view? Although Saettler seemed to say so in the first portion of his book, he now says "the theories and techniques of cognitive science are still not highly developed for practical application in educational technology ... although some significant developments have already taken place." As I indicated earlier, I would agree with this viewpoint.

After discussing the influence of cognitive science on our field, Saettler focuses on the history of instructional design. I had a little difficulty following the flow of this chapter, as Saettler moves from the work of Gagné, to a variety of theories of instructional design, to a discussion of instructional systems design and instructional systems design theory. With regard to this matter, let me say that when I wrote my chapter on the history of the field, I had difficulty deciding what to include in my discussion of the history of the systems approach. I finally settled on tracing the history of empirical approaches to the design and improvement of instruction. I am not sure whether this is a better framework within which to view the history of instructional design, but I did find it helpful as I put my chapter together.

Saettler closes his discussion of the history of instructional systems design by stating that "instructional systems design models typically focus on producing and validating instructional products, rather than [trying] ... to gain a better understanding of why and how schools function as they do." I would point out that while this may be a shortcoming of some instructional systems design models, a number of professionals in the field are really concerned about this issue. Indeed, a number of them have recently written articles which focus on the need to get a clearer picture of the reality of schools before trying to change them (e.g., Martin and Clemente 1990; Reiser and Radford 1990).

In the last portion of his book, Saettler looks at educational technology in the 1980s, 1990s, and beyond. Saettler makes a number of interesting observations in this section, and I would like to briefly comment upon a few of them.

One of the points Saettler makes is that "beginning with the instructional slide, a kind of media bandwagon syndrome has influenced educators' decisions about new media ... implying that existing educational ills or problems could be cured by the use of this new medium ... [but] these technological innovations have achieved marginal instructional benefits and have often ended in disillusionment." Later on, Saettler states that the newer technologies, like computer-based instruction and interactive video, may meet the same fate. He states, "unfortunately, microcomputer developments are bringing back an emphasis on devices rather than on the process of educational technology." I, too, am concerned about this renewed emphasis on the products associated with our field. What is especially troublesome to me is that in spite of the new technological products and processes that have been developed during the past few decades, instruction in the schools remains virtually unchanged.

Why has the manner in which instruction is delivered in schools remained virtually the same for at least the last 100 years? Saettler addresses this issue by citing the work of Larry Cuban, who has written a fascinating book entitled *Teachers and Machines: The Classroom Use of Technology Since 1920* (1986). In summarizing Cuban's ideas, Saettler states that many attempts have been made to explain the failure of technological innovations and educational reform.... [P]revailing explanations refer to insufficient funds, lack of adequate time, poor teacher preparation, or the persistent resistance of teachers to change ... but [these explanations] appear to overlook the basic behavior patterns of individual teachers operating within the school organization.

In other words, the use of technology in the classroom does not fit in well with the way teachers typically conduct their professional activities.

I wish Saettler had spent a little more time discussing Cuban's viewpoint, because I believe Cuban provides an excellent analysis of why media have not played a greater role in public education. Here, for example, is a statement from Cuban's book: "[T]eachers' repertoires, both resilient and efficient, have been shaped by the crucible of experience and the culture of teaching.... [T]hose who have tried to convince teachers to adopt technological innovations over the last century have discovered the durability of classroom pedagogy." Cuban's book is loaded with insightful statements like this one. So, in addition to Saettler's book, I would highly recommend that you add Cuban's book to your required reading list.

In order to overcome the problems cited by Cuban, Saettler calls for the development of experimental laboratory schools where the majority of the instructional staff would be nonteaching members, and where the bulk of the instruction would presumably be delivered by well-designed instructional media. A number of others have called for similar efforts (e.g., Branson 1987; Reigeluth 1987). I think that such efforts may work on a trial basis, but I question whether any large-scale attempts to implement a system like this are likely to work, given how impervious schools are to major changes.

Turning to the last chapter of Saettler's book, here he examines the state of the art of selected aspects of educational technology, and again, in many instances, he seems to be right on the mark. For example, with regard to instructional theory and instructional design, Saettler states, "[M]ost instructional theories which underlie current models of instructional design were developed more than two decades ago and are highly inadequate in prescribing instruction for interactive new technologies." Indeed, a number of professionals in our field have recognized this as a problem and are trying to develop new models. Perhaps the most prominent work in this area has been done by David Merrill and his colleagues (e.g., Merrill, Li, and Jones 1990), as they attempt to go about developing models of what they call "second generation instructional design."

Will the development of such models, or other developments, result in dramatic changes in our field? At the close of this book, Saettler responds to this question by saying, "[In the future] any change in educational technology will be evolutionary, rather than revolutionary," and I think he is right.

Regardless of whether the changes in our field are evolutionary or revolutionary, I doubt that anyone will be able to do a better job of describing those changes than Paul Saettler. I hope he will continue to write about the history of our field and I would like to encourage you to read what he has already written. I believe you will find his most recent effort to be highly enlightening *and* very enjoyable.

REFERENCES

Branson, R. K. (1987). Why the schools can't improve: The upper-limit hypothesis. *Journal of Instructional Development*, 10(4): 15-26.

Commission on Instructional Technology. (1970). *To improve learning: An evaluation of instructional technology.* New York: R. R. Bowker.

Cuban, L. (1986). *Teachers and machines: The classroom use of technology since 1920.* New York: Teachers College Press.

Martin, B. L., and Clemente, R. (1990). Instructional systems design and public schools. *Educational Technology Research & Development*, 38: 61-75.

Merrill, M. D., Li, Z., and Jones, M. K. (1990). Second generation instructional design. *Educational Technology*, 30(2): 7-14.

Reigeluth, C. M. (1987). The search for meaningful reform: A third-wave educational system. *Journal of Instructional Development*, 10(4): 3-14.

Reiser, R. A. (1987). Instructional technology: A history. *Instructional technology: Foundations*, ed. R. M. Gagné. Hillsdale, N.J.: Lawrence Erlbaum.

Reiser, R. A., and Radford, J. P. (1990). Preparing preservice teachers to use the systems approach. *Performance Improvement Quarterly*, 3(4): 40-52.

Saettler, P. (1968). *A history of instructional technology.* New York: McGraw-Hill.

Saettler, P. (1990). *The evolution of American educational technology.* Englewood, Colo.: Libraries Unlimited.

Response

Paul Saettler

PRELIMINARY REMARKS OF AUTHOR

The Evolution of American Educational Technology constitutes the culmination of over 40 years of systematic study of the history of educational technology for this author. This author has conducted more than 400 personal interviews with key figures in the field and has seen and read hundreds of original documents which have amplified the history of the field. Personal interviews have been wide and diverse, including such important figures as John Dewey, Edward Thorndike, Jean Piaget, B. F. Skinner, Mario Montessori (the son of Maria Montessori), and W. W. Charters. Pehaps, more importantly, Professor F. Dean McClusky has helped bridge the period from the early 1920s to the 1940s by providing intimate personal accounts and numerous original documents going back to the early years of this century. Whenever possible, primary sources have been sought and utilized in order to avoid the misconstructions of others.

RESPONSE OF AUTHOR TO CRITIQUE OF PROFESSOR G. M. TORKELSON

Professor Torkelson has made a number of perceptive remarks and observations which generally reflect the view of this author. For example, it is apparent, as Torkelson points out, "that there is an obvious trend toward cognitive processes as a substitute for behavioristic psychology and that the fashionable paradigm for research of the past, comparing relative merits of different forms of media, has virtually disappeared." Torkelson calls attention to the need to incorporate communication theories into educational technology in a more systematic and deliberate manner. He says, "There is implicit in the scope of communications theories a broader inclusion of factors affecting educational practice than are usually associated with the functions of educational technologists."

RESPONSE OF AUTHOR TO CRITIQUE OF PROFESSOR REISER

Professor Reiser indicated his disappointment that this author did not provide a definition of educational technology of his own. Although this author considered doing this in the book, it was omitted because definitions tend to be self-limiting. Moreover, this author takes the position that the citing of his own definition is outside the function of a historian. However, if required, this author would fashion a definition based on the original technological concepts of the early Greeks (Plato and Aristotle) that technology is "a systematic use of knowledge for intelligent human action." In educational terms, a possible definition might be that "educational technology is a process which applies scientific knowledge and other *relevant* knowledge (i.e., the humanities) to the problems of learning and education." But this definition is really not complete in modern-day terms. As Professor Torkelson pointed out in his critique, unless "AECT and associated professions become cognizant of the social and political factors blocking a full promise of educational technologies' potentials, and take actions to incorporate efforts toward changes in the instructional climate of most public schools, we may find our efforts towards more effective education even farther from being realized."

Professor Reiser criticized the assertion that cognitive theory was beginning to replace behavioristic theory in educational technology during the 1980s. Although behavioristic theory and practice may be embedded in certain quarters, particularly in the industrial sphere, this author takes strong exception to this criticism, because the theoretical and research literature as well as practice indicate otherwise. It appears to this author that this critic is viewing educational technology in a narrow manner and not viewing it with a broad perspective.

Professor Reiser points out that my advocacy of an experimental, laboratory approach to educational problems is unrealistic in terms of the constraints of the public school. This author would be the first to admit that we can hardly expect experimental conditions in the public schools, but that should not and ought not to prevent us as educational technology professionals beginning a concerted effort to develop laboratory situations outside of the political and financial restraints of the public school. It was thought that the laboratories and R&D institutions sponsored by the federal government in the 1960s would pursue this effort, but unfortunately they only tended to reinforce the status quo. If we cannot find some way to do this, we cannot begin to implement something approximating a science and technology of instruction.

Professor Reiser proposed the discussion of instructional design and systems design be placed in a historical framework consonant with the history of empiricism. This author totally disagrees with this notion. If the history of instructional and systems design is correctly understood, it does not necessarily reflect an empirical history, because the total history does not fit this context. Instructional and systems design need to be approached historically in terms of different theoretical orientations and therefore they cannot be placed in either a behavioristic or cognitive context. For example, an empirical historical analysis of instructional and systems design can tell us nothing about the basic characteristics of living educational systems that are maintained in a continuous exchange of human components in an open system.

Part Five
Leadership Profiles

Introduction

For the past five years, one of the features of the *Yearbook* has been this part highlighting the people who have made significant contributions to the field of educational media and technology. Each person appearing here has made special contributions through research, writing, and service to the profession. The names each year are selected by the editors. There is no nomination process, no voting, no awards—only the recognition of unique individuals who have reached the pinnacle of the profession through their achievements and personal influence on colleagues and students.

Each "portrait" is painted by a person who knows the leader well. In most cases, the authors are, or have been, colleagues. Their articles are labors of love, respect, and admiration. They offer genuine insights into the leader that go beyond the usual biographical sketch.

It is difficult to single out characteristics in common for the three who are profiled this year. *Robert Gagné* is well known for his influential research and writings, *Robert Heinich* for his philosophical analyses of the profession, and *Charles Schuller* for his influence on federal legislation affecting the field. The list goes on for each person; for example, Heinich and Schuller are past presidents of the Association for Educational Communications and Technology, and Gagné was influential in the American Psychological Association. Each article describes fully the person and his contributions.

Each edition of the *Yearbook* will continue to carry leadership profiles. At the risk of creating a contest, the editors would like to invite nominations for individuals who deserve to be honored in this fashion.

Robert Mills Gagné

Robert Mills Gagné

Robert M. Morgan
Professor
Florida State University

In 1990, after having served 21 years on the faculty of the Department of Educational Research, Robert M. Gagné became an Emeritus Professor at Florida State University. This 50-year milestone in his professional life did not result, however, in his retirement, but only a shift in the locus of his research work from Tallahassee to an Air Force research center in San Antonio, Texas. There one of the most productive and highly respected careers in the field of educational psychology continued without having been seriously interrupted.

Bob Gagné was born on August 21, 1916, the son of a North Andover, Massachusetts, candy maker. He was an exemplary high school and undergraduate student and graduated Phi Beta Kappa from Yale in 1937 with a major in psychology. Gagné's undergraduate adviser at Yale was Edward S. Robinson, whose counsel during these early years continued to influence his subsequent work. Three years later, in 1940, he had completed Master of Science and Ph.D. degrees at Brown University, also in the field of psychology. As Gagné has noted, many graduate students during this period were unmarried and spent most of their time in the psych labs, as did many of their professors. His special interest, then and for the remainder of his professional life, was the phenomenon of learning. Working with Clarence H. Graham, his graduate adviser, Gagné was interested in finding whether precise mathematical formulations could be employed in the field of learning. His studies of the "conditioned operant response" under various incentive conditions were done as part of his doctoral research.

In 1940 Gagné was appointed instructor of psychology at Connecticut College for Women. Here he began his interest in human learning, shifting away from white rats as experimental subjects. At this point he was called up for what was to have been a short term of military service, which in December of 1941 became long-term after the Japanese attack on Pearl Harbor and the beginning of World War II. The first world war had created an urgent need for psychological work, particularly in the area of tests and measurement. The same was to be true for World War II, except this time there were additional needs for psychological applications to training and human performance systems. Upon completion of his basic training, Gagné was assigned to Psychological Research Unit No. 1 at Maxwell Field, Alabama, which had the responsibility for administering and scoring aptitude tests for the selection and classification of air crew personnel—pilots, bombardiers, navigators, gunners. This was interesting and exciting work for a young behavioral scientist.

In 1942 Gagné attended Officer Candidate School and was commissioned a second lieutenant. For a short time he was assigned to a headquarters at Fort Worth, Texas, and then was transferred to the School of Aviation Medicine at Randolph Field, Texas. In a group headed by Arthur W. Melton, Gagné was involved in the development of psychomotor tests to be used in air crew classification. Later he was assigned to the Psychological Testing Film Unit at the Santa Ana Army Air Base, headed by James J. Gibson, which was engaged in developing film tests of perceptual abilities. Gagné ended his military service as a first lieutenant at the Psychology Branch, Aero Medical Laboratory, Wright Field, with a unit headed by Paul M. Fitts. The work led there by Fitts came to be called *human engineering*.

Also in 1942 Gagné made what many of his long-time friends have felt was his most brilliant move. He married Harriet Towle, who is called "Pat" by everyone.

Upon his discharge from the military, Gagné accepted a temporary appointment to the faculty of Pennsylvania State University before returning to Connecticut College in 1946. For the next three years he was engaged in studies of learning and transfer of training in multidiscrimination motor tasks, under a grant from the Navy Special Devices Center. In 1949 he was persuaded by Arthur Melton to join a new U.S. Air Force organization—the Human Resources Research Center—which later became the Air Force Personnel and Training Research Center. His first assignment was as research director of the Perceptual and Motor Skills Laboratory. The influence of his experiences during this period is evident in the textbook he co-authored with Edwin A. Fleishman; the book had a strong human performance orientation.

Gagné's next post was as technical director of the Maintenance Laboratory at Lowry Air Force Base, Colorado. This unit conducted research on the training of electronic maintenance personnel and associated specialties. In addition to training research, the laboratory was a leader in the development of a technology for predicting human resource requirements for newly developed weapon systems. The basic elements of this technology are still being used by the Air Force. Gagné has commented that his colleagues at Lowry were unusually talented research psychologists and have remained outstanding contributors in behavioral research. He looks back on this eight years of civilian service in the Air Force as one of "peak enjoyment" in his professional life, because of his association with such stimulating research scientists.

Following his Air Force years, Gagné was appointed a professor of psychology at Princeton University. While at Princeton, from 1958 through 1962, his research included studies of problem solving and the learning of mathematical skills. It is understandable that in this post-Sputnik era, when so much national attention was focused on the problems of education, Gagné's research interests shifted toward the learning of school subjects. He participated in the University of Maryland Mathematics Project and in the development of the elementary science program, "Science—A Process Approach," a project sponsored by the American Association for the Advancement of Science. It was during this time that Gagné observed the phenomenon of "learning hierarchies," during his research on intellectual skills and their prerequisites.

His interest in research on the applied problems of education and training continued when, in 1962, he became director of research at the American Institutes for Research (AIR), whose president and founder was the former military psychologist, John C. Flanagan. AIR was heavily involved in research on training, human performance assessment, the evaluation of educational programs, and related problem areas. At that time AIR had three office locations with multiple research teams at work, all under the monitorship of Gagné. This was a busy but highly rewarding time for him, enriched by an expanding array of colleagues and friends representing many different disciplines. It was during this time that what was to be his best-known book, *The Conditions of Learning*, was first published. This book was eventually published in virtually every major language on the planet and it has gone through several revisions and updates. By this time Gagné's scientific contributions to education, training, and human resources development were recognized worldwide.

Gagné returned to the campus in 1966, accepting an appointment as professor of educational psychology at the University of California at Berkeley. In addition to his research, teaching, and advisory responsibilities at Berkeley, he was given a special assignment to act as founding director of the Far West Laboratory for Educational Research and Development during its initial organizational stage. A half year later, John

Hemphill was appointed as the permanent director of the lab and the hectic startup activities gave way to more routine and order. Gagné's research at Berkeley continued to focus on learning hierarchies and rule learning. Collaborating with W. F. Rohwer, Jr., Gagné coauthored "Instructional Psychology," the first chapter on this subject for the 1969 *Annual Review of Psychology*.

By 1969, nearly 30 years had elapsed since Gagné had completed his doctoral work. He had been a prolific researcher and writer during these three decades. Thus, his stated intention to "slow down and not work so hard," when invited by the Florida State University to join its educational research faculty, was believable. Moving to FSU, Gagné found his most lasting professional home. With Leslie J. Briggs, he wrote *Principles of Instructional Design* and produced the second and third editions of *Conditions of Learning*. During his years at FSU, he authored, or co-authored with colleagues in the Department of Edcucational Research and the Learning Systems Institute, a number of other books that helped shape the new discipline of instructional systems design. He also played a leadership role in the development of a new graduate program in this area and supervised a number of doctoral students who themselves became productive researchers and scholars. Before his retirement at FSU, he produced *Studies of Learning — 50 Years of Research*, a topical compilation of his own research publications over the past half-century. Not many scholars could do this.

It is interesting to note that, despite his saying that he intended to slow down, Gagné produced about 60 percent of his scholarly writing while at FSU, the duration of which was roughly 40 percent of his career.

Gagné received many honors and awards during his active career: the Phi Delta Kappa Award for Distinguished Educational Research from the American Educational Research Association (AERA); the Eminent Lectureship Award from the Society of Engineering Education; the E. L. Thorndike Award in Educational Psychology; the John Smyth Award from the Victorian Institute of Educational Research; and election to the National Academy of Education. In addition, he was named by Florida State University the Robert O. Lawton Distinguished Professor, that university's highest recognition given to a member of the faculty. He also served as president of AERA and president of the American Psychological Association's divisions of military psychology and educational psychology.

In June 1992, Gagné concluded his work with the Air Force in San Antonio and he and Pat moved to their retirement home in the southern mountains of North Carolina, where they look forward to visits from their financial analyst son, Sam, their educational psychologist daughter, Ellen, and their grandchildren. He insists that he is now finally fully retired and will be devoting more time to his woodworking and fine clock making.

Robert Heinich

Robert Heinich

Michael Molenda
Associate Professor
Department of Instructional Systems Technology
Indiana University
Bloomington, Indiana

Robert Heinich was born May 31, 1923, in Ridgewood in the borough of Queens, New York City. He was one of five sons of a couple whose parents had emigrated to the United States from Germany. He showed an early aptitude for science and mathematics and was admitted to Stuyvesant High School, a magnet school for young people gifted and talented in math and science.

As is characteristic of many instructional media professionals, Bob had an unusually avid interest in the artistic and expressive side of media to go with his scientific curiosity. The artistic side found voice thanks to the serendipity of the elevated train schedule. During his sophomore year of high school, as he rode from Queens to Manhattan every morning—a 45-minute trip—he struck up an acquaintance with another young man who shared an interest in poetry, not just in reading, but in oral presentation. Somehow they discovered a music store in Astoria with a disc recorder in the back room. The owner gave music lessons and often recorded his students' playing. For 50 cents an hour Bob and his friend were able to rent the facilities (including the proprietor as recording engineer!) to record their oral interpretations of such romantic classics as Poe's "The Raven," "The Bells," and "Annabel Lee," and FitzGerald's "Rubaiyat of Omar Khayyam." When they expanded into Poe's short stories, they drafted friends to come in and flesh out the cast of voices.

This led to an interest in the "art" films of that time, such as Cocteau's "Blood of the Poet," Renoir's "Grande Illusion," and Ivens' "The Spanish Earth," all of which could be seen at the Fifth Avenue Playhouse in Manhattan. Here one could experience the dramatic power that could be achieved when poetry, music, drama, and visual art were combined. That 1930s period was also a time of ferment in political ideas; the New Deal, conservative isolationism, Marxism, and fascism contended on the street corners and in the halls of The Cooper Union, where Heinich was beginning his college studies in engineering. World War II intervened, however, to pluck Heinich out of this formative period of his education.

From early in 1943 until early in 1946, Bob had what he likes to refer to as "a loose association with the Army Air Corps." The inclinations and habits of mind that he had already developed did not jibe well with the Army's preferences for discipline and bureaucracy. He and the Army survived his three-year hitch, mutually agreeing that he should remain at the rank of private. One of the happy accidents of his service was that, having been stationed in Denver, San Antonio, and Carlsbad (New Mexico), he discovered the Southwest, particularly Colorado.

After discharge, he enrolled at Colorado State College (now the University of Northern Colorado) at Greeley, where he helped form the campus chapter of the American Veteran's Committee, a political activist group (and the only veteran's group that accepted women and blacks into its ranks) that served as an alternative to the conformist values of other veterans' organizations. At one of these meetings, Heinich happened to sit next to the campus Audio-Visual Center director, who offered him a part-time job. There he discovered a coterie of devotees of the media arts among whom he felt at home. He decided then and there to abandon his plans to become a college math professor and to find a career in the applications of media to education.

The audiovisual connection led Heinich into contact with James D. Finn, who was then head of the audiovisual program at Colorado State College. Finn had attracted a covey of bright students, many of whom—such as Lou Forsdale, Fred Harcleroad, and Bob Wagner, in addition to Heinich—went on to play prominent roles in the field. It was also at Greeley that Heinich met Christine Rebecca Finegan, with whom he formed a happy, lifelong partnership that continues to this writing.

In the fall of 1949, Heinich took his first full-time position, as Audio-Visual Director of the Colorado Springs public schools. He was armed not only with a B.A. and M.A. from Colorado State College, but also with the nascent intellectual urges that were to dominate his work for the next 40 years. These were shaped by a unique combination of talents—aesthetic, engineering, and political.

One sees these themes interwoven through all Heinich's work. The aesthetic: One cannot activate the full educational power of a medium without feeling and appreciating its capacity to tell a story, to move the heart, to sway the mind. The engineering: One cannot build an instructional system without attention to its infrastructure and its connections to the larger system of which it is part. The political: One cannot predict or control the future of a technology until one understands the dynamics of the social, political, and economic milieu in which that technology operates; who has an interest in its success and who in its failure?

Between 1949 and 1962 Heinich built a strong foundation for the school district, and for himself, in Colorado Springs. His program was recognized as the outstanding one in Colorado and eventually gained regional and national repute. Indeed, his accomplishments at Colorado Springs alone would be enough to constitute a full and rich career. For these he was made an honorary life member of the Colorado Educational Media Association. During those years he also found time to serve as first president of the Colorado Springs Friends of the Library, to serve five years as president of the local credit union, to write a regular column of record reviews for the city's newspaper, and to act in an amateur theatrical group.

In 1962 he decided to pursue his Ph.D. under Jim Finn, who was by that time at the University of Southern California. This, too, he accomplished with distinction when his dissertation, "Instructional Technology and Instructional Management: A Proposal for a New Theoretical Structure," was recognized as the outstanding dissertation of 1967 at USC. The thesis was later published by the Association for Educational Communications and Technology (AECT) as one of its major theoretical underpinnings.

Developing new theoretical constructs has been a hallmark of Heinich's work. He is well known and frequently cited for his definitions of *instructional technology, technologies of instruction*, and related terms. He is less known for, but equally proud of, a construct in research methodology—the John Henry effect—which he conceived of and named. In his work with implementing innovations such as televised courses, he noticed a tendency for teachers in the control group to be keenly aware that their work was being compared with that of a machine in the experimental treatment. He saw teachers, like John Henry in the legend, working extra hard to make sure that their teacher-led class outperformed the other one. Heinich hypothesized that this tendency could account for part of the "no significant difference" so often found in studies comparing instructional methods. Under Heinich's tutelage, Gary Saretsky investigated and validated the John Henry effect as a research-biasing factor in his 1977 dissertation, "The Application of Facet Design and 'Modus Operandi' Methodologies to the Explication of a Research Biasing Factor: The John Henry Effect."

About the time Heinich completed his doctoral studies, there was a surge of interest among textbook publishers in branching into the publication of complete systems of instruction. One of the publishers experimenting with this notion was Doubleday and Co., which convinced Bob to become director of its Educational Systems Division in 1967. During his two years there he produced a number of films, audiotapes, filmstrip sets, and reading programs.

In 1969, he decided to return to the education field, joining the Instructional Systems Technology faculty at Indiana University, where he was to remain until his retirement. It was during this period that his leadership in professional associations was beginning to crest. In 1971-72 he served as president of the Association for Educational Communications and Technology (AECT). During his presidency, the association set up a parallel foundation, the ECT Foundation, of which Heinich became the first president. He remained so for 10 years, from 1972 to 1982.

Like his mentor, Jim Finn, Heinich's engagement with the big ideas in the field led him to many editorial positions, instigating and guiding the intellectual development of the field. His contributions as consulting editor to half-a-dozen journals were more than honorary; he provided true mentoring to those who sought his counsel. His most prominent editorial position was as editor of *A V Communication Review*, which under his 13-year stewardship evolved into *Educational Communication and Technology Journal (ECTJ)*.

Heinich's insights into the influence of structural features on the uses of technology are well summarized in two award-winning articles published in *ECTJ*: "The Proper Study of Instructional Technology" (1984) and "Instructional Technology and the Structure of Education" (1985). In these widely cited articles he demonstrates how the very organizational structure of schools and universities militates against their acceptance of technology-based instruction. He contrasts "crafts" organization with "technology" organization to explain why educators tend to resist innovations that would fundamentally affect their day-to-day way of working. He also shows how the craft mentality is embedded in the legal structure of education as well as its other policies, procedures, and ways of thinking. The latter article concludes with a call for a reexamination of the research agenda for the field:

> By using analytical techniques from other disciplines and by treating the institutions themselves as variables, we can come to a better understanding of why some technologies are accepted and others are not. Because the stock-in-trade of educators is knowledge, we instructional technologists operate on the belief that knowledge in itself will change their behavior. We must realize that educators, the same as other professionals and tradesmen, respond to the organizational structures of which they are a part. To change their behaviors in regard to technology, the organizational structures may have to change. *How* is what we need to determine.

Despite these many and visible practical and theoretical accomplishments, Heinich's name is probably best known to most people because of his co-authorship with Michael Molenda and James D. Russell of *Instructional Media and the New Technologies of Instruction*. In its first edition in 1982, this textbook not only garnered "book of the year" honors from both major professional associations, but also rapidly became the most widely adopted textbook for introductory instructional media courses. The fourth edition is in preparation in 1992. This textbook reflects the theme, running through Heinich's career, of a synthesis between the aesthetic/humanistic realm and the scientific/technological realm, which may account for some part of its success.

He has been generous in sharing his knowledge with the field, in many ways other than his writings. For example, he worked behind the scenes for years in the early 1970s, leading the AECT team that collaborated with the American Association of School Librarians (AASL) to produce national standards for school media programs, published in 1975 as *Media Programs: District and School*. He served on many teams that visited and evaluated school media programs as well as university instructional technology departments. For nearly 20 years he was a field and proposal evaluator for the Bureau of Education for the Handicapped. Drawing on his broad perspective and deep experience in the field, he can be counted on to ask the hard, insightful questions.

Heinich's achievements have been recognized by the two most prominent professional associations in instructional media and technology. The National Society for Performance and Instruction (NSPI) granted him a Presidential Citation and AECT granted him the Distinguished Service Award, emblematic of a career that is unusually distinguished in terms of both the quality and quantity of his professional contributions.

Biographies of professors tend to focus on their accomplishments away from the university, since these are the activities most visible to the rest of the world. Like other professors, though, Heinich did also stay home and do his job of teaching, research, and service at Indiana University. In fact, from 1979 to 1984 he chaired the Instructional Systems Technology (IST) department; his was the longest term of leadership other than that of L. C. Larson, the founder of the program in 1940. He directed more than 15 dissertations, preferring to work closely with a few students who were interested in questions that inquired deeply into the heart of instructional technology: what it really means, where it comes from, and where it is going. As a teacher, his favorite class was always one he originated at Indiana, "Filmic Expression," which featured the viewing and analysis of films that exemplify a wide array of forms and inquired into why they work and how they work.

The moving image has continued to hold a fascination for Bob since those teenage years at the Fifth Avenue Playhouse. He has for many years been a juror at the American Film and Video Festival, continuing to attend the annual conferences even after his retirement. He also served a term as president of the Indiana Film and Video Association.

Bob, with his wife Chris, remains active since his retirement in 1990. They belong to several square-dancing and ballroom-dancing clubs, spending the summers dancing in Colorado and the rest of the year dancing in Indiana. He continues to do photography and to expand his formidable collection of recorded classical music, poetry, and drama. Those hobbies that became a profession still fascinate as a hobby.

Charles Francis Schuller

Charles Francis Schuller

The Man and His Legacy

Kent L. Gustafson
Department of Instructional Technology
The University of Georgia
Athens, Georgia

Charles Francis Schuller has always lived up to the rather impressive name given him at birth. Before retiring, he was always Dr. Schuller to his students, despite his never demanding such formality. It was simply their recognition of his stature in the profession and on the campus at Michigan State University that prevented them from calling him by any other name. He just looked and acted like a "Doctor." His colleagues have always known him as "Charlie" in person and as "CFS" in written communication. These little facts speak reams about one of the most influential pioneers in the field of educational media and instructional development and technology. Charlie has never been one to stand on formality; rather, he depends on the quality of his ideas and powers of persuasion to get things done. In an insightful comment on his persuasive skills, one of the faculty with whom he worked recently reported, "Charlie never gave me an order—of course he sometimes hinted about things he hoped would get done!"

Getting things done is what he is still remembered for even 15 years after his retirement. Today he and his wife Charlotte are enjoying life as active senior citizens in Long Boat Key, Florida, but even there he cannot stop being a leader and organizer. Almost immediately upon his arrival there, he helped organize a homeowners association and provided valuable guidance and managerial skill during its formative years. Recently he turned over those responsibilities to Charlotte, but no doubt is busy looking for another opportunity to apply his organizational skills.

Charlie became acquainted with the field of educational media through his work in naval training during World War II. Like many of the other influential pioneers in this area (Jim Finn, Charlie Hoban, Floyd Brooker, and Paul Witt), Charlie recognized the important role media and technology could play in education and training as a result of the massive education task faced by both the military and civilian sectors during that great conflict. One cannot help but wonder how different the field might be (or how much longer it might have taken to emerge) had it not been for the experience, insights, and motivation these individuals carried with them after being discharged from their respective branches of military and government service.

Numerous descriptors come to mind when describing Charlie: committed, persuasive, high standards, warm, and able to command great loyalty are among those most frequently heard from former colleagues and students asked to comment for this article. Charlie was committed to improving schools long before it came into vogue. He has always firmly believed, from the very depths of his soul, that public education is the foundation of a free, democratic, and prosperous society. He worked with teachers, administrators, and media personnel from his earliest days following the war. His passion was contagious and inspired many to carefully examine what could be possible if not rooted to the past. For example, he and Walter Wittich, with whom he had worked at the University of Wisconsin, created a college-level audiovisual course for teachers, to be delivered via distance education, as early as 1958. Filmed and then transferred to kinescope for broadcast on television, this course was used in several states and served as a model for later distance education efforts in other fields. Charlie was also committed to making the world a better place through international activities. Projects such as the one he established and designated Horace Hartsell to conduct in Brazil and another with National Iranian Radio and Television in Iran always received his staunch backing, despite the controversy the latter created on campus.

Persuasiveness is another of Schuller's defining attributes. Although many individuals have sound ideas, few have the energy and persuasive powers to bring them to reality. Whether it was lobbying Congress on behalf of the National Defense Education Act (NDEA), selling the merits of investing in technology to the administration at Michigan State University (where he created and headed one of the largest instructional media operations in the world), or convincing an individual student that instructional development was the wave of the future, Charlie had few equals. The passage of the NDEA resulted in fellowships in designated critical fields, of which media and technology became one largely through the efforts of Schuller, Finn, Larson, and Ely. The NDEA fellows were part of the new wave of doctoral programs that helped establish the academic heritage of the field and laid the groundwork for its rapid expansion in the decades of the 1960s, 1970s, and 1980s. Along the way, Charlie in 1958 served as president of the Department of AudioVisual Instruction (DAVI), which is now known as the Association for Educational Communications and Technology (AECT), and was an active voice in other national and state professional organizations. Charlie also took the lead in working with the U.S. Commissioner of Education and other leaders in the media field to promote the inclusion of media and technology in the programs offered in the various academic disciplines. For many faculty in these disciplines, the push from NDEA and related federal programs provided the impetus to examine how technology could reform instruction and revitalize their teaching. This was true at both the college and public school levels, as significant funds were allocated for the purchase of equipment and materials and to provide inservice education programs for faculty.

The Instructional Media Center (IMC) at Michigan State was another of Charlie's creations. When he arrived at Michigan State, his office by one report was a "cubbyhole." By the time he had completed his building efforts, the Instructional Media Center, as it came to be called, offered an extensive array of media services to faculty, including what was the largest university-based closed-circuit television system in the world. Complete film production, graphics facilities, equipment circulation, a rental film library, and consulting services were available at no charge to faculty for instructional purposes. Classroom setup services were also provided by a fleet of IMC trucks that circled the campus from early morning to late at night. But even this large and smoothly functioning system was not enough to satisfy Charlie. Believing that quality utilization of this technology required the application of systematic processes, Charlie and his colleagues, working with Leonard Silvern, began to experiment with what they would later call instructional development. John Barson was named to head the Instructional Systems Development Project, which became the first major test of the concepts of systematic development in education and from which was derived a model and set of heuristics that drove much of the thinking in this new field for several years. Meanwhile, and apparently in his spare time (of which it is hard to believe he had any), Charlie and Walter Wittich authored *Instructional Technology, Its Nature and Use*, one of the major textbooks in the field. Published by Harper and Row, it went through six editions, which included major revisions and updating before its authors took their well-deserved retirements. Charlie published two other books, one with William Sur entitled *Music Education for Teenagers*, and the other, published by the

National Education Association, entitled *The School Administrator and His Audio-visual Program*.

Both these titles address other key areas of interest to Charlie: music and administration. Speaking of spare time, Charlie continues to play golf, his major nonprofessional obsession in life. According to reports, he is as competitive as ever, although his game has fallen off a bit in his eighth decade. He may even occasionally wear the custom-made cuff links given to him by the IMS staff that had a golf ball, telephone, and airplane mounted on them to signify the three activities that seemed to occupy most of his waking hours.

Charlie influences those around him by model and direct contact. He never fails to greet people with a smile and can find the positive note in even the most gloomy of circumstances. Stranded by bad weather with this author in a distant city, Charlie noted that it was an opportunity to get better acquainted and also to get some work done. Personally, I was more interested in getting home, but his everpresent smile and good sense in accepting a situation that could not be changed turned the trip into one of my more enjoyable experiences in his company. He was, however, as any of his doctoral advisees can testify, a ruthless editor. With a well-tuned sense of the language and solid knowledge of its mechanics, he could turn our poor prose into sparkling poetry. What little writing skill I have today is testimony to his artful command of language and his ability to destroy my meager efforts while reworking them, and at the same time making me feel I was still competent. Many people possess one of these skills; Charlie is one of the rare individuals who possesses both.

Of the many legacies Charlie has bestowed on the field, the greatest is the cadre of graduates of the professional preparation program he established and led for so many years. They have gone on to create and head numerous other programs around the country and the world. From Georgia, to Detroit, to San Diego, to Manila, and back to East Lansing, they keep alive the quest for improving education that was the driving force for Charlie Schuller. We feel blessed that our lives were influenced by this giant in the field and work to continue the heritage he helped establish.

Part Six
Organizations and Associations
in North America

Introduction

This part of *EMTY 1992* includes annotated entries for several hundred associations and organizations headquartered in North America whose interests are in some manner significant to the fields of instructional technology/educational media, library and information science, communication, computer technology, training/management in business/industry, publishing, and others. They are organized into two general geographic areas: the United States and Canada. The section on the United States includes a classified list with headings designed to be useful in finding subject leads to the alphabetical list. Readers who know only the acronym for an association or organization of interest to them may refer to the index to obtain its full name.

It was not deemed necessary to include a classified list for Canada, because the overall number of organizations listed is considerably smaller than for the United States.

All organizations listed in part 6 were sent a copy of the entry describing the organization that appeared in *EMTY 1991*. Respondents were invited to update and edit these entries, with the proviso that, if no response was received, information included in *EMTY 1991* would be repeated so that the organization or association would be represented in this directory. Entries for organizations that did not respond are indicated by an asterisk before the name of the organization. Any organization that has had a name change since the 1991 edition is listed under the new name; a note referring the user to the new name appears under the former name. If information was received that an organization had ceased operations, a note to this effect appears under the organization name in the alphabetical listing.

The reader is reminded that changes in communications and media are frequent and extensive and that information in this directory is as accurate as possible at the time of publication.

CLASSIFIED LIST

Adult, Continuing, Distance Education
Audio (Records, Audiocassettes and Tapes, Telephone, Radio); Listening
Audiovisual (General)
Censorship
Children-, Youth-Related Organizations
Communication
Community Resources
Computers, Computer Software, Computer Hardware
Copyright
Databases; Networks
Education (General)
Education (Higher)
Equipment (Manufacturing, Maintenance, Testing, Operating)
ERIC-Related
Films—Educational/Instructional/Documentary
Films—Theatrical (Film Study, Criticism, Production)
Films—Training
Futures
Games, Toys, Drama, Play, Simulation, Puppetry

Graphics
Health-Related Organizations
Information Science
Instructional Technology/Design/Development
International Education
Libraries—Academic, Research
Libraries—Public
Libraries—Special
Libraries and Media Centers—General, School
Microforms; Micrographics
Museums; Archives
Photography
Print—Books
Production (Media)
Publishing
Religious Education
Research
Selection, Collections, Processing (Materials)
Special Education
Training
Video (Cassette, Broadcast, Cable, Satellite, Videodisc, Videotex)

Adult, Continuing, Distance Education

(ALA) Reference and Adult Services Division (RASD)

Association for Continuing Higher Education (ACHE)

Association for Educational Communications and Technology (AECT)

ERIC Clearinghouse on Adult, Career, and Vocational Education (CE)

National University Continuing Education Association (NUCEA)

Network for Continuing Medical Education (NCME)

Superintendent of Documents

Audio (Records, Audiocassettes and Tapes, Telephone, Radio); Listening

American Women in Radio and Television (AWRT)

Clearinghouse on Development Communication

Corporation for Public Broadcasting (CPB)

Federal Communications Commission (FCC)

National Association for Better Broadcasting (NABB)

National Association of Broadcasters (NAB)

National Association of Business and Educational Radio (NABER)

National Public Radio (NPR)

Oral History Association

Radio Free Europe/Radio Liberty (RFE-RL)

Recording for the Blind

Recording Industry Association of America, Inc. (RIAA)

Audiovisual (General)

Association for Educational Communications and Technology (AECT)

(AECT) Division of Educational Media Management (DEMM)

(AECT) Division of School Media Specialists (DSMS)

Association of Audio-Visual Technicians

HOPE Reports

Censorship

Freedom of Information Center (FOL)

Children-, Youth-Related Organizations

(ALA) Association for Library Service to Children (ALSC)

(ALA) Young Adult Library Services Association (YALSA)

Association for Childhood Education International (ACEI)

Children's Television International, Inc.

Close Up Foundation

Council for Exceptional Children (CEC)

(CEC) Technology and Media Division (TAM)

ERIC Clearinghouse on Elementary and Early Childhood Education (PS)

ERIC Clearinghouse on Handicapped and Gifted Children (EC)

National Association for the Education of Young Children (NAEYC)

National PTA

Communication

ERIC Clearinghouse on Information Resources (IR)

ERIC Clearinghouse on Languages and Linguistics (FL)

ERIC Clearinghouse on Reading and Communication Skills (CS)

Freedom of Information Center (FOL)

International Association of Business Communicators (IABC)

International Communication Association

International Communications Industries Association (ICIA)

National Council of the Churches of Christ—Communication Unit

Speech Communication Association (SCA)

Women in Film (WIF)

Community Resources

Teachers and Writers Collaborative (T&W)

Computers, Computer Software, Computer Hardware

(AECT) Division of Interactive Systems and Computers (DISC)

Association for the Development of Computer-Based Instructional Systems (AD-CIS)

Computer-Based Education Research Laboratory (CERL); PLATO and NovaNet

International Association for Computer Information Systems (formerly Association for Computer Educators (ACE)

International Society for Technology in Education (ISTE)

MECC (Minnesota Educational Computing Corporation)

OCLC (Online Computer Library Center)

SOFTSWAP

SpecialNet

Copyright

Copyright Clearance Center (CCC)

International Copyright Information Center (INCINC)

Databases; Networks
ERIC (Educational Resources Information Center) (See separate entries for the various clearinghouses.)
ERIC Document Reproduction Service (EDRS)
ERIC Processing and Reference Facility
SpecialNet

Education (General)
American Association of School Administrators (AASA)
American Montessori Society (AMS)
American Society of Educators (ASE)
Association for Childhood Education International (ACEI)
(AECT) Minorities in Media (MIM)
Association for Experiential Education (AEE)
Association of Teacher Educators (ATE)
Center for Instructional Research and Curriculum Evaluation
Council for Basic Education
Education Development Center, Inc.
ERIC Clearinghouse on Counseling and Personnel Services (CG)
ERIC Clearinghouse on Educational Management (EA)
ERIC Clearinghouse on Elementary and Early Childhood Education (PS)
ERIC Clearinghouse on Handicapped and Gifted Children (EC)
ERIC Clearinghouse on Rural Education and Small Schools (RC)
ERIC Clearinghouse for Science, Mathematics, and Environmental Education (SE)
ERIC Clearinghouse for Social Studies/Social Science Education (ERIC/ChESS)
ERIC Clearinghouse on Teacher Education (SP)
ERIC Clearinghouse on Urban Education (UD)
National Association of Secondary School Principals (NASSP)
National Association of State Boards of Education (NASBE)
National Association of State Educational Media Professionals (NASTEMP)
National Association of State Textbook Administrators (NASTA)
National Center for Appropriate Technology (NCAT)
National Clearinghouse for Bilingual Education
National Council for Accreditation of Teacher Education (NCATE)
National Education Association (NEA)
National Endowment for the Arts (NEA)

National Endowment for the Humanities (NEH)
National Science Foundation (NSF)
National Science Teachers Association (NSTA)
Project in Distance Education
Project in Educational Technology
Social Science Education Consortium (SSEC)

Education (Higher)
American Association of Community and Junior Colleges (AACJC)
American Association of State Colleges and Universities
Association for Continuing Higher Education (ACHE)
(AECT) Community College Association for Instruction and Technology (CCAIT)
(AECT) Northwest College and University Council for the Management of Educational Technology
ERIC Clearinghouse for Junior Colleges (JC)
ERIC Clearinghouse on Higher Education (HE)
University Film and Video Association (UFVA)

Equipment (Manufacturing, Maintenance, Testing, Operating)
(ALA) Library and Information Technology Association (LITA)
American National Standards Institute (ANSI)
Association of Audio-Visual Technicians (AAVT)
EPIE Institute
ERIC Clearinghouse on Tests, Measurement, and Evaluation (TM)
International Association of Magnetic and Optical Media Manufacturers and Related Industries (formerly International Tape/Disc Association (ITA)
International Communications Industries Association (ICIA)
National School Supply and Equipment Association (NSSEA)
Society of Motion Picture and Television Engineers (SMPTE)

ERIC-Related
ACCESS ERIC
Adjunct ERIC Clearinghouse for Art Education (ADJ/AR)
Adjunct ERIC Clearinghouse for United States-Japan Studies (ADJ/JS)
Adjunct ERIC Clearinghouse on Literacy Education for Limited-English-Proficient Adults (ADJ/LE)

Adjunct ERIC Clearinghouse on Chapter 1 (Compensatory Education) (ADJ/Chapter 1)
Adjunct ERIC Clearinghouse on Consumer Education (ADJ/CN)
ERIC (Educational Resources Information Center)
ERIC Clearinghouse for Junior Colleges (JC)
ERIC Clearinghouse for Science, Mathematics, and Environmental Education (SE)
ERIC Clearinghouse for Social Studies/Social Science Education (SO)
ERIC Clearinghouse on Adult, Career, and Vocational Education (CE)
ERIC Clearinghouse on Counseling and Personnel Services (CG)
ERIC Clearinghouse on Educational Management (EA)
ERIC Clearinghouse on Elementary and Early Childhood Education (PS)
ERIC Clearinghouse on Handicapped and Gifted Children (EC)
ERIC Clearinghouse on Higher Education (HE)
ERIC Clearinghouse on Information Resources (IR)
ERIC Clearinghouse on Languages and Linguistics (FL)
ERIC Clearinghouse on Reading and Communication Skills (CS)
ERIC Clearinghouse on Rural Education and Small Schools (RC)
ERIC Clearinghouse on Teacher Education (SP)
ERIC Clearinghouse on Tests, Measurement, and Evaluation (TM)
ERIC Clearinghouse on Urban Education (UD)
ERIC Document Reproduction Service (EDRS)
ERIC Processing and Reference Facility

Films—Educational/Instructional/Documentary
Anthropology Film Center (AFC)
Association of Independent Video and Filmmakers and the Foundation for Independent Video and Film
Children's Television International, Inc.
CINE Information
Council on International Non-theatrical Events (CINE)
Film Advisory Board (FAB)
Film Arts Foundation (FAF)
Film/Video Arts, Inc.
National Aeronautics and Space Administration (NASA)

National Alliance of Media Arts Centers (NAMAC)
National Audiovisual Center (NAC)
National Film Board of Canada (NFBC)
National Information Center for Educational Media (NICEM)
Pacific Film Archive (PFA)
PCR: Films and Video in the Behavioral Sciences

Films—Theatrical (Film Study, Criticism, Production)
Academy of Motion Picture Arts and Sciences (AMPAS)
American Society of Cinematographers
Film Advisory Board (FAB)
Film Arts Foundation (FAF)
Hollywood Film Archive
International Film and TV Festival of New York
National Film Information Service (NFIS)

Films—Training
American Film and Video Association (AFVA)
(AECT) Industrial Training and Education Division (ITED)
Association of Independent Video and Filmmakers and the Foundation for Independent Video and Film
Children's Film and Television Center of America (CFTCA)
Council on International Non-theatrical Events
Great Plains National ITV Library (GPN)
National Audiovisual Center (NAC)
National Film Board of Canada (NFBC)
Training Media Association

Futures
Institute for the Future (IFTF)
Office of Technology Assessment (OTA)
World Future Society (WFS)

Games, Toys, Drama, Play, Simulation, Puppetry
North American Simulation and Gaming Association (NASAGA)
Puppeteers of America
Society for Computer Simulation (SCS)

Graphics
International Graphic Arts Education Association (IGAEA)

Health-Related Organizations
Health Science Communications Association
(HeSCA)
Lister Hill National Center for Biomedical
Communications of the National
Library of Medicine
Medical Library Association (MLA)
National Association for Visually Handi-
capped (NAVH)
National Library of Medicine
Network for Continuing Medical Education
(NCME)

Information Science
International Information Management
Congress (IMC)

**Instructional Technology/Design/Develop-
ment**
Agency for Instructional Technology (AIT)
Association for Educational Communications
and Technology (AECT)
(AECT) Community College Association for
Instruction and Technology (CCAIT)
(AECT) Division of Educational Media Man-
agement (DEMM)
(AECT) Division of Instructional Develop-
ment (DID)
Association for the Development of Com-
puter-Based Instructional Systems
(ADCIS)
National Society for Performance and Instruc-
tion (NSPI)
Office of Technology Assessment (OTA)
Professors of Instructional Design and Tech-
nology (PIDT)
Society for Applied Learning Technology
(SALT)

International Education
(AECT) International Division (ITNL)
(AECT) International Visual Literacy Asso-
ciation, Inc. (IVLA)
Institute of Culture and Communication (East-
West Center)
Institute of International Education
Office for International Networks in Educa-
tion and Development (INET)
United Nations Department of Public Infor-
mation, Dissemination Division

Libraries—Academic, Research
American Library Association (ALA)
(ALA) Association of College and Research
Libraries (ACRL)

ERIC Clearinghouse on Information
Resources (IR)

Libraries—Public
American Library Association (ALA)
(ALA) Association for Library Service to
Children (ALSC)
(ALA) Audiovisual Committee (of the Public
Library Association)
(ALA) Library Administration and Manage-
ment Association (LAMA)
(ALA) Library and Information Technology
Association (LITA)
(ALA) Public Library Association (PLA)
(ALA) Reference and Adult Services Divi-
sion (RASD)
(ALA) Technology in Public Libraries Com-
mittee (of the Public Libraries Associa-
tion)
(ALA) Young Adult Library Services Asso-
ciation (YALSA)
ERIC Clearinghouse on Information
Resources (IR)

Libraries—Special
American Library Association (ALA)
(ALA) Association for Library Service to
Children (ALSC)
(ALA) Association of Specialized and Coop-
erative Library Agencies (ASCLA)
ERIC Clearinghouse on Information
Resources (IR)
Special Libraries Association (SLA)
Theater Library Association

**Libraries and Media Centers—General,
School**
American Library Association (ALA)
(ALA) American Association of School Li-
brarians (AASL)
(ALA) American Library Trustee Association
(ALTA)
(ALA) Association for Library Service to
Children (ALSC)
(ALA Round Table) Continuing Library Edu-
cation Network and Exchange
(CLENE)
Association for Educational Communications
and Technology (AECT)
(AECT) Division of School Media Specialists
(DSMS)
(AECT) National Association of Regional
Media Centers (NARMC)
Catholic Library Association (CLA)
Consortium of College and University Media
Centers

Council of National Library and Information
Associations
ERIC Clearinghouse on Information
Resources (IR)
International Association of School Librarian-
ship (IASL)
Library of Congress
National Alliance of Media Arts Centers
(NAMAC)
National Association of State Educational
Media Professionals (NASTEMP)
National Commission on Libraries and Infor-
mation Science (NCLIS)
National Council of Teachers of English
(NCTE) Commission on Media
On-Line Audiovisual Catalogers (OLAC)

Microforms; Micrographics
See ERIC-Related entries.

Museums; Archives
(AECT) Archives
American Federation of Arts (AFA)
Association of Systematics Collections
Computer Museum
Hollywood Film Archive
International Museum of Photography at
George Eastman House
Lawrence Hall of Science
Museum Computer Network, Inc. (MCN)
Museum of Holography
Museum of Modern Art
Museum of Television and Radio
National Gallery of Art (NGA)
Smithsonian Institution

Photography
International Center of Photography (ICP)
International Museum of Photography at
George Eastman House
Museum of Holography
National Press Photographers Association,
Inc. (NPPA)
Photographic Society of America (PSA)
Society for Imaging Science and Technology
(IS&T)
Society for Photographic Education (SPE)
Society of Photo Technologists (SPT)

Print—Books
American Library Association (ALA)
Association for Educational Communications
and Technology (AECT)
Smithsonian Institution
United Nations Department of Public Information

Production (Media)
American Society of Cinematographers
Association for Educational Communications
and Technology (AECT)
(AECT) Media Design and Production Divi-
sion (MDPD)
Association of Independent Video and Film-
makers and the Foundation for Inde-
pendent Video and Film
Film Arts Foundation (FAF)
Women in Film (WIF)

Publishing
Association of American Publishers (AAP)
Government Printing Office (US GPO)
Magazine Publishers of America (MPA)
National Association of State Textbook
Administrators (NASTA)

Religious Education
Catholic Library Association (CLA)
National Religious Broadcasters (NRB)

Research
American Educational Research Association
(AERA)
(AECT) ECT Foundation
(AECT) Research and Theory Division (RTD)
Center for Advanced Visual Studies
Center for Instructional Research and Curricu-
lum Evaluation
Clearinghouse on Development Communica-
tion
Council for Educational Development and
Research (CEDaR)
Education Development Center, Inc.
ERIC Clearinghouses. See ERIC-Related
entries.
Far West Laboratory for Educational Re-
search and Development (FWL)
HOPE Reports
Institute for Development of Educational
Activities, Inc. (IDEA)
Institute for Research on Teaching
National Technical Information Service
(NTIS)
National Technology Center (NTC)
The NETWORK
Northwest Regional Educational Laboratory
(NWREL)

Selection, Collections, Processing (Materials)
National Information Center for Educational
Media (NICEM)

Special Education
Council for Exceptional Children (CEC)
ERIC Clearinghouse on Handicapped and
Gifted Children (EC)
National Association for Visually Handi-
capped (NAVH)
National Technology Center (NTC)

Training
American Management Association (AMA)
American Society for Training and Develop-
ment (ASTD)
Association for Educational Communications
and Technology (AECT)
(AECT) Federal Educational Technology
Association (FETA)
(AECT) Industrial Training and Education
Division (ITED)
ERIC Clearinghouse on Adult, Career, and
Vocational Education (CE)
National Society for Performance and Instruc-
tion (NSPI)
Training Modules for Trainers (TMT)

**Video (Cassette, Broadcast, Cable, Satel-
lite, Videodisc, Videotex)**
Agency for Instructional Technology (AIT)
American Women in Radio and Television
(AWRT)
Association for Educational Communications
and Technology (AECT)
(AECT) Division of Telecommunications (DOT)
(AECT) National ITFS Association
(NIA/ITFS)
Association of Independent Video and Film-
makers and the Foundation for Inde-
pendent Video and Film

Central Educational Network (CEN)
Children's Film and Television Center of
America (CFTCA)
Children's Television International, Inc.
Close Up Foundation
Corporation for Public Broadcasting (CPB)
Federal Communications Commission (FCC)
Great Plains National ITV Library (GPN)
International Association of Magnetic and
Optical Media Manufacturers and
Related Industries (formerly Interna-
tional Tape/Disc Association (ITA))
International Telecommunications Satellite
Organization (INTELSAT)
International Teleconferencing Association
(ITCA)
International Television Association (ITVA)
National Association for Better Broadcasting
(NABB)
National Association of Broadcasters (NAB)
National Cable Television Institute (NCTI)
National Federation of Community Broadcast-
ers (NFCB)
National Telemedia Council, Inc. (NTC)
Nebraska Videodisc Design/Production
Group (VD-PG)
PBS ENCORE
PBS VIDEO
Public Broadcasting Service (PBS)
Public Service Satellite Consortium (PSSC)
Society of Cable Television Engineers (SCTE)
Society of Motion Picture and Television
Engineers (SMPTE)
Telecommunications Research and Action
Center (TRAC)
Women in Film (WIF)

ALPHABETICAL LIST

Academy of Motion Picture Arts and Sciences (AMPAS). 8949 Wilshire Blvd., Beverly Hills, CA 90211. (310) 247-3000. An honorary organization composed of outstanding individuals in all phases of motion pictures. Seeks to advance the arts and sciences of motion picture technology and artistry. Presents annual film awards; offers artist-in-residence programs; operates reference library and National Film Information Service. *Publications: Annual Index to Motion Picture Credits; Academy Players Directory.*

*Agency for Instructional Technology (AIT). Box A, Bloomington, IN 47402. (812) 339-2203; (800) 457-4509. Michael F. Sullivan, Exec. Dir. Established to strengthen education through technology. In cooperation with state and provincial agencies, AIT develops instructional materials using video, computers, and other emerging technologies. AIT also acquires and distributes a wide variety of video, computer, and related print materials for use as major learning resources. From April 1973 to July 1984, AIT was known as the Agency for Instructional Television. Its predecessor organization, National Instructional Television, was founded in 1962. *Publications: AIT Newsletter; AIT Catalog.*

*American Association of Community and Junior Colleges (AACJC). One Dupont Circle NW, Suite 410, Washington, DC 20036-1176. (202) 728-0200. Dale Parnell, Pres. AACJC serves the nation's 1,211 community, technical, and junior colleges through advocacy, professional development, publications, and national networking. The annual convention draws more than 4,000 mid- and top-level administrators of two-year colleges. Staff and presidents offer expertise in all areas of education. Sixteen councils and six commissions address all areas of education. *Membership*: 1,110 institution, 150 international, 4 foundation, 75 corporate, 103 educational association. *Dues*: Vary for institutions, corporations, foundations, and individuals. *Publications: Community, Technical and Junior College Journal* (bi-mo.); *AACJC Letter* (mo.); *College Times*; Community College Press (books, monographs, etc.); publications program (directories, books, monographs, policy statements, etc.).

American Association of School Administrators (AASA). 1801 N. Moore St., Arlington, VA 22209. (703) 528-0700. Fax (703) 528-2146. Richard D. Miller, Exec. Dir. Represents professional administrators and managers in education in the United States and overseas; provides an extensive program of professional development through the National Academy for School Executives (NASE). Also produces publications and audiovisual programs to increase knowledge and skills of administrators. *Membership:* 18,500. *Dues:* $199. *Publications: The School Administrator; Leadership News*; numerous books and video programs.

American Association of State Colleges and Universities. One Dupont Cir. NW, Suite 700, Washington, DC 20036-1192. (202) 293-7070. James B. Appleberry, Pres. Membership is open to any regionally accredited institution of higher education, and those in the process of securing accreditation, which offers programs leading to the degree of bachelor, master, or doctor, and which are wholly or partially state-supported and state-controlled. Organized and operated exclusively for educational, scientific, and literary purposes, its particular purposes are to improve higher education within its member institutions through cooperative planning, studies, and research on common educational problems and the development of a more unified program of action among its members; and to provide other needed and worthwhile educational services to the colleges and universities it may represent. *Membership:* 375 institutions (university), 28 system, and 7 associate members. *Dues:* Based on current student enrollment at institution. *Publications: MEMO: To the President; The Center Associate; Office of Federal Program Reports; Office of Federal Program Deadlines.* (Catalogs of books and other publications available upon request.)

American Educational Research Association (AERA). 1230 17th St. NW, Washington, DC 20036. (202) 223-9485. Fax (202) 775-1824. William J. Russell, Exec. Dir. A national professional organization of educators and behavioral scientists active and/or interested in educational research and its application to educational problems. Sponsors annual meetings featuring presentations of original research findings. *Membership:* 18,000. *Dues:* $45. *Publications: Educational Researcher; American Educational Research Journal; Journal of Educational Statistics; Educational Evaluation and Policy Analysis; Review of Research in Education; Review of Educational Research.*

The American Federation of Arts (AFA). Headquarters, 41 E. 65th St., New York, NY 10021. (212) 988-7700. Fax (212) 861-2487. Serena Rattazzi, Dir. National nonprofit museum service that organizes and circulates exhibitions of fine arts and media arts to museums, university art galleries, and art centers throughout the United States and abroad. Also provides specialized services to member museums, including reduced-rate programs of fine art insurance, air and surface transport of art, and professional management training. *Institutional Membership:* 520. *Publications:* Newsletter: *ART* (3/yr.); *MEMO TO MEMBERS* (for institutional members only) (6/yr.).

American Film and Video Association (AFVA). 8050 N. Milwaukee Ave., P.O. Box 48659, Niles, IL 60648. (708) 698-6440. Kathryn Osen, Acting Exec. Dir.; Lawrence Skaja, Managing Dir. Formerly the Educational Film Library Association, the AFVA is recognized as the authoritative organization in assembling data about the 16mm and video fields, in encouraging quality production and appreciation of film generally, and in providing guidance in the proper use of these media. Serves as a national clearinghouse of information about films, conducts workshops on a variety of media-related topics, and sponsors the annual American Film and Video Festival. *Membership:* 1,300. *Dues:* $55 individual, $210 institution. *Publications: SightLines; AFVA Bulletin; AFVA Evaluations.*

American Library Association (ALA). 50 E. Huron St., Chicago, IL 60611. (312) 944-6780. Fax (312) 440-9374. Linda F. Crismond, Exec. Dir. The ALA is the oldest and largest national library association. Its 52,000 members represent all types of libraries—state, public, school, and academic, as well as special libraries serving persons in government, commerce, the armed services, hospitals, prisons, and other institutions. Chief advocate of achievement and maintenance of high-quality library information services through protection of the right to read, educating librarians, improving services, and making information widely accessible. *Membership:* 52,000. *Dues:* Basic dues $38 first year, $75 renewing members. *Publications: American Libraries; Booklist; Choice; Book Links.*

(ALA) American Association of School Librarians (AASL). 50 Huron St., Chicago, IL 60611. (312) 944-6780. Fax (312) 664-7459. Ann Carlson Weeks, Exec. Dir. Seeks general improvement and extension of school library/media services as a means of strengthening education. Gives special attention to evaluation, selection, interpretation, and use of library media. Activities and projects of the association are divided among 55 committees and 3 sections. *Membership:* 7,300. *Dues:* Membership in ALA plus $35, $105 renewing member, $34 student member. *Publications: School Library Media Quarterly;* others.

(ALA) American Library Trustee Association (ALTA). 50 E. Huron St., Chicago, IL 60611. (312) 280-2160. Fax (312) 280-3257. Sharon L. Jordan, Exec. Dir. Interested in the development of effective library service for people in all types of communities and libraries. Members, as policymakers, are concerned with organizational patterns of service, the development of competent personnel, the provision of adequate financing, the passage of suitable legislation, and the encouragement of citizen support for libraries. *Membership:* 1,710. *Dues:* $40 plus membership in ALA. *Publications: ALTA Newsletter, Trustee Digest.*

(ALA) Association for Library Collections and Technical Services (ALCTS). 50 E. Huron St., Chicago, IL 60611. (312) 944-6780. Karen Muller, Exec. Dir; Arnold Hirshon, Pres., July 1991-June 1992. Dedicated to acquisition, identification, cataloging, classification, and preservation of library materials, the development and coordination of the country's library resources, and aspects of selection and evaluation involved in acquiring and developing library materials and resources. Sections include Acquisition of Library Materials, Cataloging and Classification, Collection Management and Development, Preservation of Library Materials, Reproduction of Library Materials, and Serials. *Membership:* 5,854. *Dues:* $35 plus membership in ALA. *Publications: Library Resources & Technical Services* (q.); *ALCTS Newsletter* (8/yr.).

(ALA) Association for Library Service to Children (ALSC). 50 E. Huron St., Chicago, IL 60611. (312) 280-2163. Fax (312) 280-3257. Susan Roman, Exec. Dir. Interested in the improvement and extension of library services for children in all types of libraries, evaluation and selection of book and nonbook library materials, and improvement of techniques of library services for children from preschool through the eighth grade or junior high school age. Annual conference and midwinter meeting with the ALA. Committee membership open to ALSC members. *Membership:* 3,600. *Dues:* $35 plus membership in ALA. *Publications: Journal of Youth Services in Libraries; ALSC Newsletter.*

(ALA) Association of College and Research Libraries (ACRL). 50 E. Huron St., Chicago, IL 60611-2795. (312) 280-3248. Fax (312) 280-3257. Althea H. Jenkins, Exec. Dir. Represents librarians and promotes libraries of postsecondary, research, and specialized institutions. Has available library standards for colleges, universities, and two-year institutions. Publishes statistics on academic libraries. Committees include Academic Status, Audiovisual, Professional Education, Legislation, Publications, and Standards and Accreditation. Free list of materials available. *Membership:* 11,000. *Dues:* $35 (in addition to ALA membership). *Publications: College & Research Libraries; College & Research Libraries News; Rare Books and Manuscripts Librarianship;* 11 section newsletters; *Choice.*

(ALA) Association of Specialized and Cooperative Library Agencies (ASCLA). 50 E. Huron St., Chicago, IL 60611. (800) 545-2433, ext. 4399. Fax (312) 280-3257. Andrew Hansen, Exec. Dir. Represents state library agencies, multitype library cooperatives, and libraries serving special clienteles to promote the development of coordinated library services with equal access to information and materials for all persons. The activities and programs of the association are carried out by 21 committees, 3 sections, and various discussion groups. Write for free checklist of materials. *Membership:* 1,300. *Dues:* (in addition to ALA membership) $30 for personal members, $50 for organizations, $500 for state library agencies. *Publications: Interface.*

(ALA) Library Administration and Management Association (LAMA). 50 E. Huron St., Chicago, IL 60611. (312) 280-5038. Karen Muller, Exec. Dir.; Susanne Stroyan, Pres., July 1991-June 1992. Provides an organizational framework for encouraging the study of administrative theory, for improving the practice of administration in libraries, and for identifying and fostering administrative skills. Toward these ends, the association is responsible for all elements of general administration that are common to more than one type of library. These may include: Buildings and Equipment Section (BES); Fundraising & Financial Development Section (FRFDS); Library Organization & Management Section (LOMS); Personnel Administration Section (PAS); Public Relation Section (PRS); Systems & Services Section (SASS); Statistic Section (SS). *Membership:* 5,223. *Dues:* $35 (in addition to ALA membership). *Publication: Library Administration & Management* (q.).

(ALA) Library and Information Technology Association (LITA). 50 E. Huron St., Chicago, IL 60611. (312) 280-4270; (voice) (800) 545-2433, ext. 4270. Fax (312) 280-3257. Linda J. Knutson, Exec. Dir. Concerned with library automation, the information sciences, and the design, development, and implementation of automated systems in those fields, including systems development, electronic data processing, mechanized information retrieval, operations research, standards development, telecommunications, video communications, networks and collaborative efforts, management techniques, information technology, optical technology, artificial intelligence and expert systems, and other related aspects of audiovisual activities and hardware applications. *Membership:* 5,000. *Dues:* $35 plus membership in ALA, $15 for library school students. *Publications: Information Technology and Libraries; LITA Newsletter.*

(ALA) Public Library Association (PLA). 50 E. Huron St., Chicago, IL 60611. (312) 280-5752; (800) 545-2433 ext. 5PLA. Fax (312) 280-5029. Eleanor Jo Rodger, Exec. Dir.; June M. Garcia, Pres. Concerned with the development, effectiveness, and financial support of public libraries. Speaks for the profession and seeks to enrich the professional competence and opportunities of public libraries. Sections include Adult Lifelong Learning, Community Information, Metropolitan Libraries, Public Library Systems, Small and Medium-sized Libraries, and Marketing of Public Library Services. *Membership:* 7,000. *Dues:* $35, open to all ALA members. *Publications: Planning and Role Setting for Public Libraries: A Manual of Options and Procedures; Output Measures for Public Libraries: A Manual of Standardized Procedures* (2d ed.); *Public Library Data Service, Statistical Report.*

(ALA) Audiovisual Committee (of the Public Library Association). 50 E. Huron St., Chicago, IL 60611. (312) 280-5752. Promotes use of audio-visual materials in public libraries.

(ALA) Technology in Public Libraries Committee (of the Public Library Association). 50 E. Huron St., Chicago, IL 60611. (312) 944-6780. Collects and disseminates information on technology applications in public libraries.

(ALA) Reference and Adult Services Division (RASD). 50 E. Huron St., Chicago, IL 60611. (312) 280-5752; (800) 545-2433, ext. 4398. Fax (312) 280-3257. Andrew M. Hansen, Exec. Dir. Responsible for stimulating and supporting in every type of library the delivery of reference information services to all groups and of general library services and materials to adults. *Membership:* 5,201. *Dues:* $35 plus membership in ALA. *Publications: RQ; RASD Update;* others.

(ALA) Young Adult Library Services Association (YALSA) (formerly Young Adult Services Division). 50 E. Huron St., Chicago, IL 60611. (312) 280-4390. Mary Elizabeth Wendt, Pres. Seeks to improve and extend library services to young people, assumes responsibility within the ALA to evaluate and select books and nonbook media and to interpret and make recommendations regarding their use with young adults. Committees include Best Books for Young Adults, Recommended Books for the Reluctant Young Adult Reader, Media Selection and Usage, Publishers' Liaison, and Selected Films for Young Adults. *Membership:* 2,400. *Dues:* $35 (in addition to ALA membership), $15 for students. *Publications: Journal of Youth Services in Libraries; Best Books; Youth Participation in Libraries: A Training Manual; Outstanding Books for the College Bound;* many others.

(ALA Round Table) Continuing Library Education Network and Exchange. 50 E. Huron St., Chicago, IL 60611. (312) 280-3213. M. Kent Mayfield, Pres. Seeks to provide access to quality continuing education opportunities for librarians and information scientists and to create an awareness of the need for such education in helping individuals in the field to respond to societal and technological changes. *Membership:* 350. *Dues:* Open to all ALA members; individual members $15, $50 for organizations. *Publications: CLENExchange* (q.), available to nonmembers by subscription at $20/yr. U.S. zip, $25 non-U.S. zip.

American Management Association (AMA). 135 W. 50th St., New York, NY 10020. (212) 586-8100. David Fagiano, Chairman and CEO. The AMA is an international educational organization—membership-based and not-for-profit—dedicated to broadening the management knowledge and skills of people and, by so doing, strengthening their organizations. The AMA operates management centers and offices in the United States and, through AMA/International, in Brussels, Belgium; Sao Paulo, Brazil; Toronto, Canada; and Mexico City, Mexico. The AMA offers public meetings through the Center for Management Development, Padgett-Thompson, Presidents Association, AMA/International, AMA On-Site, and Operation Enterprise (young adult program), and provides interchange of management information, ideas, and experience in a wide variety of management topics through national conferences, seminars, and membership briefings. Services offered include the Extension Institute (self-study programs in both print and audio formats); the Information Resource Center (for members only), a management information and library service; and four AMA bookstores. The AMA publishes approximately 60 books per year as well as numerous research surveys, research reports, and management briefing reports; AMA Video (based in Boston) produces a variety of videotapes. *Membership:* approx. 70,000. *Publications* (periodicals): *Management Review* (membership); *The President; Personnel; Organizational Dynamics; Service Savvy; Small Business Reports; Supervisory Management; Supervisory Sense; Trainer's Workshop.*

American Montessori Society (AMS). 150 5th Ave., New York, NY 10011. (212) 924-3209. Fax (212) 727-2254. Bretta Weiss, Natl. Dir. Dedicated to promoting better education for all children through teaching strategies consistent with the Montessori system. Membership is composed of schools in the private and public sectors employing this method, as well as individuals. It serves as a resource center and clearinghouse for information and data on Montessori, affiliates teacher training programs in different parts of the country, and conducts a consultation service and accreditation program for school members. Sponsors two regional and one national educational conference per year and four professional development symposia under the auspices of the AMS Teachers' Section. Dues: Teachers, schoolheads, $33.50/yr.; parents, $26.50/yr.; institutions, from $215/yr. and up. *Publications: AMS Montessori LIFE* (q.); *Schoolheads* (newsletter); occasional papers.

American National Standards Institute (ANSI). 11 West 42nd Street, New York, NY 10036. (212) 642-4900. Fax (212) 302-1286. Manuel Peralta, Pres.; James N. Pearse, Chairman of the Board. ANSI is the coordinator of the U.S. voluntary standards system, approves American National Standards, and represents the United States in the International Organization for Standardization (ISO) and the International Electrotechnical Commission (IEC). The Institute does not write standards or codes but coordinates those developed through an open consensus process by the more than 240 organizations, 1,000 businesses, and 20 government agencies that comprise its membership. *Publications: Catalog of Standards* (annual) lists more than 8,000 standards for all topic areas; *ANSI Reporter* (m.), newsletter of the national and international standards community; *Standards Action* (biweekly), listing of status of revisions on standards in the United States, international communities, Europe, and other foreign national bodies.

American Society for Training and Development (ASTD). 1640 King St., Box 1443, Alexandria, VA 22313. (703) 683-8100. Fax (703) 683-8103. Curtis E. Plott, Exec. V.P. Leading professional organization for individuals engaged in employee training and education in business, industry, government, and related fields. Members include managers, program developers, instructors, consultants, counselors, suppliers, and academics. The purpose of its extensive professional publishing program is to build an essential body of knowledge for advancing the competence of training and development practitioners in the field. Many special-interest subgroups relating to industries or job functions are included in the organization. *Membership:* 55,000 national plus chapter. *Dues:* $150/yr. individual (group discounts available). *Publications: Training and Development Magazine; Info-Line; ASTD Video Directories; Competency Analysis for Trainers: A Personal Planning Guide; ASTD Directory of Academic Programs in T&D/HRD; Evaluating Training Programs; Training and Development Handbook; National Report; Technical & Skills Training Magazine.* Newsletters: *Focus* (chapter newsletter); *Management Development Report; The Business of Training; Technical Trainer/Skills Trainer.* ASTD also has recognized professional areas, networks, and industry groups, most of which produce newsletters.

American Society of Cinematographers. 1782 N. Orange Dr., Hollywood, CA 90078. (213) 876-5080. Leonard South, Pres. *Membership:* 271. *Publication: American Cinematographers Magazine.*

American Society of Educators (ASE). 1429 Walnut St., Philadelphia, PA 19102. (215) 563-3501. Fax (215) 563-1588. Andrea Epstein, Mng. Ed. A multifaceted professional organization that serves the nation's teachers by providing information and evaluation of media resources and technologies for effective classroom use. *Membership:* 41,000. *Dues:* $29/yr., $47/yr. foreign. *Publications: Media and Methods; School Executive.*

American Women in Radio and Television (AWRT). 1101 Connecticut Ave. NW, Suite 700, Washington, DC 20036. (202) 429-5102. Susan Kudla Finn, Exec. Dir. Organization of professionals in the electronic media, including owners, managers, administrators, and those in creative positions in broadcasting, satellite, cable, advertising, and public relations. The objectives are to work worldwide to improve the quality of radio and television; to promote the entry, development, and advancement of women in the electronic media and allied fields; to serve as a medium of communication and idea exchange; and to become involved in community concerns. Organized in 1951. Student memberships available. *Membership:* 52 chapters. *Dues:* $105/yr. *Publications: News and Views; Resource Directory; Careers in the Electronic Media.*

Anthropology Film Center (AFC). Box 493-87504, 1626 Canyon Rd., Santa Fe, NM 87501. (505) 983-4127. Carroll Williams, Dir. Offers the Documentary Film Program, a 34-week full-time course in 16mm film production and theory and summer workshops. Also provides consultation, research, 16mm film equipment sales and rental, facilities rental, occasional seminars and workshops, and a specialized library. *Publications: An Ixil Calendrical Divination* (16mm color film); *First Impressions of Ixil Culture* (16mm color film).

Association for Childhood Education International (ACEI). 11501 Georgia Ave., No. 315, Wheaton, MD 20902. (301) 942-2443. Lucy Prete Martin, Ed. and Dir. of Publications. Concerned with children from infancy through early adolescence. ACEI publications reflect careful research, broad-based views, and consideration of a wide range of issues affecting children. Many are media-related in nature. The journal (*Childhood Education*) is essential for teachers, teachers-in-training, teacher educators, day care workers, administrators, and parents. Articles focus on child development and emphasize practical application. Regular departments include book reviews (child and adult); reviews of films, pamphlets, and software; research; and classroom idea-sparkers. Articles address timely concerns: of the five issues published yearly, one is a theme issue devoted to critical concerns. *Membership:* 15,000. *Dues:* $45/yr. *Publications: Childhood Education* (official journal); *ACEI Exchange* (newsletter); *Journal of Research in Childhood Education.*

Association for Computer Educators (ACE). See listing for International Association for Computer Information Systems.

Association for Continuing Higher Education (ACHE). 620 Union Dr., Rm. 143N, Indiana University, Purdue University at Indianapolis, Indianapolis, IN 46202. (317) 274-2637. Fax (317) 274-4016. Dr. Scott Evenbeck, Exec. V.P. An association of institutions and individuals having a commitment to providing opportunities in higher education for adults in traditional and nontraditional programs. *Membership:* 1,556 individuals representing 622 institutions. *Dues:* $50/yr. professional, $225/yr. institutional. *Publications: 5 Minutes with ACHE; The Journal of Continuing Higher Education; Proceedings.*

Association for Educational Communications and Technology (AECT). 1025 Vermont Ave. NW, Suite 820, Washington, DC 20005, (202) 347-7834. Fax (202) 347-7839. Stanley Zenor, Exec. Dir; Larry Kitchens, Pres. AECT is an international professional association concerned with the improvement of learning and instruction through media and technology. It serves as a central clearinghouse and communications center for its members, who include instructional technologists; media or library specialists; university professors and researchers; industrial/business training specialists; religious educators; government media personnel; school, school district, and state department of education media program administrators and specialists; and educational/training media producers. AECT members also work in the armed forces, in public libraries, in museums, and in other information agencies of many different kinds, including those related to the emerging fields of computer technology. The AECT annual convention features the nation's largest instructional media exposition, InfoCOMM International Exposition, held jointly with the International Communications Industries Association (ICIA). The next convention will be held January 5-9, 1993, in New Orleans, Louisiana. *Membership:* 5,000, plus 9,000 additional subscribers, 9 divisions, 15 national affiliates, 46 state affiliates, Puerto Rico, Guam, and more than 30 national committees and task forces. *Dues:* $65/yr. regular, $26/yr. student and retired. *Publications: TechTrends* (6/yr., free with membership, $30/yr. nonmembers); *Report to Members* (6/yr., newsletter); *Educational Technology Research and Development* (4/yr., $30/yr.

member, $20/yr. student and retired, $45/yr. nonmembers); various division publications; several books and videotapes.

Because of similarity of interests, the following organizations have chosen to affiliate with the Association for Educational Communications and Technology. (As many as possible have been polled for inclusion in *EMTY*.)

- Association for Multi-Image (AMI)
- Association for Special Education Technology (ASET)
- Community College Association for Instruction and Technology (CCAIT)
- Consortium of University Film Centers (CUFC)
- Federal Educational Technology Association (FETA)
- Health Science Communications Association (HeSCA)
- International Association for Learning Laboratories (IALL)
- International Visual Literacy Association (IVLA)
- Minorities in Media (MIM)
- National Association of Regional Media Centers (NARMC)
- National Instructional Television Fixed Service Association (NIA/ITFS)
- New England Educational Media Association
- Northwest College and University Council for the Management of Educational Technology
- Southeastern Regional Media Leadership Council (SRMLC)
- State University of New York Educational Communications Center

Two additional organizations are also related to the Association for Educational Communications and Technology:

- AECT Archives
- AECT ECT Foundation

Association for Educational Communications and Technologies (AECT) Divisions:

(AECT) Division of Educational Media Management (DEMM). 1025 Vermont Ave. NW, Suite 820, Washington, DC 20005. (202) 347-7834. Jacquelyn Hill, Pres. Seeks to develop an information exchange network and to share information about common problems, solutions, and program descriptions of educational media management. Develops programs that increase the effectiveness of media managers, initiates and implements a public relations program to educate the public and administrative bodies as to the use, value, and need for educational media management, and fosters programs that will help carry out media management responsibilities effectively. *Membership:* 1,024. *Dues:* One division membership included in the basic AECT membership; additional division memberships $10/yr. *Publication: Media Management Journal.*

(AECT) Division of Interactive Systems and Computers (DISC). 1025 Vermont Ave. NW, Suite 820, Washington, DC 20005. (202) 347-7834. Annette Lamb, Pres. Concerned with the generation, access, organization, storage, and delivery of all forms of information used in the processes of education and training. The Division promotes the networking of its members to facilitate sharing of expertise and interests. *Membership:* 512. *Dues:* One division membership included in the basic AECT membership; additional division memberships $10/yr. *Publication:* Newsletter.

(AECT) Division of Instructional Development (DID). 1025 Vermont Ave. NW, Suite 820, Washington, DC 20005. (202) 347-7834. Phillip Doughty, Pres. DID is composed of individuals from business, government, and academic settings concerned with the systematic design of instruction and the development of solutions to performance problems. Members' interests include the study, evaluation, and refinement of design processes; the creation of new models of instructional development; the invention and improvement of techniques for managing the development of instruction; the development and application of professional ID competencies; the promotion of academic programs for preparation of ID professionals; and the dissemination of research and development work in ID. *Membership:* 765. *Dues:* One division membership included in the basic AECT membership; additional division memberships $10/yr. *Publications: DID Newsletter;* occasional papers.

(AECT) Division of School Media Specialists (DSMS). 1025 Vermont Ave. NW, Suite 820, Washington, DC 20005. (202) 347-7834. Burton Brooks, Pres. DSMS promotes communication among school media personnel who share a common concern in the development, implementation, and evaluation of school media programs; and strives to increase learning and improve instruction in the school setting through the utilization of educational media and technology. *Membership:* 860. *Dues:* One division membership included in the basic AECT membership; additional division memberships $10/yr. *Publication:* Newsletter.

(AECT) Division of Telecommunications (DOT). 1025 Vermont Ave. NW, Suite 820, Washington, DC 20005. (202) 347-7834. Savan Wilson, Pres. Seeks to improve education through use of television and radio, video and audio recordings, and autotutorial devices and media. Aims to improve the design, production, evaluation, and use of telecommunications materials and equipment; to upgrade competencies of personnel engaged in the field; to investigate and report promising innovative practices and technological developments; to promote studies, experiments, and demonstrations; and to support research in telecommunications. Future plans call for working to establish a national entity representing instructional television. *Membership:* 695. *Dues:* One division membership included in the basic AECT membership; additional division memberships $10/yr. *Publication:* Newsletter.

(AECT) Industrial Training and Education Division (ITED). 1025 Vermont Ave. NW, Suite 820, Washington, DC 20005. (202) 347-7834. Joanne Willard, Pres. Seeks to promote the sensitive and sensible use of media and techniques to improve the quality of education and training; to provide a professional program that demonstrates the state of the art of educational technology as a part of the AECT convention; to improve communications to ensure the maximum use of educational techniques and media that can give demonstratable, objective evidence of effectiveness. *Membership:* 250. *Dues:* One division membership included in the basic AECT membership; additional division memberships $10/yr. *Publication:* Newsletter.

(AECT) International Division (INTL). 1025 Vermont Ave. NW, Suite 820, Washington, DC 20005. (202) 347-7834. Mary Lou Shippe, Pres. Seeks to improve international communications concerning existing methods of design; to pretest, use, produce, evaluate, and establish an approach through which these methods may be improved and adapted for maximum use and effectiveness; to develop a roster of qualified international leaders with experience and competence in the varied geographic and technical areas; and to encourage research in the application of communication processes to support present and future international social and economic development. *Membership:* 200. *Dues:* One division membership included in the basic AECT membership; additional division memberships $10/yr. *Publication:* Newsletter.

(AECT) Media Design and Production Division (MDPD). 1025 Vermont Ave. NW, Suite 820, Washington, DC 20005. (202) 347-7834. Karen Miller, Pres. Seeks to provide formal, organized procedures for promoting and facilitating interaction between commercial and noncommercial, nontheatrical filmmakers, and to provide a communications link for filmmakers with people of similar interests. Also seeks to provide a connecting link between creative and technical professionals of the audiovisual industry. Advances the informational film producer's profession by providing scholarships and apprenticeships to experimenters and students and by providing a forum for discussion of local, national, and universal issues. Recognizes and presents awards for outstanding films produced and for contributions to the state of the art. *Membership:* 300. *Dues:* One division membership included in the basic AECT membership; additional division memberships $10/yr. *Publication:* Newsletter.

(AECT) Research and Theory Division (RTD). 1025 Vermont Ave. NW, Suite 820, Washington, DC 20005. (202) 347-7834. Rhonda Robinson, Pres. Seeks to improve the design, execution, utilization, and evaluation of audiovisual communications research; to improve the qualifications and effectiveness of personnel engaged in communications research; to advise the educational practitioner as to use of the results of research; to improve research design, techniques, evaluation, and dissemination; and to promote both applied and theoretical research on the systematic use of all forms of media in the improvement of instruction. *Membership:* 337. *Dues:* One division membership included in the basic AECT membership; additional division memberships $10/yr. *Publication:* Newsletter.

Association for Educational Communications and Technology (AECT)
Affiliate Organizations:

(AECT) Community College Association for Instruction and Technology (CCAIT). New Mexico Military Institute, 101 W. College Blvd., Roswell, NM 88201. (505) 624-8381. Bruce McLaren, Pres. A national association of community and junior college educators interested in the discovery and dissemination of information about problems and processes of teaching, media, and technology in community and junior colleges. Facilitates member exchange of data, reports, proceedings, personnel, and other resources; sponsors AECT convention sessions and social activities. *Membership:* 200. *Dues:* $10.00. *Publications:* Regular newsletter; irregular topical papers.

(AECT) Federal Educational Technology Association (FETA). U.S. Office of Personnel Management, P.O. Box 7559 (1100TC), Washington, DC 20044-7559. Sue Middendorf, Pres. FETA is dedicated to the improvement of education and training through research, communication, and practice. It encourages and welcomes members from all government agencies—federal, state, and local; from business and industry; and from all educational institutions and organizations. FETA encourages interaction among members to improve the quality of education and training in any arena, but with specific emphasis on government-related applications.

(AECT) Health Science Communications Association (HeSCA). *See* separate listing.

(AECT) International Visual Literacy Association, Inc. (IVLA). Department of Media Educational Technology, East Texas State University, E.T. Station, Commerce, TX 75428. (214) 886-5496. Roberts Braden, Pres. Provides a multidisciplinary forum for the exploration of modes of visual communication and their application through the concept of visual literacy; promotes development of visual literacy, and serves as a bond between the diverse organizations and groups working in that field. *Dues:* $40, regular; $20, student. *Publications: Journal of Visual Literacy; Readings from Annual Conferences.*

(AECT) Minorities in Media (MIM). University of South Alabama, Instructional Media Center, Mobile, AL 36688. (205) 460-7029. Dr. Joaquin M. Holloway, Jr., Pres. Seeks to encourage the effective use of educational media in the teaching/learning process; provide leadership opportunities in advancing the use of technology as an integral part of the learning process; provide a vehicle through which minorities might influence the use of media in institutions; develop an information exchange network to share information common to minorities in media; study, evaluate, and refine the educational technology process as it relates to the education of minorities; and encourage and improve the production of materials for the education of minorities. *Membership:* 100. *Dues:* $10. *Publication:* Annual newsletter.

(AECT) National Association of Regional Media Centers (NARMC). Bucks County Intermediate Unit 22, 705 Shady Retreat Rd., Doylestown, PA 18901. (215) 348-2940. Shirley D. Crehan, Pres. Seeks to foster the exchange of ideas and information among educational communications specialists responsible for the administration of regional media centers through workshops, seminars, and national meetings. Studies the feasibility of developing joint programs that could increase the effectiveness and efficiency of regional media services. Disseminates information on successful practices and research studies conducted by regional media centers. *Membership:* 268 regional centers, 70 corporations. *Dues:* $45. *Publications: etin* (q. newsletter); *Annual Report.*

(AECT) National ITFS Association (NIA/ITFS). Academic Media Services, University of Colorado, Campus Box 379, Boulder, CO 80309-0379. (303) 492-7345. Fax (303) 492-7017. Dr. Daniel Niemeyer, Pres. Established in 1978, NIA/ITFS is a nonprofit, professional organization of Instructional Television Fixed Service (ITFS) licensees, applicants, and others interested in ITFS broadcasting. The goals of the Association are to gather and exchange information about ITFS, to gather data on utilization of ITFS, and to act as a conduit for those seeking ITFS information or assistance. The NIA/ITFS provides members with information on excess capacity leasing and license and application data, and represents ITFS interests for the FCC, technical consultants, and equipment manufacturers. *Publications:* Newsletter (q.); FCC regulation update.

(AECT) Northwest College and University Council for the Management of Educational Technology. Instructional Resources Center, Northrup Library, Linfield College, McMinnville, OR 97128. (503) 472-4121, ext. 264. Susan Davis DeHut, Pres. The first regional group representing institutions of higher education in Alberta, Alaska, British

Columbia, Idaho, Montana, Oregon, and Washington to receive affiliate status in AECT. Membership is restricted to media managers with campus-wide responsibilities for educational technical services in the membership region. Corresponding membership is available to those who work outside the membership region. An annual conference and business meeting is held the last weekend of October each year, rotating throughout the region. Current issues under consideration include managing emerging telecommunication technologies, copyright, accreditation, and certification. Organizational goals include identifying the unique status problems of media managers in higher education and improving the quality of the major publication. *Membership:* approx. 85. *Dues:* $35. *Publication: NW/MET Bulletin.*

Other AECT-Related Organizations:

(AECT) Archives. University of Maryland at College Park, The University Libraries, c/o Lauren Brown, Curator, Historical Mss. & Archivist, College Park, MD 20742. (301) 405-9059. A collection of media, manuscripts, and related materials representing important developments in visual and audiovisual education and in instructional/educational technology. The collection is housed as part of the National Public Broadcasting Archives. Maintained by the University of Maryland at College Park in cooperation with AECT. Open to researchers and scholars.

(AECT) Archives. University of Iowa, c/o Barry Bratton, N. 304 Lindquist Center, Iowa City, IA 52242. (319) 335-5566. A collection of historical media and audiovisual projection devices. Maintained by the University of Iowa in cooperation with AECT. Open only to researchers and scholars.

(AECT) ECT Foundation. 1025 Vermont Ave. NW, Suite 820, Washington, DC 20005. Robert E. de Kieffer, Chair. The ECT Foundation is a nonprofit organization whose purposes are charitable and educational in nature. Its operation is based on the conviction that improvement of instruction can be accomplished, in part, by the continued investigation and application of new systems for learning and by periodic assessment of current techniques for the communication of information. In addition to awarding scholarships, internships, and fellowships, the Foundation develops and conducts leadership training programs for emerging professional leaders.

Association for Experiential Education (AEE). CU Box 249, Boulder, CO 80309. (303) 492-1547. Fax (303) 492-7090. Daniel Garvey, Exec. Dir. The AEE believes that the learner and the teacher should use the most powerful and effective means to interact with each other and their environments, and to deal with the tasks at hand. Experience-based education emphasizes direct experience to increase the quality of learning. The AEE helps to advance, expand, conceptualize, and formalize this learning process. *Membership:* 1,600. *Dues:* $35-$50 individual, $125 institutional. *Publications: Jobs Clearinghouse; The Journal of Experiential Education;* books and directories.

Association for Library and Information Science Education. c/o Sally Nicholson, 4101 Lake Boone Trail, Suite 201, Raleigh, NC 27607-4916. Seeks to advance education for library and information science and produces annual *Library and Information Science Education Statistical Report.* Open to professional schools offering graduate programs in library and information science; personal memberships open to educators employed in such institutions; other memberships available to interested individuals. *Membership:* 650 individuals, 85 institutions. *Dues:*

institutional, $250 full; $150 associate; $75 international; personal, $40 full-time; $20 part-time, student, retired. *Publications: Journal of Education for Library and Information Science*; directory; *Library and Information Science Education Statistical Report.*

Association for the Development of Computer-Based Instructional Systems (ADCIS). International Headquarters, 1601 West Fifth Ave., Suite 111, Columbus, OH 43212. (614) 488-1863. Carol Norris, Contact Person. Lloyd Rieber, Pres. International association with a worldwide membership of professionals who are actively involved in the development and use of computer-based instructional technologies. Members work in business and industry; elementary and secondary schools; junior colleges, colleges, and universities; vocational and specialized schools; and the military and the government. An annual international conference, membership in special interest groups, and networking for members provides an international forum for intellectual leadership in the field, professional growth opportunities, and the integration of theory and practice. *Publications: ADCIS News; The Journal of Computer-Based Instruction (JCBI).*

Association of American Publishers (AAP). 220 E. 23rd St., New York, NY 10010. (212) 689-8920. Ambassador Nicholas A. Veliotes, Pres. A group of approximately 250 companies whose members produce the majority of printed materials sold to U.S. schools, colleges, libraries, and bookstores, as well as to homes. Range of member interests is reflected in textbooks; religious, scientific, and media books; instructional systems; software audio and videotapes; records; cassettes; slides; transparencies; and tests. Provides its members with information concerning trade conditions, markets, copyrights, manufacturing processes, taxes, duties, postage, freight, censorship movements, government programs, and other matters of importance. *Membership:* 250 companies. *Dues:* Vary. *Publication: AAP Monthly Report.*

Association of Audio-Visual Technicians (AAVT). 2378 S. Broadway, Denver, CO 80210. (303) 698-1820. Fax (303) 777-3261. Elsa C. Kaiser, Exec. Dir. Proposes to increase communication and to assist audiovisual services and production technicians in their work; holds seminars in conjunction with most of the major audiovisual shows. Also has a lending library of old service manuals for rent by AAVT members. *Membership:* 1,200. *Dues:* $35 individuals, $65 institutions. *Publication: Fast Forword.*

Association of Independent Video and Filmmakers and the Foundation for Independent Video and Film. 625 Broadway, 9th Floor, New York, NY 10012. (212) 473-3400. Fax (212) 677-8732. Martha Gever, Exec. Dir. The national trade association for independent video and filmmakers, representing their needs and goals to industry, government, and the public. Programs include domestic and foreign festival liaison for independents, screenings and seminars, insurance for members, group, and information and referral services. Recent activities include monitoring status of independent work on public television, advocacy for cable access, and lobbying for modifications in copyright law. *Dues:* $45 individual, $85 institutional, $60 libraries, $25 students. *Publication: The Independent Film and Video Monthly.*

Association of Systematics Collections. 730 11th St. NW, 2nd Floor, Washington, DC 20001. (202) 347-2850. K. Elaine Hoagland, Exec. Dir. Promotes the care, management, and improvement of biological collections, provides information on biological collections and biologists who offer taxonomic services, and publishes current information on government permit regulations regarding the scientific use of plants and animals. *Membership:* 80 institutions and scientific societies. *Dues:* After election to membership. *Publications: Biogeography of the Tropical Pacific; Crocodilian, Tuatara, and Turtle Species of the World; Collections of Frozen Tissues, Controlled Wildlife II, III; Sources of Federal Funding in the Biological Sciences, Guidelines to* *the Acquisition and Management of Biological Specimens*; *ASC Newsletter*; *A Guide to Museum Pest Control*; *Systematics: Relevance, Resources, Services, and Management* (a bibliography); *Foundations for a National Biological Survey*. *Newsletter subscription:* $17/yr. individual, $32/yr. libraries.

Association of Teacher Educators (ATE). 1900 Association Dr., Suite ATE, Reston, VA 22091. (703) 620-3110. Fax (703) 620-9530. Gloria Chernay, Exec. Dir. Annual conference, usually held in February, and annual summer workshops. *Membership:* 4,000. *Dues:* $60. *Publications: Action in Teacher Education*; *ATE Newsletter*; other miscellaneous publications.

Catholic Library Association (CLA). 461 W. Lancaster Ave., Haverford, PA 19041. (215) 649-5250. Anthony Prete, Exec. Dir. Seeks to improve libraries in general and religion-oriented libraries in particular and promotes discriminating taste in literature and other communication media. Encourages compilation, publication, and use of religious reference tools, seeks to attract persons into librarianship through scholarships, fosters research and developments in librarianship and communication, and encourages cooperation with associations interested in the field. Produces continuing education programs on videotape. *Membership:* 3,000. *Dues:* $45-$500. *Publications: CLA Handbook and Membership Directory* (annual); *Catholic Library World* (6/yr.); *Catholic Periodical and Literature Index* (6/yr.).

Center for Advanced Visual Studies. MIT Building W11, 40 Massachusetts Ave., Cambridge, MA 02139. (617) 253-4415. Otto Piene, Dir. Founded by Gyorgy Kepes in 1968, the Center offers a unique situation in which artists explore and realize artwork in collaboration with scientists and engineers. Has done significant work on lasers, holography, video, kinetics, environmental art, and sky art.

Center for Instructional Research and Curriculum Evaluation. 1310 S. 6th St., Champaign, IL 61820. (217) 333-3770. Robert E. Stake, Dir. A unit within the College of Education, University of Illinois, the Center is primarily active in conducting curriculum research in the United States, but has been of considerable interest to program evaluation specialists in foreign countries.

Central Educational Network (CEN). 1400 E. Touhy, Suite 260, Des Plaines, IL 60018-3305. (708) 390-8700. Fax (708) 390-9435. James A. Fellows, Pres. Manages interactive telecommunications network. Provides general audience and instructional television programming and ITV services. *Membership:* PTV stations and educational agencies.

Children's Film and Television Center of America (CFTCA). USC School of Cinema-Television, 850 W. 34th St., University Park, Los Angeles, CA 90089-2211. (213) 743-8632. Shanta Herzog, Exec. Dir. All CFTCA activities have been suspended.

Children's Television International, Inc. 8000 Forbes Pl., Suite 201, Springfield, VA 22151. (703) 321-8455. Ray Gladfelter, Pres.; Karla Ray, Dir. of Customer Services. An educational organization that develops, produces, and distributes a wide variety of color television programming and television-related materials as a resource to aid children's social, cultural, and intellectual development. Program areas cover language arts, science, social studies, and art for home, school, and college viewing. *Publications:* teacher's guides that accompany instructional TV series and catalogues.

CINE Information. 215 W. 90th St., New York, NY 10024. (212) 877-3999. Barbara Margolis, Exec. Dir. CINE Information is a nonprofit educational organization established to develop sound methods and tools for the more effective use of film by community groups and educational programmers. It produces and distributes materials about film and videotape use and produces films on topics of social and cultural importance. Newest releases include an Academy Award nominee for Best Documentary feature in "Adam Clayton Powell," which was also broadcast on PBS's "The American Experience" series, and American Film Festival winner, "Are We Winning, Mommy? America and the Cold War." "Mommy" was also featured at the Berlin, Toronto, Chicago, and Park City, Utah Film Festivals. *Publication: In Focus: A Guide to Using Films*, by Linda Blackaby, Dan Georgakas, and Barbara Margolis, a complete step-by-step handbook for film and videotape users with detailed discussions of how to use film and tape in educational, cultural, and fundraising activities.

Clearinghouse on Development Communication. 1815 N. Fort Myer Dr., 6th Floor, Arlington, VA 22209. (703) 527-5546. Fax (703) 527-4661. Michael Laflin, Dir. A center for materials and information on applications of communication technology to development problems. Operated by the Institute for International Research and funded by the Bureau for Science and Technology of the U.S. Agency for International Development. Visitors and written requests for information are welcome. *Dues:* Subscription, $10. *Publications: Development Communication Report* (q.); other special reports.

Close Up Foundation. 44 Canal Center Plaza, Alexandria, VA 22314. (703) 706-3726; (800) 765-3131. Fax (703) 706-0002. Stephen A. Janger, Pres.; Lynn Page Whittaker, Dir. of Publications. A nonprofit, nonpartisan civic education organization promoting informed citizen participation in public policy and community service. Programs reach more than a million participants a year. *Publications: Current Issues; The Bill of Rights: A User's Guide; Perspectives; International Relations; The American Economy;* documentary videotapes on domestic and foreign policy issues. Close Up brings 24,000 students and teachers a year to Washington, D.C. for week-long government studies programs, produces television programs on the C-SPAN cable network for secondary school and home audiences, and conducts the Citizen Bee for high school students and the Civic Achievement Award Program for middle school students.

Computer-Based Education Research Laboratory (CERL). University of Illinois, 252 Engineering Research Lab, 103 South Mathews Ave., Urbana, IL 61801. (217) 333-6210. Fax (217) 244-0793. Dr. Edwin L. Goldwasser, Acting Dir. CERL is a research laboratory dedicated to research on and development of systems for the delivery of cost-effective, interactive, computer-based education (CBE). CERL is best known for its PLATO and NovaNET systems used by colleges and universities, businesses and government installations, and by public schools (PLATO originated at the University of Illinois in 1960, NovaNET in 1986). Both of these are large-scale, mainframe-based systems with thousands of users; but CERL has also worked on stand-alone and local-area CBE delivery. NovaNET, the newest development, uses a custom-designed, low-cost mainframe and satellite communications for continent-wide availability. It is capable of simultaneously serving a mix of students, teachers, educational administrators, and courseware developers numbering several thousands. *Publications:* department and professional journals; publications list available on request.

The Computer Museum. 300 Congress St., Boston, MA 02210. (617) 426-2800. Fax (617) 426-2943. Dr. Oliver Strimpel, Exec. Dir. The world's only computer museum occupies 55,000 square feet in a renovated historic building on Boston's waterfront. The museum presents the past, present, and future of the information revolution, from mammoth vacuum-tube computers to state-of-the-art technology, through over 100 interactive exhibits, including a giant walk-through computer™, displays, films and animation, recreations of vintage computer installations, and the most extensive collection of computers and robots ever assembled. *Membership:* 2,000. *Dues:* $30 individual, $45 family. *Publications: The Computer Museum Annual* (an. journal); *The Computer Museum News* (q. newsletter); *Educational Group Tour Planner; Educational Activities Kit;* gift and educators' catalogs.

Consortium of College and University Media Centers. 121 Pearson Hall-MRC, Iowa State University, Ames, IA 50011. (515) 294-8022. Fax (515) 294-8089. Don Rieck, Exec. Dir. A professional group of higher education media personnel whose purpose is to improve education and training through the effective use of educational media. Assists educational and training users in business on making films, video, and educational media more accessible. Fosters cooperative planning among university media centers. Gathers and disseminates information on improved procedures and new developments in educational media and media center management. *Membership:* 350. *Dues:* $125/yr. constituents; $35 active; $125 sustaining (commercial); $15 students, $35 associates. *Publications: The Leader* (newsletter to members); *16mm Film Maintenance Manual.*

Copyright Clearance Center (CCC). 27 Congress St., Salem, MA 01970. (508) 744-3350. Fax (508) 741-2318. Eamon T. Fennessy, Pres. An organization through which corporations, academic and research libraries, information brokers, government agencies, and other users of copyrighted information may obtain authorizations and pay royalties for photocopying these materials in excess of exemptions contained in the U.S. Copyright Act of 1976. In addition to offering a Transactional Reporting Service, CCC also operates an Annual Authorization Service, which is an annual-license program serving photocopy permissions needs of large U.S. corporations. *Membership:* 2,500 users, approx. 8,000 foreign and domestic publishers, 1.5 million publications. *Publications: CCC Report* (q. newsletter, $10/yr., $12 foreign); *COPI: Catalog of Publisher Information* (4 issues/yr., $35 issue, $115/yr.).

Corporation for Public Broadcasting (CPB). 901 E. St. NW, Washington, DC 20004. (202) 879-9800. Donald E. Ledwig, Pres. and CEO. A private, nonprofit corporation authorized by the Public Broadcasting Act of 1967 to develop noncommercial television and radio services for the American people, while insulating public broadcasting from political pressure or influence. CPB supports station operations and funds radio and television programs for national distribution. CPB sets national policy that will most effectively make noncommercial radio and television and other telecommunications services available to all citizens. *Publications: CPB Report* (biweekly, 3 yrs. for $25); *Annual Report; CPB Public Broadcasting Directory* ($10 plus $2 postage and handling).

Council for Basic Education. 725 15th St. NW, Washington, DC 20036. (202) 347-4171. A. Graham Down, Exec. Dir. A vocal force advocating a broadly defined curriculum in the liberal arts for all students in elementary and secondary schools. *Membership:* 4,000. *Dues:* $40/yr. members; $25/yr. subscribers. *Publication: Basic Education; Perspective* (q., 2 yrs. for $75 members or $45 subscribers); various reports and books.

Council for Educational Development and Research (CEDaR). 1201 16th St. NW, Suite 305, Washington, DC 20036. (202) 223-1593. Dena G. Stoner, Exec. Dir. Members are educational research and development institutions. Aims to advance the level of programmatic, institutionally based educational research and development and to demonstrate the importance of research and development in improving education. Provides a forum for professional personnel in member institutions. Coordinates national dissemination program. Other activities include research, development, evaluation, dissemination, and technical assistance on educational issues. *Membership:* 14. *Publications: R&D Preview; Directory.*

Council for Exceptional Children (CEC). 1920 Association Dr., Reston, VA 22091. (703) 620-3660. Fax (703) 264-9494. Jeptha Greer, Exec. Dir. A membership organization providing information to teachers, administrators, and others concerned with the education of handicapped and gifted children. Maintains a library and database on literature on special education; prepares books, monographs, digests, films, filmstrips, cassettes, and journals; sponsors annual convention and conferences on special education; provides on-site and regional training on various topics and at varying levels; provides information and assistance to lawmakers on the education of the handicapped and gifted; coordinates Political Action Network on the rights of exceptional persons. *Membership:* 55,000. *Dues:* Professional, $60-80, depending on state of residence; student, $26-26.50, depending on state of residence. *Publications: Exceptional Children; Teaching Exceptional Children; Exceptional Child Educational Resources;* numerous other professional publications dealing with the education of handicapped and gifted children.

(CEC) Technology and Media Division (TAM). Council for Exceptional Children, 1920 Association Dr., Reston, VA 22091. (703) 620-3660. The Technology and Media Division (TAM) of the Council for Exceptional Children (CEC) encourages the development of new applications, technologies, and media for use as daily living tools by special populations. This information is disseminated through professional meetings, training programs, and publications. TAM members receive four issues annually of the *Journal of Special Education Technology* containing articles on specific technology programs and applications, and five issues of the TAM newsletter providing news of current research, developments, products, conferences, and special programs information. *Membership:* 1,500. *Dues:* $10 in addition to CEC membership.

Council of National Library and Information Associations. St. John's University, Library Room 322, Grand Central & Utopia Parkways, Jamaica, NY 11439. (718) 990-6735. D. Sherman Clarke, Chair. The council is a forum for discussion of many issues of concern to library and information associations. Current committees at work are the Joint Committee on Association Cooperation and the Ad Hoc Committee on Copyright Implementation. *Membership:* 21 associations. *Dues:* Inquire.

Council on International Non-theatrical Events (CINE). 1001 Connecticut Ave. NW, Suite 1016, Washington, DC 20036. (202) 785-1136. Fax (202) 785-4114. Richard Calkins, Exec. Dir. Coordinates the selection and placement of U.S. documentary, television, short subject, and didactic films in more than 200 overseas film festivals annually. A Golden Eagle Certificate is awarded to each professional film considered most suitable to represent the United States in international competition. A CINE Eagle Certificate is awarded to winning adult amateur, youth, and university student-made films. Prizes and certificates won at overseas festivals are presented by embassy representatives at an annual awards luncheon. Deadlines for receipt of entry forms are 1 February and 1 August. *Publications: CINE Yearbook; Annual International U.S. Film Festival Directory.*

Education Development Center, Inc. 55 Chapel St., Newton, MA 02160. (617) 969-7100. Janet Whitla, Pres. Seeks to improve education at all levels, in the United States and abroad, through curriculum development, institutional development, and services to the school and the community. Produces filmstrips and videocassettes, primarily in connection with curriculum development and teacher training. *Publications: Annual Report*; occasional papers.

EPIE Institute (Educational Products Information Exchange). 103 West Montauk Highway, Hampton Bays, NY 11946. (516) 728-9100. P. Kenneth Komoski, Exec. Dir. Involved primarily in assessing educational materials and providing product descriptions/ citations of virtually all educational software. All of EPIE's services, including its Curriculum Alignment Services for Educators, are available to schools and state agencies as well as individuals. *Publications: Parents Guide to Educational Software*; *The Educational Software Selector (T E.S.S.)*; *EPIE Report on Integrated Instructional Systems*; *EPIE Report on Instructional Management Systems*. EPIE's newsletter, *EPIEgram*, is published by Sterling Harbor Press, Box 28, Greenport, NY 11944.

ERIC (Educational Resources Information Center). U.S. Department of Education/OERI, 555 New Jersey Ave. NW, Washington, DC 20208-5720. (202) 219-2289. Fax (202) 219-1817. Robert Stonehill, Dir. ERIC is a nationwide information network that provides access to the English-language education literature. The ERIC system consists of 16 Clearinghouses, 5 adjunct Clearinghouses, and system support components that include the ERIC Processing and Reference Facility, ACCESS ERIC, and the ERIC Document Reproduction Service (EDRS). ERIC actively solicits papers, conference proceedings, literature reviews, and curriculum materials from researchers, practitioners, educational associations and institutions, and federal, state, and local agencies. These materials, along with articles from nearly 800 different journals, are indexed and abstracted for entry into the ERIC database. The ERIC database—the largest education database in the world—now contains over 700,000 records of documents and journal articles. Users can access the ERIC database online, on CD-ROM, or through print and microfiche indexes. ERIC microfiche collections, which contain the full text of most ERIC documents, are available for public use at nearly 900 locations worldwide. Reprints of ERIC documents, on microfiche or in paper copy, can also be ordered from EDRS. A list of the ERIC Clearinghouses, together with full addresses, telephone numbers, and brief scope notes describing the areas they cover, follows here. *Dues:* None. *Publications: Resources in Education*; *Current Index to Journals in Education*.

ERIC Clearinghouse on Adult, Career, and Vocational Education (CE). Ohio State University, Center on Education and Training for Employment, 1900 Kenny Rd., Columbus, OH 43210-1090. (614) 292-4353; (800) 848-4815. Fax (614) 292-1260. All levels and settings of adult and continuing, career, and vocational/technical education. Adult education, from basic literacy training through professional skill upgrading. Career education, including career awareness, career decision making, career development, career change, and experience-based education. Vocational and technical education, including new subprofessional fields, industrial arts, corrections education, employment and training programs, youth employment, work experience programs, education/business partnerships, entrepreneurship, adult retraining, vocational rehabilitation for the handicapped, and workplace literacy.

ERIC Clearinghouse on Counseling and Personnel Services (CG). University of Michigan, School of Education, Rm. 2108, 610 East University St., Ann Arbor, MI 48109-1259. (313) 764-9492. Fax (313) 747-2425. Preparation, practice, and supervision of counselors at all educational levels and in all settings; theoretical development of counseling and guidance; personnel procedures such as testing and interviewing and the analysis and dissemination of the resultant information; group work and case work; nature of pupil, student, and adult characteristics; personnel workers and their relation to career planning, family consultations, and student orientation activities.

ERIC Clearinghouse on Educational Management (EA). University of Oregon, 1787 Agate St., Eugene, OR 97403-5207. (503) 346-5043. Fax (503) 346-5890. The leadership, management, and structure of public and private educational organizations; practice and theory of administration; preservice and inservice preparation of administrators; tasks and processes of administration; methods and varieties of organization and organizational change; and the social context of educational organizations. Sites, buildings, and equipment for education; planning, financing, constructing, renovating, equipping, maintaining, operating, insuring, utilizing, and evaluating educational facilities.

ERIC Clearinghouse on Elementary and Early Childhood Education (PS). University of Illinois, College of Education, 805 W. Pennsylvania Ave., Urbana, IL 61801-4897. (217) 333-1386. Fax (217) 333-3767. The physical, cognitive, social, educational, and cultural development of children from birth through early adolescence; prenatal factors; parental behavior factors; learning theory research and practice related to the development of young children, including the preparation of teachers for this educational level; educational programs and community services for children; and theoretical and philosophical issues pertaining to children's development and education.

ERIC Clearinghouse on Handicapped and Gifted Children (EC). Council for Exceptional Children, 1920 Association Dr., Reston, VA 22091-1589. (703) 264-9474. Fax (703) 264-9494. All aspects of the education and development of the handicapped and gifted, including prevention, identification, assessment, intervention, and enrichment, in both special and integrated settings.

ERIC Clearinghouse on Higher Education (HE). George Washington University, One Dupont Cir. NW, Suite 630, Washington, DC 20036-1183. (202) 296-2597. Fax (202) 296-8379. Topics relating to college and university conditions, problems, programs, and students. Curricular and instructional programs and institutional research at the college or university level. Federal programs, professional education (medicine, law, etc.), professional continuing education, collegiate computer-assisted learning and management, graduate education, university extension programs, teaching-learning, legal issues and legislation, planning, governance, finance, evaluation, interinstitutional arrangements, management of institutions of higher education, and business or industry educational programs leading to a degree.

ERIC Clearinghouse on Information Resources (IR). Syracuse University, Huntington Hall, Rm. 030, Syracuse, NY 13244-2340. (315) 443-3640. Fax (315) 443-5448. Educational technology and library and information science at all levels. Instructional design, development, and evaluation are the emphases within educational technology, along with the media of educational communication—computers and microcomputers, telecommunications (cable, broadcast, satellite), audio and video recordings, film, and other audiovisual materials—as they pertain to teaching and learning. Within library and information science, the focus is on the operation and management of information services for education-related organizations. All aspects of information technology related to education are considered within the scope.

ERIC Clearinghouse for Junior Colleges (JC). University of California at Los Angeles (UCLA), Math-Sciences Bldg., Rm. 8118, 405 Hilgard Ave., Los Angeles, CA 90024-1564. (212) 825-3931. Fax (212) 206-8095. Development, administration, and evaluation of two-year public and private community and junior colleges, technical institutes, and two-year branch university campuses. Two-year college students, faculty, staff, curricula, programs, support services, libraries, and community services. Linkages between two-year colleges and business/industrial organizations. Articulation of two-year colleges with secondary and four-year postsecondary institutions.

ERIC Clearinghouse on Languages and Linguistics (FL). Center for Applied Linguistics, 1118 22nd St. NW, Washington, DC 20037-0037. (202) 429-9551. Fax (202) 659-5641. Languages and language sciences; theoretical and applied linguistics; all areas of foreign language, second language, and linguistics instruction, pedagogy, or methodology; psycholinguistics and the psychology of language learning; cultural and intercultural context of languages; application of linguistics in language teaching; bilingualism and bilingual education; sociolinguistics; study abroad and international exchanges; teacher training and qualifications specific to the teaching of foreign languages and second languages; commonly and uncommonly taught languages, including English as a second language; related curriculum developments and problems.

ERIC Clearinghouse on Reading and Communication Skills (CS). Indiana University, Smith Research Center, Suite 150, 2805 East 10th St., Bloomington, IN 47408-2698. (812) 855-5847; (812) 855-7901. Reading, English, and communication skills (verbal and nonverbal), preschool through college, and adults working with their children. Includes family literacy. Research and instructional development in reading, writing, speaking, and listening; identification, diagnosis, and remediation of reading problems; speech communication (including forensics); mass communication; interpersonal and small group interaction; interpretation; rhetorical and communication theory; and theater and drama. Preparation of instructional staff and related personnel in these areas. Includes all aspects of reading behavior, with emphasis on physiology, psychology, and sociology; instructional materials, curricula, tests/measurements, and methodology; and the role of libraries and other agencies in fostering and guiding reading. To obtain list of most recent publications, write to ERIC/RCS at preceding address.

ERIC Clearinghouse on Rural Education and Small Schools (RC). Appalachia Educational Laboratory, 1031 Quarrier St., P.O. Box 1348, Charleston, WV 25325-1348; (800) 624-9120. Fax (304) 347-0487. Economic, cultural, social, or other factors related to educational programs and practices for rural residents; American Indians/Alaska Natives, Mexican-Americans, and migrants; educational practices and programs in all small schools; outdoor education.

ERIC Clearinghouse for Science, Mathematics, and Environmental Education (SE). Ohio State University, 1200 Chambers Rd., Rm. 310, Columbus, OH 43212-1792. (614) 292-6717. Fax (614) 292-0263. Science, mathematics, environmental, and engineering education at all levels. Within these three broad subject areas, the following topics:

development of curriculum and instructional materials; teachers and teacher education; learning theory/outcomes (including the impact of parameters such as interest level, intelligence, values, and concept development upon learning in these fields); educational programs; research and evaluative studies; media applications; computer applications.

ERIC Clearinghouse for Social Studies/Social Science Education (ERIC/ ChESS). Indiana University, Social Studies Development Center, Suite 120, 2805 East Tenth St., Bloomington, IN 47408-2698. (812) 855-3838, (812) 855-7901. All levels of social studies/social science education; contents and contributions of the social science disciplines (anthropology, economics, geography, civics, sociology, social psychology, political science) and selected humanities disciplines (history, art, music); education as a social science; comparative education (K-12); content and curriculum materials on social topics such as law-related education, ethnic studies, bias and discrimination, aging, adoption, women's equity, and sex education.

ERIC Clearinghouse on Teacher Education (SP). American Association of Colleges for Teacher Education, One Dupont Cir. NW, Suite 610, Washington, DC 20036-1186. (202) 293-2450, (202) 457-8095. School personnel at all levels; teacher selection and training, preservice and inservice preparation, and retirement; the theory, philosophy, and practice of teaching; curricula and general education not specifically covered by other clearinghouses; all aspects of physical, health, recreation, and dance education.

ERIC Clearinghouse on Tests, Measurement, and Evaluation (TM). American Institutes for Research (AIR), Washington Research Center, 3333 K St. NW, Washington, DC 20007-3541. (202) 342-5060. Fax (202) 342-5033. Tests and other measurement devices; methodology of measurement and evaluation; application of tests, measurement, or evaluation in educational projects or programs; research design and methodology in the area of testing and measurement/evaluation; learning theory in general.

ERIC Clearinghouse on Urban Education (UD). Teachers College, Columbia University, Institute for Urban and Minority Education, Main Hall, Rm. 303, Box 40, 525 W. 120th St., New York, NY 10027-9998. (212) 678-3433. Fax (212) 678-4048. Programs and practices in public, parochial, and private schools in urban areas and the education of particular children and youth of the various racial and ethnic groups in various settings—local, national, and international; the theory and practice of educational equity; urban and minority experiences; and urban and minority social institutions and services.

ACCESS ERIC. Aspen Systems Corp., 1600 Research Blvd., Rockville, MD 20850-3166. 1-800-USE-ERIC [873-3742]. Fax (301) 251-5212. Beverly Swanson, ERIC Project Dir. Toll-free service provides access to the information and services available through the ERIC system. Staff will answer questions as well as refer callers to education sources. ACCESS ERIC also produces several publications and reference and referral databases that provide information both about the ERIC system and current education-related issues and research. *Publications: A Pocket Guide to ERIC; All About ERIC; The ERIC Review;* the Conclusion Brochure series; *Catalog of ERIC Clearinghouse Publications; ERIC Calendar of Education-Related Conferences; ERIC User's Interchange; Directory of ERIC Information Service Centers. Databases:* ERIC Digests Online (EDO); Education-Related Information Centers; ERIC Information Service Providers; ERIC Calendar of Education-Related Conferences. (The databases are available through GTE Education Services on a subscription basis.)

Adjunct ERIC Clearinghouse for Art Education (ADJ/AR). Indiana University, Social Studies Development Center, 2805 East 10th St., Suite 120, Bloomington, IN 48408-2373. (812) 855-3838. Fax (812) 855-7901. Gilbert Clark, Dir.

Adjunct ERIC Clearinghouse for United States-Japan Studies (ADJ/JS). Indiana University, Social Studies Development Center, 2805 East 10th St., Suite 120, Bloomington, IN 48408-2373. (812) 855-3838. Fax (812) 855-7901. C. Frederick Risinger, Dir.

Adjunct ERIC Clearinghouse on Chapter 1 (Compensatory Education) (ADJ/ Chapter 1). Chapter 1 Technical Assistance Center, PRC Inc., 2601 Fortune Cir. E., One Park Fletcher Bldg., Suite 300-A, Indianapolis, IN 46241. (317) 244-8160; (800) 456-2380. Fax (317) 244-7386. Mary Quilling, Dir.

Adjunct ERIC Clearinghouse on Consumer Education (ADJ/CN). National Institute for Consumer Education, 207 Rackham Bldg., West Circle Dr., Eastern Michigan University, Ypsilanti, MI 48197. (313) 487-2292. Fax (313) 487-7153. Rosella Bannister, Dir.

Adjunct ERIC Clearinghouse on Literacy Education for Limited-English-Proficient Adults (ADJ/LE). Center for Applied Linguistics, 1118 22nd St. NW, Washington, DC 20037. (202) 429-9292. Fax (202) 659-5641. JoAnn Crandall, Dir.

ERIC Document Reproduction Service (EDRS). 7420 Fullerton Rd., Suite 110, Springfield, VA 22153-2852. 1-800-443-ERIC [3742]. Fax (703) 440-1408. Operates the document delivery arm of the ERIC system. Furnishes microfiche and/or paper copies of most ERIC documents. Address purchase orders to the preceding address. Fax order and delivery service available.

ERIC Processing and Reference Facility. 1301 Piccard Dr., Suite 300, Rockille, MD 20850-4305. (301) 258-5500. Fax (301) 948-3695. Ted Brandhorst, Dir. A centralized information processing facility serving all components of the ERIC network under policy direction of Central ERIC. Services provided include: acquisitions, editing, receiving and dispatch, document control and analysis, lexicography, computer processing, file maintenance, database management, and others. Receives and edits abstracts from 16 ERIC Clearinghouses for publication in *Resources in Education* (RIE), updates and maintains the *Thesaurus of ERIC Descriptors*. *Publications: Resources in Education*; *Source Directory*; *Report Number Index*; *Clearinghouse Number/ED Number Cross Reference Listing*; *Title Index*; *ERIC Processing Manual*; numerous other listings and indexes.

Far West Laboratory for Educational Research and Development (FWL). 1855 Folsom St., San Francisco, CA 94103. (415) 565-3000. Dr. Dean Nafziger, Exec. Dir. Far West Laboratory for Educational Research and Development serves the four-state region of Arizona, California, Nevada, and Utah, working with educators at all levels to plan and carry out school improvements. The mission of FWL is to challenge and enable educational organizations and their communities to create and sustain improved learning and development opportunities for their children, youth, and adults. To accomplish its mission, FWL directs resources toward: advancing knowledge; developing products and programs for teachers and learners; providing assistance to educational agencies; communicating with outside audiences to remain informed and to inform others about the results of research, development, and exemplary practice; and creating an environment where diverse educational and societal issues can be addressed and resolved. Far West Laboratory maintains a reference library with a complete ERIC microfiche collection and conducts information searches. *Publications:* books, newsletters; handbooks, guides; research syntheses; reports; training materials. See also Council for Educational Development and Research (CEDaR).

Federal Communications Commission (FCC). 1919 M St. NW, Washington, DC 20554. (202) 632-7000. Patti Grace Smith, Chief, Consumer Assistance & Small Business Div. An agency that regulates radio, television, telephone, and telegraph operations within the United States. Allocates frequencies and channels for different types of communications activities, issues amateur and commercial operators' licenses, and regulates rates of interstate communication services of many different kinds. *Publications:* bulletins pertaining to educational broadcasting and general information about FCC-regulated services.

Film Advisory Board (FAB). 1727-1/2 Sycamore, Hollywood, CA 90028. (213) 874-3644. Elayne Blythe, Pres. Previews and evaluates films and film-type presentations in all formats, makes recommendations for improved family entertainment fare, and presents awards of excellence to outstanding motion pictures, television programs, and videos, and for innovations in these industries. Technical awards are also presented, as are awards for outstanding contributions to the entertainment industry and for the most promising newcomers. Awards of excellence are presented for videocassettes; the FAB Winner Seal is featured worldwide on many of the family and child videocassettes for Prism, RCA Columbia, Rhino, and others. Supplies film list to many national organizations, encouraging them to support FAB award-winning products. *Membership:* 450. *Dues:* $40/yr. *Publication:* monthly film list distributed to studios, libraries, churches, public relations firms, youth groups, PTAs, clubs, and colleges. Now rating home videos with Film Advisory Board (FAB) rating system.

Film Arts Foundation (FAF). 346 9th St., 2d Floor, San Francisco, CA 94103. (415) 552-8760. Gail Silva, Dir. Service organization designed to support and promote independent film and video production. Services include low-cost 16mm and Super-8 editing facility, skills file, festivals file, resource library, group legal plan, seminars, workshops, annual film and video festival, grants program, monthly publication, work-in-progress screenings, proposal and distribution consultation, nonprofit sponsorship of selected film and video projects, and advocacy for independent film and video. *Membership:* 2,000 plus. *Dues:* $35. *Publication: Release Print.*

Film/Video Arts, Inc. (F/VA). 817 Broadway, New York, NY 10003. (212) 673-9361. Fax (212) 475-3467. Film/Video Arts is a nonprofit media arts center dedicated to the advancement of emerging and established media artists of diverse backgrounds. Provides support services that include low-cost production equipment and facilities, education and training, exhibition, and grant and employment opportunities. Offers scholarship assistance to women, African-Americans, Latinos, Asians, and Native Americans. *Membership fee*: $40/individual, $60/nonprofit organizations (Oct. 1-Sept. 30).

Freedom of Information Center (FOI). 20 Walter William Hall, University of Missouri, Columbia, MO 65211. (314) 882-4856. Kathleen Edwards, Center Mgr. Collects and indexes material on actions by government, media, and society affecting the flow of information at international, national, state, and local levels. The center answers questions on the federal FOI Act, censorship issues, access to government at all levels, privacy, ethics, bar-press guidelines, and First Amendment issues. *Publications:* Back issues of FOI publications available for purchase.

Government Printing Office (US GPO). N. Capitol and H Sts. NW, Washington, DC 20401. (202) 512-2395. Fax (202) 512-2250 (for publications and order information). The GPO provides printing and binding services to Congress and the agencies of the federal government. Distributes and sells government publications through its Superintendent of Documents' sales and depository library programs.

Great Plains National ITV Library (GPN). P.O. Box 80669, Lincoln, NE 68501. (402) 472-2007; (800) 228-4630. Fax (402) 472-1785. Lee Rockwell, Dir. Distributor of instructional television courses and videos produced by organizations across the country. Offers more than 100 videotape (videocassette) courses and related teacher utilization materials. Available for purchase or, in some instances, lease. Also distributes instructional videodiscs. *Publications:* quarterly newsletter; annual catalog; occasional flyers and brochures.

Health Science Communications Association (HeSCA). 6105 Lindell Blvd., St. Louis, MO 63112. (314) 725-4722. Lionelle Elsesser, Exec. Dir. Draws together people with a wide variety of knowledge, professions, and experience in work toward the common goal of improved instructional design in all areas of the health sciences communications. Recognizes excellence in biocommunications through its media festivals and awards programs. *Membership:* 500. *Dues:* $100 individual; $145 institutional (1st yr.); $1,000 sustaining; $35 students (without journal); $40 retired members. For additional categories, contact association office. *Publications: Patient Education Sourcebook; Feedback* (newsletter); *Journal of Biocommunications*; directory of accredited institutions with programs in biomedical communications.

*Hollywood Film Archive. 8344 Melrose Ave., Hollywood, CA 90069. (213) 933-3345. D. Richard Baer, Dir. Archival organization for information about feature films produced worldwide, from the early silents to the present. Offers comprehensive movie reference works for sale, including *Variety Film Reviews* (1907-1989), as well as copyright records. *Publications:* reference books.

HOPE Reports. 1600 Lyell Ave., Rochester, NY 14606-2396. (716) 458-4250. Thomas W. Hope, Pres. and Chair. Provides reports for the presentation audiovisual/video communication field, covering statistical and financial status, sales, salaries, trends, and predictions. Also provides calendar scheduling service of national/international events. Makes private surveys and has consulting service. *Publications: Contract Production for the '90s; Video Post-Production; Media Market Trends V; LCD Panels and Projectors; Overhead Projection System; Slides and Computer Graphics; Educational Media Trends; Understanding Electronic Photography; Producer & Video Post Wages & Salaries.*

Institute for Development of Educational Activities, Inc. (IDEA). 259 Regency Ridge, Dayton, OH 45459. (513) 434-6969. Fax (513) 434-5203. Action-oriented research and development organization, originating from the Charles F. Kettering Foundation, established to assist the educational community in bridging the gap that separates research and innovation from actual practice in the schools. Goal is to design and test new responses to improve education and to create arrangements that support local application. Main activities include: developing new and improved processes, systems, and materials; training local facilitators to use the change processes; providing information and services about improved methods and materials. Sponsors an annual fellowship program for administrators and conducts seminars for teachers.

*Institute for Research on Teaching. College of Education, MSU, East Lansing, MI 48824. (517) 353-6413. Penelope Peterson and Jere Brophy, Co-Dirs. Funded primarily by the U.S. Department of Education and Michigan State University. Conducts research on the continuing problems of practice encountered by teaching professionals, the teaching of subject matter disciplines in elementary schools (through the Center for the Learning and Teaching of Elementary Subjects), and publishes numerous materials detailing this research. *Publications:* Research series; occasional papers; newsletter; Elementary Subjects Center research series; annual catalog.

Institute for the Future (IFTF). 2740 Sand Hill Rd., Menlo Park, CA 94025-7020. (415) 854-6322. Fax (415) 854-7850. J. Ian Morrison, Pres. Works with organizations to plan their long-term futures. Helps them to evaluate the external environment and take advantage of the opportunities offered by new technologies. Founded in 1968, IFTF has emerged as a leader in action-oriented research for business, industry, and governments, having worked with more than 300 organizations. Typical projects include environmental scanning, strategic planning assistance, policy analyses, and market outlooks and evaluations for new products and next-generation technologies. The success of the organization is based on several unique strengths, including a pragmatic futures orientation, studies of emerging technologies, networking of ideas and people, and use of scenarios to identify and analyze issues and options. *Publications:* list available from IFTF free of charge.

Institute of Culture and Communication. East-West Center, 1777 East-West Rd., Honolulu, HI 96848. (808) 944-7666. Larry E. Smith, Interim Dir. A program of the East-West Center, which was established by the U.S. Congress "to promote better relations and understanding among the nations of Asia, the Pacific, and the United States through cooperative study, training and research." The Institute is organized around four programs: Multiculturalism; Core Values; Cultural Change; and Culture and Development.

*Institute of International Education. 809 United Nations Plaza, New York, NY 10017. (212) 883-8200. Richard Krasno, Pres. A private, nonprofit organization administering public and private grants to enable U.S. students to study abroad and foreign students to study at universities in this country. *Membership:* 650 U.S. universities. *Publications: Academic Year Abroad*; *Vacation Study Abroad*; *Open Doors: Report on International Educational Exchange*; *English Language and Orientation Programs in the United States*; numerous publications and directories for foreign nationals interested in study in the United States and for U.S. nationals interested in study abroad.

International Association for Computer Information Systems (formerly Association for Computer Educators (ACE)). Department of Accounting, University of Wisconsin-Eau Claire, Eau Claire, WI 54702. (715) 836-2952. Dr. Susan Haugen, Treas.; Dr. Thomas Seymour, Pres. Membership for those who teach or have an interest in computers and information systems. *Membership:* 1,000-plus libraries. *Dues:* $35/yr. *Publication: The Journal of Computer Information Systems.*

International Association of Business Communicators (IABC). One Hallidie Plaza, Suite 600, San Francisco, CA 94102. (415) 433-3400. Fax (415) 362-8762. Norman G. Leaper, Pres. IABC is the worldwide association for the communication and public relations profession. It is founded on the principle that the better an organization communicates with all its audiences, the more successful and effective it will be in meeting its objectives. IABC is dedicated to fostering communication excellence, contributing more effectively to organizations' goals worldwide, and being a model of communication effectiveness. *Membership:* 11,000 plus. *Dues:* $180 in addition to local and regional dues. *Publication: Communication World.*

International Association of Magnetic and Optical Media Manufacturers and Related Industries (formerly International Tape/Disc Association (ITA)). 505 Eighth Avenue, New York, NY 10018. (212) 643-0620. Henry Brief, Exec. V.P. Primary goals include the collection and dissemination of research and information; operation of forums and seminars to encourage interaction and understanding of issues and trends; fostering the development of technical standardization relating to marketing and maintenance of product quality; and identification of, monitoring, and response to public policies that impact the magnetic and optical media and related industries. *Membership:* Over 450 companies worldwide. *Dues:* Based upon annual gross dollar volume in the audio/video/data area. *Publications: ITA Membership Newsletter; Seminar Proceedings; ITA Source Directory.*

International Association of School Librarianship (IASL). Box 1486, Kalamazoo, MI 49005. (616) 343-5728. Jean E. Lowrie, Exec. Secy. Seeks to encourage development of school libraries and library programs throughout the world, to promote professional preparation of school librarians and continuing education programs, to achieve collaboration among school libraries of the world, and to facilitate loans and exchanges in the field. *Membership:* 900 plus. *Dues:* $20 personal and institution; based on membership for associations. *Publications: IASL Newsletter; Annual Proceedings; Persons to Contact; Indicators of Quality for School Library Media Programs;* occasional papers.

International Center of Photography (ICP). 1130 Fifth Ave., New York, NY 10128. (212) 860-1777. Fax (212) 360-6490, and ICP Midtown, 1133 Avenue of the Americas, New York, NY 10036. (212) 768-4680. Fax (212) 768-4688. Cornell Capa, Dir. A comprehensive photographic institution whose exhibitions, publications, collections, and educational programs embrace all aspects of photography from aesthetics to technique; from the eighteenth century to the present; from master photographers to newly emerging talents; from photojournalism to the avant garde. Changing exhibitions, lectures, seminars, workshops, museum shops, and screening rooms make ICP a complete photographic resource. *Membership:* 7,000. *Dues:* $40 individual membership, $50 double membership, $100 supporting, $250 Photography Circle, $500 Silver Card, $1,000 Gold Card; corporate memberships available. *Publications: Library of Photography; Encyclopedia of Photography—Master Photographs from PFA Collection; Man Ray in Fashion.*

International Communication Association. Box 9589, Austin, TX 78766. (512) 454-8299. Fax (512) 454-4221. Robert L. Cox, Exec. Dir. Established to study human communication and to seek better understanding of the process of communication. Engages in systematic studies of communication theories, processes, and skills, and disseminates information. *Membership:* 2,200. *Dues:* $40-$1,450. *Publications: Human Communication Research* (9); *A Guide to Publishing in Scholarly Communication Journals; Communication Theory* (q.); *Journal of Communication* (q.); *Communication Yearbook.*

*International Communications Industries Association (ICIA). 3150 Spring St., Fairfax, VA 22031. (703) 273-7200. Kenton Pattie, Exec. V.P. An international association of media hardware and software producers and manufacturers, dealers, representatives, and others involved with educational, communications, and information activities and services and products. Maintains close liaison with Congress in matters pertaining to small business media legislation. Annual convention and exhibit, "INFOCOMM International"™ Exposition each winter brings together over 10,000 manufacturers, dealers, producers, and equipment users in a show with over 90,000 square feet of communications products. *Publications: Equipment Directory of Audio-Visual, Computer and Video Products; Communications Industries Report;* various market research studies in the video industry.

International Copyright Information Center (INCINC). c/o Association of American Publishers, 1718 Connecticut Ave. NW, 7th Floor, Washington, DC 20009-1148. (202) 232-3335. Fax (202) 745-0694. Carol A. Risher, Dir. Assists developing nations in their efforts to translate and/or reprint copyrighted works published in the United States.

International Film and TV Festival of New York. Admin. offices: 780 King St., Chappaqua, NY 10514. (914) 238-4481. Gerald M. Goldberg, Pres. An annual, competitive festival for industrial and educational film and video productions, filmstrips and slide programs, multi-image and multi-media presentations, and television programs. Entry fees begin at $100. First entry deadline is August 1.

*International Graphic Arts Education Association (IGAEA). 4615 Forbes Ave., Pittsburgh, PA 15213. (412) 682-5170. Virgil Pufahl, Pres. The president's address is Department of Communication, University of Wisconsin, Platteville, WI 53818. An organization of professionals in graphic arts education and industry, dedicated to promoting effective research and disseminating information concerning graphic arts, graphic communications, and related fields of printing. *Dues:* $15 regular; North America, add $2.00. *Publications: Visual Communications Journal*; *Research and Resource Reports*.

International Information Management Congress (IMC). 345 Woodcliff Dr., Fairport, NY 14450. (716) 383-8330. George D. Hoffman, Exec. Dir. An educational association supporting education in the information management field, exchange of information, and publications. Organizes yearly conferences and exhibits in different parts of the world. *Membership:* 30 associations, 70 sustaining company members. *Dues:* $120 affiliates; $200 associations; varies for sustaining members. *Publication: IMC Journal* (bi-monthly).

International Museum of Photography at George Eastman House. 900 East Ave, Rochester, NY 14607. (716) 271-3361. Fax (716) 271-3970. James L. Enyeart, Dir. World-renowned museum of photographic and cinematographic history established to preserve, collect, and exhibit photographic technology and film materials and to understand and appreciate photographic art and imaging science. Services include archives, traveling exhibitions, library regional center for the conservation of photographic materials, and photographic print service. Educational programs, films, symposia, and internship stipends offered. *Dues:* $35 libraries; $45 families; $35 individual; $25 students or senior citizens; $75 Contributor; $125 Sustainer; $250 Patron; $500 Benefactor. *Publications: IMAGE*; *Microfiche Index to Collections*; Newsletter.

International Society for Technology in Education (ISTE) (formerly International Council for Computers in Education (ICCE)). University of Oregon, 1787 Agate St., Eugene, OR 97403-9905. (503) 346-4414. Fax (503) 346-5890. David Moursund, CEO. *Membership:* 13,000. *Dues:* $36 U.S., $43 outside U.S. *Publications:* Guides to the instructional use of computers at pre-college level and in teacher training. Materials available include 12 different periodicals, about 50 books, and a range of independent study courses that carry graduate-level credit.

*International Telecommunications Satellite Organization (INTELSAT). 3400 International Dr. NW, Washington, DC 20008. (202) 944-6800. Public Relations (202) 944-7500. Dean Burch, Dir. Gen. Dedicated to the design, development, construction, establishment, operation, and maintenance of the global, international telecommunications satellite system that currently provides two-thirds of the world's international overseas telecommunications links and virtually all live international television services. *Membership:* 119 countries.

International Teleconferencing Association (ITCA). 1150 Connecticut Ave. NW, Suite 1050, Washington, DC 20036. (202) 833-2549; (202) 833-1308. Jodi S. Noon, Managing Dir. Seeks to provide a clearinghouse for the exchange of information between users, researchers, and providers in the field of teleconferencing. *Membership:* 1,200 plus. *Dues:* $500 organizational; $100 individual; $250 small business; $1,000 sustaining; $2,000 Gold Sustaining; $30 Student. *Publications: ITCA Insider Newsletter* (mo.); *Videoconferencing Room Directory.*

*International Television Association (ITVA). 6311 N. O'Connor Rd., Suite 230, LB 51, Irving, TX 75039. (214) 869-1112. Fred M. Wehrli, Exec. Dir. ITVA is the only organization dedicated to serving the needs of the professional video communicator in nonbroadcast settings. It has more than 100 chapters in North America and there are 3,000 international affiliate members in 14 countries around the world. *Membership:* 9,000. *Dues:* $125/yr. individual. *Publication: International Television News* (ITN).

Lawrence Hall of Science. University of California, Berkeley, CA 94720. (510) 642-3167. Dr. Marian Diamond, Dir. A center for research and public education. Its Math Education Project (Linda Lipner, Dir.) introduces visitors and teachers to computers through classes, workshops, exhibits, and the publication of software packages. *Publications: Teaching Basic Bit by Bit* (book only); *Creative Play*; *What's in Your Lunch?*; *Micros for Micros: Estimation, Numbers, Words, Music.*

Library of Congress. James Madison Bldg., 101 Independence Ave. SE, Washington, DC 20540. As the research arm of Congress and the national library, the Library of Congress provides materials on interlibrary loan and prepares traveling exhibits of photographs. Cataloging data are available in card, book, and machine-readable formats. The American Folklife Center provides for the preservation and dissemination of folklife through research, performances, exhibits, publications, and recordings. The Copyright Office catalogs copyright entries. Many other divisions are of interest to media specialists. *Publications:* Listed in *Library of Congress Publications in Print.*

*Lister Hill National Center for Biomedical Communications of the National Library of Medicine. Bldg. 38A, 8600 Rockville Pike, Bethesda, MD 20894. (301) 496-4441. Daniel R. Masys, M.D., Dir. Conducts research and development programs in three major categories: computer and information science as applied to the problems of medical libraries, of biomedical research, and of health care delivery; biomedical image engineering, including image acquisition, processing, storage retrieval, and communications; and use of new technologies for health professions education. It carries on research in the use of computer-assisted videodisc technology and has a Learning Center for Interactive Technology, which demonstrates new applications for health sciences education.

Magazine Publishers of America (MPA). 575 Lexington Ave., Suite 540, New York, NY 10022. (212) 752-0055. Fax (212) 888-4217. Donald D. Kummerfeld, Pres. MPA is the trade association of the consumer magazine industry. Promotes the greater and more effective use of magazine advertising, with ad campaigns in the trade press and in MPA member magazines, presentations to advertisers and their ad agencies, and magazine days in cities around the United States. Runs educational seminars, conducts surveys of its members on a variety of topics, represents the magazine industry in Washington, D.C., maintains an extensive library on magazine publishing, and carries on other activities. *Membership:* 230 publishers representing over 1,200 magazines. *Publications: Newsletter of Research; Newsletter of International Publishing*; Magazine.

Medical Library Association (MLA). 6 N. Michigan Ave., Suite 300, Chicago, IL 60602. (312) 419-9094. Richard A. Lyders, Pres.; Raymond A. Palmer, Exec. Dir. A group of professionals in the health sciences library field dedicated to fostering medical and allied scientific libraries, promoting educational and professional growth of health sciences librarians, and exchanging medical literature among members. *Membership:* 5,000. *Dues:* $105 individual, $315 sustaining. *Publications: MLA News; Bulletin of the Medical Library Association*; monographs.

Minnesota Educational Computing Corporation (MECC). 6160 Summit Dr. North, Minneapolis, MN 55430-4003. (612) 481-3500. Dale LaFrenz, Pres. Since its inception in 1973, MECC has remained committed to serving education by listening and responding to the diverse and changing needs of students and educators. MECC promotes effective learning by developing high-quality, curriculum-based software in all major subject areas, and by making it affordable through a variety of purchase plans. Approximately one-third of the nation's school districts have joined MECC through the membership program, permitting them to duplicate MECC software products on site. MECC products are also available through authorized dealers nationwide or can be ordered directly from the MECC catalog. In addition to software products, MECC offers instructional management, emerging technology products, and an annual international conference. MECC Center for the Study of Educational Technology conducts a variety of studies on the impact of technology on education. MECC respects the challenges faced by modern educators and pledges to remain on the cutting edge of technology.

Museum Computer Network, Inc. (MCN). 5001 Baum Blvd., Pittsburgh, PA 15213-1851. (412) 681-1818. Fax (412) 681-5758. Lynn W. Cox, Exec. Dir. As a not-for-profit professional association, membership in MCN means access to professionals committed to using computer technology to achieve the cultural aims of museums. Members include novices and experts, museum professionals, vendors and consultants, working in application areas from collections management to administrative computing. Activities include an annual conference, educational workshops, advisory services, special projects, and publication of a quarterly newsletter. *Membership Dues*: Sponsor $250; vendor $150; institution $100; individual $40. *Publication: Spectra* (newsletter). Subscription to *Spectra* is available to libraries only for $30.

Museum of Holography. 11 Mercer St., New York, NY 10013. (212) 925-0581. Fax (212) 334-8039. Martha Tomko, Dir. Housed in a landmark cast-iron building, the museum boasts the world's largest collection of holograms, or three-dimensional images. Through its extensive exhibition and education programs, the museum shows the work of artists working in the medium and explains how holograms are made, how they work, and how they have become useful tools in art, science, and technology. The museum also maintains a library, a collection of slides and photographs, and an artist-in-residence program. *Publication: Holosphere.*

Museum of Modern Art, Circulating Film and Video Library. 11 W. 53rd St., New York, NY 10019. (212) 708-9530. Fax (212) 708-9531. William Sloan, Libr. Sponsors film study programs and provides film rentals and sales. *Publication: Circulating Film and Video Catalog.*

Museum of Television and Radio (formerly The Museum of Broadcasting, MB). 25 W. 52nd St., New York, NY 10019. Office (212) 621-6600; Information Tape (212) 621-6800. Fax (212) 621-6700. William S. Paley, Founder; Dr. Robert M. Batscha, Pres. A nonprofit institution with three equally important missions: to collect and preserve radio and television programs; to make these programs available to the public; and to explore and interpret radio and television's heritage through public exhibitions of the collection. The Museum houses a collection of 40,000 radio and television programs, including 10,000 commercials, which reflects more than 70 years of broadcasting history. The fully computerized catalog is used for selecting programs for individual listening and viewing at easy-to-use consoles. Because each program in the Museum's collection is extensively documented, the catalog itself serves as a significant research tool. The Museum also presents major exhibitions and seminars that highlight various aspects of radio and television. Exhibitions focus on topics of social, historical, popular, or artistic interest; seminars feature in-person discussions with writers, producers, directors, actors, and others who have created landmark programming. The Museum has a variety of educational programs for groups of all ages and interests, as well as a visiting scholars program. The Museum is supported by daily contributions, membership fees, and grants by individuals, corporations, foundations, and government agencies. The new museum building opened in September 1991. *Publications:* exhibition catalogs; screening schedules; flyers.

National Aeronautics and Space Administration (NASA). Office of Human Resources and Education, Education Division, Washington, DC 20546. (202) 453-8388. Fax (202) 755-2979. Dr. Malcolm Phelps, contact person. From elementary through postgraduate school, NASA's educational programs are designed to capture students' interest in science, mathematics, and technology at an early age; to channel more students into science, engineering, and technology career paths; and to enhance the knowledge, skills, and experiences of teachers and university faculty. NASA's educational programs include NASA Spacelink (an electronic information system); videoconferences (90-minute interactive staff development videoconferences to be delivered to schools via satellite); NASA Select (informational and educational television programming); and ISY (International Space Year) Videoconferences (two live, interactive videoconferences that provide an opportunity for secondary school students to interact with space scientists and engineers). Additional information is available from the Education Division at NASA headquarters and counterpart offices at the nine NASA field centers.

National Alliance of Media Arts Centers (NAMAC). 1212 Broadway, Suite 816, Oakland, CA 94612. (415) 451-2717. Fax (415) 834-3741. Julian Low, Dir. A nonprofit organization dedicated to increasing public understanding of and support for the field of media arts in the United States. Members include media centers, cable access centers, universities, and media artists, as well as other individuals and organizations providing services for production, education, exhibition, distribution, and preservation of video, film, audio, and intermedia. NAMAC's information services are available to the general public, arts and nonarts organizations, businesses, corporations, foundations, government agencies, schools, and universities. *Membership:* 250 organizations, 200 individuals. *Dues:* Institutional ranges from $50-$250/yr. depending on annual budget; $35/yr. individual. *Publications: Media Arts Information Network; NAMAC Directory* (published every other year).

*National Association for Better Broadcasting (NABB). 7918 Naylor Ave., Los Angeles, CA 90045. (213) 641-4903. Frank Orme, Pres. Promotes the public interest in broadcasting through the development of greater awareness of the public's rights and responsibilities in broadcasting. *Publications: Better Radio and Television; You Own More Than Your Set!*

*National Association for the Education of Young Children (NAEYC). 1834 Connecticut Ave. NW, Washington, DC 20009. (202) 232-8777; (800) 424-2460. Offers professional development opportunities to early childhood educators designed to improve the quality of services to children from birth through age eight, the critical years of development. *Membership:* 70,000 in 390 local and state affiliate groups. *Dues:* $25 regular; $50 comprehensive. *Publications: Young Children* (journal); over 60 books, posters, videos, and brochures.

National Association for Visually Handicapped (NAVH). 22 W. 21st St., New York, NY 10010. (212) 889-3141. Lorraine H. Marchi, Pres. (or) 3201 Balboa Street, San Francisco, CA 94121. (415) 221-3201. Debra Strom, contact person for 11 western states, Alaska and Hawaii. Publishes and distributes newsletters at irregular intervals (*Seeing Clearly* for adults and *In Focus* for youth). Informational literature, most of which is in large print, is available to visually impaired individuals, their families, and the professionals and paraprofessionals who work with them. Maintains a loan library (free) by the U.S. Postal Service of large-print books. Offers counsel and guidance to visually impaired adults and their families and to the parents of visually-impaired children. *Membership:* 10,350. *Publications: Catalog of Large Print Materials; Selected List of LPM for Adults; Loan Library List.*

National Association of Broadcasters (NAB). 1771 N St. NW, Washington, DC 20036-2891. (202) 429-5300. Edward O. Fritts, Pres. and CEO. A trade association that represents commercial broadcasters. Encourages development of broadcasting arts and seeks to protect its members and to strengthen and maintain the industry so that it may best serve the public. *Membership:* radio and television stations, and all the major networks. *Dues:* Based on station revenue for radio and on market size for television. *Publications: Telemedia,* a video journal for members; weekly newsletters: *TV Today; RadioWeek;* industry monographs.

*National Association of Business and Educational Radio (NABER). 1501 Duke St., Alexandria, VA 22314. (703) 739-0300; (800) 759-0300. John Sherlock, Dir., Membership/Communications. Represents individuals whose business and professional needs interest them in the uses of TV-shared UHF, and 800 Mhz channels for communication purposes. *Membership:* 5,000. *Publications: Business Radio; ShopTalk; TechTalk; SMR Letter; Private Carrier Pages.*

*National Association of Secondary School Principals (NASSP). 1904 Association Dr., Reston, VA 22091. (703) 860-0200. Thomas F. Koerner, Ed. and Dir. Provides a national voice for secondary education, supports promising and successful educational practices, conducts research, examines issues, and represents secondary education at the federal level. *Membership:* 40,000. *Publications: NASSP Bulletin; NASSP NewsLeader; Curriculum Report; Legal Memorandum; Schools in the Middle; TIPS for Principals; AP Special; Practitioner and Leadership Magazine.*

*National Association of State Boards of Education (NASBE). 1012 Cameron St., Alexandria, VA 22314. (703) 684-4000. Gene Wilhoit, Exec. Dir. Studies problems and improves communication among members, exchanges information, provides educational programs and activities, and serves as a liaison with other educators' groups. *Membership:* 562. *Publication: The State Board Connection.*

*National Association of State Educational Media Professionals (NASTEMP). New Mexico Department of Education, Education Building, Santa Fe, NM 87501-2786. (505) 827-6562. Mary Jane Vinella, Library Media Consultant. The National Association of State Boards of Education is a nonprofit association that represents state and territorial boards of education. Its primary objectives are to strengthen state leadership in education policymaking, to promote excellence in the education of all students, to advocate equality of access to educational opportunity, and assure responsible lay governance of public education. *Membership:* open to U.S. Department of Education and state and district agencies. *Membership:* 110. *Dues:* $10. *Publications: Aids to Media Selection for Students and Teachers; Quarterly Newsletter.*

National Association of State Textbook Administrators (NASTA). Gordon Persons Bldg., Rm. 5157, 50 North Ripley St., Montgomery, AL 36130-3901. Barry L. Buford, Pres. NASTA's purposes are (1) to foster a spirit of mutual helpfulness in adoption, purchase, and distribution of textbooks; (2) to arrange for study and review of textbook specifications; (3) to authorize special surveys, tests, and studies; and (4) to initiate action leading to better quality textbooks. NASTA is not affiliated with any parent organization; it works with the Association of American Publishers and the Book Manufacturers Institute. Services provided include a working knowledge of text construction, monitoring lowest prices, sharing adoption information, identifying trouble spots, and discussions in the industry. *Membership:* Approx. 22.

National Audiovisual Center (NAC). National Archives and Records Administration, 8700 Edgeworth Dr., Capitol Heights, MD 20743. (301) 763-1896. Fax (301) 763-6025. George Ziener, Dir. Central information and distribution source for more than 8,000 audiovisual programs produced by or for the U.S. government. Materials are made available for sale or rent on a self-sustaining basis, at the lowest price possible. *Publications: Media Resource Catalog* (1991) listing 600 of the latest and most popular programs, is available free. Also available free are specific subject listings such as science, history, medicine, and safety and health.

National Cable Television Institute (NCTI). P.O. Box 27277, Denver, CO 80227. (303) 761-8554. Fax (303) 761-8556. Tom Brooksher, Gen. Mgr. Provides educational materials and services for the upgrading of professional competencies of cable television personnel.

National Center for Appropriate Technology (NCAT). P.O. Box 3838, Butte, MT 59702. (406) 494-4572. Fax (406) 494-2905. George Turman, Pres. A nonprofit corporation with a mission to advance the research, development, and widespread adoption of appropriate technologies in the four major program areas of sustainable energy and agriculture, affordable housing, and environmental protection. NCAT operates national technical assistances and distributes several how-to and educational publications. *Publications: Connections: A Curriculum in AT for the Fifth and Sixth Grades*; *Energy Education Guidebook*; *Photovoltaics in the Pacific Islands*; others. Free publications catalog is available from NCAT Publications, P.O. Box 4000, Dept. EMTY, Butte, MT 59702.

National Clearinghouse for Bilingual Education. 1118 22nd St. NW, Washington, DC 20037. (202) 467-0867; (800) 321-6223. Joel Gomez, Dir. National information center for the education of language-minority students from kindergarten to adult and a producer of various publications related to the field of bilingual education. *Dues:* None. *Publication: FORUM* (bi-monthly newsletter).

National Commission on Libraries and Information Science (NCLIS). 1111 18th St. NW, Suite 310, Washington, DC 20036. (202) 254-3100. Fax (202) 254-3111. Peter R. Young, Exec. Dir. An agency in the executive branch of the U.S. government charged with advising Congress and the President in the entire field of library and information services. The commission has four major roles: to advise the President and Congress on the implementation of national policy; to conduct studies and analyses of the library and information needs of the nation; to promote research and development activities that will improve the nation's library and information services; and to conduct the White House Conference on Library and Information Services.

National Council for Accreditation of Teacher Education (NCATE). 2010 Massachusetts Ave., NW, Suite 200, Washington, DC 20036. (202) 466-7496. Fax (202) 296-6620. Arthur E. Wise, Pres. A consortium of professional organizations that establishes standards of quality and accredits professional education units in schools, colleges, and departments of education. Interested in the self-regulation and improvement of standards in the field of teacher education. *Membership:* 520 colleges and universities, 26 educational organizations. *Publications: Standards, Procedures and Policies for the Accreditation of Professional Education Units; Annual List* of accredited programs/units; *Quality Teaching* (newsletter, 3/yr.).

National Council of Teachers of English (NCTE). Commission on Media, 1111 Kenyon Rd., Urbana, IL 61801. (217) 328-3870. Fax (217) 328-9645. Miles Myers, Exec. Dir. An advisory body that identifies key issues in the teaching of media. Reviews current projects and recommends new directions and personnel to undertake them, monitors NCTE publications on media, and suggests program ideas for the annual convention. *Publications: English Journal; College English; Language Arts; English Education: Research in the Teaching of English; Teaching English in the Two-Year College.*

National Council of the Churches of Christ Communication Unit. 475 Riverside Dr., New York, NY 10115. (212) 870-2227. Fax (212) 870-2030. Rev. Dr. J. Martin Bailey, Dir. of Communication. Ecumenical arena for cooperative work of Protestant and Orthodox denominations and agencies in broadcasting, film, cable, and print media. Offers advocacy to government and industry structures on media services. Services provided include liaison to network television and radio programming; film sales and rentals; distribution of information about syndicated religious programming; syndication of some programming; cable television and emerging technologies information services; news and information regarding work of the National Council of Churches, related denominations, and agencies. Works closely with other faith groups in Interfaith Broadcasting Commission. Online communication via Ecunet/NCCLink. *Membership:* 32 denominations. *Publication: EcuLink.*

*National Education Association (NEA). 1201 16th St. NW, Washington, DC 20036. (202) 833-4000. Kerth Geiger, Pres. The world's largest advocacy organization of teachers, other school employees, and college faculty. Seeks to improve American public education, conducts research on school problems and professional teacher welfare, maintains lobby relationships with the federal government, and provides information to the public about education and educational needs. *Membership:* 2 million. *Dues:* $75 active membership.

National Endowment for the Arts (NEA). 1100 Pennsylvania Ave. NW, Washington, DC 20506. The NEA is a grant-making agency. For a guide to programs, contact the Public Information Office at (202) 682-5400.

National Endowment for the Humanities (NEH). 1100 Pennsylvania Ave. NW, Rm. 426, Washington, DC 20506. (202) 786-0278. James Dougherty, Asst. Dir. for Media. Offers limited support for the planning, scripting, and production of radio and television projects pertaining to the humanities. Grants are available for children's, as well as adult, programming. The program has two deadlines each year, in March and in September. For further information, contact Media Program, Division of General Program, NEH. *Publication: Guidelines for Applications.*

National Federation of Community Broadcasters (NFCB). 666 11th St. NW, Suite 805, Washington, DC 20001. (202) 393-2355. Lynn Chadwick, Pres. NFCB represents its members in public policy development at the national level and provides a wide range of practical services. *Membership:* 70 stations, 100 (associate) stations and production groups. *Dues:* Based on income, from $75 to $500 for associations; $300 to $2,000 for participants. *Publications: Legal Handbook; Audio Craft* (1989 edition); *Community Radio Monthly.*

*National Film Board of Canada (NFBC). 1251 Avenue of the Americas, New York, NY 10020. (212) 586-5131. John Sirabella, Nontheatrical Rep. Established in 1939, the NFBC's main objective is to produce and distribute high-quality audiovisual materials for educational, cultural, and social purposes. *Publication: U.S. Film Resource Guide.*

National Film Information Service (NFIS). 8949 Wilshire Blvd., Beverly Hills, CA 90211. (213) 247-3000. Provides an information service on film. All inquiries must be accompanied by SASE.

National Gallery of Art (NGA). Department of Education Resources and Extension Programs, Washington, DC 20565. (202) 842-6273. Ruth R. Perlin, Head. This department of NGA is responsible for the production and distribution of educational audiovisual programs including interactive technologies. Materials available (all loaned free to schools, community organizations, and individuals) range from films, videocassettes, and color slide programs to videodiscs. A free catalog of programs is available upon request. Two videodiscs in the Gallery's collection are available for long-term loan. *Publication: Catalogue of Programs.*

*National Information Center for Educational Media (NICEM). P.O. Box 40130, Albuquerque, NM 87196. (505) 265-3591; (800) 468-3453. Marjorie M. K. Hlava, Pres. NICEM, in conjunction with the Library of Congress, is a centralized facility that collects, catalogs, and disseminates information about nonbook materials of many different kinds. Its mission is to build and expand the database to provide current and archival information about nonbook educational materials; to apply modern techniques of information dissemination that meet user needs; and to provide a comprehensive, centralized nonbook database used for catalogs, indexes, multimedia publications, special search services, machine-readable tapes, and online access. *Publications:* indexes to audiovisual educational materials.

National Library of Medicine. 8600 Rockville Pike, Bethesda, MD 20894. (301) 496-6308. Donald A. B. Lindberg, M.D., Dir. Collects, organizes, and distributes literature on biomedicine; seeks to apply modern technology to the flow of biomedical information to health professionals; and supports development of improved medical library resources for the country. Responsible for MEDLINE, SDILINE, CATLINE, SERLINE, CANCERLIT, AVLINE, and TOXLINE. Maintains a collection of 20,000 health science audiovisual materials; supervises the Lister Hill Center for Biomedical Communications and the National Center for Biotechnology Information. Maintains seven regional medical libraries. *Publication: National Library of Medicine Audiovisuals Catalog.*

National Press Photographers Association, Inc. (NPPA). 3200 Croasdaile Dr., Suite 306, Durham, NC 27705. (919) 383-7246. Fax (919) 383-7261. Charles Cooper, Exec. Dir. An organization of professional news photographers who participate in and promote photojournalism in publications and through television and film. Sponsors workshops and contests; maintains a tape library and collections of slides in the field. *Membership:* 11,000. *Dues:* $55 professional, $30 student. *Publications: News Photographer;* membership directory; *Best of Photojournalism Books.*

National PTA. 700 N. Rush St., Chicago, IL 60611. (312) 787-0977. Fax (312) 787-8342. Pat Henry, Pres. A child advocacy association dedicated to improving the lives of our country's children through the school, home, community, and place of worship. Strengthens laws for the care and protection of children and youth. *Membership:* 7 million. *Dues:* Vary, established by local units. *Sample Publications: PTA Today Magazine; Kids with Keys, Parents with Jobs: Who's in Charge?* (English and Spanish); *Home Helps for Learning; How to Talk to Your Child About*

Sex; *Drug Abuse and Your Teens: What Parents Should Know*; *Young Children and Drugs: What Parents Can Do*; *What's Happening in Washington.*

National Public Radio (NPR). 2025 M Street NW, Washington, DC 20036. (202) 822-2300. Douglas J. Bennet, Pres. Through member stations in 48 states, Puerto Rico, and the District of Columbia, NPR reaches a broad segment of the population. Its award-winning programming—"All Things Considered," "Morning Edition," "Performance Today," "Car Talk," and "Blues Stage"—has helped build an audience base of more than 13 million weekly listeners. With programs such as "Horizons," "Afropop Worldwide," "Crossroads," and "National Native News," NPR acknowledges the diversity in American society and provides programs that focus on minorities, the elderly, and the disabled. In addition to programming, NPR provides more than 430 member stations with distribution and representation support services.

National Religious Broadcasters (NRB). 299 Webro Rd., Suite 250, Parsippany, NJ 07054. (201) 428-5400. Fax (201) 428-1814. E. Brandt Gustavson, Exec. Dir. Holds an annual national convention and seven regional conventions. *Membership:* 850 stations, individuals, and agencies. *Dues:* Based on income. *Publications: Religious Broadcasting Magazine*; *Annual Directory of Religious Broadcasting*; *Religious Broadcasting Cassette Catalog.*

National School Supply and Equipment Association (NSSEA). 8300 Colesville Rd., Suite 250, Silver Spring, MD 20910. (301) 495-0240. Fax (301) 495-3330. Tim Holt, Exec. V.P. A service organization of 1,000 manufacturers, distributors, retailers, and independent manufacturers' representatives of school supplies, equipment, and instructional materials. Seeks to maintain open communications between manufacturers and dealers in the school market, to find solutions to problems affecting schools, and to encourage the development of new ideas and products for educational progress. *Publications: Tidings*; *Annual Membership Directory.*

*National Science Foundation (NSF). Washington, DC 20550. (202) 357-9498. Primary purposes are to increase the nation's base of scientific knowledge; encourage research in areas that can lead to improvements in economic growth, productivity, and environmental quality; promote international cooperation through science; and develop and help implement science education programs to aid the nation in meeting the challenges of contemporary life. Grants go chiefly to colleges and other research organizations. Applicants should refer to the *NSF Guide to Programs.* Scientific material and media reviews are available to help the public learn about NSF-supported programs.

National Science Teachers Association (NSTA). 1742 Connecticut Ave. NW, Washington, DC 20009. (202) 328-5800. Fax (202) 328-0974. Bill Aldridge, Exec. Dir. International nonprofit association of science teachers ranging from kindergarten through university level. *Membership:* 50,000. *Dues:* $50/yr. individual (includes one journal), $50/yr. institutional (includes one journal). *Publications: Science and Children*; *The Science Teacher*; *Journal of College Science Teaching*; *Science Scope*; *Quantum.*

National Society for Performance and Instruction (NSPI). 1300 L Street, NW, Suite 1250, Washington, DC 20005. (202) 408-7969. Fax (202) 408-7972. Paul Tremper, Exec. Dir. NSPI is an international association dedicated to increasing productivity in the workplace through the application of performance and instructional technologies. Founded in 1962, its members are located throughout the United States, Canada, and 30 other countries. Offers an awards program recognizing excellence in the field. The Annual Conference and Expo is held in the spring. *Membership:* 5,000. *Dues:* $95, active member; $40, students and retirees. *Publications:*

Performance & Instruction Journal, (10/yr.); *Performance Improvement Quarterly*; *News & Notes*, newsletter, 10/yr.; *Annual Membership Directory*.

National Technical Information Service (NTIS). Springfield, VA 22161. (703) 487-4650. Fax (703) 321-8547. NTIS is a self-supporting agency of the U.S. Department of Commerce that actively collects, organizes, and distributes technical information generated by the United States and foreign governments in all areas of science and technology. There are 2 million titles in the NTIS permanent archives, some of which date as far back as 1945, with approximately 63,000 new titles added annually. Reprints from the entire collection are available at any time, whether a report dates from 20 years ago or last month. In addition, NTIS provides government-generated computer software and computerized data files, on both tape and diskette, through its Federal Computer Products Center. To keep pace with technology transfer activities, the NTIS Center for the Utilization of Federal Technology licenses federal inventions and makes them available to private industry. In the area of foreign technology, NTIS has recently increased its holdings—up to a third of the reports entering the collection are now from foreign sources. Access to the collection is through a printed catalog, *The Government Reports Announcements & Index*, online, or via CD-ROM of the NTIS Bibliographic Database. Most main commercial online services and optical disk publishers offer access to the NTIS Bibliographic Database. To request a free 32-page catalog describing NTIS products and services, contact the NTIS Order Desk at the preceding address and ask for PR827/NCB.

National Technology Center (NTC). American Foundation for the Blind, 15 W. 16th St., New York, NY 10011. (212) 620-2080. Evaluations Laboratory: (212) 620-2051. Fax (212) 620-2137. Eliot M. Schreier, Dir. The Center has three components: National Technology Information System, Evaluations Laboratory, and Research and Development Laboratory. Provides a resource for blind and visually impaired persons and professionals in education, rehabilitation, and employment; their families; and rehabilitation professionals, educators, researchers, manufacturers, and employers. The NTC also develops products to enhance education, employment, mobility, and independent living opportunities for blind and visually impaired people worldwide.

National Telemedia Council Inc. (NTC). 120 E. Wilson St., Madison, WI 53703. (608) 257-7712. Dr. Marti Tomas, Pres.; Marieli Rowe, Exec. Dir. An organization working to develop a better-informed, more evaluative public through media literacy, working with teachers, parents, and others concerned with children. Sponsor organization of KIDS-4, a Sun Prairie, Wisconsin, cable television channel produced by and for children. Every fall, NTC conducts Project LOOK-LISTEN-THINK-RESPOND, a classroom television evaluation activity. Other NTC activities include conferences and workshops, the Teacher Idea Exchange (T.I.E.), Sponsor Recognition Awards for excellence in telemedia programming, the newsletters *Telemedium* and *Telemedium Update*, and the development of a media literacy clearinghouse. *Dues:* $20 and up. *Publications: Telemedium; Telemedium UPDATE; Annual Report of Project LOOK-LISTEN-THINK-RESPOND; Media Literacy Clearinghouse Directory*.

National University Continuing Education Association (NUCEA). One Dupont Cir. NW, Suite 615, Washington, DC 20036. (202) 659-3130. Calvin Stockman, Pres.; Kay J. Kohl, Exec. Dir. An association of public and private institutions concerned with making continuing education available to all population segments and to promoting excellence in the continuing higher education community. NUCEA has an annual national conference and several professional development seminars throughout the year, and many institutional members offer university and college film rental library services. *Membership:* 400 institutions; 2,000 professionals. *Dues:* Vary according to membership category. *Publications:* monthly newsletter; quarterly occasional papers;

scholarly journal; *Independent Study Catalog*; *Guide to Certificate Programs at American Colleges and Universities*; *Conferences and Facilities Directory*; NUCEA-ACE/Macmillan Continuing Higher Education book series; *Lifelong Learning Trends* (a statistical factbook on continuing higher education); *Directory of Black Professionals in Continuing Education*; membership directory; other publications relevant to the field.

*Nebraska Videodisc Design/Production Group (VD-PG). KUON-TV, University of Nebraska, Box 83111, Lincoln, NE 68501. (402) 472-3611. Ron Nugent, Group Dir. A group of designers and producers concerned with the development and production of programs that exploit the unique capabilities of the videodisc. Holds annual symposium and workshops.

*The NETWORK. 300 Brickstone Square, Suite 900, Andover, MA 01810. (508) 470-1080. D. Max McConkey, Dir. A research and service organization providing consultation, training, assistance, and materials to schools, other educational institutions, and private sector firms with educational interests. *Publications: Administering Writing Programs: A Training Package for the Coordination of Writing Programs*; *The Cumulative Writing Folder*; *Nutrition Education Curriculum*; *Sex Equity Curriculum*; *The Effective Writing Teacher*; *Eighteen Strategies: An Action Guide to School Improvement*; *People, Policies and Practices; Examining the Chain of School Improvement*, vols. I-X. See also Council for Educational Development and Research.

*Network for Continuing Medical Education (NCME). One Harmon Plaza, Secaucus, NJ 07094. (201) 867-3550; (800) 223-0272; in NJ, (800) 624-2102. Jim Disque, Exec. Dir. Produces and distributes videocassettes to hospitals for physicians' continuing education. *Membership:* by subscription. *Dues:* Subscription fees: VHS—$1,820; 3/4-inch film—$2,020.

North American Simulation and Gaming Association (NASAGA). c/o Pentathalon Institute, P.O. Box 20590, Indianapolis, IN 46220. (317) 782-1553. Provides a forum for the exchange of ideas, information, and resources among persons interested in simulation and games. Assists members in designing, testing, using, and evaluating simulations and/or games and in using these as research tools. A computerized mailing list and cross-referencing service are available through national headquarters and UNC-Asheville. Sponsors various conferences. *Membership:* 800. *Dues:* $35 regular, $10 student. *Publication: Simulation and Games.*

Northwest Regional Educational Laboratory (NWREL). 101 SW Main St., Suite 500, Portland, OR 97204. (503) 275-9500. Fax (503) 275-9489. Robert R. Rath, Exec. Dir. Assists education, government, community agencies, and business and labor in bringing about improvement in educational programs and processes by developing and disseminating effective educational products and procedures, including applications of technology. Provides technical assistance and training in educational problem solving. Evaluates effectiveness of educational programs and processes. *Membership:* 817. *Dues:* None. *Publication: Northwest Report* (newsletter).

OCLC Online Computer Library Center, Inc. 6565 Frantz Rd., Dublin, OH 43017-3395. (614) 764-6000. Fax (614) 764-6096. A nonprofit membership organization that engages in computer library service and research and makes available computer-based processes, products, and services for libraries, other educational organizations, and library users. From its facility in Dublin, Ohio, OCLC operates an international computer network that libraries use to catalog books, order custom-printed catalog cards and machine-readable records for local catalogs, arrange interlibrary loans, and maintain location information on library materials. OCLC also provides online and offline reference products and services for the electronic delivery of information. More than 13,000 libraries contribute to and/or use information in the OCLC Online Union Catalog.

Publications: OCLC Newsletter (6/yr.); OCLC Reference News (6/yr.); Annual Report; Annual Review of Research.

Office for International Networks in Education and Development (INET). College of Education, Michigan State University, 238 Erikson, East Lansing, MI 48824-1034. (517) 355-5522. Anne Schneller, Mgr. The INET office makes a number of publications available to development planners and practitioners working on behalf of persons in Africa, Asia, Latin America, and the Middle East. Such materials are distributed for sale or on an exchange basis; that is, the office sends publications in hopes that recipients will give the office further materials, especially those of a "fugitive" nature. Such materials may be in the form of books, working papers, surveys, occasional papers, annual reports, journals, or newsletters that are relevant to education and development. The INET office strongly encourages participants to continue this exchange of publications, which has proved to be so important to low-cost dissemination of information throughout the Third World. INET is interested particularly in matters and materials related to formal and nonformal education for development. *Membership:* Free. *Dues:* None.

Office of Technology Assessment (OTA). U.S. Congress, Washington, DC 20510-8025. (202) 224-9241. Fax (202) 228-6098. John Gibbons, Dir. Established by Congress to study, report on, and assess the significance and probable impact of new technological developments on U.S. society and to advise Congress on public policy implications and options. Recent assessments focusing on technology and education issues include *Elementary and Secondary Education for Science and Engineering, A Technical Memorandum* (1989); *Higher Education for Science and Engineering, A Background Paper* (1989); *Linking for Learning: A New Course for Education* (1989); *Critical Connections: Communication for the Future* (1990); *Computer Software and Intellectual Property, A Background Paper* (1990). In addition, the assessment, *Power On! New Tools for Teaching & Learning* (1988), includes an interim staff paper on "Trends and Status of Computers in Schools: Use in Chapter 1 Programs and Use with Limited English Proficient Students" (March 1987). The OTA is currently preparing a study of educational assessment tools, to be released early in 1992, and a report on the use of technology to meet adult literacy needs (Winter 1992). *Publications:* For a list, contact the publishing office at (202) 224-8996.

On-line Audiovisual Catalogers (OLAC). 285 Sharp Rd., Baton Rouge, LA 70815. (504) 342-4938. Bobby Ferguson, Treas. Formed as an outgrowth of the ALA conference, OLAC seeks to permit members to exchange ideas, computer files, and information and to interact with other agencies that influence audiovisual cataloging practices. *Membership:* 725. *Dues:* Available for single or multiple years, ranges from $10-$27 individual, $16-$45 institutional. *Publication:* OLAC Newsletter.

Oral History Association. 1093 Broxton Ave, No. 720, Los Angeles, CA 90024. (310) 825-0597. Fax (310) 206-1864. Richard Candida Smith, Exec. Sec. Seeks to develop the use of oral history as primary source material and to disseminate oral history materials among scholars. *Membership:* 1,400. *Publications: Oral History Newsletter; Oral History Review; Oral History Evaluation Guidelines; Annual Report and Membership Directory; Oral History and the Law; Oral History in Secondary Education; Oral History for Community History Projects.*

Pacific Film Archive (PFA). University Art Museum, 2625 Durant Ave., Berkeley, CA 94720. (510) 642-1437. Fax (510) 642-4889. Sponsors the exhibition, study, and preservation of classic, international, documentary, animated, and avant-garde films. Provides media research and a service to locate film sources, books, and addresses.

PCR: Films and Video in the Behavioral Sciences. Special Services Bldg., Pennsylvania State University, University Park, PA 16802. (814) 863-3102; purchasing info. (800) 826-0132. Fax (814) 863-2574. Thomas McKenna, Mng. Ed. Collects and makes available to professionals 16mm films and video in the behavioral sciences judged to be useful for university teaching and research. A free catalog of the films in PCR is available. The PCR catalog now contains some 1,400 films in the behavioral sciences (psychology, psychiatry, anthropology, animal behavior, sociology, teaching and learning, and folklife). Some 7,000 professionals now use PCR services. Films and tapes are available on loan for a rental charge. Many films may also be purchased. Films may be submitted for international distribution. Contact the managing editor through PCR.

Photographic Society of America (PSA). 3000 United Founders Blvd., Suite 103, Oklahoma City, OK 73102. (405) 843-1437. Terry S. Stull, Operations Manager. A nonprofit organization for the development of the arts and sciences of photography and for the furtherance of public appreciation of photographic skills. Its members, largely amateurs, consist of individuals, camera clubs, and other photographic organizations. Divisions include color slide, motion picture, nature, photojournalism, travel, pictorial print, stereo, and techniques. Sponsors national, regional, and local meetings, clinics, and contests. Request dues information from preceding address. *Publication: PSA Journal.*

*Professors of Instructional Design and Technology (PIDT). Audio-Visual Center, Indiana University, Bloomington, IN 47405-5901. (812) 855-2854. Dr. Tom Schwen, contact person. An organization designed to encourage and facilitate the exchange of information among members of the instructional design and technology academic and corporate communities. Also serves to promote excellence in academic programs in instructional design and technology and to encourage research and inquiry that will benefit the field while providing leadership in the public and private sectors in its application and practice. Membership consists of faculty employed in higher education institutions whose primary responsibilities are teaching and research in this area; their corporate counterparts; and other persons interested in the goals and activities of the PIDT.

*Project in Distance Education. *One key component of the OAS Multinational Project on Secondary and Higher Education.* Organization of American States, Department of Educational Affairs, 1889 F St. NW, Washington, DC 20006. (202) 458-3309. Arturo Garzon, contact person. Promotes development of distance education in Latin American and Caribbean countries through technical cooperation, planning, human resource and institution building and research. Main projects in Argentina, Brazil, Colombia, Costa Rica, El Salvador, and Panama.

*Project in Educational Technology. *One key component of the OAS Multinational Project on Secondary and Higher Education.* Organization of American States, Department of Educational Affairs, 1889 F St. NW, Washington, DC 20006. (202) 458-3309. Arturo Garzon, contact person. Maintains support, information, and personnel exchanges among educational technology centers in Brazil, Argentina, and Chile, with tie-ins to other Latin American countries. Emphasizes development of human resources through a variety of programs, seminars, short courses, on-site training, and technical cooperation. Also disseminates information through its journal. *Publication: Revista de Tecnologia Educativa.*

Public Broadcasting Service (PBS). 1320 Braddock Pl., Alexandria, VA 22314. (703) 739-5000. Bruce Christensen, Pres. Serves as a distributor of national public television programming, obtaining all programs from the stations or independent producers; PBS is not a production facility. Owned and operated by licensees through annual membership fees. Funding for technical distribution facilities in part by the Corporation for Public Broadcasting. PBS services include national promotion, program acquisition and scheduling, legal services, development and fundraising support, engineering and technical studies, and research. Of special interest are the Adult Learning Service, which offers telecourses through college, public television station partnerships, and PBS VIDEO, which offers PBS programs for rent or sale to educational institutions. PBS is governed by a board of directors elected by licensees for 3-year terms. *Membership:* 172 licensees; 337 stations.

> **PBS ENCORE.** 1320 Braddock Pl., Alexandria, VA 22314. (703) 739-5225. Michael Patterson, Manager. Distributes PBS programs with extant broadcast rights to public television stations. *Publications: PBS Encore Catalog; Monthly News & Update Memo.*

> ***PBS VIDEO.** 1320 Braddock Pl., Alexandria, VA 22314. (800) 424-7963 or (703) 739-5380. Jon Cecil, Dir. Markets and distributes PBS television programs for sale on videocassette to colleges, public libraries, schools, government, and other organizations and institutions. Top-selling programs include "Moyers: The Power of the Word," "Middle Ages School Kit," "Thinking Your Way to Better SAT Scores," "American Experience II," "The Mind," "Eyes on the Prize II," and "The Civil War." *Publications: PBS VIDEO Program Catalog; PBS VIDEO Check It Out Catalog; PBS Video News.*

Public Service Satellite Consortium (PSSC). 1235 Jefferson Davis Highway, Suite 904, Arlington, VA 22202. (703) 979-0801. Louis A. Bransford, Pres. Represents the telecommunication interests of nonprofit organizations; provides members with information, consultation, educational briefings, and representation to federal agencies and other organizations; assists members in contracting for operational functions such as systems engineering and networking; conducts workshops on new technologies and telecommunications issues. PSSC is also the headquarters of the National Center for Telecommunications Information Policy. *Publications: Report to Members Newsletter; Teleguide: A Handbook on Video-Teleconferencing.* In service until May 31, 1992.

Puppeteers of America. 5 Cricklewood Path, Pasadena, CA 91107. (818) 797-5748. Gayle Schulter, Membership Chair. Founded in 1937 to promote and develop the art of puppetry. It has a large collection of films and videotapes for rent in its audiovisual library and offers books, plays, and related items from the Puppetry Store. Puppeteers is a national resource center that offers workshops, exhibits, a puppetry exchange, and regional festivals. *Dues:* Various classes of membership which range from $15-$40. *Publications: Puppeteering Journal* (annual directory); bi-monthly newsletter; quarterly journals.

*Radio Free Europe/Radio Liberty (RFE-RL, Inc.). 1201 Connecticut Ave. NW, Washington, DC 20036. (202) 457-6900. An independent radio broadcast service funded by federal grants, which broadcasts to the nations of the former Soviet Union; Bulgaria, Czechoslovakia, Hungary, Poland, and Romania; the Baltic States; and Afghanistan.

*Recording for the Blind. 20 Roszel Rd., Princeton, NJ 08540. (609) 452-0606. Supported by volunteers and contributions from individuals, corporations, and foundations. Supplies free recordings of educational books for visually, perceptually, and physically disabled students and professionals.

*Recording Industry Association of America, Inc. (RIAA). 1020 19th St. NW, Suite 200, Washington, DC 20036. (202) 775-0101. Jason S. Berman, Pres. Compiles and disseminates U.S. industry shipment statistics by units and wholesale/retail dollar equivalents; establishes industry technical standards; conducts audits for certification of gold and platinum records and video awards; acts as the public information arm on behalf of the U.S. recording industry; provides antipiracy intelligence to law enforcement agencies; presents an RIAA cultural award for contributions to cultural activities in the United States; and acts as a resource center for recording industry research projects. *Membership:* 50 sound recording manufacturers. *Publications: Statistical Report; Industry Sourcebook;* newsletter; press releases.

Smithsonian Institution. c/o Smithsonian Information, Smithsonian Institution, Washington, DC 20560. (202) 357-2700. Robert McCormick Adams, Secy. An independent trust instrumentality of the United States that conducts scientific, cultural, and scholarly research; administers the national collections; and performs other educational public service functions, all supported by Congress, trusts, gifts, and grants. Includes 15 museums, including the National Museum of Natural History, the National Museum of American History, and the National Air and Space Museum. Museums are free and open daily except December 25. The Smithsonian Institution Traveling Exhibition Service (SITES) organizes exhibitions on art, history, and science and circulates them across the country and abroad. *Membership:* Smithsonian Associates (Resident and National and Air and Space). *Dues:* Vary. *Publications: Smithsonian; Air & Space/Smithsonian.*

*Social Science Education Consortium (SSEC). 3300 Mitchell Lane, Suite 240, Boulder, CO 80301-2272. (303) 492-8154. James R. Giese, Exec. Dir. The major goal of SSEC is to improve social studies instruction at all levels—elementary, secondary, and college. The consortium disseminates information about social studies materials, instructional methods, and trends. It assists educators in identifying, selecting, and using new ideas and methods in social studies and provides a forum for social scientists and educators to exchange ideas and views. A free catalog of publications and services is available on request. *Membership:* 140.

Society for Applied Learning Technology (SALT). 50 Culpeper St., Warrenton, VA 22186. (703) 347-0055. Raymond G. Fox, Pres. Seeks to advance the development of highest standards and practices in the application of technology to learning, to foster wide dissemination of understanding and knowledge in actual and potential uses of technology in learning, and to provide an effective educational channel among scientists, managers, and users of training and learning technology. *Membership:* 800. *Dues:* $45. *Publications: Journal of Educational Technology Systems; Journal of Interactive Instructional Development; Journal of Medical Education Technologies.* Send for list of books.

Society for Computer Simulation (SCS). P.O. Box 17900, San Diego, CA 92177-7900. (619) 277-3888. Fax (619) 277-3930. Chip G. Stockton, Exec. Dir. Founded in 1952, SCS is a professional-level technical society devoted to the art and science of modeling and simulation. Its purpose is to advance the understanding, appreciation, and use of all types of computer models for studying the behavior of actual or hypothesized systems of all kinds. Sponsors standards and local, regional, and national technical meetings and conferences such as Eastern & Western Simulation Multiconferences, Summer Computer Simulation Conference, Winter Simulation Conference, International Simulation Technology Conference (SIMTEC), National Educational Computing Conference (NECC), and others. *Membership:* 1,900. *Dues:* $50. *Publications: Simulation* (monthly); Simulation series (q.); *Transactions of SCS* (q.). Additional office in Ghent, Belgium.

Society for Imaging Science and Technology (IS&T) (formerly Society of Photographic Engineering). 7003 Kilworth Lane, Springfield, VA 22151. (703) 642-9090. Fax (703) 642-9094.

Calva Lotridge, Exec. Dir. Seeks to advance the science and engineering of imaging materials and equipment and to develop means for applying and using imaging techniques in all branches of engineering and science. *Membership:* 3,000; 17 chapters. *Publication: Journal of Imaging Science and Technology.*

*Society for Photographic Education (SPE). Campus Box 318, University of Colorado, Boulder, CO 80309. (303) 492-0588. Judith Thorpe, Exec. Dir. An association of college and university teachers of photography, museum photographic curators, writers, and publishers. Promotes higher standards of photographic education. *Membership:* 1,700. *Dues:* $50. *Publications: Exposure*; newsletter.

Society of Cable Television Engineers (SCTE). 669 Exton Commons, Exton, PA 19341. (215) 363-6888. William W. Riker, Exec. V.P. SCTE is dedicated to the technical training and further education of members. A nonprofit membership organization for persons engaged in engineering, construction, installation, technical direction, management, or administration of cable television and broadband communication technologies. Also eligible for membership are students in communications, educators, government and regulatory agency employees, and affiliated trade associations. *Membership:* 9,000. *Dues:* $40/yr. *Publication: The Interval.*

Society of Motion Picture and Television Engineers (SMPTE). 595 W. Hartsdale Ave., White Plains, NY 10607-1824. (914) 761-1100. Fax (914) 761-3115. Lynette Robinson, Exec. Dir. Fosters the advancement of engineering and technical aspects of motion pictures, television, and allied arts and sciences; disseminates scientific information in these areas; and sponsors lectures, exhibitions, classes, and conferences. Open to those with clearly defined interest in the field. *Membership:* 9,500. *Dues:* $65. *Publications:* Booklets and reports related to nonbook media, such as *SMPTE Journal; Special Effects in Motion Pictures*; test films.

*Society of Photo Technologists (SPT). 6535 S. Dayton, Suite 2000, Englewood, CO 80111. (303) 799-0667. Karen A. Hone, contact person. An organization of photographic equipment repair technicians which improves and maintains communications between manufacturers and independent repair technicians. *Membership:* 1,000. *Dues:* $60-$250. *Publications: SPT Journal; SPT Parts and Services Directory; SPT Newsletter, SPT Manuals—Training and Manufacturer's Tours.*

*SOFTSWAP. P.O. Box 271704, Concord, CA 94527-1704. (415) 685-7289. Hal Gibson, contact person. SOFTSWAP is an inexpensive, yet high-quality library of many teacher-developed and commercial educational programs for use in the Apple, IBM, and MAC computers. These copyrighted programs are organized onto disks that are sold for a nominal charge with permission to copy. *Publications:* Catalog; newsletter.

Special Libraries Association (SLA). 1700 18th St. NW, Washington, DC 20009-2508. (202) 234-4700. Fax (202) 265-9317. David R. Bender, Exec. Dir. SLA is an international professional organization of more than 13,000 librarians, information managers, and brokers serving business, research, government, universities, media, museums, and institutions that use or produce specialized information. Founded in 1909, the goal of the Association is to advance the leadership role of special librarians in the information society. SLA encourages its members to increase their professional competencies and performance by offering continuing education courses, workshops, and middle management and executive management courses. *Membership:* 13,000 plus. *Publications: SpeciaList* (mo. newsletter); *Special Libraries* (q.); bibliographic aids in library and information services.

SpecialNet. Part of the GTE Education Service Network. 1090 Vermont Ave. NW, Suite 800, Washington, DC 20005. (202) 408-7021; (800) 659-3000. Fax (202) 628-8216. Brenda Jacobs, contact person. A computerized, fee-charging information database emphasizing special education resources.

Speech Communication Association (SCA). 5105 Backlick Rd., Bldg. E, Annandale, VA 22003. (703) 750-0533. James L. Gaudino, Exec. Dir. A voluntary society organized to promote study, criticism, research, teaching, and application of principles of communication, particularly of speech communication. *Membership:* 7,000. *Dues:* $75. *Publications: Spectra Newsletter* (mo.); *Quarterly Journal of Speech; Communication Monographs; Communication Education; Critical Studies in Mass Communication; Speech Communication Teacher; Index to Journals in Communication Studies through 1985; Speech Communication Directory of SCA and the Regional Speech Communication Organizations* (CSSA, ECA, SSCA, WSCA). For additional publications, request brochure.

Superintendent of Documents. U.S. Government Printing Office, Washington, DC 20402. (202) 783-3238. Fax (202) 512-2250. Functions as the principal sales agency for U.S. government publications. Has over 20,000 titles in its active sales inventory. For information on the scope of its publications, write for the free Subject Bibliography index listing of over 240 subject bibliographies on specific topics. Of particular interest are SB 258, *Grants and Awards;* SB 114, *Directories and Lists of Persons and Organizations;* SB 73, *Motion Pictures, Films and Audiovisual Information;* SB 207, *Small Business;* SB 85, *Financial Aid for Students.*

Teachers and Writers Collaborative (T&W). 5 Union Square West, New York, NY 10003. (212) 691-6590. Nancy Larson Shapiro, Dir. Sends writers and other artists into New York public schools to conduct long-term projects with classroom teachers and students and publishes materials on how to teach creative writing based on these workshops. *Dues:* $35/yr. basic membership. *Publications: Teachers & Writers* (magazine); *The T&W Guide to Walt Whitman; Playmaking; Blazing Pencils; The List Poem; The Whole Word Catalogue,* vols. 1 & 2; *Personal Fiction Writing; The Writing Workshop,* vols. 1 & 2; *The T&W Handbook of Poetic Forms; The Art of Science Writing; Like It Was: A Complete Guide to Writing Oral History; Origins; Moving Windows: Evaluating the Poetry Children Write; Poetic Forms: 10 Audio Programs; Acrostic* and *Pantoum* (software packages). Free publications catalog available.

*Telecommunications Research and Action Center (TRAC). Box 12038, Washington, DC 20005. (202) 462-2520. Samuel Simon, counsel. Seeks to educate telecommunications consumers, to improve broadcasting, and to support local and national media reform groups and movements. *Dues:* $25/yr. *Publications: After Divestiture: What the AT&T Settlement Means for Business and Residential Telephone Service; Citizens' Media Directory; A Citizens' Primer on the Fairness Doctrine; Phonewriting: A Consumer's Guide to the New World of Electronic Information Services.*

Theater Library Association (TLA). 111 Amsterdam Ave., Rm. 513, New York, NY 10023. (212) 870-1670. Richard M. Buck, Secy. Treas. Seeks to further the interests of collecting, preserving, and using theater, cinema, and performing arts materials in libraries, museums, and private collections. *Membership:* 500. *Dues:* $20 individual, $25 institutional. *Publications: Broadside* (q.); *Performing Arts Resources* (membership annual).

Training Media Association. 198 Thomas Johnson Dr., Suite 206, Frederick, MD 21702. (301) 662-4268. Robert A. Gehrke, Exec. Dir. An organization dedicated to the protection of film and videotape copyright and copyright education. *Membership:* 75. *Dues:* Based on number of employees. *Publication: The Monthly.*

*Training Modules for Trainers (TMT). School of Education, University of Michigan, Ann Arbor, MI 48109. (313) 763-4668. Dr. Carl F. Berger, Dir. Funded by the Michigan Department of Education, the TMT Project was conceived to provide materials for use by trainers in addressing the computing needs of the educational community. The materials consist of a set of modules, each containing an overview, goals, training leader prerequisites, competency list, issues narrative, references, activities, blackline masters, and a feedback form. In addition, there is a videotape and set of slides available to supplement certain modules. Module topics include training methods, district planning, instructional methods, applications concepts, software evaluation, hardware configuration, basic technical skills, instructional management, software design, computers in the curriculum, computer-mediated communication, administrative uses, future images, computers and media services, emerging technology, artificial intelligence, CD-ROM, distance education, and videodiscs. *Publications: Training Modules for Trainers: A Resource for Training Leaders in The Educational Use of Computers* (set of 19).

United Nations Department of Public Information, Dissemination Division. Vadim Perfiliev, Dir. United Nations, Rm. S-1037 A, New York, NY 10017. (212) 963-6835. Fax (212) 963-6914. Chief, Information Dissemination Service, Rm. S-0260. (212) 963-6824. Fax (212) 963-4642. Film, Video and Radio Distribution, Rm. S-0805. (212) 963-6982, Fax (212) 963-6869. Print and Electronic Materials Distribution, Rm. S-0260. (212) 963-1258. Fax (212) 963-4642. The Department of Public Information produces and distributes films, radio, video, still pictures, charts, posters, and various publications on the United Nations and its activities. Distribution is worldwide and is done in part through a network of United Nations information centers, as well as via distributors and direct from U.N. Headquarters in New York. Information products are provided in a number of different languages, mainly in the six official U.N. languages: Arabic, Chinese, English, French, Russian, and Spanish.

University Film and Video Association (UFVA). c/o Loyola Marymount University, Communication Arts Department, Los Angeles, CA 90045. (310) 338-3033. Fax (310) 338-3030. Donald J. Zirpola, Pres. Members are involved in the arts and sciences of film and video. Promotes film and video production in educational institutions, fosters study of world cinema and video in scholarly resource centers, and serves as central source of information on film/video instruction, festivals, grants, jobs, production, and research. *Membership:* Approx. 800. *Dues:* Individual $35; student $15; institutional $75; commercial firm $150. *Publications: Journal of Film and Video; UFVA Digest;* membership directory.

*Women in Film (WIF). 6464 Sunset Blvd., No. 900, Hollywood, CA 90028. (213) 463-6040. Marcy Kelly, Pres. For women in film and television, a communications and support network, an education and advocacy resource, and a showcase for outstanding work being done by women directors, producers, and writers. The mission of WIF is to advance the employment, position, and depiction of women. Annually produces the Women in Film Festival (four days of premiere, documentary, video, and animation screenings, awards in 11 categories, special events and seminars); The Crystal Awards (recognizing contributions in film and television that promote the organization's mission); a program of film-finishing grants and scholarships for women through the Women in Film Foundation; a series of workshops on subjects related to improving the image and increasing the participation of women in the industry. *Membership criteria:* Three years' professional experience in film and television. *Dues:* $125/yr. *Publication:* Newsletter (mo.).

Women's Media Project (WMP). This project of the NOW Legal Defense and Education Fund has ceased operations.

World Future Society (WFS). 4916 St. Elmo Ave., Bethesda, MD 20814-6089. (301) 656-8274. Edward Cornish, Pres. Organization of individuals interested in the study of future trends and possibilities. *Membership:* 30,000. *Dues:* For information, please write to preceding address. *Publications: The Futurist: A Journal of Forecasts, Trends and Ideas about the Future; Futures Research Quarterly; Future Survey.* The society's bookstore offers audio- and videotapes, books, and other items.

This section on Canada includes information on 11 Canadian organizations whose principal interests lie in the general fields of education, educational media, instructional technology, and library and information science. Organizations listed in the 1991 *EMTY* were contacted for updated information and changes have been made accordingly. If no response was received, the entry for 1991 is repeated and indicated by an asterisk.

ACCESS NETWORK. 16930 114 Ave., Edmonton AB T5M 3S2, Canada. (403) 451-7272. Fax (403) 452-7233. Peter L. Senchuk, Pres. and CEO; Jean Campbell, Gen. Mgr. (Acting), Educational Services; Malcolm Knox, Gen. Mgr., Television; Don Thomas, Gen. Mgr., ACCESS NETWORK-CKUA Radio. ACCESS NETWORK is the registered trade name of the Alberta Educational Communications Corporation, which was established October 17, 1973, to consolidate and upgrade a variety of educational media services developing at that time within the province. ACCESS NETWORK acquires, develops, produces, and distributes television and radio programs, microcomputer courseware, multimedia kits, and related printed support materials for educational purposes. In 1985, the Corporation launched a province-wide educational television service, which is available by cable, satellite, and off-air transmitters to 82% of Alberta's population. ACCESS NETWORK-CKUA AM/FM broadcasts through a province-wide AM and FM radio network. Intended primarily for use in Alberta classrooms, ACCESS NETWORK productions are now available for national and international distribution.

Association for Media and Technology in Education in Canada (AMTEC). Instructional Technology Centre, University of Alberta, Faculty of Education, B-117 Education Centre, Edmonton, AB T6G 2G5, Canada. David Mappin, Pres. Promotes applications of educational technology in improving education and the public welfare. Fosters cooperation and interaction; seeks to improve professional qualifications of media practitioners; organizes and conducts media and technology meetings, seminars, and annual conferences; stimulates and publishes research in media and technology. *Membership:* 550. *Publications: Canadian Journal of Educational Communication* (q.); *Media News* (q.); *Membership Directory* (with membership).

*Canadian Association of Broadcasters/Association canadienne des radiodiffusers (CAB/ACR). Box 627, Station B, Ottawa, ON KIP 5S2, Canada. (613) 233-4035. Fax (613) 233-6961. A nonprofit trade association representing the majority of Canada's local-serving, advertising-supported radio and television stations.

*Canadian Book Publishers' Council (CBPC). 250 Merton St., Suite 203, Toronto, ON M4S 1B1, Canada. (416) 322-7011, (416) 322-6999. Jacqueline Hushion, Exec. Dir. CBPC members publish and distribute an extensive list of Canadian and imported materials to schools, universities, bookstores, and libraries. CBPC provides exhibits throughout the year and works through a number of subcommittees and groups within the organization to promote effective book publishing. *Membership:* 40 companies, educational institutions, and government agencies that publish books as an important facet of their work.

Canadian Broadcasting Corporation (CBC). 1500 Bronson Ave., Box 8478, Ottawa, ON K1G 3J5, Canada. (613) 724-1200. The CBC is a publicly owned corporation established in 1936 by an Act of the Canadian Parliament to provide a national broadcasting service in Canada in the two official languages. The CBC is financed mainly by public funds voted annually by Parliament.

*Canadian Education Association/Association canadienne d'education (CEA). 252 Bloor St. W., Suite 8-200, Toronto, ON M5S 1V5, Canada. (416) 924-7721. Robert E. Blair, Exec. Dir. The Canadian equivalent of the U.S. National Education Association. *Publications: CEA Handbook; Education Canada; CEA Newsletter; An Overview of Canadian Education; Women and Men in Education: A National Survey of Gender Distribution in School Systems; Marketing the School System; School Board Leave Policies; Dollars and Sense: How School Boards Save Money; Evaluation for Excellence: The Price of Quality; The Public Finance of Elementary and Secondary Education in Canada; Student Transportation in Canada: Facts and Figures; Federal Involvement in Public Education; Canada and Citizenship Education.*

Canadian Film Institute (CFI). 2 Daly, Ottawa, ON KIN 6E2, Canada. (613) 232-6727. Fax (613) 232-6315. Serge Losique, Exec. Dir. Established in 1935, the Institute promotes the study of film and television as cultural and educational forces in Canada. It distributes over 6,000 films and videos on the sciences and the visual and performing arts through the Canadian Film Institute Film Library. *Publications: The Guide to Film, Television, and Communications Studies in Canada 1989-* (bilingual); *Canadian Film* series (monographs); *Northern Lights* (programmer's guide to the Festival of Festivals Retrospective); *Switching on to the Environment* (critical guide).

Canadian Library Association. 200 Elgin St., Suite 602, Ottawa, ON K2P IL5, Canada. Marnie Swanson, Pres.; Margaret Andrews, Pres.-Elect (officers change July 1992); Karen Adams, Exec. Dir.

Canadian Museums Association/Association des musées canadiens (CMA/AMC). 280 Metcalfe St., Suite 400, Ottawa, ON K2P 1R7, Canada. (613) 233-5653. Fax (613) 233-5438. John G. McAvity, Exec. Dir. Seeks to advance public museum service in Canada. *Membership:* 2,000. *Publications: Museogramme* (mo. newsletter); *Muse* (q. journal); *Directory of Canadian Museums* (listing all museums in Canada plus information on government departments, agencies, and provincial and regional museum associations). CMA offers a correspondence course that serves as an introduction to museum operations and philosophy through selected readings.

*National Film Board of Canada (NFBC). 1251 Ave. of the Americas, New York, NY 10020. (212) 586-5131. John Sirabella, Nontheatrical Rep. Established in 1939, the NFBC's main objective is to produce and distribute high-quality audiovisual materials for educational, cultural, and social purposes. *Publication: U.S. Film Resource Guide.*

Ontario Film Association, Inc. 3-1750 The Queensway, Suite 1341, Etobicoke, ON M9C 5H5, Canada. A nonprofit organization whose primary objective is to promote the sharing of ideas and information about film and video through seminars, workshops, screenings, and publications. Sponsors the annual Grierson Documentary Seminar on film and video subjects and the Annual Showcase of film and video, a marketplace for buyers. *Publication: Visual Media/Visuels Miedias.*

Part Seven
Graduate Programs

Doctoral Programs in
Instructional Technology

This directory presents information on 62 doctoral (Ph.D. and Ed.D.) programs in instructional technology, educational communications/technology, media services, and closely allied programs throughout the United States and the District of Columbia. Information in this section was obtained from, and updated by, the institutional deans, chairpersons, or their representatives, in response to an inquiry-questionnaire mailed to them during the fall of 1991. Updated information was requested with the proviso that, if no reply was received, the information from the 1991 edition would be used to insure that the program would be represented in the listing. Programs for which no response was received are indicated by an asterisk.

Entries provide the following data: (1) name and address of the institution; (2) chairperson or other individual in charge of the doctoral program; (3) types of degrees offered and specializations, including information on positions for which candidates are prepared; (4) special features of the degree program; (5) admission requirements, including minimal grade point average; (6) number of faculty; (7) number of full-time and part-time students participating in the program; (8) details of available financial assistance; (9) doctoral program trends; and (10) the total number of men (m), total number of women (w), and the number of foreign nationals who graduated with doctorates during the one-year period between 1 July 1990 and 30 June 1991.

Directors of advanced professional programs for instructional technology/media specialists should find this information useful as a means of comparing their own offerings and requirements with those of institutions offering comparable programs. This listing should also assist individuals seeking a school at which to pursue advanced graduate studies in locating institutions that best suit their interests and requirements.

Additional information on the programs listed, including instructions on applying for admission, may be obtained by contacting individual program coordinators. General or graduate catalogs usually are furnished for a minimal charge; specific program information normally is sent at no charge.

In endeavoring to provide complete listings, we are greatly indebted to those individuals who responded to our requests for information. We are also indebted to Mark Bugler of the University of Iowa, who shared with us the results of his recent survey of doctoral programs in the United States.

Although considerable effort has been expended to ensure completeness of the listings, there may be institutions within the United States or its territories that now have programs or that have been omitted. Readers are encouraged to furnish new information to the publisher who, in turn, will follow up for the next edition of *EMTY*.

Institutions in this section are listed alphabetically by state.

ALABAMA

University of Alabama. School of Library and Information Services, Tuscaloosa, AL 35487. (205) 348-4610. Fax (205) 348-3746. J. Gordon Coleman, Jr., Coord., Doctoral Program, School of Library and Information Services. *Specialization:* Ph.D. in Library and Information Science with specializations in school library media, youth services, library management, information studies, and historical studies. *Features:* Program is designed to fit the needs of the student using the resources of the entire university. Students may prepare for careers in teaching and research in colleges and universities or for innovative practice in the profession. *Admission Requirements:* Master's in library science, instructional technology, or equivalent, Miller Analogy score of 55 or GRE score of 1,650, 3.5 graduate QPA, three letters of recommendation, writing sample, curriculum vitae, and statement of purpose. *Faculty:* 10 full-time; 1 part-time. *Students:* 7 full-time; 9 part-time. *Assistance:* Six 20-hour assistantships paying $622/ month with all tuition waived (in-state and out-of-state); some scholarships. *Doctoral Program Trends*: Doctoral program initiated in August 1988. *Doctorates Awarded 1990-91:* 0 (relatively new program).

ARIZONA

*Arizona State University. College of Education, Tempe, AZ 85287-0611. (602) 965-7485. Fax (602) 965-9144. Howard Sullivan, Prof., Div. of Psychology in Education, College of Education. *Specialization:* School offers program of study leading to the Ph.D. degree in educational technology. Primary content focus is on instructional design and development, with strong research emphasis. Students may complement this focus with concentrated work in such areas as instructional media, computer-based education, training, etc. Preparation is for work as university faculty and instructional designers and trainers in business, industry, the military, and higher education. *Features:* Instructional development internships in higher education or in business, industry, and the military. *Admission Requirements:* Three months prior to enrollment: all university application forms, two transcripts from each institution in which previous academic work has been completed, three letters of reference, a score report for either the Miller Analogies Test (65 or higher) or the GRE (1,200 or higher verbal plus quantitative), statement of professional goals, and undergraduate GPA of 3.0 or better. *Faculty:* 3 full-time. *Students:* 12 full-time; 12 part-time. *Assistance:* Graduate assistantships $2,750-10,000 per academic year; summer assistantship opportunities; fellowships; scholarships; loans administered through the university financial aid office. *Doctoral Program Trends:* More than half of program graduates obtain university positions. *Doctorates Awarded 1989-90:* 2w.

CALIFORNIA

United States International University. School of Education, San Diego, CA 92131. (619) 693-4595. *Specializations:* The Ed.D. Program is designed to attract students interested in a variety of emphases: computer literacy, teaching with or about computers, computer program coordination, instructional systems development, distance education, and microcomputer management. Prepares individuals to serve in a variety of positions: school district coordinators for instructional computing, specialists in designing learning strategies and training programs, university directors of learning resources, and change agents in industry and the military having teaching or training as a primary concern. *Features:* Program involves required core courses in human behavior and futuristics; concentration courses in leadership, cognitive theory, global education, statistics; and elective specialization courses including computer literacy, problem solving, microcomputer programming, microcomputer applications, issues in computer education, curriculum theory and design, and instructional systems development. The development of independent microcomputer use skills is emphasized. *Admission Requirements:* Admission to graduate program recommended by committee of faculty to the Dean of the School of Education. Evaluation of GRE or MAT test score, candidate's vita, three letters of recommendation, statement of purpose for study, and final committee interview. *Faculty:* 15 full-time; 5 part-time. *Students:* 40 full-time; 10 part-time. *Assistance:* A limited number of graduate assistantships offered in conjunction with research and development work undertaken at the university. *Doctoral Program Trends:* Increasing enrollment of international students from Taiwan interested in infusing computer technology into Taiwanese public schools. *Doctorates Awarded 1987-88:* 4m, 4w, including 4 foreign nationals.

University of California at Berkeley. School of Library and Information Studies, Berkeley, CA 94720. Robert Harlan, Prof., Coord., School of Library and Information Studies. *Specialization:* School offers the Ph.D. degree in library and information studies. *Features:* Ph.D. requires original piece of research revealing high critical ability and powers of imagination and synthesis. The program stresses the need for familiarity with information processing technology, educational technology, database management systems, etc. *Admission Requirements:* Contingent upon admission to graduate standing, including graduation from an accredited master's degree program with at least a B average. *Faculty:* 12 full-time. *Students:* Approximately 34. *Assistance:* Scholarships, fellowships, assistantships (research and teaching), and readerships. *Doctoral Program Trends:* Cognitive science now a Ph.D. subfield. *Doctorates Awarded 1990-91:* 2m, 0w.

University of California at Los Angeles. Department of Education, Los Angeles, CA 90024-1521. (310) 825-6608. Fax (310) 206-6293. Aimee Dorr, Prof. of Education, Learning and Instruction Specialization, Div. of Educational Psychology, Dept. of Education. *Specializations:* Offers Ph.D. and Ed.D. programs. Ph.D. program prepares graduates for research, teaching educational technology, and consultancies in the development of instructional materials. Ed.D. program prepares graduates for leadership roles in the development of instructional materials and educational technologies. *Features:* The program addresses the design and utilization principles and processes underlying all effective applications of instructional technologies and their products. Television, microcomputer-based, and multimedia systems are encouraged. *Admission Requirements:* Superior academic record, combined GRE score of 1,000 or better. For the Ed.D. program, two or more years of relevant field experience is desirable. *Faculty:* 8 faculty participate in learning and instruction, of whom 2 teach full-time in instructional technology and the remaining 6 (all with full-time academic appointments) teach part-time in instructional technology and part-time in other areas in the department. *Students:* 10 full-time. *Assistance:* Includes fellowships, tuition remission, and some paid research and teaching assistantships. *Doctoral Program Trends:* Doctoral applications from high-quality students have increased in recent years, and more students are interested in the instructional uses of computers and multimedia. *Doctorates Awarded 1990-91:* 0.

University of Southern California. School of Education, Los Angeles, CA 90089-0031. (213) 740-3476. Fax (213) 946-8142. Edward J. Kazlauskas, Assoc. Prof., Prog. Chair., Instructional Technology. *Specializations:* M.A., Ph.D., Ed.D. to prepare individuals to teach instructional technology; manage educational media/training programs in business or industry, research and development organizations, and higher educational institutions; perform research in instructional technology and media; and deal with computer-driven technology. *Features:* Special emphasis upon instructional design, systems analysis, and computer-based training. *Admission Requirements:* A bachelor's degree and satisfactory performance (combined score of 1,000) on the GRE aptitude test. *Faculty:* 5 cooperative faculty with joint appointments. *Students:* 10 full-time; 20 part-time. *Assistance:* Part-time work available (instructional technology-related) in the Los Angeles area and on the university campus. *Doctoral Program Trends:* Enrollments of students seeking position placements in business/industry, instructional design/development, media production, and computer education.

COLORADO

University of Colorado at Denver. School of Education, Campus Box 106, P.O. Box 173364, Denver, CO 80217-3364. (303) 556-4881. Fax (303) 556-4822. David H. Jonassen, Prof., Chair. of Instructional Technology Program, School of Education. *Specializations:* Ph.D. in instructional technology, in instructional development, and/or instructional computing for use in business/industry and higher education. *Features:* Courses in management and consulting, emphasizing instructional development, interactive video technologies, evaluation, and internship opportunities in a variety of agencies. *Admission Requirements:* Satisfactory GPA, GRE, writing/publication background, letters of recommendation, transcripts, and application form. *Faculty:* 5½ full-time; 4 part-time. *Students:* 12 part-time; 3 full-time. *Assistance:* Corporate internships are available. *Doctoral Program Trends:* Research on emerging technologies (hypermedia, expert systems, networking, and mapping strategies), development of constructivist instructional design models and evaluation methods, use of computer-based cognitive tools for learning. *Doctorates Awarded 1989-90:* 0 (relatively new program).

University of Northern Colorado. College of Education, Greeley, CO 80639. (303) 351-2687. Fax (303) 351-2377. Edward P. Caffarella, Prof., Chair, Educational Technology, College of Education. *Specializations:* Ph.D. in Educational Technology with emphasis areas in instructional development/design, interactive technology, and technology integration. *Features:* Graduates are prepared for careers as instructional technologists, course designers, trainers, instructional developers, media specialists, and human resource managers. *Admission Requirements:* GPA of 3.2, three letters of recommendation, congruency between applicant's statement of career goals and program goals, GRE combined test score of 1,650, and interview with faculty. *Faculty:* 6 full-time; 2 part-time. *Students:* 28 doctoral, 48 M.A., 15 graduate certification. *Assistance:* A limited number of Colorado Fellowships are available for full-time incoming students; graduate and teaching assistantships are available for full-time students. *Doctorates Awarded 1990-91:* 1m, 2w.

CONNECTICUT

University of Connecticut. Storrs, CT 06269-2001. (203) 486-2530. Fax 486-1766. Phillip Sleeman, Dir., University Center for Instructional Media and Technology, and Prof. of Education. *Specializations:* Ph.D. degree program involving advanced instructional media and technology to prepare individuals for instructional technology positions of major responsibility in universities, colleges, community colleges, large school systems, state departments of education, government, industry, and other educational and media organizations of national scope. *Features:* The program seeks an optimum mix of competencies involved in solving instructional media and technology problems, with competencies in several fields of professional education (psychological foundations, social foundations, research and evaluation, business administration, curriculum and supervision, instructional media and technology, interactive video, computers, videodiscs, teleconferencing, computer graphics, and data processing). *Admission Requirements:* Admission to graduate school; undergraduate GPA above 3.0; filing of Miller Analogies Test; evidence of scholarly attainments, interests, and potential for growth; strength and validity of career motive;

previous significant experience in the instructional media field; and at least five years of highly successful teaching experience (of which one or more years of administrative or supervisory experience would be desirable). *Faculty:* 2 full-time; 4 part-time. *Students:* Data not available. *Assistance:* A number of graduate assistantships, predoctoral fellowships, research fellowships, and federal and minority fellowships available competitively. *Doctoral Program Trends:* Interactive video, teleconferencing, advanced learning theory, computer graphics, videodisc, and research. *Doctorates Awarded 1990-91:* 2m, 2w.

FLORIDA

*Florida State University. College of Education, Tallahassee, FL 32306. (904) 644-8789. Fax (904) 644-8776. Walter Wager, Prof. and Program Leader, Instructional Systems Program, Department of Educational Research, College of Education. *Specializations:* Ph.D. in instructional systems with specializations for persons planning to work in academia, business, industry, government, or the military. *Features:* Core courses include systems and materials development, analysis of media, project management, psychological foundations, current trends in instructional design, and research and statistics. Internships are also required. *Admission Requirements:* Total score of 1,000 on the verbal and quantitative sections of the GRE, or a GPA of 3.0 for the last two years of undergraduate study, 3.3 GPA graduate. International students must provide TOEFL scores. *Faculty:* 10. *Assistance:* University and college fellowships; grant- and contract-funded assistantships. *Doctoral Program Trends:* Increased enrollments of students interested in position placements in business and industry. *Doctorates Awarded 1990-91:* 7m, 8w, including 4 foreign nationals.

Nova University. Center for Computer and Information Sciences, 3301 College Ave., Fort Lauderdale, FL 33314. (800) 541-6682, ext. 1984; (305) 475-7563. Fax (305) 476-1982. Dr. Edward Simco, Dean, Center for Computer and Information Sciences. *Specializations:* Sc.D. in the areas of Information Systems, Information Science, and Training and Learning; Ed.D. in Computer Education. *Features:* Minimal residency requirements; three-year program; course requirements are completed using online interaction, institutes, regional symposia, audiobridge, videotapes, and ECRs (Electronic Classroom Sessions). Current students are located throughout the country and the world. *Admission Requirements:* Master's degree from an accredited university, appropriate work experience and related credentials, and demonstrated computer literacy. *Faculty:* 10 full-time. *Students:* Full-time in each of the following programs: Computer Education, 116; Training and Learning, 30; Information Systems, 115; Information Science, 29; total 290. *Assistance:* Guaranteed student loan program. *Doctoral Program Trends:* This program continues to expand rapidly. *Doctorates Awarded 1990-91:* 12m, 5w.

University of Florida. College of Education, Gainesville, FL 32611. (904) 392-0705, ext. 600. Fax (904) 392-7159. Lee Mullally, Assoc. Prof., Chair., Educational Media and Instructional Design Program, College of Education. *Specializations:* Ph.D. and Ed.D. programs that stress theory, research, training, teaching, evaluation, and instructional development. *Admission Requirements:* A composite score of at least 1,100 on the GRE, an undergraduate GPA of 3.0 minimum and a graduate GPA of 3.5 minimum, and three letters of recommendation. *Faculty:* 2 full-time. *Students:* 4 full-time; 9 part-time. *Assistance:* 2 graduate assistantships. *Doctoral Program Trends:* Increasing enrollments of students interested in position placements in business/industry, instructional design/development, and computer education and public school emphases, i.e., district-wide positions and D.O.E. positions. *Doctorates Awarded 1990-91:* 3.

GEORGIA

Georgia State University. University Plaza, Atlanta, GA 30303. (404) 651-2510. Fax (404) 651-2546. Francis Atkinson, Coord., Dept. of Curriculum and Instruction. *Specializations:* Ph.D. in instructional technology, development, media management in schools, special libraries, or business. *Admission Requirements:* Three letters of recommendation, handwritten and autobiographical sketch, admission tests, and acceptance by department. *Faculty:* 3.5 full-time equivalent. *Students:* 18 full- and part-time. *Assistance:* Graduate research assistantships. *Doctoral Program Trends:* Budget has remained about the same; facilities, including space, hardware, and software, have been upgraded while faculty and staff have decreased slightly. *Doctorates Awarded 1988-89:* 0.

University of Georgia. College of Education, 607 Aderhold Hall, Athens, GA 30602. (404) 542-3810. Fax (404) 542-2321. Murray H. Tillman, Chair, Dept. of Instructional Technology. *Specializations:* M.Ed., Ed.S., and Ed.D. for leadership positions as specialists in instructional design and development. The program offers advanced study for individuals with previous preparation in instructional media and technology, as well as a preparation for personnel in other professional fields requiring a specialty in instructional systems/instructional technology. Representative career fields for graduates include designing/developing/evaluating new courses, tutorial programs, and instructional materials in a number of different settings; military/industrial training; medical/dental/nursing professional schools; allied health agencies; teacher education/staff development centers; state/local school systems; higher education/teaching/research; and publishers/producers of instructional products (textbooks, workbooks, films, etc.). *Features:* Minor areas of study available in a variety of other departments. Personalized programs are planned around a common core of courses; practica, internships, and/or clinical experiences. Research activities include special assignments, applied projects, and task forces, as well as thesis and dissertation studies. *Admission Requirements:* Application to graduate school, satisfactory GRE score, other criteria as outlined in Graduate School Bulletin. *Faculty:* 10 full-time. *Students:* 21 full-time. *Assistance:* Graduate assistantships available. Doctoral Program Trends: Increasing enrollments of students interested in placements in business/industry. *Doctorates Awarded 1990-91:* 1m, 3w.

ILLINOIS

Northern Illinois University. College of Education, DeKalb, IL 60115. (815) 753-0464. Fax (815) 753-2100. Dr. Gary L. McConeghy, Chair, Instructional Technology, College of Education—LEPS. *Specializations:* Ed.D. in instructional technology, emphasizing instructional design and development, computer education, media administration, production, and preparation for careers in business, industry, and higher education. *Features:* Considerable flexibility in course selection, including advanced seminars, internships, individual study, and research. Program is highly individualized. A total of 60 courses offered by several departments, including Library Science, Radio/Television/Film, Art, Journalism, Educational Psychology, and Research and Evaluation. *Admission Requirements:* 2.75 undergraduate GPA, 3.5 M.S. GPA; combined score of 1,000 on GRE; a writing sample; and three references. *Faculty:* 6 full-time, with courses in other departments taught by several members of the graduate faculty; 3 part-time. *Students:* 65 part-time. *Assistance:* 9 assistantships available involving laboratory supervision, instruction, and instructional development activities on and off campus. Some additional fellowships and grants possible, especially for minority students. *Doctoral Program Trends:* Increasing enrollments of students interested in positions in business/industry, health, instructional design/development, and computer education. *Doctorates Awarded 1990-91:* 2.

Southern Illinois University. College of Education, Carbondale, IL 62901. (618) 536-2441. Fax (618) 453-1646. Billy G. Dixon, Prof., Chair, Dept. of Curriculum and Instruction, College of Education. *Specializations:* Ph.D. and M.S. in education with specialty areas in instructional technology, instructional development, computer-based education, and school library media. *Features:* All specializations are oriented to multiple education settings. *Admission Requirements:* M.S., 2.7 GPA or better; Ph.D., 3.25 GPA or better; MAT or GRE score; letters of recommendation; and writing sample. *Faculty:* 5 full-time; 5 part-time. *Students:* Approximately 140 current graduate students in these specialty areas. *Assistance:* Six graduate scholarships available plus university fellowship program. *Doctoral Program Trends:* Graduate student enrollment has continued to increase. *Doctorates Awarded 1989-90:* 4m, 3w.

*Southern Illinois University. School of Education, Edwardsville, IL 62026. (618) 692-3277. Fax (618) 692-3359. Orville Joyner, Prof., Chair., Dept. of Educational Leadership. School of Education. *Specializations:* Ed.D. (all-school degree) in instructional processes emphasizing theory and research, teaching, evaluation, and instructional systems design and development. *Admission Requirements:* GRE, undergraduate GPA of B+. *Faculty:* 6 full-time; 1 part-time. *Students:* 4 full-time; 10 part-time. *Assistance:* 4 graduate assistantships, 2 fellowships. *Doctoral Program Trends:* Increasing enrollments of students interested in position placements in business/industry, health, government, instructional design/development, and computer education. *Doctorates Awarded 1989-90:* 5m, including 1 foreign national.

University of Illinois at Urbana-Champaign. College of Education, Champaign, IL 61820. (217) 244-3391. Fax (217) 244-4572. J. Richard Dennis, Assoc. Prof., Dept. of Curriculum and Instruction. College of Education. *Specializations:* Ph.D., Ed.D. programs (including advanced certificate program) with emphasis in the following areas: preparation of university research faculty, materials/training designers, computer resources managers, and continuing professional teacher training. *Features:* Programs designed to accommodate individuals with diverse background preparations. *Admission Requirements:* Master's degree, 4.0 out of 5.0 GPA, GRE at least 50 percentile in two of Verbal, Quantitative, and Analytic; a sample of scholarly writing in English; TOEFL scores, including scores on Test of Written English for non-English-speaking students. *Faculty:* 8 full-time. *Students:* 60 full-time and part-time, including 20 foreign nationals. *Assistance:* Limited fellowships available; some assistantships; non-English applicants for assistantships must also submit TOEFL Test of Spoken English scores; tuition waiver support available for highly qualified applicants. *Doctoral Program Trends:* Increasing emphasis on application of artificial intelligence, the design of intelligence tutoring systems, telecommunications, and interactive multimedia. *Doctorates Awarded 1990-91:* 4m, 1w, including 2 foreign nationals.

University of Illinois at Urbana-Champaign. Department of Educational Psychology, 220 A Ed., 1310 S. 6th St., Champaign, IL 61820. Charles K. West, Prof., Div. of Learning and Instruction, Dept. of Educational Psychology. *Specialization:* Ph.D. in educational psychology with emphasis in educational computing. *Features:* Individually tailored program. Strongly research-oriented with emphasis on applications of cognitive science to instruction. *Admission Requirements:* Flexible: good academic record, high GRE scores, and strong letters of recommendation. *Faculty:* 17. *Students:* 1991-92, 29 enrolled. *Assistance:* Scholarships, research assistantships, and teaching assistantships available. *Doctoral Program Trends:* Data not available. *Doctorates Awarded 1990-91:* 3.

INDIANA

Indiana University. School of Education, Bloomington, IN 47405. (812) 855-1791. Fax (812) 855-3044. Charles Reigeluth, Prof., Chair., Dept. of Instructional Systems Technology, School of Education. *Specializations:* Ph.D. and Ed.D. *Features:* Three major emphasis areas—instructional design and development, message design and production, and organizational change. Students draw on all areas when planning their academic programs. Virtually all students are full-time residents. Many opportunities for students to combine practice with study by working in the AV center and other appropriate agencies on and off campus. *Admission Requirements:* Satisfactory GPA, verbal, quantitative, and analytical sections of the GRE. *Faculty:* 10 full-time equivalent. *Students:* Approximately 100 doctoral students, 83 master's students. *Assistance:* Graduate assistantships, associate instructorships, fellowships, scholarships, and fee remissions. *Doctoral Program Trends:* Increasing enrollments of students interested in position placements in business/industry, instructional design/development, and computer education. *Doctorates Awarded 1988-89:* 5m, 3w, including 3 foreign nationals.

Purdue University. School of Education, West Lafayette, IN 47907. (317) 494-5669. Fax (317) 494-0587. James D. Russell, Prof. of Educational Computing and Instructional Development, Dept. of Curriculum and Instruction. *Specialization:* Ph.D. programs to prepare individuals to direct instructional development in school districts, health, business, government, and industry. *Admission Requirements:* GPA of 3.0 or better, three recommendations, scores of at least 1,000 on the GRE, statement by the applicant concerning his or her proposed goals and time schedule, and acceptance by the Department of Curriculum and Instruction. *Faculty:* 6 full-time. *Students:* 16 full-time. *Assistance:* Graduate teaching assistantships and graduate laboratory assistantships. *Doctoral Program Trends:* Increasing enrollments of students interested in position placements in business/industry, health, instructional design/development, and computer education. *Doctorates Awarded 1990-91:* 4m, 4w.

IOWA

Iowa State University. College of Education, Ames, IA 50011. (515) 294-6840. Fax (515) 294-9284. Michael Simonson, Prof., Curriculum and Instruction, College of Education. *Specializations:* Master's or Ph.D. in education with an emphasis on media, computers, curriculum and instruction for public school and private corporate training, college and university supervision of media use, operation of an instructional materials center, and instructional development; higher education research and teaching, and teacher education programs; and positions in business, industry, or public and private agencies concerned with communications and teaching processes. *Features:* Practicum experiences related to professional objectives, supervised study and research projects tied to long-term studies within the program, development and implementation of new techniques, teaching strategies, and operational procedures in instructional resources centers and four computer labs. *Admission Requirements:* Admission to graduate school, GRE, top half of undergraduate class. *Faculty:* 5 full-time. *Students:* 20 full-time; 20 part-time. *Assistance:* Graduate assistantships. *Doctoral Program Trends:* Increasing enrollments of students interested in industry positions. *Doctorates Awarded: 1990-91:* 2m, 3w.

University of Iowa. College of Education, Iowa City, IA 52242. (319) 335-5577. Fax (319) 335-5386. Leonard S. Feldt, Prof., Psychological and Quantitative Foundations, College of Education. *Specializations:* Computer applications, instructional development, training and human resource development. *Features:* Flexibility in planning to fit individual needs, backgrounds, and career goals. The program is interdisciplinary, involving courses within divisions of the College of Education, as well as in the schools of Business, Library Science, Radio and Television, Linguistics, and Psychology. *Admission Requirements:* A composite score of at least 1,000 on GRE (verbal and quantitative) and a 3.2 GPA on all previous graduate work for regular admission. (Conditional admission may be granted.) Teaching or relevant experience may be helpful. *Faculty:* 4 full-time; 3 part-time. *Students:* 40 full-time and part-time. *Assistance:* Special assistantships (in the College of Education) for which students in any College of Education program may compete. Application deadlines for the special assistantships is 1 February. *Doctoral Program Trends:* Increasing enrollments of students interested in position placements in business/industry, instructional design/development, and computer education. *Doctorates Awarded: 1990-91:* 2m, 4w.

KANSAS

*Kansas State University. College of Education, Manhattan, KS 66506-5301. (913) 532-5556. Fax (913) 532-7304. Jackson Byars, Prof., Dept. of Educational Media and Technology, College of Education. *Specializations:* Ph.D. and Ed.D. programs. *Admission Requirements*: Offered on a semester basis and require 90 credit hours, including 60 in media and technology, one year of residency, and a dissertation. *Students:* 26. *Faculty:* 4, 0, 6. *Program Trends:* Increasing enrollments of students interested in position placements in business/industry, health, college teaching, instructional design/development, and computer education. *Doctorates Awarded 1987-88:* 4m, 4w.

*University of Kansas. Instructional Technology Center, Lawrence, KS 66045. (913) 864-3057. Ronald Aust, Asst. Prof., Curriculum and Instruction, Dir., Instructional Technology Center. *Specializations:* Ph.D., Ed.D. and Ed.S., and M.S. to prepare instructional technologists to serve in leadership roles in a variety of educational settings. Emphasis is on the use of research-based data to guide decision making in the various roles required of instructional technologists. Special attention is given to the principles of and procedures for designing instruction with computers, video, interactive video, and distance-learning applications. *Features:* The Instructional Technology Center provides a laboratory setting to assist in research projects and in the acquisition of production, instructional development, and media management skills. The department's microcomputer laboratories provide access to current equipment and software. Students are encouraged to work with faculty on appropriate projects. In addition to a common core, flexibility is built into the program so students may pursue their own interests. *Admission Requirements:* Regular admission, 3.5 GPA and 900 GRE; Provisional, 3.25 GPA and 900 GRE or 3.5 GPA with less than 900 GRE. *Faculty:* 3. *Students:* 5 full-time; 12 part-time. *Assistance:* 4 graduate teaching assistantships (apply by 1 March). *Doctoral Program Trends:* Increasing enrollment of students interested in position placements in college teaching, in business and industry training, and in computer education. *Doctorates Awarded 1988-89:* 2m, 1w.

KENTUCKY

*University of Kentucky. College of Education, Lexington, KY 40506. (606) 257-4661. Gary Anglin, Assoc. Prof., Dept. of Curriculum and Instruction, College of Education. *Specializations:* Ed.D. program emphasizing instructional design/instructional technology, research, and teaching. *Features:* Data not available. *Admission Requirements:* A minimum composite score (verbal and quantitative) of 1,000 on the GRE, minimum undergraduate GPA of 2.5, minimum graduate GPA of 3.4. Concurrent applications to the graduate school and department are required, including letters of recommendation. *Faculty:* 2 full-time. *Students:* 12. *Assistance:* A limited number of teaching associateships and research assistantships are awarded on a competitive basis. Applicants for available minority fellowships are encouraged. Financial assistance package includes tuition remission. *Doctoral Program Trends:* Increasing enrollments of students interested in positions in business/industry, college teaching, instructional design/development, and computer education. *Doctorates Awarded 1988-89:* 0.

MARYLAND

*The Johns Hopkins University. School of Continuing Studies, Baltimore, MD 21218. (301) 338-8273. Fax (301) 338-8424. Diane Tobin, Coord., Div. of Education, School of Continuing Studies. *Specializations:* Ed.D. in human communications and its disorders—a dual-major degree in technology and one of the following areas: mild-moderate handicapped and severely/profoundly handicapped. The program requires 99 semester hours beyond the baccalaureate, including 12 hours of dissertation research and 27 hours in computers and related rehabilitation educational technology. (A master's level program is also offered.) *Features:* Computer courses, including but not limited to assistive technology, authoring programs and systems, LOGO, interactive videodisc, hardware and adaptive devices, software selection/evaluation, expert systems, robotics, networking, and computerized information and data management in special education. Internships and practicum opportunities in special education and rehabilitation settings. *Admission Requirements:* Master's or doctorate from an accredited institution. *Faculty:* 3 full-time; 12 part-time. *Students:* 30 full-time and part-time. *Doctoral Program Trends:* Emphasis on applications of microcomputers and related technology. *Doctorates Awarded 1989-90:* 1.

*University of Maryland. College of Library and Information Services, College Park, MD 20742. (301) 405-2051. Fax (301) 314-9145. James Liesener, Coord., College of Library and Information Services. *Specialization:* Ph.D. in Library Science and Educational Technology/Instructional Communication. *Features:* Program is broadly conceived and interdisciplinary in nature, using the resources of the entire campus. The student and the advisor design a program of study and research to fit the student's background, interests, and professional objectives. Students prepare for careers in teaching and research in information science and librarianship and elect concentrations including educational technology/instructional communication. *Admission Requirements:* Baccalaureate degree (the majority enter with master's degrees in library science, educational technology, or other relevant disciplines), GRE general tests, three letters of recommendation, and a statement of purpose. Interviews required when feasible. *Faculty:* 15½ with doctorates and 16 part-time. *Students:* 22 full-time. *Assistance:* Some fellowships starting at $8,800, with remission of tuition; some assistantships also available. *Doctorates Awarded 1988-89:* 3.

MASSACHUSETTS

*Boston University. School of Education, Boston, MA 02215. (617) 353-3519. Fax (617) 353-3924. Gaylen B. Kelley, Prof., Chair, Program in Educational Media and Technology, School of Education. *Specializations:* Ed.D. for developing and teaching academic programs in instructional technology in community colleges and universities; or specialization in such application areas as business and industrial training, biomedical communication, or international development projects. Program specializations in instructional development, media production and design, and instructional facilities design for media and technology. Students participate in mandatory research sequence and may elect courses in other university schools and colleges. *Features:* Doctoral students have a great deal of flexibility in program planning and are encouraged to plan programs that build on prior education and experience that lead to specific career goals; there is strong faculty participation in this process. *Admission Requirements:* Three letters of recommendation, Miller Analogies Test score, copies of undergraduate and graduate transcripts, complete application form with statement of goals, and a personal interview with the department chair (may be waived). Minimum GPA is 2.7 with Miller Analogy Score of 50. *Faculty:* 3 full-time; 13 part-time. *Students:* 10 full-time; 57 part-time. *Assistance:* A number of assistantships and part-time instructor positions. *Doctoral Program Trends:* Increasing enrollments of students interested in position placements in business/industry, health, government, program administration, instructional design/development, media production, and computer education. *Doctorates Awarded 1989-90:* 4m, 2w, including 2 foreign nationals.

MICHIGAN

*Michigan State University. College of Education, East Lansing, MI 48824. (517) 355-8538. Fax (517) 354-6393. Leighton A. Price, Prof., Coord. of the Educational Systems Development Program in the Department of Counseling, Educational Psychology and Special Education. *Program Basis:* Quarter. *Specializations:* Ph.D. and Ed.D. to prepare individuals to improve the quality and effectiveness of instructional delivery systems, to improve learning at all educational and training levels, and to serve as instructional developers and highly qualified training personnel. Emphasis is given to systems design and analysis, to selection and evaluation of instructional computing and other educational technologies, to design and validation of instructional materials, and to research on attributes of teaching strategies and supporting technologies. *Features:* Individually designed doctoral programs, guided field experience in instructional design projects, and cognitive work in areas such as communication, higher education, or instructional resource management. *Admission Requirements:* Master's degree with an acceptable academic record, transcripts, teaching credentials (preferred), three letters of recommendation, acceptable verbal and quantitative GRE scores, statement describing professional goals and ways that the doctoral program may contribute to their achievement, and a personal interview. *Faculty:* 9 full-time; 1 part-time. *Students:* 15 Ph.D. candidates. *Assistance:* Some fellowship and graduate assistantship opportunities in instructional development and technology are available for qualified applicants. *Trends:* The program is responding to rapid developments in the field of educational technology. *Doctorates Awarded 1987-88:* 2m, 1w, including 1 foreign national.

*University of Michigan. Department of Educational Studies, Ann Arbor, MI 48109-1259. (313) 747-0612. Fax (313) 763-1229. Patricia Baggett, Assoc. Prof., Chair., Computers and Education. *Programs:* M.A., Ed.D. and joint M.A. and Ph.D. with the Computer Science Department. *Minimum Degree Requirements:* 30 credit hours for master's, 60 for doctorate. *Faculty:* 2 full-time; several partial appointments. *Graduate students:* approximately 15.

Wayne State University. College of Education, Detroit, MI 48202. (313) 577-1728. Fax (313) 577-3606. Rita C. Richey, Prof., Program Coord., Instructional Technology Programs, Div. of Administrative and Organizational Studies, College of Education. *Specializations:* Ed.D. and Ph.D. programs to prepare individuals for leadership in business, industry, health care, and the K-12 school setting as instructional development specialists; media or learning resources managers or consultants; specialists in instructional video, and computer-assisted specialists. *Features:* Guided field experience and participation in instructional development activities in business and industry. *Admission Requirements:* Master's, GPA of 3.5, GRE, and Miller Analogy Test, strong professional recommendations, and an interview. *Faculty:* 3 full-time; 5 part-time. *Students:* 135

full-time and part-time. *Assistance:* Contract industrial internships, university scholarships. *Doctoral Program Trends:* Increased enrollments of students seeking position placements in college teaching, instructional design/development, and computer education. *Doctorates Awarded 1990-91:* 6m, 9w.

MINNESOTA

University of Minnesota. College of Education, Minneapolis, MN 55455. (612) 624-2034. Fax (612) 626-7496. Gregory C. Sales, Assoc. Prof., Curriculum and Instructional Systems, College of Education. *Specializations:* M.A. and Ph.D. in education are offered through the graduate school. Areas of study include instructional design and technology, computer-based instruction, and curriculum systems and instruction research. *Features:* Internships and special field experiences. *Admission Requirements:* General requirements for admission. *Faculty:* 4 full-time; 4 associate. *Students:* 115 full- and part-time. *Assistance:* Teaching fellowships, research, project assistantships, and internships are available on a limited basis. *Doctoral Program Trends:* Increasing enrollments of students interested in position placements in college teaching, business/industry, instructional design/development, and computer education. *Doctorates Awarded 1990-91:* 3w.

MISSOURI

*University of Missouri-Columbia. College of Education, Columbia, MO 65211. (314) 882-3832. Fax (314) 882-5071. John F. Wedman, Assoc. Prof., Educational Technology Program, Curriculum and Instruction Dept., College of Education. *Specializations:* Ph.D. and Ed.D. programs to prepare individuals for positions in higher education and instructional development positions in both industry and the military. *Features:* Program deals with educational computing, instructional design, and media development. Support areas, such as communications and management, are integrated with educational technology courses to form a degree plan that is both focused and broad-based. An internship experience, in a setting consistent with the career goals of the student, is also included. *Admission Requirements:* Graduate GPA above 3.5 and a combined score of 1,350 or better on the GRE or a graduate GPA of 3.2 and a combined score of 1,500 or better on the GRE. Minimum of two years of appropriate professional experience, letters of recommendation, and statement of purpose. A TOEFL score of 550 or better is required for students whose native language is not English. *Faculty:* 3 full-time; 3 part-time, plus selected faculty in interdisciplinary fields. *Students:* 14 students are currently active in the doctoral program. *Assistance:* Scholarships and fellowships, ranging from $200 to $8,000, available from several sources. Teaching and research assistantships available to qualifed individuals. Special financial support available for minority and foreign national students. *Doctoral Program Trends:* Research and development activities related to distance learning technologies used in various educational settings. *Doctorates Awarded 1989-90:* 2m (foreign nationals).

NEBRASKA

*University of Nebraska. Teachers College, Lincoln, NE 68588-0515. (402) 472-2018. Fax (402) 472-8317. David Brooks, Prof., Coord., Teachers College. *Specializations and Features:* Ph.D. and Ed.D. programs are in administration, curriculum, and instruction with an emphasis in instructional technology (IT). Students in these programs demonstrate competencies for professions in instructional design, research in IT, and training by developing appropriate portfolios. Within the context of a balanced graduate experience in IT, extensive experiences in the use of videodisc technologies are possible. *Admission Requirements:* Admission standards are set by the graduate college. *Faculty:* 3 full-time faculty teach in the IT program; 5 are involved in videodisc design and production. *Assistance:* Scholarship and externally based funding support available. *Doctoral Program Trends:* Program emphasizes design and theory in the area of instructional technology. *Doctorates Awarded 1989-90:* 1.

NEW JERSEY

Rutgers-The State University of New Jersey. The Graduate School, New Brunswick, NJ 08903. (908) 932-7447. Fax (908) 932-6916. Brent D. Ruben, Prof., Dir., Ph.D. Program, School of Communication, Information and Library Studies, The Graduate School. *Specializations:* Ph.D. programs in communication; information and communication in management and organizational processes; information systems, structures and users; information and communication policy and technology; and library and information services. *Features:* Program provides doctoral-level coursework for students seeking theoretical and research skills for scholarly and professional leadership in the information and communication fields. *Admission Requirements:* Typically, students should have completed a master's degree in information studies, communication, library science, or related field. The undergraduate GPA should be 3.0 or better. The GRE is required; TOEFL is also required for foreign applicants whose native language is not English. *Faculty:* 42 full-time. *Students:* 82 full-time and part-time. *Assistance:* Teaching assistantships and Title II-B Fellowships available per year for full-time students. Research assistantships and other work opportunities are also available. *Doctoral Program Trends:* Increasing emphasis on relationship between communication and information and the impact of both on human behavior. *Doctorates Awarded 1990-91:* 2m, 1w.

NEW YORK

*Columbia University, Teachers College, New York, NY 10027. (212) 678-3344. Fax (212) 678-4048. John B. Black, Prof. and Chair. *Specialization:* Ed.D. for individuals seeking careers in instructional technology; programs in instructional technology (in a department that also includes communication and computing in education). *Features:* Part-time employment is available and encouraged as part of the coursework of 90 semester hours (in addition to the dissertation). Programs are individually planned, interdisciplinary, and based on prior and present interests and anticipated future developments in instructional technology. Up to 45 credits of relevant coursework may be transferred. *Admission Requirements:* A record of outstanding capability, potential for leadership and creativity as indicated from academic records, recommendations, score on the GRE, statement of expressed interest and future plans. *Faculty:* 5 full-time; 2 part-time. *Students:* 12 full-time; 32 part-time. *Assistance:* Limited scholarships (applications must be received before 1 January for the following September semester) and work-study financial aid for qualified applicants. *Doctoral Program Trends:* Increasing enrollments of students interested in position placements in business/industry, instructional design/development, and computer education. *Doctorates Awarded 1987-88:* 3w.

*New York University. New York, NY 10003. (212) 998-5177. Donald T. Payne, Assoc. Prof., Dir., Educational Communication and Technology Program. *Specializations:* Preparation of individuals to perform as instructional media designers, developers, and producers in education, business and industry, health and medicine, community services, government, and other fields; to coordinate media communications programs in educational television centers, museums, schools, corporations, health and medicine, and community organizations; to serve as directors and supervisors in audiovisual programs in all settings listed; and to teach in educational communications and instructional technology programs in higher education. *Features:* Emphasizes theoretical foundations, in particular a cognitive perspective of learning and instruction and their implications for designing media-based learning environments; participation in special research and production projects in multi-image, television, microcomputers, and computer-based interactive multimedia systems. *Admission Requirements:* Combined score of 1,000 minimum on GRE, interview related to academic and/or professional preparation and career goals. *Faculty:* 2 full-time; 7 part-time. *Students:* 100. *Assistance:* Some financial aid and work-study programs. *Doctoral Program Trends:* Increasing enrollments of students interested in position placements in business, industry, health, instructional design/development, media production, and computer education. *Doctorates Awarded 1989-90:* 1m, 1w; *Masters of Arts awarded 1989-90:* 1m, 9w.

State University of New York at Buffalo. Graduate School of Education, Buffalo, NY 14214. (716) 636-3164. T. A. Razik, Prof. of Education, Dept. of Educational Organization, Administration and Policy. *Specializations:* Ph.D., Ed.D., and Ed.M. to educate graduate students in the theories, resources, and dynamics of instructional design and management. Emphasis is on the systems approach, communication, and computer-assisted instruction and model building, with a specific focus on the efficient implementation of media in instruction. *Features:* The program is geared to instructional development, systems analysis, systems design and management in educational and noneducational organizations; research is oriented to the analysis of communication and information theory. Laboratories are available to facilitate student and faculty research projects in educational and/or training settings. Specifically, the knowledges and skills are categorized as follows: planning and designing; delivery systems and managing; and evaluating. *Admission Requirements:* Satisfactory scores on the Miller Analogies Test and/or GRE, master's degree or equivalent in field of specialization, and minimum 3.0 GPA. *Faculty:* 3 full-time; 3 part-time. *Students:* 20 full-time; 33 part-time. *Assistance:* 3 graduate assistantships (apply by 10 March). *Doctoral Program Trends:* Increasing enrollments of students interested in position placements in business/industry, health, university teaching, instructional design/development, and computer application. *Doctorates Awarded 1990-91:* 3m, 2w, including 1 foreign national.

Syracuse University. School of Education, Syracuse, NY 13244-2340. (315) 443-3703. Fax (315) 443-5732. Donald P. Ely, Prof., Chair., Instructional Design, Development, and Evaluation Program, School of Education. *Specializations:* Ph.D., Ed.D., and M.S. programs for instructional design of programs and materials, educational evaluation, human issues in instructional development, media production (including computers and videodisc), and educational research and theory (learning theory, application of theory, and educational and media research). Graduates are prepared to serve as curriculum developers, instructional developers, program and product evaluators, researchers, resource center administrators, communications coordinators, trainers in human resource development, and higher education instructors. *Features:* Field work and internships, special topics and special issues seminar, student- and faculty-initiated minicourses, seminars and guest lecturers, faculty-student formulation of department policies, and multiple international perspectives. *Admission Requirements:* A bachelor's degree from an accredited institution. *Faculty:* 5 full-time; 4 part-time. *Students:* 68 full-time; 65 part-time. *Assistance:* Some fellowships (competitive) and graduate assistantships entailing either research or administrative duties in instructional technology. *Doctoral Program Trends:* Increasing enrollments of students interested in position placements in business/industry, program administration, instructional design/development, and computer education. *Doctorates Awarded 1990-91:* 4m, 3w, including 3 foreign nationals.

OHIO

Kent State University. Instructional Technology Program, White Hall 405, Kent, OH 44242. (216) 672-2294. Fax (216) 672-3407. Dr. David Dalton, Program Coordinator. *Program Basis:* Semester. *Tuition per credit:* $117 in-state, $209 out-of-state. *Summer:* Two 5-week sessions. *Specializations:* Ph.D. in Educational Psychology with courses in research methods, new technologies, instructional design, production and evaluation of media programming, change strategies, etc. *Features:* Program encourages students to take elective courses in relevant departments in the College of Education and across the university (for example in communications, psychology, technology, etc.). *Admission Requirements:* Obtain a doctoral program application packet from the Graduate School of Education, White Hall 306. Send two completed copies of the application, a $10 application fee, transcripts, 5 letters of recommendation (at least 2 from previous instructors), score on one of the following: Miller Analogies Test, Terman Concept Mastery Test, or GRE. *Assistance:* Graduate assistantships and teaching assistantships available. *Faculty:* 4. *Graduates:* a few each year.

Ohio State University. College of Education, Columbus, OH 43210. (614) 292-4872. Fax (614) 292-7900. Marjorie Cambre, Assoc. Prof., Contact Person, Instructional Design and Technology Program, College of Education. *Degrees offered:* M.A. and Ph.D. in instructional and interactive technologies, within the program area of Instructional Design and Technology. *Specializations:* Ph.D. in instructional design and technology for preparation of individuals to perform research and to teach in higher education, administer comprehensive media services, or engage in research, production, and development of leadership functions in higher education and related educational agencies. *Features:* Interdisciplinary work in other departments (journalism, communications, radio and television, computer and information science); individual design of doctoral programs according to candidate's background, experience, and goals; and internships provided on campus in business and industry and in schools; integrated school media laboratory, microcomputer, and videodisc laboratories. *Admission Requirements:* Admission to graduate school and specific program area in the College of Education, GRE general test (Ph.D. only), minimum 2.7 GPA, and satisfactory academic and professional recommendations. *Faculty:* Regular faculty—7 full-time and 1 part-time. *Students:* 52 master's; 35 doctoral; 11 international. *Assistance:* Graduate fellowships and scholarships are often available, as well as departmental teaching and research assistantships and assistantship opportunities in media facilities on campus. *Doctoral Program Trends:* Increasing enrollments of students interested in position placements in business/industry, instructional design/development, computer education, and multimedia. *Other:* Quarter credit basis. Tuition per credit: 1 credit Ohio resident, $152; out-of-state, $345; 10 or more credits Ohio resident, $1,213; out-of-state, $3,143.

University of Toledo. College of Education and Allied Professions, Toledo, OH 43606. (419) 537-4266. Fax (419) 537-3853. Amos C. Patterson, Prof., Chair., Dept. of Curriculum and Educational Technology, College of Education and Allied Professions. *Features:* Research and theory in the areas of instructional design, development, evaluation, computers, video, and training and human resources. Emphasis is in the empirical study of systematic processes and procedures in instructional technology, 135 quarter hours beyond the baccalaureate degree or 116 quarter hours beyond the master's degree, including tool skill courses and dissertation credit. Residency requirement of one year or three full-time summer quarters, depending on Ph.D. or Ed.D. option. Option of one or two minor areas of study to be included in total program hours. *Admission*

Requirements: GRE score of 1,000, combined totals, Miller Analogies Test at or above 50th percentile, three letters of recommendation, official transcripts of undergraduate and graduate work, and autobiographical sketch. *Tuition and Fees:* $89.50 per quarter hour. *Faculty:* 8, 5, 1. *Students:* 10 full-time; 21 part-time. *Assistance:* Graduate assistantships require 20 hours of work per week. Basic stipend for assistantships of $5,200 with full tuition remission. *Doctoral Program Trends:* Increasing enrollments of students seeking position placements in business/industry, health, government, college teaching, program administration, instructional design/development, media production, and computer education. *Doctorates Awarded 1990-91:* 5m, 1w, including 1 foreign national.

OKLAHOMA

Oklahoma State University. College of Education, Stillwater, OK 74078. (405) 744-7125. Fax (405) 744-7713. Bruce Petty, Coord., Dept. of Curriculum and Instruction, College of Education. *Specializations:* M.S. and Ed.D. programs in educational technology: microcomputers, media management/administration, materials production, utilization/application, theory and research, selection, college teaching, evaluation, instructional systems design, instructional development, curriculum foundations, and learning theory. *Admission Requirements:* Minimum of 3.0 GPA on undergraduate work (master's), Miller Analogies Test, and minimum of one year teaching experience (doctorate). *Faculty:* 2 full-time; 2 part-time. *Students:* 14 full-time, 18 part-time M.S. candidates; 8 full-time, 12 part-time Ed.D. candidates. *Assistance:* 8 graduate assistantships. *Doctoral Program Trends:* Increasing enrollments of students interested in position placements in business/industry, college teaching, program administration, and instructional design/development. *Doctorates Awarded 1990-91:* 1w.

*University of Oklahoma. College of Education, Norman, OK 73069. (405) 325-5974. Fax (405) 325-3242. Tillman J. Ragan, Prof., Head, Dept. of Educational Psychology, Educational Technology Program Area, College of Education. *Specializations:* Ph.D. and Ed.D. leading to specializations for research, teaching, management, and consulting in instructional technology (including preparation in instructional design and development, computer, video, computer-assisted video instruction and preparation in management of instructional systems and programs). *Features:* Programs are designed through the vehicle of an advisory conference in which the student's background and goals are translated into a program of study and research proficiencies; a practicum is included to provide experiences resembling those related to the individual's career objectives. Computer emphasis area now available. *Admission Requirements:* Evidence of potential for contribution to the field, satisfactory performance on the GRE aptitude test, satisfactory performance on advisory conference in second semester of post-master's work. *Faculty:* 3 full-time; 3 part-time. *Assistance:* Graduate assistantships involving teaching and service or research are available. *Doctoral Program Trends:* Increasing interest in instructional psychology, management and change, interactive multimedia, and instructional design. *Doctorates Awarded 1989-90:* 3m, 2w.

OREGON

*University of Oregon. Division of Teacher Education, Eugene, OR 97401. Judith Grosenick, Assoc. Dean, Division of Teacher Education. *Specializations:* Ph.D. or Ed.D. in Curriculum and Instruction leading to public school, junior college, college, and university supervision of media use and instructional development; higher education research and teaching; and positions in business, industry, and public and private agencies concerned with instructional development, computers in education, product development, and training. *Features:* A flexible program designed to meet a specific student's needs. *Admission Requirements:* Master's degree. *Faculty:* 2 full-time; 4 part-time. *Students:* 87. *Assistance:* Graduate assistantships available in Curriculum and Instruction. *Doctoral Program Trends:* Increasing enrollments of students interested in computers in education and in locating positions in nontraditional learning environments such as business and industry. *Doctorates Awarded 1988-89:* 4m, 2w.

PENNSYLVANIA

Pennsylvania State University. Division of Adult Education and Instructional Systems, University Park, PA 16802. (405) 325-1521. Fax (405) 325-3242, Dept. (405) 325-5974. Kyle L. Peck, Prof. in Charge. *Specializations:* Ph.D. and Ed.D. for individuals seeking professional pursuits in instructional systems design, development, management, evaluation, and research in instructional endeavors within business, industrial, medical, health, religious, higher education, and public school settings. Present research emphases are on instructional development, dissemination, implementation, and management; interactive video; computer-based education; and visual learning. *Features:* A common thread throughout all programs is that candidates have basic competencies in the understanding of human learning; curriculum; instructional design, development, evaluation; and research procedures. Practical experience is available in mediated independent learning, research, instructional development, computer-based education, and dissemination projects. *Admission Requirements:* GRE or MAT and acceptance as a prospective candidate by a graduate faculty member. *Faculty:* 7 full-time. *Students:* 75. *Assistance:* Graduate assistantships in managing mediated independent study courses, operating media facilities, assisting in research projects, and participating in university instructional development projects and computer-based education. *Doctoral Program Trends:* Increasing enrollments of students interested in position placements in business/industry, program administration, instructional design/development, interactive video, and computer education. *Doctorates Awarded 1990-91:* 5m, 2w.

*Temple University. College of Educational Media Program, College of Education, Dept. of Curriculum, Instruction and Technology, Philadelphia, PA 19122. (215) 787-6001. Elton Robertson, Prof., Dept. of Educational Media. *Specializations:* Ed.D. in Curriculum, Instruction, and Technology with emphasis in educational media for proficiency in employing instructional technology to enhance learning and teaching at elementary, secondary, and university levels, as well as in industrial training situations. *Features:* The program is designed to take into account the candidate's personal and professional goals. Practical experience is provided for those wishing to (1) teach media-related courses, (2) apply the newer interactive technology to enhance the instructional development process, and (3) function in various administrative roles in support of learning resource and instructional resource centers. *Admission Requirements:* Bachelor's degree, master's degree, or 24 credits in educational media, admission to the graduate school, media experience, and a satisfactory interview with the faculty. *Faculty:* 2 full-time. *Students:* 3 full-time; 27 part-time. *Assistance:* 4 departmental assistantships, fellowships. *Doctoral Program Trends:* Increasing enrollments of students interested in position placements in business/industry, government, instructional design/development, media production, and computer education. *Doctorates Awarded 1989-90:* 1m, 3w.

University of Pittsburgh. School of Education, Pittsburgh, PA 15260. (412) 612-7254. Fax (412) 648-5911. Barbara Seels, Assoc. Prof., Prog. Coord., Program in Instructional Design and Technology, Dept. of Instruction and Learning, School of Education. *Specializations:* Ed.D. and M.Ed. programs for the preparation of instructional technologists with skills in designing, developing, using, evaluating, and managing processes and resources for learning. Certification option for instructional technologists available. Program prepares people for positions in which they can effect educational change through instructional technology. Program includes three competency areas: instructional design, technological delivery systems, and communications research. *Admissions Requirements:* Submission of written statement of applicant's professional goals, three letters of recommendation, demonstration of English proficiency, satisfactory GPA, sample of professional writing, GRE, and personal interviews. *Faculty:* 3 full-time. *Students:* 20 full-time, 40 part-time, of which approximately 20 are foreign nationals. *Assistance:* Tuition scholarships and assistantships may be available. *Doctoral Program Trends:* Increasing enrollments of students interested in instructional design. *Doctorates Awarded 1990-91:* 4m, 7w, including 2 foreign nationals.

TENNESSEE

Memphis State University. College of Education, Memphis, TN 38152. (901) 678-2365. Fax (901) 678-4778. Thomas Rakes, Prof., Chair, Dept. of Curriculum and Instruction. *Specialization:* Ed.D. offered in instructional design with career emphasis in schools, health care, and business and industry. *Features:* Internship, special projects, and research opportunities. *Admission Requirements:* Master's degree or equivalent and acceptable GRE scores. *Faculty:* 3 full-time; 2 part-time. *Students:* Data not available. *Assistance:* Assistantships. *Doctoral Program Trends:* Applied instructional design research and applied CBI research. *Doctorates Awarded 1990-91:* 2m, 3w.

University of Tennessee. College of Education, Dept. of Curriculum and Instruction, Knoxville, TN 37996-3400. Dr. Al Grant, Coord., Instructional Media and Technology Program. *Media Concentration Areas:* M.S. in Ed. and Ed.S. in the Department of Curriculum and Instruction, concentration in Instructional Media and Technology; Ph.D., College of Education, concentration in Instructional Media and Technology, Ed.D. in Curriculum and Instruction, concentration in Instructional Media and Technology. Coursework in media management, advanced software production, utilization, research, theory, psychology, instructional computing, television, and instructional development. Coursework will also meet the requirements for state certification as Instructional Materials Supervisor in the public schools of Tennessee. *Admission Requirements:* Send for the Graduate Catalog, The University of Tennessee. *Media Faculty:* 1 full-time, with additional assistance from Dept. of Curriculum and Instruction and university faculty. *Program Trends:* Graduate students are seeking professional media positions in medicine/health, corporations, and higher education. *Doctorates Awarded 1989-90:* 0.

TEXAS

*East Texas State University. Dept. of Secondary and Higher Education, Commerce, TX 75429. (903) 886-5504. Fax (903) 886-5039. Ron Johnson, Coord., Dept. of Secondary and Higher Education. *Specializations:* Ed.D. is offered for individuals interested in emphasizing educational technology within the broad areas of supervision, curriculum, and instruction; M.S. with majors in educational technology or library science is offered. Programs are designed to prepare professionals in instructional design, production of instructional materials, and teaching and leadership in public schools and higher education. *Features:* Programs are designed to meet professional goals of individuals. Opportunities are provided for practical applications through internships, practicums, and assistantships. *Admission Requirements:* Satisfactory GPA and GRE scores, evidence of literary and expository skills and aptitudes, and recommendations. *Faculty:* 8 full-time; 2 part-time.

Texas A&M University. College of Education, College Station, TX 77843. (409) 845-7276. Fax (409) 845-9663. Ronald D. Zellner, Assoc. Prof., Coord., Educational Technology Program, College of Education. *Specializations:* Ph.D. and Ed.D. programs to prepare individuals to teach college and university courses in educational technology, manage learning resource centers, and apply educational technology skills and knowledge in various settings related to communication and instructional processes in higher education, public education, business and industry, and public and private agencies. *Features:* The doctoral programs are flexible and interdisciplinary; degrees are established and granted in conjunction with the Department of Curriculum and Instruction and other departments in the College of Education; specialization areas include computer applications (CAI, CMI, interactive video), media, and video production; program provides laboratories, equipment, and a PBS television station. *Admission Requirements:* A bachelor's degree, admission to graduate college (which includes satisfactory performance on the GRE); some requirements may vary with respect to the particular program in which the degree is housed. *Faculty:* 4 full-time. *Students:* 4 full-time; 2 part-time. *Assistance:* Several graduate assistantships (teaching and project) and a limited number of fellowships; part-time employment on campus, in local school districts, and in surrounding communities. *Doctoral Program Trends:* Increasing emphasis on placement in government, industry, and computer education settings. *Doctorates Awarded 1990-91:* 1m, 1w.

The University of Texas. College of Education, Austin, TX 78712. (512) 471-5211. Fax (512) 471-4607. DeLayne Hudspeth, Assoc. Prof., Area Coord. at Austin, Instructional Technology, Dept. of Curriculum and Instruction, College of Education. *Specialization:* Ph.D. program emphasizes research, design, and development of instructional systems and communications technology. *Features:* The program is interdisciplinary in nature, although certain competencies are required of all students. Programs of study and dissertation research are based on individual needs and career goals. Learning resources include a model LRC, computer labs and classrooms, a color television studio, interactive multimedia lab, and access to a photo and graphics lab. *Admission Requirements:* Minimum 3.0 GPA and a score of at least 1,100 on the GRE. *Faculty:* 4 full-time; 2 part-time. Many courses are offered cooperatively by other departments, including Radio-TV Film, Computer Science, and Educational Psychology. *Students:* 24. *Assistance:* Assistantships are available in planning and developing instructional materials, teaching undergraduate computer literacy, and assisting with research in instructional technology; there are also some paid internships. *Doctoral Program Trends:* Increasing enrollments of students seeking positions in business/industry, health, program administration, instructional design/development, and computer education. *Doctorates Awarded 1990-91:* 6.

UTAH

*Brigham Young University. Department of Instructional Science, Provo, UT 84602. (801) 378-5097. Fax (801) 378-4017. Paul F. Merrill, Prof., Chair. *Specializations:* M.S. and Ph.D. offered in instructional science and technology. In the M.S. program, students may specialize in instructional design and production, computers in education, or research and evaluation. In the Ph.D. program, students may specialize in instructional design, instructional psychology, or research and evaluation. *Features:* Course offerings include principles of learning, instructional design, assessing learning outcomes, evaluation in education, empirical inquiry in education, project and instructional resource management, quantitative reasoning, microcomputer materials production, naturalistic inquiry, and more. Students are required to participate in internships and projects related to development, evaluation, measurement, and research. *Admission Requirements:* For further information, write to Dr. Paul F. Merrill at the preceding address. *Faculty:* 10 full-time. *Students:* 20 M.S., 40 Ph.D. *Doctoral Program Trends:* Increasing enrollments of students interested in position placements in business/industry, health, college teaching, instructional design/development, and computer education. *Doctorates Awarded 1989-90:* 6.

Utah State University. College of Education, Logan, UT 84322-2830. (801) 750-2694. Fax (801) 750-2693. Don C. Smellie, Prof., Chair, Dept. of Instructional Technology, College of Education. *Specializations:* Ph.D. in educational technology. Offered for individuals seeking to become professionally involved in instructional development and administration of media programs in public schools, community colleges, and universities. Teaching and research in higher education is another career avenue for graduates of the program. *Features:* The doctoral program is built on a strong master's and specialist's program in instructional technology. All doctoral students complete a core with the remainder of the course selection individualized, based upon career goals. *Admission Requirements:* 3.0 GPA, successful teaching experience or its equivalent, a combined verbal and quantitative score of 1,100 on the GRE, written recommendations, and a personal interview. *Faculty:* 9 full-time; 7 part-time. *Students:* 120 M.S./M.Ed. candidates; 5 Ed.S. candidates; 25 Ph.D. candidates. *Assistance:* Approximately 18 to 26 assistantships (apply by 1 June). *Doctoral Program Trends:* Increasing enrollments of students seeking position placements in business/industry, college teaching, instructional design/development, and computer education. *Doctorates Awarded 1990-91:* 2m.

VIRGINIA

University of Virginia. Curry School of Education, Charlottesville, VA 22903. (804) 924-7471. Fax (804) 924-0747. John B. Bunch, Assoc. Prof. of Education, Dept. of Educational Studies, School of Education. *Specializations:* Ed.D. or Ph.D. program for well-qualified students seeking professional training in the design, production, and evaluation of instructional programs and materials in school or nonschool settings. Students may also work with faculty to conduct research on the effective uses of technology for instruction or information exchange. Graduates are placed as instructional developers or media specialists in education; as training developers in business, industry, or government agencies; or as university faculty. *Features:* A relatively small program that enables the department to tailor programs to the needs and goals of individual students (including options of minor area concentrations in other professional schools). Specializations are available in interactive technologies (a multimedia approach employing computer-, compact disc-, and videodisc-based materials), or media production (including video and photography). *Admission Requirements:* Satisfactory performance on the GRE, written recommendations, and a personal interview. *Faculty:* 3 full-time. *Students:* 15 full-time; 25 part-time. *Assistance:* A number of graduate assistantships are available as well as a limited number of fellowships (application must be made prior to 1 April). *Doctoral Program Trends:* Increasing enrollments of students seeking positions in business/industry, health, college teaching, instructional design/development, media production, and computer education. *Doctorates Awarded 1990-91:* 4.

***Virginia Polytechnic Institute and State University.** College of Education, Blacksburg, VA 24061. (703) 231-5587. Fax (703) 231-3717. John K. Burton, Prof., Program Area Leader, Instructional Systems Development, Curriculum and Instruction. *Specializations:* M.A., M.S., and Ed.D. programs in instructional technology. Preparation for education, business, and industry. *Features:* Areas of emphasis are instructional design, educational computing, evaluation, and media management. Psychology is the disciplinary theory/research perspective. The Instructional Systems Development Program houses the Self-Instructional Curriculum Lab (SICL) and the Education Microcomputer Lab (EML), which contains some 70 microcomputers (Apple, IBM, and Macintosh) including interactive video and speech synthesis capabilities. The program is also affiliated with the university's Learning Resources Center (LRC), which houses production services for graphics and video as well as satellite communications. Doctoral students are expected to intern either on campus (e.g., LRC) or off campus (e.g., Arthur Andersen Associates, AT&T, etc.) or both. *Admission Requirements:* 3.3 GPA for master's degree, three letters of recommendation, all transcripts. Experience in education recommended but not required. *Faculty:* 10 full-time; 2 split; 4 adjunct. *Students:* 10 full-time; 12 part-time. *Assistance:* Seven graduate assistantships; three tuition waivers; 2-4 additional graduate assistantships usually available from contracts and grants. *Doctoral Program Trends:* Increasing use of computers for most production. Increasing liaison with private sector, although most doctorates still take academic positions. Continued emphasis on graduate student research and publication presentation. *Doctorates Awarded 1989-90:* 4m, 3w.

WASHINGTON

*University of Washington. College of Education, Seattle, WA 98195. (206) 543-1877. Fax (206) 543-8439. William D. Winn, Prof. of Education, College of Education. *Specializations:* Ph.D. and Ed.D. for individuals in business, industry, higher education, public schools, and organizations concerned with education or communication (broadly defined). *Features:* Emphasis on instructional design as a process of making decisions about the shape of instruction; additional focus on research and development in such areas as message design (especially graphics and diagrams); electronic information systems; interactive instruction via videodisc, videotex, and computers. *Admission Requirements:* GRE scores, letters of reference, transcripts, personal statement, master's degree or equivalent in field appropriate to the specialization, 3.5 GPA in master's program, two years of successful professional experience and/or experience related to program goals. *Faculty:* 2 full-time; 3 part-time. *Students:* 12 full-time; 32 part-time. *Assistance:* Assistantships awarded competitively and on basis of program needs; other assistantships available depending on grant activity in any given year. *Doctoral Program Trends:* Students increasingly interested in applying ID principles to interactive instructional environments. *Doctorates Awarded 1989-90:* 3.

WEST VIRGINIA

*West Virginia University. College of Human Resources and Education, Morgantown, WV 26506. (304) 293-3803. David McCrory Prof., Chair, George Maughan, Coord., Technology Education, Communication and Information Systems Sequence of Study. *Specializations:* M.A. and Ed.D. programs in history of technical development, research, college teaching, instructional systems design, instructional development, and communication and information systems. *Admission Requirements:* GRE and Miller Analogies Test, minimum 3.0 GPA. *Faculty:* 4 full-time; 2 part-time. *Students:* 10 full-time; 6 part-time. *Assistance:* Two teaching assistantships, three research assistantships. *Doctoral Program Trends:* Increasing enrollments of students seeking position placements in business/industry, government, program management, educational delivery systems, and computer education. *Doctorates Awarded 1988-89:* 2m.

WISCONSIN

University of Wisconsin-Madison. School of Education, Madison, WI 53706. (608) 263-4670. Michael Streibel, Prof., Dept. of Curriculum and Instruction, School of Education. *Specializations:* Ph.D. programs to prepare college and university faculty. *Features:* The program is coordinated with media operations of the university. Traditional instructional technology courses are processed through a social, cultural, and historical frame of reference. Current curriculum emphasizes communication, perception, and cognitive theories, critical cultural studies, and theories of textual analysis and instructional development. Strength in small-format video production and computers. *Admission Requirements:* Previous experience in instructional technology preferred, previous teaching experience, minimum 2.75 GPA on all undergraduate work completed, acceptable scores on either Miller Analogies Test or GRE, and a minimum 3.0 GPA on all graduate work. (Note: Exceptions may be made on some of these requirements if all others are acceptable.) *Faculty:* 3 full-time; 1 part-time. Students: 21 Ph.D., 27 M.S. *Assistance:* A few stipends of approximately $1,000 a month for 20 hours of work per week; other media jobs are also available. *Doctoral Program Trends:* Preparation of academics with strengths in social/cultural aspects of educational technology and the role of media in education.

WYOMING

University of Wyoming. College of Education, Box 3374, Laramie, WY 82071. (307) 766-3896. Fax (307) 766-6668. Patricia McClurg, Prog. Area Coordinator, Instructional Technology. Specializations: The College of Education offers both the Ed.D. and the Ph.D. programs. Students select areas of specialization and Instructional Technology as one option. *Faculty:* 6 full-time. *Doctorates Awarded 1989-90:* 0. For additional information, contact Dr. Patricia McClurg and see the university's master's degree programs.

Master's Degree and Six-Year Programs
in Instructional Technology

Program data for this yearbook were updated by program chairpersons or their representatives in response to an inquiry-questionnaire submitted to them during the fall semester of 1991.

Six-year specialist/certificate programs in instructional technology and related media are included in this directory, as was the case in 1991. Each of these specialist/certificate programs is described in a separate paragraph following the individual institution's master's degree program.

Each entry in the directory contains the following information: (1) name and mailing address of the institution; (2) name, academic rank, and title of program head; (3) name of the administrative unit offering the program; (4) minimum degree requirements; (5) number of faculty (reported either as full-time and part-time or total full-time, full-time with doctorates, and part-time with doctorates); (6) the number of men (m) and the number of women (w) who graduated with master's degrees from the program during the one-year period between 1 July 1990 and 30 June 1991; and (7) identification of institutions offering six-year specialist degree programs in instructional technology.

Several institutions appear in both this list and the list of graduate programs in educational computing, since their computer technology programs are offered separately from the educational/instructional technology programs.

To ensure completeness of this directory, considerable effort has been expended. However, readers who know of either new programs or omissions are encouraged to provide information to the publisher who, in turn, will follow up on them for the next edition of *EMTY*. In those instances where updated information was not received, the entry which appeared in *EMTY 1991* is included in order to have the program represented; such entries are indicated by an asterisk before the name of the institution. In some cases, additional or more recent information from other sources has been added; programs new to the listing are indicated by two asterisks. For such additional information we are particularly indebted to Jenny Johnson (*Graduate Curricula in Educational Communications and Technology; A Descriptive Directory,* 4th ed., Association for Educational Communications and Technology, February 1992) and Mark Bugler, from the University of Iowa, who shared the results of his recent survey of doctoral programs in the United States.

Individuals who are interested in any of these graduate programs are encouraged to make direct contact with the head of the program to obtain the most recent information available.

Institutions in this section are arranged alphabetically by state.

ALABAMA

Alabama State University. Library Education Media, School of Education, Montgomery, AL 36195. Fax (205) 262-0474. Katie R. Bell, Prof., Coord., Library Education Media, School of Education. *Program Basis:* Semester. *Minimum Degree Requirements:* 36 semester hours including 18 in media; thesis optional. *Faculty:* 2. *Graduates:* 2m, 20w.

The school also offers a six-year specialist degree program in instructional technology and library media. This 36-42 semester program includes 18 semester hours in an instructional support area; 12 hours in education, including statistics on human development and behavior; and 3 hours in a research project. *Graduates 1990-91:* 3.

Auburn University. Educational Foundations, Leadership, and Technology, Auburn, AL 36849. Fax (205) 844-5785. Jeffrey Gorrell, Prof., Dept. Head. *Program Basis:* Quarter. *Minimum Degree Requirements:* 48 credit hours including 36 in media. *Faculty:* 24, 14, 10. *Graduates:* 1m, 3w.

The school also offers a six-year specialist degree program in instructional technology. Program is offered as either a degree or a nondegree option. The program serves either to improve the certification of school media specialists or to provide higher-level study in instructional design and/or the application of computers in the learning environment.

*Jacksonville State University. Instructional Media Division, Jacksonville, AL 36265. (205) 782-5096. Stanley Easton, Dept. Head, Dept. of Educational Resources, Instructional Media Division. *Program Basis:* Semester. *Minimum Degree Requirements:* 33 credit hours including 18 in media; thesis optional. *Faculty:* 3 full-time. *Graduates 1989-90:* 10w.

University of Alabama. School of Library and Information Studies, Tuscaloosa, AL 35487-0252. (205) 348-4610. Fax (205) 348-3746. Philip M. Turner, Prof., Dean. *Program Basis:* Semester. *Minimum Degree Requirements:* 36 credits including 21 in media. *Faculty:* 4 full-time. *Graduates:* 6m, 40w, including 2 foreign nationals.

The school also offers a six-year specialist degree program in instructional technology which is highly flexible and tailored to the students' educational needs. The program, leading to an Ed.S., consists of 30 semester hours of coursework, does not require a thesis, and requires that 12 of the 30 hours be taken in library media. *Graduates:* 1m, 1w.

University of South Alabama. College of Education, Mobile, AL 36688. (205) 460-6221. Fax (205) 460-7830. John G. Baylor, Assoc. Prof., Dept. of Behavioral Studies and Educational Technology, College of Education. *Program Basis:* Quarter. *Minimum Degree Requirements:* 58 credit hours including 42 in media; thesis optional. M.Ed. program in educational media is for state school library media certification; M.S. program in instructional design is for employment in business, industry, the military, etc.; the Ed.S. in educational media leads to higher certification in library media. *Faculty:* 5 full-time. *Graduates:* 6m, 6w.

The school also offers a six-year specialist degree program in instructional technology for the improvement of teaching. The specific course offerings relating to the specialty field of educational media add to and complement the common core of the program and provide additional information and skills the media specialist needs to support the classroom teacher's efforts. *Admission to Candidacy:* Refer to the College of Education general section of the school's Bulletin for specific requirements for admission. *Ed.S. Graduates:* 1w.

ARIZONA

*Arizona State University. College of Education, FMC Payne 148, Tempe, AZ 85287-0111. (602) 965-7192. Fax (602) 967-8887. Gary G. Bitter, Coord. Educational Media and Computers. *Program Basis:* Semester. *Minimum Degree Requirements:* 33 semester hours; comprehensive exam required; a project; thesis not required. *Faculty:* 9 full-time.

*Arizona State University. Learning and Technology, 322 Payne, Tempe, AZ 85287-0611. (602) 965-4963. Vernon S. Gerlach, Prof., Coord., Learning and Technology, Division of Psychology in Education. *Program Basis:* Semester. *Minimum Degree Requirements:* 30 credit hours; comprehensive exam required; thesis optional. *Faculty:* 3 full-time. *Graduates 1989-90:* M.A. degree: 6m, 4w; M.Ed. degree: 5m, 11w.

University of Arizona. Graduate Library School, 1515 East First St., Tucson, AZ 85719. (602) 621-3565. Fax (602) 621-3279. C.D. Hurt, Prof. and Dir., Graduate Library School. *Program Basis:* Semester. *Minimum Degree Requirements:* 38 graduate credit hours including 12 hours of core courses and a computer proficiency requirement; comprehensive required. *Faculty:* 9, 0, 0. *Graduates 1990-91:* 17m, 77w, including 6 foreign nationals (1989 calendar year).

ARKANSAS

Arkansas Tech University. Department of Instructional Technology, Russellville, AR 72801. (501) 968-0434. Fax (501) 968-9811. Connie Zimmer, Asst. Prof. of Secondary Education and Coord. of Master of Education in Instructional Technology, School of Education. *Specializations*: M.Ed. in Instructional Technology, six-year program. *Features*: Program includes Library Media Education, Training Program, Media Production, and Computer Education. *Requirements for Admission*: Bachelor's degree from a regionally accredited institution, cumulative GPA of 2.50 on a 4.00 scale or a GPA of 3.00 on final 30 hours of undergraduate work, and the GRE (no minimum score established at this time). *Minimum Degree Requirements:* 36 credit hours for M.Ed., thesis optional. *Faculty:* 1 full-time, 2 part-time. *Students*: 59 part-time, 1 foreign national. *Graduates:* 2m, 6w.

*University of Arkansas. College of Education 350, Fayetteville, AR 72701. Jacqueline O'Dell, Prog. Coordinator for Educational Technology. *Graduate Degree:* M.S. in Education. *Requirements:* 33 credit hours, 18 in educational technology. *Faculty:* 3 full-time, 2 part-time. *Graduates 1989-90:* 8m, 12w.

University of Central Arkansas. Library Science Department, Conway, AR 73032. Selvin W. Royal, Prof., Chair, Educational Media/Library Science Dept. *Program Basis:* Semester. *Minimum Degree Requirements:* 36 credit hours. *Faculty:* 5 full-time, 3 part-time. *Graduates:* 1m, 32w.

CALIFORNIA

California State University-Chico. College of Communication, Chico, CA 95929-0504. John Ittelson, Prof., Advisor, Instructional Technology Program and Communication Design. *Program Basis:* Semester. *Minimum Degree Requirements:* 30 credit hours; thesis or project required. *Faculty:* 3 full-time. *Graduates 1989-90:* 2m, 5w, including 1 foreign national.

California State University-Dominguez Hills. School of Education, Carson, CA 90747. Fax (213) 516-3449. Peter Desberg, Prof., Coord., Computer-Based Education, Graduate Education Department. *Program Basis:* Semester. *Minimum Degree Requirements:* 30 credit hours including 9 hours of educational common core units and 21 units of educational technology/computers; thesis optional. *Faculty:* 4 full-time. *Graduates:* 30m, 38w, including 7 foreign nationals.

*California State University-Long Beach. Instructional Media, Long Beach, CA 90840. (213) 985-4966. Fax (213) 985-1753. Richard J. Johnson, Prof., Chair, Dept. of Instructional Systems Technology. *Program Basis:* Semester. *Minimum Degree Requirements:* 30 credit hours including 21 in media; thesis optional. *Faculty:* 6 full-time, 4 part-time. *Graduates 1989-90:* 7m, 12w, including 2 foreign nationals.

California State University-Los Angeles. School of Education, Los Angeles, CA 90032-8143. (213) 343-4346; (213) 343-4330. Fax (213) 343-4318. James H. Wiebe, Prof., Div. of Educational Foundations, School of Education. *Program Basis:* Quarter. *Minimum Degree Requirements:* 45 credit hours including 33 in media, and 2 options in the M.A. degree program: (1) computer education, and (2) instructional media and design. *Admission Requirements*: B.A. or B.S., 2.75 GPA, GRE not required. *Assistance*: Contact Student Financial Services Office at (213) 343-3240 for information. *Faculty:* 6 full-time. *Graduates:* 12m, 13w, including 2 foreign nationals.

*California State University-Northridge. School of Communication, Health and Human Services, Northridge, CA 91330. Judith Marlane, Prof., Chair, Dept. of Radio-Television-Film. Master's program is in mass communication, offered jointly with Department of Journalism, R-TV-F Prog. Coord., John Allyn, Prof. Emphasis on theory and criticism and instructional media available within the Mass Communication program. *Program Basis:* Semester. *Minimum Degree Requirements:* 30 credit hours plus needed prerequisites for students lacking needed undergraduate preparation. Seven three-unit instructional media-oriented course offerings available to students. *Faculty:* 10, 4, 2. *Graduates:* 1m, 2w.

California State University-San Bernardino. Television Center, San Bernardino, CA 92407. R. A. Senour, Prof., Dir., Audiovisual and Instructional Television Center. *Program Basis:* Quarter. *Minimum Degree Requirements:* 48 credit hours including 28 in media/computers in education; plus 4 hours in graphics and telecommunications and 4 hours in interactive mulitmedia. Elective in information systems advised. Project for M.A. required. *Faculty:* 1, 2, 3. *Graduates:* 8.

The school also offers technical certificate programs in computer education and educational technology. *Graduates:* Data not available.

National University. School of Education, Vista, CA 92083. (619) 945-6430. Fax (619) 945-6398. James R. Brown, Dir., Dept. of Instructional Technology, School of Education. *Program Basis:* Quarter. *Minimum Degree Requirements:* The equivalent of 60 quarter hours with media courses tailored to meet student needs; thesis required. *Faculty:* 1 full-time. *Graduates 1989-90:* 26m, 11w.

Pepperdine University. Graduate School of Education and Psychology, 400 Corporate Pointe, Culver City, CA 90230. (213) 568-5600. Fax (213) 568-5727. Dr. Robert C. Paull, Chair., M.A. in Education with Concentration in Educational Technology; Terence R. Cannings, Ed.D., Dir., M.S. in School Administration with Concentration in Educational Technology. *Specializations:* M.A. in Education with Concentration in Educational Technology, M.S. in School Administration with Concentration in Educational Technology. *Features:* Programs can be completed in 12 to 18 months; evening and weekend classes. *Admission Requirements:* 3.0 GPA in undergraduate major;

2.5 cumulative GPA, GRE waived with 3.0 GPA; 2 letters of recommendation. *Faculty:* 4 full-time, 2 part-time. *Students*: Approximately 25 students enroll per year in this concentration; 50 percent full-time, 50 percent part-time. Approximately 3 international students per year. *Assistance*: University, state, and federal financial aid available. *Graduates 1991:* 5m, 15w.

*San Diego State University. Educational Technology, San Diego, CA 92182-0311. (619) 594-6718. Patrick Harrison, Prof., Chair, Dept. of Educational Technology. *Program Basis:* Semester. *Minimum Degree Requirements:* 30 credit hours including 27 in educational technology, instructional design, and training. *Faculty:* 6 full-time. *Graduates 1989-90:* 20m, 30w, including 5 foreign nationals.

San Francisco State University. Center for Educational Technologies, San Francisco, CA 94132. (415) 338-1509. Eugene Michaels, Coord. & Prof. *Specializations*: Training and Designing Development, Instructional Computing, and Instructional and Interactive Video. *Program Basis:* Semester. *Minimum Degree Requirements:* 30 credit hours, field study thesis or project required. *Faculty:* 2 full-time, 3 part-time. *Students*: 110. *Graduates:* l0m, 12w.

The school also offers an 18-unit Graduate Certificate in Training Systems Development, which can be incorporated into the master's program.

*San Jose State University. Instructional Technology Program, School of Education, San Jose, CA 95192-0076. (408) 924-3620. Fax (408) 924-3713. Robert Stephens, Assoc. Prof., Chair., Instructional Technology Program, Educational Leadership and Development Div. *Program Basis:* Semester. *Minimum Degree Requirements:* 30 credit hours including 20 in media; thesis program. *Faculty:* 11 full-time. *Graduates 1989-90:* 11m, 29w, including 78 foreign nationals.

United States International University. School of Education, San Diego, CA 92131. Dr. Maria T. Fernandez-Wilson, Acting Prog. Coord. and Asst. Prof., School of Education. *Program Basis:* Quarter. *Minimum Degree Requirements:* 45 quarter hours and 9 courses. *Specialization*: M.A. in Computer Education. *Features*: Tailored to meet computer literacy, problem solving, software applications, curriculum development, and integrating microcomputers into instructional needs of classroom teachers, curriculum coordinators, and district-level specialists from the United States and a number of international countries. (International Summer 3-3-3 Maste.'s Program available for candidates who wish to study abroad for one or two summers with a one-course-per-quarter load during the academic year.) *Faculty:* 12 full-time. *Graduates:* l0m, 24w, including 5 foreign nationals.

*University of California-Berkeley. School of Library and Information Studies, Berkeley, CA 94720. Charlotte Nolan, Assoc. Dean, Library and Information Studies, School of Library and Information Studies. *Program Basis:* Semester. *Minimum Degree Requirements:* 28 credit hours in library science, computer science, and related. *Faculty:* 12, 6, 2. *Graduates:* 31m, 60w, including 8 foreign nationals.

The school also offers a six-year specialist degree certificate program. Twenty semester credit hours are required for each of the following four certificate programs: library and information studies; bibliography; library automation and information science; and library management. Students are expected to carry out an independent research or design project. There are no language requirements, qualifying examinations, or final comprehensive examinations to be met or passed in any of the programs. Each program of study is drawn up by individual students in consultation with a faculty counselor. *Graduates:* 1m, 1w.

University of California-Los Angeles. Graduate School of Education, Los Angeles, CA 90024-1521. (310) 825-8326; (310) 825-1838. Fax (310) 206-6293. Aimee Dorr, Prof., Learning and Instruction Specialization, Div. of Educational Psychology, Graduate School of Education. *Specialization:* M.A. only. *Program Basis:* Quarter. *Minimum Degree Requirements:* 36 credit hours with emphasis on all media of communication and instruction. *Faculty:* 4 full-time, 2 part-time. *Graduates 1990-91:* 1m, 2w.

*University of California-Santa Barbara. Department of Education, Santa Barbara, CA 93106. (805) 893-3102. Willis D. Copeland, Prof., Program Leader, Instruction, Dept. of Education. *Program Basis:* Quarter. *Minimum Degree Requirements:* 40 credit hours including 28 required and 12 elective; thesis required. *Faculty:* 1 full-time, 2 part-time. *Graduates 1989-90:* 8m, 8w, including 3 foreign nationals.

*University of Southern California. Instructional Technology, Div. of Curriculum and Instruction, Los Angeles, CA 90007-0031. Ed Williams, Prof., Chair., Dept. of Educational Psychology and Technology, School of Education. *Program Basis:* Semester. *Minimum Degree Requirements:* 31 credit hours including 12 hours in media; thesis optional. *Faculty:* 5, 11, 2. *Graduates:* 11m, 13w, including 8 foreign nationals.

COLORADO

University of Colorado-Denver. Instructional Technology Program, School of Education, Denver, CO 80217-3364. (303) 556-4881. Fax (303) 556-4822. David H. Jonassen, Prof. and Chair., Instructional Technology Program, School of Education. *Program Basis:* Semester. *Minimum Degree Requirements:* For several tracks, including instructional computing, corporate training and development, library/media and instructional technology, 36 credit hours including comprehensive; project or internship required. *Program Trends:* Hypermedia/multimedia design, interactive video, technology and school restructuring, management of instructional design. *Faculty:* 9 full-time, 1 part-time. *Graduates:* 6m, 23w.

University of Northern Colorado. College of Education, Greeley, CO 80639. (303) 351-2687. Fax (303) 351-2377. David H. Roat, Prof., Chair., Educational Technology, Div. of Research, Evaluation and Development, College of Education. *Program Basis:* Semester. *Minimum Degree Requirements:* For M.A. in Educational Media, 36 semester hours; for M.A. in Educational Technology, 30 semester hours; comprehensive required; thesis optional. *Admission Requirements:* GPA of 3.0, GRE combined test score of 1,500 for full-time students. *Faculty:* 5 full-time. *Students:* 28 doctoral, 48 M.A., 15 graduate certification. *Assistance:* Graduate and teaching assistantships are available for full-time students. *Graduates:* 25.

CONNECTICUT

*Central Connecticut State University. Department of Educational Technology and Media, New Britain, CT 06050. (203) 827-7671. Mary Ann Pellerin, Assoc. Prof., Chair., Dept. of Educational Technology and Media. *Program Basis:* Semester. *Minimum Degree Requirements:* 33-36 credit hours of which the number taken in media varies. *Faculty:* 2 full-time, 6 part-time. *Graduates 1989-90:* 3m, 6w, M.S.; 2m, 4w, Certified Library Media Specialists; 2w, Elementary Education with Specialization in Educational Technology; 1w, M.S. without certification.
  The school offers fifth- and sixth-year planned programs in educational media.

Fairfield University. Computers in Education, Fairfield, CT 06430. Dr. Ibrahim Hefzallah, Dir. of Media/Educational Technology, (203) 254-4000. *Specializations*: M.A. in media/educational technology (includes instructional development, television production, or a customized course of study). *Minimum Degree Requirements:* 33 semester hours and comprehensive exam. *Admission Requirements*: Bachelor's degree and, for foreign students, TESOL exam minimum score of 550. *Faculty:* 2 full-time, number of part-time varies.

School also offers Certificate of Advanced Study in media management, which includes instructional development and television production. Customized course of study is also available.

Southern Connecticut State University. School of Library Science and Instructional Technology, New Haven, CT 06515. (203) 397-4530. Fax (203) 397-4677. Nancy Disbrow, Chair., School of Library Science and Instructional Technology. *Program Basis:* Semester. *Minimum Degree Requirements:* For instructional technology only, 30 credit hours including 21 in media with comprehensive examination; 36 hours without examination. *Admission Requirements*: For M.S. in Instructional Technology: QPR of 2.5 on 4-point scale overall or 3.0 in major area of study.

The school also offers Professional Diploma in Library Information Studies; students may select instructional technology as area of specialization. Thirty credit hours with 6 credit hours of core requirements, 9-15 credit hours in specialization. *Faculty:* 1 full-time, 3 part-time. *Graduates:* 1w, 2m.

University of Connecticut. Center for Instructional Media, Storrs, CT 06268. Phillip J. Sleeman, Prof., Dir., Univ. Center for Instructional Media and Technology. M.A. and sixth-year program have been discontinued; for information on the Ph.D. program, see the doctoral program listing.

DISTRICT OF COLUMBIA

Gallaudet University. School of Education, Washington, DC 20002. (202) 651-5536 (voice or TDD). Ronald E. Nomeland, Prof., Chair., Dept. of Educational Technology, School of Education and Human Services. *Program Basis:* Semester. *Specializations*: M.S. in Special Education/Deafness with specialization in Educational Computing, Instructional Design, and Media Product Development. *Features:* Combines educational technology skills with study in special education and deafness to prepare graduates for positions in programs serving deaf and other handicapped learners as well as in regular education programs, or in government and industry. *Minimum Degree Requirements:* 36 credit hours including 26 in educational media and a related practicum. *Students*: 10 full-time, 4 part-time, 4 foreign nationals. *Faculty:* FTE 3 full-time, 1 part-time. *Graduates:* 2m, 7w.

*Howard University. School of Education, Washington, DC 20059. John W. Greene. Prof., Chair, Dept. of Educational Leadership and Community Services, School of Education, and Coord., Educational Technology Prog. *Program Basis:* Semester. *Minimum Degree Requirements:* 36 credit hours for M.Ed., including introduction to educational technology; computer-assisted instruction; individualized instruction; and instructional systems development; thesis required for M.A. *Faculty:* 3, 3, 5. *Graduates:* 6m, 7w, including 1 foreign national.

The school also offers a certificate of advanced graduate study usually totalling 30 credit hours, of which 12-20 hours are in educational technology. Foundation courses in philosophy, sociology, and human learning are also required. *Graduates:* Data not available.

*University of the District of Columbia (UDC). College of Education and Human Ecology, 800 Mount Vernon Pl. NW, Washington, DC 20747. (202) 727-2756. Leo Pickett, Assoc. Prof. and Chair., Dept. of Media/Library and Instructional Systems, College of Education and Human

Ecology. *Program Basis:* Semester. *Minimum Degree Requirements:* For M.S. degree in Instructional Systems, 30 hours of required courses and 6 hours of electives; for M.S. degree in Library and Information Science, 30 hours of required courses and 6 hours of electives. *Faculty:* 5 full-time, 2 part-time. *Graduates 1989-90:* 11m, 10w, including 6 foreign nationals.

FLORIDA

Barry University. School of Education, 11300 N.E. Second Ave., Miami Shores, FL 33161. (305) 463-1360. Fax (305) 849-3608. Sister Evelyn Piche, Dean, School of Education and Joel S. Levine, Prof. and Dir. of Computer Education Programs. *Specializations:* Computer Science Education and Computer Applications in Education. *Admission Requirements:* 3.0 GPA; GRE or MAT score required. *Program Basis:* Four nine-week cycles plus two intensive three-week and one two-week summer cycle. *Minimum Degree Requirements:* 36 semester credit hours including 6 credits in one of the following: practicum, internship, or thesis. *Faculty:* 3 full-time. *Graduates:* 15m, 25w, including 4 foreign nationals.

The school also offers 36 credit hours above the master's degree leading to a specialist degree in computer education. This program, while adhering to the master's program description, emphasizes in-depth studies in the area of specialized technology and related applications. *Graduates:* 9m, 20.

*Florida Atlantic University. College of Education, Boca Raton, FL 33431. (407) 367-3602. Dan Kauffman, Prof., Cognitive Science and Artificial Intelligence, College of Education. *Program Basis:* Semester. *Minimum Degree Requirements:* 33 credit hours with emphasis on cognitive science and educational technology; thesis optional but recommended. Graduates must demonstrate competence in learning theory, research methodology, future technologies, hypertext/hypermedia, computer applications, chaos theory, and two computer languages. *Faculty:* 2 full-time, 1 part-time. *Graduates:* 8w.

*Florida State University. College of Education, Tallahassee, FL 32306. (904) 644-4592. Walter Wager, Prof. and Prog. Leader, Instructional Systems Prog., Dept. of Educational Research, College of Education. *Program Basis:* Semester. *Minimum Degree Requirements:* 36 hours; no thesis required. *Faculty:* 6 full-time, 5 part-time. *Graduates 1989-90:* 6m, 5w, including 2 foreign nationals.

*Jacksonville University. Div. of Education, Jacksonville, FL 32211. (904) 744-3950. Fax (904) 744-0101. Daryle C. May, Prof. and Dir. of Teaching Prog. in Computer Education, Div. of Education. *Program Basis:* Semester. *Minimum Degree Requirements:* 36 credit hours including 18 in computer-related major. *Faculty:* 7 full-time. *Graduates 1989-90:* 8m, 9w.

*Nova University. Center for Advancement of Education, 3301 College Ave., Fort Lauderdale, FL 33314. (800) 541-NOVA. Fax (305) 370-5698. Donald Stanier, Dir. of GEM Programs. M.S. and Ed.S. in Educational Media. *Program Basis:* Modules. *Minimum Degree Requirements:* 39 credit hours all in media; practicum required instead of thesis. *Faculty:* Information not available. *Graduates 1980-90:* 3m, 22w, including 15 foreign nationals. (Refer to Nova's doctoral program listing for additional information.)

University of Central Florida. College of Education, Orlando, FL 32816. (407) 275-2153. Fax (407) 823-5135. Donna Baumbach, Assoc. Prof., Dept. of Educational Services, Educational Media/Instructional Technology Programs, College of Education. *Program Basis:* Semester. *Minimum Degree Requirements:* 39-45 semester hours including 30 in technology/media; thesis, project, or research options required. *Admission Requirements*: GPS 3.0; minimum GRE score, 1,000. *Students:* 10 full-time, 96 part-time. *Faculty:* 2 full-time, 1 part-time, 7 adjuncts.

University of Florida. Educational Media and Instructional Design, Gainesville, FL 32611. (904) 392-0705. Lee J. Mullally, Assoc. Prof. and Prog. Leader, Educational Media and Instructional Design. *Program Basis:* Semester. *Minimum Degree Requirements:* 36 credit hours including 24 in educational media and instructional design; thesis optional. *Faculty:* 2 full-time. *Graduates:* 3m, 3w. The Education Specialist Program is an advanced degree program and has the same requirements for admission as the Ph.D. and Ed.D. programs. A special research and/or development project is required for the Ed.S. It also requires 72 semester hours beyond the B.E.

*University of Miami. School of Education and Allied Professions, Coral Gables, FL 33124. (305) 284-3005. Fax (305) 284-3023. Charles E. Hannemann, Assoc. Prof., Area Coord. for Educational Technology, Dept. of Teaching and Learning, School of Education. *Program Basis:* Semester. *Minimum Degree Requirements:* 30 credit hours including 12 hours in media for M.S. Ed. in organizational training; 30 credit hours including 15 hours in media for M.S. Ed. in instructional design; no thesis required but comprehensive written exam required. *Faculty:* 2 full-time. *Graduates 1989-90:* 6m, 5w.

*University of South Florida. School of Library and Information Science, Tampa, FL 33620. (813) 974-3520. Fax (813) 974-3826. John McCrossan, Prof., Dir., School of Library and Information Science. *Program Basis:* Semester. *Minimum Degree Requirements:* 36 hours, thesis optional. *Faculty:* 9 full-time, 1 part-time. *Graduates 1989-90:* 12m, 67w, including 2 foreign nationals. The sixth-year specialist program allows students to specialize in areas such as services for special clientele and library management. Students pursue work in the School of Library and Information Science and in other departments depending on the student's particular needs and interests, i.e., communications, aging studies, guidance, and public administration. The 36 hours include 9 hours for a thesis or project. Application procedures are similar to those for the master's program. Admission requirements are (1) an undergraduate GPA of 3.0, a minimum grade of B on the last half of the baccalaureate degree, or minimum GRE aptitude score of 1,000 (quantitative and verbal); (2) three letters of recommendation; and (3) a master's degree from an ALA-accredited library school. *Graduates:* Data not available.

GEORGIA

*Georgia Southern University. School of Education, Statesboro, GA 30460. (912) 681-5203. Jack A. Bennett, Assoc. Prof., Dept. of Educational Leadership, Technology, and Research. *Program Basis:* Quarter. *Minimum Degree Requirements:* 60 quarter-credit hours including a varying number of hours of media for individual students. *Faculty:* 3 full-time. *Graduates 1989-90:* M.Ed., 6w.

The school also offers a six-year specialist degree program. This program is designed to extend the leadership preparation of school media specialists through a combination of courses in administration, supervision, and advanced media processes. *Graduates 1989-90:* 4w.

*Georgia State University. School of Education, Atlanta, GA 30303. (404) 651-2510. Francis T. Atkinson, Coord., Library, Media and Technology, Dept. of Curriculum and Instruction, School of Education. *Program Basis:* Quarter. *Minimum Degree Requirements:* 60 credit hours including 45 hours in media; thesis optional. *Faculty:* 4 full-time. *Graduates 1989-90:* 14w.

The school also offers a 50-hour six-year specialist degree program in educational media, designed for practicing media specialists who have a master's degree. Research, education, content courses, and a research paper are required. *Graduates 1989-90:* 5m, 7w.

University of Georgia. College of Education, 607 Aderhold Hall, Athens, GA 30602. (404) 542-3810. Fax (404) 542-2321. Murray H. Tillman, Prof., Chair., Dept. of Instructional Technology, College of Education. *Program Basis:* Quarter. *Minimum Degree Requirements:* 60 credit hours including 25 in media; thesis optional. *Faculty:* 10 full-time. *Graduates:* 1m, 15w, including 3 foreign nationals.

The school also offers a 45-hour six-year specialist degree program in instructional technology and a doctoral program. Master's program is designed to meet certification requirements for those seeking to work in Georgia schools. Coursework includes educational psychology, curriculum design, instructional design, production, media center management, and an applied project. *Graduates:* 16w, including 1 foreign national.

**Valdosta State College. School of Education, 1500 N. Patterson St., Valdosta, GA 31698. (912) 333-5927. Fax (912) 333-7408. Catherine Price, Assoc. Prof., Dept. of Instructional Technology. *Program Basis:* Quarter. *Minimum Degree Requirements:* 65 quarter credits. *Admission Requirements:* Bachelor's degree in education, undergraduate GPA of at least 2.5, MAT score, and GRE aptitude score. *Faculty:* 3 full-time, 2 part-time.

West Georgia College. Dept. of Media Education, Education Center, Carrollton, GA 30118. Fax (404) 836-6729. Price Michael, Prof., Chair., Media Education Dept. *Specializations:* M.Ed. with major in Media. *Program Basis:* Quarter. *Minimum Degree Requirements:* 60 quarter hours. *Admission Requirements:* GRE score of 800 or minimum of 550 on NTE Core Exam, undergraduate GPA of 2.5. *Faculty:* 3 full-time. *Graduates:* 7w.

The school also offers a six-year specialist degree program. *Features:* This program is designed to develop advanced competencies in such areas as curriculum design, information retrieval, development of instructional systems, design of media programs and facilities, skills in media research, and management. The Ed.S. consists of 45 quarter hours of approved coursework beyond the M.Ed. *Admission Requirements:* Graduate GPA of 3.25 and a GRE score of 900 or a minimum of 575 on the NTE Core Exam, or a score at or above the 53rd percentile on the Library Media Specialist NTE Specialty Area Test.

HAWAII

University of Hawaii-Manoa. Educational Technology Department, 1776 University Ave., Honolulu, HI 96822. (808) 956-7671 or 956-3910. Fax (808) 956-3905. Geoffrey Z. Kucera, Prof., Chair, Educational Technology Dept. *Program Basis:* Semester. *Minimum Degree Requirements:* 39 credit hours, including 33 in educational technology; thesis and nonthesis available. *Faculty:* 4 full-time, 2 part-time. *Students:* 21. *Graduates:* 2m, 2w.

IDAHO

*Boise State University. College of Technology, Boise, ID 83725. (208) 385-1312. Fax (208) 385-1856. Mark E. Eisley, Dir., Instructional/Performance Technology Program, College of Technology. *Program Basis:* Semester. *Minimum Degree Requirements:* 33 credit hours in instructional/performance technology and related coursework; project or thesis required (included in 33 credit hours). Program is also delivered through computer-mediated conferencing to students located anywhere in North America. *Faculty:* 2 full-time, 5 part-time. *Graduates 1989-90:* 8. Relatively new program.

ILLINOIS

*Chicago State University. Department of Library Science and Communications Media, Chicago, IL 60628. (312) 995-2278. Harry Liebler, Prof., Chair., Dept. of Library Science and Communications Media. *Program Basis:* Semester. *Minimum Degree Requirements:* 36 credit hours; thesis optional. *Faculty:* 4 full-time. *Graduates 1989-90:* 7m, 41w, including 1 foreign national.

*Eastern Illinois University. Buzzard Bldg., Rm. 213, Charleston, IL 61920. (213) 581-5931. John T. North, Prof., Chair, Dept. of Information Services and Technology. *Program Basis:* Semester. *Minimum Degree Requirements:* 32 credit hours including 24 in library/media; thesis optional. *Faculty:* 3 full-time, 1 part-time. *Graduates 1989-90:* 3m, 7w, including 1 foreign national.

Governors State University. College of Arts and Sciences, University Park, IL 60466. (708) 534-5000, ext. 2432. Fax (708) 534-0054. Michael Stelnicki, Prof., Instructional and Training Technology, College of Arts and Sciences. *Specialization:* M.A. in Communication with I and IT major. *Features:* Emphasizes three professional areas—Instructional Design, Performance Analysis, and Design Logistics. *Program Basis:* Trimester. *Minimum Degree Requirements:* 36 credit hours, all in instructional and performance technology. *Admission Requirements:* Bachelor's degree, no minimal GPA, no GRE score. *Faculty:* 2 full-time, 1 part-time. *Students:* 4 full-time, 32 part-time. *Graduates:* 4m, 8w.

*Illinois State University. Department of Communication, Normal, IL 61761. Vincent Hazelton, Prof., Chair., Dept. of Communication. *Program Basis:* Semester. *Minimum Degree Requirements:* 32 credit hours including 18 in media; thesis optional. Faculty: 2, 0, 0. *Graduates 1989-90:* 4m, 6w.

*Northeastern Illinois University. Instructional Media, Chicago, IL 60625. Christine Swarm, Prof., Assistant Chair., Curriculum and Instruction, Coord. of Instructional Media, Coord. of Secondary Education. *Program Basis:* Semester. *Minimum Degree Requirements:* 33 credit hours including 21 in media; thesis optional. *Faculty:* 2, 2, 0. *Graduates 1989-90:* 10m, 52w, including 2 foreign nationals.

Northern Illinois University. College of Education, DeKalb, IL 60115. (815) 753-0464. Fax (815) 753-2100. Dr. Gary L. McConeghy, Chair., Instructional Technology, College of Education-LEPS. *Program Basis:* Semester. *Minimum Degree Requirements:* 39 credits including 30 in instructional technology; thesis optional. *Faculty:* 5 full-time, 1 part-time. *Students:* 98, including 16 foreign nationals. *Graduates:* 21.

Rosary College. Graduate School of Library and Information Science, River Forest, IL 60305. (708) 366-2490. Fax (708) 366-5360. Michael E. D. Koenig, Dean. *Program Basis:* Semester. *Minimum Degree Requirements:* 36 credit hours including media; nonthesis. *Admission Requirements:* Entrance examinations may include GRE and TOEFL. *Faculty:* 11 full-time, 16 part-time. *Graduates:* 16m, 74w.

    The school also offers certificate programs in law librarianship, library administration, and technical services and several joint-degree programs.

Southern Illinois University-Carbondale. College of Education, Carbondale, IL 62901. (618) 453-4218. Fax (618) 453-1646. Billy G. Dixon, Chair.; Sharon A. Shrock, Assoc. Prof., Coord., Instructional Development, Div. of Curriculum and Instruction, College of Education. *Specializations:* M.S. in Instructional Development, Computer-Based Instruction, or School Library Media. *Program Basis:* Semester. *Minimum Degree Requirements:* 32 credit hours plus thesis or 36 credit hours without thesis. *Admission Requirements:* Bachelor's degree and 2.70 GPA; GRE not required. *Assistance:* Graduate assistantships, scholarships, and other financial aid available. *Master's Program Trends:* International enrollment is increasing and there are employment opportunities available in numerous fields. *Faculty:* 5 full-time, 3 part-time. *Students:* 57 full-time, 15 part-time, 22 foreign nationals. *Graduates:* 7m, 11w.

*Southern Illinois University-Edwardsville. Instructional Technology Program, School of Education, Edwardsville, IL 62026-1125. (618) 692-3277. Charles Nelson, Coord., Dept. of Educational Leadership. *Program Basis:* Quarter. *Minimum Degree Requirements:* 52 degree credit hours including 36 in instructional technology; thesis optional. *Faculty:* 6 part-time. *Graduates 1989-90:* 12m, 17w, including 2 foreign nationals.

University of Illinois at Urbana-Champaign. College of Education, Champaign, IL 61820. (217) 244-3391. Fax (217) 244-4572. J. Richard Dennis, Assoc. Prof., Dept. of Curriculum and Instruction, College of Education. *Program Basis:* Semester. *Minimum Degree Requirements:* 32 credit hours with emphasis on theory and design of interactive instructional systems, educational psychology, and educational policy studies; 4.0 minimum GPA required; TOEFL scores for non-English-speaking students, including scores for Test of Written English; and GRE of at least 50th percentile in two of Verbal, Quantitative, and Analytic. *Faculty:* 15 part-time. *Graduates:* 5m, 8w, including 6 foreign nationals.

The school also offers a six-year specialist degree program in instructional technology. This program requires two years of demonstrated professional service and admission requirements comparable to those required for the master's degree. This program also requires 32 credit hours beyond the master's, of which 16 are at the most advanced graduate level. *Graduates:* 1w.

University of Illinois at Urbana-Champaign. Department of Educational Psychology, Champaign, IL 61820. Charles K. West, Prof., Div. of Learning and Instruction, Dept. of Educational Psychology. *Program Basis:* Semester. *Minimum Degree Requirements:* 8 units of credit, at least 3 of which must be in 400-level courses, 2 in the major field (graduate courses are offered for 1 or 1/2 unit each); thesis required. *Faculty:* 17. *Students:* 8.

*Western Illinois University. Department of Media and Educational Technology, Macomb, IL 61455. Don Crawford, Prof., Chair, Dept. of Media and Educational Technology (offered in cooperation with Department of Educational Administration). *Program Basis:* Semester. *Minimum Degree Requirements:* 32-36 credit hours including 18 in media; thesis optional. *Faculty:* 10, 5. Note: Faculty includes individuals also teaching undergraduate courses (basic mission). Offers graduate courses in library/media and educational computing for support in other programs. *Graduates 1989-90:* 2m, 4w.

INDIANA

Indiana State University. Media Technology, Terre Haute, IN 47809. (812) 237-2930. Fax (812) 237-4348. James E. Thompson, Prof., Chair., Dept. of Educational Foundations and Media Technology. Program Basis: Semester. Minimum Degree Requirements: 32 credit hours including

18 in media; thesis optional. Faculty: 5 full-time. Graduates: 5m, 10w, including 6 foreign nationals. The school also offers a six-year specialist degree program in instructional technology.

*Indiana University. School of Education, Bloomington, IN 47405. (812) 855-1791. Fax (812) 855-3044. Charles Reigeluth, Chair and Prof., Dept. of Instructional Systems Technology. *Specialization:* M.S. in Educational Media; Post-Master's, Nondegree Program in Instructional Supervision, School Media Services; Educational Specialist in Curriculum and Instruction, Educational Media. Sixth-year program is available. *Program Basis:* Semester. *Minimum Degree Requirements:* 32 credit hours including 18 in media; thesis optional. *Admission Requirements:* GRE scores (verbal 460, quantitative 520, analytical 510); minimum 2.5 GPA. *Faculty:* 7 full-time, 10 part-time. *Students:* 83. *Assistance:* Assistantships and scholarship. *Graduates 1989-90:* 4m, 8f.

The school also offers a specialist degree program in instructional systems technology. The description of this program is the same as the school's doctoral program in instructional systems technology except for the Students, Trends, and Degrees Awarded sections. *Graduates 1989-90:* 3m, 3w, including 2 foreign nationals.

Purdue University. School of Education, West Lafayette, IN 47907. (317) 494-5669. Fax (317) 494-0587. James Russell, Prof., Educational Computing and Instructional Development, Dept. of Curriculum and Instruction. *Program Basis:* Semester. *Minimum Degree Requirements:* 30 credit hours including 20 in instructional research and development; thesis optional. *Faculty:* 6 full-time. *Graduates:* 11m, 11w, including 7 foreign nationals.

The school also offers a six-year specialist degree program in instructional technology and related fields with emphasis in instructional research and development. Admission to the program requires prior completion of a master's degree. In addition to 30 hours of coursework, each student conducts a research project. At least one unit of residence credit for this degree must be earned on campus. The degree is a terminal degree and is not an intermediate step between the master's and doctoral degrees. *Graduates 1990-91:* 1m, 1w.

*Purdue University-Calumet. Department of Education, Hammond, IN 46323. John R. Billard, Assoc. Prof., Coord., Educational Media Prog., Dept. of Education. *Program Basis:* Semester. *Minimum Degree Requirements:* 33 credit hours including 24 in media; thesis optional. *Faculty:* 2, 2, 2. *Graduates 1989-90:* 3m, 5w.

IOWA

Iowa State University. College of Education, Ames, IA 50011. (515) 294-6840. Michael Simonson and Roger Volker, Profs. and Coords., Curriculum and Instructional Technology (including media and computers), College of Education. *Program Basis:* Semester. *Minimum Degree Requirements:* 30 credit hours including 15 in media; thesis. *Faculty:* 3 full-time, 2 part-time. *Graduates:* 6m, 7w.

*Tri-College Department of Education (a consortium of Clarke College, the University of Dubuque, and Lorcas College). Clarke College, 2000 University, Dubuque, IA 52001. (319) 588-6300. Fax (319) 588-6789. Judith Decker, Prof., Coord. *Program Basis:* Semester. *Minimum Degree Requirements:* 20-22 credit hours in computers, 9 hours in education, and 2-7 hours of electives. *Faculty:* 3 part-time. *Graduates 1989-90:* 3m, 1w.

University of Iowa. College of Education, Iowa City, IA 52242. Leonard S. Feldt, Prof., Chair, Psychological and Quantitative Foundations, College of Education. *Admission Requirements*: A composite score of at least 1,000 on GRE (verbal and quantitative) and a 2.7 GPA on previous course work. *Program Basis*: Semester. *Minimum Degree Requirements:* 35 semester hours with or without thesis. *Faculty:* 4 full-time, 3 part-time. *Students*: 75 full- and part-time; number of degree candidates will be held constant for next two years. *Graduates 1990-91:* 18w, 2m.

*University of Northern Iowa. Department of Curriculum and Instruction, Cedar Falls, IA 50614. (319) 273-2309. Fax (319) 273-2917. Robert R. Hardman, Prof. and Dir., Educational Media, Dept. of Curriculum and Instruction. *Program Basis:* Semester. *Minimum Degree Requirements:* For the Educational Media Degree, 38 credit hours including 34 in media; thesis optional. For the Communications and Training Technology Degree, 38 credit hours including 32 in media; thesis optional. For the Computers Applications in Education Degree, 30 credit hours including 18 in computers; thesis optional. *Faculty:* 3 full-time, 6 part-time. *Graduates:* 3m, 1w in educational media; 6m, 8w in communications and training technology.

KANSAS

*Emporia State University. School of Library and Information Management, Emporia, KS 66801. (316) 343-5203. Martha L. Hale, Dean, School of Library and Information Management. *Program Basis:* Semester. *Minimum Degree Requirements:* Two programs—the ALA-accredited MLS requires 42 credit hours; the School Library Media Certificate Program requires approximately 27 hours and a teaching certificate. Media technology is a component of both programs. *Faculty:* 7, 0, 0. *Graduates 1989-90: 10m, 46w, including 4 foreign nationals.*

The school also offers a school library certification program which includes 27 hours of the MLS program plus technologies mainstreamed into other courses. Computer theory and use is integrated into practically every course. In addition, the program offers three 2-hour computer courses and one 3-hour course, which are combination theory and hands-on. *Graduates:* Data not available. Program is also available in Colorado and other out-of-state sites. Video courses are being developed.

*Kansas State University. College of Education, Manhattan, KS 66502. (913) 532-5551. Fax (913) 532-7304. John A. Hortin, Prof., Dept. of Curriculum and Instruction, College of Education. *Program Basis:* Semester. *Minimum Degree Requirements:* 30 credit hours including 21 in media; thesis optional. *Faculty:* 4 full-time. *Graduates 1989-90:* 7m, 24w.

The school also offers a supervisory certification program in instructional technology. *Graduates 1989-90*: 2m, 12w.

*University of Kansas. School of Education, Lawrence, KS 66045. (913) 864-3057. Fax (913) 864-3566. Ronald Aust, Asst. Prof., Dir., Instructional Technology Center, School of Education. *Program Basis:* Semester. *Minimum Degree Requirements:* 30 credit hours including 10 in media; thesis optional. *Faculty:* 2 full-time, 3 part-time. *Graduates 1989-90*: 2m, 3w, including 1 foreign national.

KENTUCKY

*University of Kentucky. College of Education, Lexington, KY 40506. (606) 257-5972. Gary Anglin, Assoc. Prof., Instructional Design, Dept. of Curriculum and Instruction, College of Education. *Program Basis:* Semester. *Minimum Degree Requirements:* 36 credit hours including

24 in instructional design and technology; no thesis required. *Faculty:* 2 full-time. *Graduates 1989-90*: 8m, 18w, including 1 foreign national.

The school also offers six-year specialist and doctoral degree programs in instructional technology. Admission requirements include a minimum grade level of 3.4 for all graduate work and 30 credit hours of work completed in education. Program requires a minimum of 30 hours beyond the master's degree including 15 hours of advanced, graduate-level courses. *Graduates:* Data not available.

*University of Louisville. School of Education, Louisville, KY 40292. Carolyn Rude-Parkins, (M.Ed., Occupational Education), Instructional Technology Concentration, School of Education. *Program Basis:* Semester. *Minimum M.Ed. Degree Requirements*: 30 credit hours; thesis optional. *Faculty:* 5 professors in 3 departments contribute to this concentration. *Graduates:* 2m, 2w. Note: Media utilization instruction is "mainstreamed" within education courses. The collaborative Technology Project with Jefferson County Public Schools supports courses in computer technology applications.

*Western Kentucky University. Department of Teacher Education, Bowling Green, KY 42101. (502) 745-3446. Fax (502) 745-6474. Robert C. Smith, Assoc. Prof., LME Coord., Dept. of Teacher Education. *Program Basis:* Semester. *Minimum Degree Requirements:* 33 credit hours including 21 in media; thesis optional. *Faculty:* 5 full-time, 2 part-time. *Graduates 1989-90*: 3m, 6w.

LOUISIANA

Louisiana State University. School of Library and Information Science, Baton Rouge, LA 70803. (504) 388-3158. Fax (504) 388-1465. Bert R. Boyce, Dean, Prof., School of Library and Information Science. *Program Basis:* Semester. *Minimum Degree Requirements:* 37 credit hours including comprehensive; residence student on full-time basis for semester or summer; and completion of degree program in five years. *Faculty:* 10. *Students*: 84 full-time, 73 part-time, 9 foreign nationals. *Graduates:* 25m, 61w. *Assistance*: A large number of graduate assistantships are available to qualified students.

*McNeese State University. Department of Administration and Educational Technology, Lake Charles, LA 70609. (318) 475-5424. Joe E. Savoie, Head., Dept. of Administration and Educational Technology. *Program Basis:* Semester. *Minimum Degree Requirements:* 30 credit hours including 15 in media; thesis not required. *Faculty:* 3 full-time. *Graduates 1989-90*: 5m, 6w.

**Northeast Louisiana University. College of Education, 700 University Ave., Monroe, LA 71209. (318) 357-3133. Bill L. Perry, Dir. Ed. Media, Dept. of Administration and Supervision. *Program Basis:* Semester. *Minimum Degree Requirements:* 36 semester credits. *Admission Requirements*: Bachelor's degree, GPA of at least 2.5, GRE score of at least 600. *Faculty:* 2 full-time.

*Southern University. College of Arts and Humanities, Baton Rouge, LA 70813. Henry Wiggins, Prof., Chair., Dept. of Mass Communications, College of Arts and Humanities. *Program Basis:* Semester. *Minimum Degree Requirements:* 30 credit hours including 21 in mass communications and instructional technology; thesis optional. *Faculty:* 4, 3, 4. *Graduates 1989-90*: 19m, 13w, including 1 foreign national.

MARYLAND

*The Johns Hopkins University. Division of Education, Baltimore, MD 21218. (301) 338-8273. Fax (301) 338-8424. Dianne Tobin, Coord., M.S. Technology for Educators, Ed.D. Technology for Special Education, Div. of Education. *Program Basis:* Semester. *Minimum Degree Requirements:* 33 credit hours, 8 required courses in computer-related technology and media, with remaining courses being electives in several broad areas. *Faculty:* 2 full-time, 8 part-time. *Graduates 1990:* 5m, 15w, including 1 foreign national.

Towson State University. College of Education, Baltimore, MD 21204. (301) 830-2576. Paul E. Jones, Assoc. Prof., Instructional Technology Program, General Education Dept. *Specializations:* Concentrations available in Instructional Development and School Library Media. *Program Basis:* Semester. *Faculty:* 5 full-time. *Graduates:* 1m, 6w, including 1 foreign national.

*University of Maryland. College of Library and Information Services, College Park, MD 20742. (301) 454-5441. Claude E. Walston, Dean and Prof., College of Library and Information Services. *Program Basis:* Semester. *Minimum Degree Requirements:* 36 credit hours including majors in library media; no thesis required. *Faculty:* 15 full-time, 13 part-time. *Graduates 1989-90:* 2m, 22w.

University of Maryland (UMBC). Department of Education, Catonsville, MD 21228. David B. Young, Coord., Instructional Systems Development Master's Degree Prog., Dept. of Education. *Program Basis:* Semester. *Minimum Degree Requirements:* 36 credit hours including 18 in systems development for each of three programs: (1) Training Systems, (2) English as a Second Language, and (3) School Instructional Systems and Post Baccalaureate Teacher Certification. *Admission Requirements:* Minimal 3.0 GPA. *Assistance:* Fellowships and graduate assistantships available. *Faculty:* 12 full-time, 2 part-time. *Students:* 300, 10 foreign nationals. *Graduates 1990-91:* 20m, 8w.

Western Maryland College. Department of Education, Westminster, MD 21157. (301) 857-2507. Paula K. Montgomery, Asst. Prof., Coord., Media/Library Science, Dept. of Education. *Program Basis:* Semester. *Minimum Degree Requirements:* 33 credit hours including 18 in media; thesis optional. *Faculty:* 1 full-time, 5 part-time. *Graduates:* 3m, 18w.

MASSACHUSETTS

*Boston College. Department of Education, McGuinn 531, Chestnut Hill, MA 02167. (617) 353-3519. Fax (617) 353-3924. Walter M. Haney, Assoc. Prof., Dir., Educational Technology Prog., 523 McGuinn Hall, Dept. of Education, Graduate School of Arts and Sciences. *Program Basis:* Semester. *Minimum Degree Requirements:* 36 credit hours including 30 in media; practicum; thesis optional. *Faculty:* 8 full-time. *Graduates 1989-90:* 4m, 5w.

The school also offers a certificate of advanced education studies degree (30 credit hours) beyond M.Ed. and a special fifth-year M.Ed. program in instructional technology for Boston College undergraduates. *Graduates:* Data not available.

*Boston University. School of Education, 605 Commonwealth Ave., Boston, MA 02215. (617) 353-3519. Gaylen B. Kelley, Prof., Prog. Dir. of Educational Media and Technology, Div. of Instructional Development, School of Education. *Program Basis:* Semester. *Minimum Degree*

Requirements: 32 credit hours; thesis optional. *Faculty:* 4 full-time, 10 part-time. *Graduates 1989-90:* 1m, 12w, including 2 foreign nationals.

The school also offers a six-year specialist degree program Certificate of Advanced Graduate Specialization (C.A.G.S.) in instructional technology and a corporate training program. This program is offered to those wishing to update their skills in instructional technology or those who wish to concentrate in a particular subdiscipline of the field. Concentrations are available in instructional television, facilities design for communications technology, instructional design, computer-based instruction, and library and information science. Program also provides a vehicle for those who wish to certify as Supervisors/Directors of Unified Media Programs for the Massachusetts public schools. Program requires 30 credit hours of course work for program completion. Students entering the program must have completed a master's degree. *Graduates 1989-90:* 1m, 1w.

*Bridgewater State College. Department of Media and Librarianship, Bridgewater, MA 02324. (508) 697-1370. Alan Lander, Prof., Chair, Dept. of Media and Librarianship. *Program Basis:* Semester. *Minimum Degree Requirements:* 33 credit hours including 27 in media; thesis optional. *Faculty:* 4 full-time. *Graduates 1989-90:* 9w.

The school also offers a Unified Media Specialist certification program that provides preparation and background in both print and nonprint resources and services. Enrollment is required in a master's degree program in instructional media, library science, or graduate school certification program to be eligible for this certification program. *Graduates:* Data not available.

Fitchburg State College. Communications/Media Department, Fitchburg, MA 01420. (508) 345-2151, ext. 3260; (508) 343-8603. Lee DeNike, David Ryder, Profs., Communications/Media Dept. *Specializations:* M.S. in Communications/Media Management. *Program Basis:* Semester. *Minimum Degree Requirements:* 36 credit hours in communications/media management including a required thesis. *Faculty:* 5. *Graduates:* 6m, 2w.

*Harvard University. Graduate School of Education, Appian Way, Cambridge, MA 02138. (617) 495-4343. Fax (617) 495-0540. David N. Perkins, Senior Research Assoc., Coord., Technology in Education, Graduate School of Education. *Program Basis:* Semester. *Minimum Degree Requirements:* 32 semester credits including emphasis in technology and educational theory and practice. *Faculty:* 3 full-time, 4 part-time. *Graduates 1989-90:* 11m, 14w, including 6 foreign nationals.

*Simmons College. Graduate School of Library and Information Science, Boston, MA 02115. (617) 738-2225. Fax (617) 738-2099. Robert D. Stueart, Dean, Graduate School of Library and Information Science. *Program Basis:* Semester. *Minimum Degree Requirements:* 36 credit hours; thesis, independent study, or field research and comprehensive examination are also required. *Areas of Emphasis:* Media management, instructional development, and information systems. *Faculty:* 9 full-time. *Graduates 1989-90:* 28m, 131w, including 18 foreign nationals.

**University of Massachusetts-Boston. School of Education, Harbor Campus, Boston, MA 02125. (617) 287-5989. Fax (617) 265-7173. Richard Kropp, Instructional Design Program. *Program Basis:* Semester. *Minimum Degree Requirements:* 36 credits, thesis or project required. *Faculty:* 1 full-time, 9 part-time.

MICHIGAN

*Eastern Michigan University. Teacher Education Department, Ypsilanti, MI 48197. (313) 487-3260. Dr. Bert Greene, Prof., Coord., Educational Technology Concentration, Teacher Education Dept. *Program Basis:* Semester. *Minimum Degree Requirements:* 30 credit hours including 18 in educational technology. *Faculty:* 8 full-time. *Graduates 1989-90:* 7m, 8w, including 8 foreign nationals.

*Michigan State University. College of Education, East Lansing, MI 48824. (517) 353-7863. Leighton A. Price, Prof., Coord., Educational Systems Development Program, Dept. of Counseling, Educational Psychology and Special Education. *Program Basis:* Quarter. *Admission Requirements:* At least a 3.0 GPA during the last two years of undergraduate study. *Minimum Degree Requirements:* 45 credit hours with emphasis in instructional design or in educational technology and instructional computing applications; no thesis required. *Faculty:* 10 full-time. *Graduates 1989-90:* 9m, 6w, including 1 foreign national.

The school also offers a six-year specialist degree program in instructional technology. The Educational Specialist Degree provides opportunities for advanced work in specialized aspects of educational systems development (e.g., instructional design and development, computer-based education, instructional program administration) as well as opportunities to broaden foundations in education, communication, applied educational technologies, and other cognate fields. *Minimum Degree Requirements:* 45 credit hours beyond the master's, written comprehensive examination, demonstrated competence in statistics where appropriate; no dissertation required. *Graduates:* Data not available.

*University of Michigan. Curriculum, Teaching and Psychological Studies, Ann Arbor, MI 48109. (313) 747-0612. Fax (313) 763-1229. Robert B. Kozma, Assoc. Prof., Chair., Instructional Technology Committee, Dept. of Curriculum, Teaching and Psychological Studies. *Program Basis:* Trimester. *Minimum Degree Requirements:* 30 credit hours including project. *Faculty:* 5 full-time, 1 part-time. *Graduates 1989-90:* 3m, 1w, including 3 foreign nationals.

Wayne State University. College of Education, Detroit, MI 48202. (313) 577-1728. Fax (313) 577-3606. Instructional Technology Program, Div. of Administrative and Organizational Studies. Rita Richey, Prof. and Program Coord. *Program Basis:* Semester. *Minimum Degree Requirements:* 36 credit hours including required project; internship recommended. *Faculty:* 3 full-time, 5 part-time. *Graduates:* 18m, 25w, including 2 foreign nationals.

The school also offers a six-year specialist degree program in instructional technology. This 36 credit-hour program includes required work in instructional design and evaluation with a core of additional work in the specialty area of concentration. Internships encouraged. *Graduates:* 1m.

MINNESOTA

Mankato State University. Library Media Education, Mankato, MN 56002. (507) 389-5210. Fax (507) 389-5751. Frank Birmingham, Prof., Chair, Library Media Education. *Program Basis:* Quarter. *Minimum Degree Requirements:* 51 credit hours including 27 in media. *Faculty:* 3 full-time. *Graduates:* 20w.

The school also offers a six-year specialist degree program in the instructional technology/media field. The library media specialist degree prepares individuals as media administrators managing the human and material resources of the media program. An individual's program seeks an in-depth knowledge in a specific area, that is, administration, materials, production. Program may or may not lead to additional certification or licensure. The 45-quarter-credit-hour program includes a research course involving library automation; 21 hours in library media education, including library/media colloquium, or educational administration or curriculum and instruction; internship; 6 hours of elective coursework outside the College of Education; thesis/field study; 6 hours of elective courses in area of media specialization; an oral examination; a comprehensive examination; and an oral thesis defense. *Graduates:* Data not available.

St. Cloud State University. College of Education, St. Cloud, MN 56301-4498. (612) 255-2022. Fax (612) 255-4778. John Berling, Prof., Dir., Center for Information Media, College of Education. *Program Basis:* Quarter. *Minimum Degree Requirements:* 48 credit hours for thesis, 51 credit hours with research paper, or 54 credit hours with portfolio. *Faculty:* 3 full-time, 26 part-time. *Graduates:* 7m, 17w, including 1 foreign national.

The school also offers a 45-quarter-credit, six-year specialist degree program in information media. This program is available to those who have completed a master's degree in media, another field, or comparable field. The program is designed to develop competencies for media supervisor licensure and administrative positions in public, academic, or school district media programs. Most students are required to take the GRE. A minimum GPA on all graduate work is 3.0. References also are required. *Graduates:* 0.

University of Minnesota. Curriculum and Instructional Systems, 130 Peik Hall, 159 Pillsbury Drive S.E., Minneapolis, MN 55455. (612) 624-2034. Fax (612) 626-7496. Gregory C. Sales, Prof., Chair, Curriculum and Instructional Systems. *Program Basis:* Quarter. *Minimum Degree Requirements:* 44 credit hours including 22 in instructional systems. *Faculty:* 4, 4 associates. *Graduates:* 3m, 3w, including 3 foreign nationals.

MISSISSIPPI

*Jackson State University. School of Education, Jackson, MS 39217-0175. (601) 968-2351. William Rush, Prof.. Chair, Dept. of Educational Foundations and Leadership, School of Education. *Program Basis:* Semester. *Minimum Degree Requirements:* 36 credit hours including 24 in media; thesis and field practicum optional. *Faculty:* 2 full-time, 1 part-time. *Graduates 1989-90:* 1m, 1w, including 1 foreign national. Two programs: B.S. Ed. and M.S. Ed. in Educational Technology.

*University of Southern Mississippi. School of Library Science, Hattiesburg, MS 39406-5146. Jeannine Laughlin, Assoc. Prof., Dir., School of Library Science. *Program Basis:* Semester. *Minimum Degree Requirements:* 41 credit hours, comprehensive required. *Faculty:* 9. *Graduates 1989-90:* 12m, 29w, including 2 foreign nationals.

MISSOURI

Central Missouri State University. Department of Special Services and Instructional Technology. Warrensburg, MO 64093. (816) 543-4341. Kenneth Brookens, Assoc. Prof., Coord., Instructional Technology. *Program Basis:* Semester. *Minimum Degree Requirements:* M.S.E., 32 credit hours in curriculum and instruction or library science with emphasis on instructional technology. *Faculty:* 1, 1 adjunct. *Students:* 4 minor, 3 graduate in Library Science with Media certification. *Graduates:* 2w.

The school also offers a certification program in learning resources by arrangement. Inquiries about the status of this program should be directed to the Chair of the Department of Special Services.

*University of Missouri-Columbia. College of Education, Columbia, MO 65211. John F. Wedman, Assoc. Prof., Coord., Educational Technology Program, Curriculum and Instruction Dept., College of Education. *Program Basis:* Semester. *Minimum Degree Requirements:* 32 credit hours including 16 hours of upper-level graduate work. *Faculty:* 3. *Graduates:* 3m, 4w, including 2 foreign nationals.

The school also offers a six-year specialist degree program in instructional technology. Program consists of 30 semester hours beyond the master's degree level and includes 15 hours of upper-level graduate work, a research course, a statistics course, and 12 hours of educational technology involving internship or equivalent (new program). *Graduates:* Data not available.

*University of Missouri-St. Louis. School of Education, St. Louis, MO 63121. (314) 553-5944. Donald R. Greer, Assoc. Prof., Coord. of Educational Technology, Dept. of Educational Studies, School of Education. *Program Basis:* Semester. *Minimum Degree Requirements:* 32 credit hours including 18 in media. *Faculty:* 1 full-time, 1 part-time. *Graduates 1989-90:* 2m, 3w.

Webster University. Instructional Technology, St. Louis, MO 63119. Fax (314) 968-7112. Paul Steinmann, Assoc. Dean and Dir., Graduate Studies and Instructional Technology. *Program Basis:* Semester. *Minimum Degree Requirements:* 33 credit hours including 24 in media; internship required. State Certification in Media Technology is a program option; six-year program not available. *Admission Requirements:* Minimal GPA of 2.5. *Faculty:* 4. *Students:* 6 full-time, 24 part-time, 3 foreign nationals. *Graduates:* 3m, 12w.

MONTANA

University of Montana. School of Education, Missoula, MT 59812. (406) 243-2563. Geneva Van Horne, Prof. of Library/Media, School of Education. *Program Basis:* Semester (beginning Fall 1992). *Minimum Degree Requirements:* 36 semester credit hours, 28 in media, thesis optional. *Faculty:* 3 full-time. *Graduates:* 3m, 12w.

The school also has an endorsement program in addition to the master's program.

NEBRASKA

University of Nebraska-Kearney. Department of Educational Administration, Kearney, NE 68849. Daniel W. McPherson, Assoc. Prof., Supervisor of Educational Media, Department of Educational Administration. *Program Basis:* Semester. *Minimum Degree Requirements:* 36 credit hours including 15 in media; thesis optional. Since this is a cooperative program, Kansas State University provides the 15 hours required for media and computer course work and the supporting faculty. *Graduates:* 2.

*University of Nebraska-Lincoln. Instructional Technology, Teachers College, Lincoln, NE 68588. (402) 472-2018. Fax (402) 472-8317. David W. Brooks, Prof., Coord., Instructional Technology, Teachers College. *Program Basis:* Semester. *Minimum Degree Requirements:* 36 credit hours including 24 in media; thesis optional. *Faculty:* 4 full-time. *Graduates:* 2m, 12w.

University of Nebraska-Omaha. Omaha, NE 68182. (402) 554-3491. Fax (402) 554-3491. Verne Haselwood, Prof., Educational Media Program in Teacher Education. *Program Basis:* Semester. *Minimum Degree Requirements:* 36 credit hours including 27 in media; thesis optional. *Faculty:* 3 full-time, 2 part-time. *Graduates:* 2m, 12w.

NEVADA

*University of Nevada-Reno. College of Education, Reno, NV 89557. (702) 784-4961. Fax (707) 784-4526. Thomas W. Sawyer, Dir. of the Learning and Resource Center, Curriculum and Instruction Dept., College of Education. *Program Basis:* Semester. *Minimum Degree Requirements:* 36 credit hours including 16 or more in (a) computer education-media or (b) library-media; thesis optional. *Faculty:* 2 full-time. *Graduates 1989-90:* 2w.

The school also offers a six-year specialist degree program in curriculum and instruction with an emphasis in (a) or (b) above. *Graduates:* Data not available. A minor is also offered in media/library science.

NEW JERSEY

Glassboro State College. School and Public Librarianship, Glassboro, NJ 08028. (609) 863-6491. Regina Pauly, Graduate Advisor and Program Coord. for School and Public Librarianship. *Program Basis:* Semester. *Minimum Degree Requirements:* 39 credit hours including required thesis project. *Faculty:* 1 full-time, 4 part-time. *Graduates:* 3m, 9w, including 1 foreign national.

*Montclair State College. Department of Reading and Educational Media, Upper Montclair, NJ 07043. Robert R. Ruezinsky, Dir. of Media and Technology. *Program Basis:* Semester. *Type of Degree Offered*: No degree program exists. Two certification programs, A.M.S. and E.M.S, exist on the graduate level. *Faculty:* includes 5 administrators and 1 adjunct, teaching on an overload basis. The school also offers Associate Media Specialist and Educational Media Certificate programs for state level certification: 18-21 credit hours of media and technology are required for the A.M.S. program and 30-33 hours for the E.M.S. program.

*Rutgers-The State University of New Jersey. School of Communication, Information and Library Studies, New Brunswick, NJ 08903. (201) 932-7500. Betty J. Turock, Chair, Dept. of Library and Information Studies, School of Communication, Information and Library Studies. *Program Basis:* Semester. *Minimum Degree Requirements:* 36 credit hours in which the hours for media vary for individual students. *Faculty:* 18. *Graduates 1989-90:* 23m, 112w, including 14 foreign nationals.

The school also offers a six-year specialist certificate program. This 24 credit-hour program must be completed within a three-year period. Some courses may be taken in library/information, an advanced curriculum that includes one or more doctoral seminars and a project culminating in a thesis, survey, film, etc. Other courses may be taken in related fields. Admission criteria include a master's degree; at least a B average and distinction in proposed area of advanced study; a minimum of two years of demonstrated successful experience; a description of applicant's area of interest; a proposed independent study project; and two letters of recommendation. *Graduates:* Data not available.

*Saint Peter's College. Computer Education, Jersey City, NJ 07306. (201) 915-9254. Henry F. Harty, Dir., Graduate Prog. in Computer Education. *Program Basis:* Semester. *Minimum Degree Requirements:* 39 credit hours including 27 in computers. *Faculty:* 7 part-time. *Graduates 1989-90:* 12m, 33w.

*Seton Hall University. Graduate Program in Educational Media, 22 Winding Way, Parsippany, NJ 07054. (201) 761-9392. Rosemary W. Skeele, Asst. Prof., Dir., Graduate Prog. in Educational Media, Div. of Educational Media, College of Education and Human Services. *Program Basis:* Semester. *Minimum Degree Requirements:* 36 credit hours including 24 in media; mediated project instead of thesis. *Faculty:* 1 full-time, 2 part-time. *Graduates 1989-90:* 1m, 4w.

The school also offers an educational specialist certificate—36 credits may lead to state certification as a media specialist.

William Paterson College. School of Education, Wayne, NJ 07470. (201) 595-2585. Fax (201) 595-2140. Amy Job, Librarian, Assoc. Prof., Coord., Prog. in Library/Media, Curriculum and Instruction Dept. *Program Basis:* Semester. *Minimum Degree Requirements:* 33 credit hours in media including research. *Faculty:* 1. *Graduates:* 4w.

NEW MEXICO

*University of New Mexico. College of Education, Albuquerque, NM 87131. (505) 277-0111. Dr. Frank Field, Chair.; Guy A. Watson, Assoc. Prof., Training and Learning Technologies, College of Education. *Program Basis:* Semester. *Minimum Degree Requirements:* Master's: 36 credit hours in Learning Technologies; Ed.D., 72 hours minimum; Ph.D., 78 hours. *Faculty:* 8 full-time, 1 part-time. *Graduates 1988-89:* 18m, 22w.

NEW YORK

Fordham University. Communications Department, Bronx, NY 10458. Donald C. Matthews, S.J., Chair.; James A. Capo, Assoc. Prof., Director of Graduate Studies, Communications Dept. *Program Basis:* Semester. *Minimum Degree Requirements:* 30 credit hours; internship or thesis required. *Faculty:* 9. *Graduates:* 4m, 5w, including 1 foreign national.

*Ithaca College. School of Communications, Ithaca, NY 14850. (607) 274-3242. Diane M. Gayeski, Assoc. Prof., Chair., Graduate Corporate Communications; Roy H. Park, School of Communications. *Program Basis:* Semester. *Minimum Degree Requirements:* 36 credit hours including 30 in communications; thesis optional. *Faculty:* 7 full-time. *Graduates 1989-90:* 4m, 17w.

New School for Social Research. Media Studies Program, New York, NY 10011. (212) 229-8903. Fax (212) 645-0661. Mark Schulman, Chair, Communication Department. *Program Basis:* Semester. *Minimum Degree Requirements:* 36 credit hours in media; thesis encouraged. *Faculty:* 6, 1, 2. *Graduates:* 69m, 111w, including 33 foreign nationals.

New York Institute of Technology. Graduate Communication Arts, Old Westbury, NY 11568. (Also in NYC). (516) 686-7777. Fax (516) 626-7602. Josefa Cubina, Dean, School of Liberal Arts, Sciences and Communication. *Program Basis:* Semester. *Minimum Degree Requirements:* 32-34 credit hours with one specialization in television, film, electronic journalism, advertising/public relations, computer graphics, studio arts or media generalist; thesis optional. *Faculty:* 3 full-time, 8 part-time. *Graduates:* 41m, 48w, including 15 foreign nationals.

*New York University. School of Education, Health, Nursing and Arts Professions. New York, NY 10003. (212) 998-5187. Fax (212) 995-4042. Donald T. Payne, Assoc. Prof. and Dir., Prog. in Educational Communication and Technology. *Program Basis:* Semester. *Minimum Degree Requirements:* 36 credit hours including 24 in media; terminal experience required; thesis optional. *Faculty:* 2 full-time, 6 part-time. *Graduates 1989-90:* 1m, 9w, including 3 foreign nationals.

The school also offers an 18 credit-hour certificate and a 30 credit-hour, six-year specialist program in educational communication and technology. Specializations for the six-year program may be found in the school's doctoral program description. Admission requirements include a master's degree with a 3.0 cumulative average. Students work closely with master's and doctoral program students who are in the same courses. *Faculty:* 2 full-time, 6 part-time. *Graduates 1989-90:* 0.

*New York University-Tisch School of the Arts. Interactive Telecommunications Program, 721 Broadway, New York, NY 10003. Red Burns, Prof., Chair, The Interactive Telecommunications Program/Institute of Film and Television. *Program Basis:* Semester. *Minimum Degree Requirements:* 60 credit hours (15 courses at 4 credit hours each; program is 2 years for full-time students) including 5-6 required courses and thesis. *Faculty:* 3, 1, 4. *Graduates 1989-90:* 20m, 20w, including 2 foreign nationals.

*Rochester Institute of Technology. Information Technology, Rochester, NY 14623-0887. Clint Wallington, Prof., Dir., Dept. of Information Technology, College of Applied Science and Technology. *Program Basis:* Quarter. *Minimum Degree Requirements:* 48 credit hours including an instructional development project (noncredit). *Faculty:* 4, 3, 1. *Graduates:* 8m, 11w.

St. John's University. Library and Information Science, Jamaica, NY 11439. Emmett Corry, O.S.F., Assoc. Prof., Dir., Div. of Library and Information Science. *Program Basis:* Semester. *Minimum Degree Requirements:* 36 credit hours including 21 in media; no thesis required. *Admission Requirements:* Bachelor's degree with a 3.0 GPA. If the average is below 3.0, it is recommended that GRE scores be submitted with the application. Graduate assistants are required to take the GRE. *Assistance:* Assistantships and fellowships are available. *Faculty:* 7, 4, 3. *Students:* 18 full-time, 144 part-time, including 20 foreign nationals. *Graduates:* 10m, 27w.

The school also offers a six-year specialist program, which is a 24 credit-hour, advanced certificate program that can be tailored to the student's individual needs. *Graduates:* Data not available.

*State University College of Arts and Science. School of Professional Studies, Potsdam, NY 13676. (315) 267-2527. Norman Licht, Prof., Coord., Instructional Technology and Media

Management, Center for Mathematics, Science and Technology. *Program Basis:* Semester. *Minimum Degree Requirements:* 33 credit hours including emphasis in instructional technology, media, and computer education; thesis optional. *Faculty:* 7 full-time, 3 part-time. *Graduates 1989-90:* 9m, 28w, including 67 foreign nationals.

*State University of New York at Albany. Department of Program Development and Evaluation, Albany, NY 12222. Instructional Design and Technology Program, Dept. of Program Development and Evaluation. *Program Basis:* Semester. *Minimum Degree Requirements:* 30 credit hours including 15 in instructional design and technology; thesis optional. *Faculty:* 2, 3, 0. *Graduates 1989-90:* 6m, 3w, including 2 foreign nationals.

State University of New York at Buffalo. Graduate School of Education, Buffalo, NY 14260. (716) 636-3164. Fax (716) 636-4281. Taher Razik, Prof., Instructional Design and Management, Dept. of Education, Organization, and Policy, Faculty of Educational Studies. *Program Basis:* Semester. *Minimum Degree Requirements:* 32 credit hours including 21 hours in instructional design and management; thesis or project required; comprehensive examination. *Faculty:* 3 full-time, 1 part-time. *Graduates:* 1m, 2w, including 1 foreign national.

Certificate program in instructional technology has been discontinued.

State University of New York at Buffalo. School of Information and Library Studies, Buffalo, NY 14260. (716) 636-2411. George S. Bobinski, Dean, School of Information and Library Studies. *Program Basis:* Semester. *Minimum Degree Requirements:* 36 credit hours including 15 in media; thesis optional. *Assistance:* Graduate and teaching assistantships available. *Faculty:* 9, 6, 0. *Graduates:* 13m, 60w, including 4 foreign nationals.

The school also offers a 6-year, 30 credit-hour certificate program in instructional technology. *Graduates:* Data not available.

State University of New York at Stony Brook. College of Engineering and Applied Sciences, Stony Brook, NY 11794-2250. (516) 632-8770. Fax (516) 632-8205. Thomas T. Liao, Prof., Chair, Dept. of Technology and Society, College of Engineering and Applied Sciences. *Program Basis:* Semester. *Minimum Degree Requirements:* 30 credit hours with emphasis in technological systems, industrial management, educational computing, and environmental and waste management. *Faculty:* 10 full-time. *Graduates:* 29m, 21w, including 10 foreign nationals.

Syracuse University. School of Education, Syracuse, NY 13244-2340. (315) 443-3703. Fax (315) 443-5732. Donald P. Ely, Prof., Chair., Instructional Design, Development and Evaluation Prog., School of Education. *Program Basis:* Semester. *Minimum Degree Requirements:* 30 credit hours. *Faculty:* 5. *Graduates:* 7m, 7w.

*Teachers College, Columbia University. Program in Communication, New York, NY 10027. (212) 678-3344. Fax (212) 678-4048. Robert P. McClintock, Chair., Dept. of Communication, Computing and Technology in Education. *Program Basis:* Semester. *Minimum Degree Requirements:* M.A., 32 credit hours including 18 in media, core courses in communication and computing, thesis optional; M.A. media specialist (certification), 36 credit hours, core in School of Library Service, internship, research paper. *Faculty:* 4 full-time. *Graduates 1989-90:* 3m, 7w, including 3 foreign nationals.

NORTH CAROLINA

*Appalachian State University. College of Education, Boone, NC 28608. Ken McEwin, Prof., Coord., Dept. of Curriculum and Instruction, Library/Media Studies, College of Education. *Program Basis:* Semester. *Minimum Degree Requirements:* 42 credit hours including selected sources in media; thesis optional. *Faculty:* 6. *Graduates 1989-90:* 8m, 17w.

*Appalachian State University. Department of Library Science and Educational Foundations, Boone, NC 28608. John H. Tashner, Prof., Coord., Department of Library Science and Educational Foundations, College of Education. *Program Basis:* Semester. *Minimum Degree Requirements:* 36 credit hours including 15 in computer education; thesis optional. *Faculty:* 4, 1, 0. *Graduates 1989-90:* 1 (new program).

East Carolina University. Department of Library and Information Studies, Greenville, NC 27858-4353. (919) 757-6621. Fax (919) 757-4368. Lawrence Auld, Assoc. Prof., Chair., Dept. of Library and Information Studies. *Specializations:* M.L.S., areas of specialization include School Media, Community College Librarianship, and Public Librarianship. M.L.S. graduates are eligible for North Carolina School Media Coordinator certification and North Carolina Public Library certification. *Program Basis:* Semester. *Minimum Degree Requirements:* Minimum of 38 credit hours in library science and media. *Faculty:* 8. *Graduates:* 2m, 14w.
   A 14-hour post-master's program for School Media Supervisor certification is also offered.

**North Carolina A&T State University. School of Education, Greensboro, NC 27411. (919) 334-7848. James N. Colt, Dept. of Curriculum and Instruction. *Program Basis:* Semester. *Minimum Degree Requirements:* 30 credits, comprehensive exam, and internship. *Areas of Emphasis:* Media management, telecommunications, instructional development, materials production, information systems, librarianship. *Faculty:* 3 full-time.

North Carolina Central University. School of Education, Durham, NC 27707. (919) 683-6218. Marvin E. Duncan, Prof., Dir., Learning Resources Center, School of Education. *Program Basis:* Semester. *Minimum Degree Requirements:* 33 credit hours including 21 in educational technology. *Features:* The master's program in educational technology is designed to prepare graduates to serve as information and communication technologists in a variety of professional ventures, among which are institutions of higher education (college resource centers), business, industry, and professional schools such as medicine, law, dentistry, and nursing. The program is also designed to develop in students the theory, practical tools, and techniques necessary to analyze, design, and manage an instructional resource program. Thesis or project required. Students who have a master's degree before entering the program who wrote a thesis or project do not have to write a thesis or project for the M.A. degree in educational technology. *Faculty:* 3 full-time, 1 part-time. *Students:* 40, including 8 foreign nationals. *Graduates:* 7m, 4w.

University of North Carolina. School of Education, Chapel Hill, NC 27514. (919) 962-3791. Fax (919) 966-4000. Ralph E. Wileman, Prof., Chair., Educational Media and Instructional Design, School of Education. *Program Basis:* Semester. *Minimum Degree Requirements:* 36 credit hours including 21 in media and comprehensive examination. *Admission Requirements:* Minimal GRE scores of 500 (quantitative) and 500 (verbal), undergraduate GPA for last two years of 3.0 out of 4.0, three strong letters of recommendation, and relevant work experience (applicants without experience will be required to take additional coursework). *Faculty:* 2 full-time, 1 part-time. *Students:* 17 full-time, 2 part-time, 1 foreign national. *Graduates:* 2m, 5w.

Western Carolina University. Department of Administration, Curriculum and Instruction, Cullowhee, NC 28723. John W. McFadden, Prof., Coord., Dept. of Administration, Curriculum and Instruction. Program has been discontinued.

OHIO

Kent State University. Instructional Technology Program, White Hall 405, Kent, OH 44242. (216) 672-2294. Dr. David Dalton, Prog. Coord. *Program Basis:* Semester. *Summer Sessions:* Two 5-week sessions. *Minimum Degree Requirements:* 34 credit hours including 14-20 hours of instructional technology coursework, depending upon certification sought. *Faculty:* 3 full-time, 4 part-time. *Graduates:* approx. 10-15 per year.

*Miami University. School of Education and Allied Professions, Oxford, OH 45056. (513) 529-3736. Joe Waggener, Assoc. Prof., Coord., Instructional Technology Program, School of Education and Allied Professions. *Program Basis:* Semester. *Minimum Degree Requirements:* 30 credit hours; thesis optional. *Faculty:* 4 full-time, 1 part-time. *Graduates:* Data not available.

*Ohio State University. College of Education, Columbus, OH 43210. (614) 292-4872. Fax (614) 292-7900. Marjorie Cambre, Assoc. Prof., Prog. contact person, Instructional Design and Technology, College of Education. *Program Basis:* Quarter. *Minimum Degree Requirements:* M.A. degree, 50 credit hours including an individualized number of hours in media; thesis optional. *Faculty:* 8 full-time. *Graduates 1989-90:* 4m, 12w.
   School media certification is available.

*Ohio University. College of Education, McCracken Hall, Athens, OH 45701-2979. (614) 593-4452. Fax (614) 593-0177. Seldon D. Strother, Prof., Dir. of Educational Media, College of Education. *Program Basis:* Quarter. *Minimum Degree Requirements:* 52 credit hours including 26 in media; thesis optional. *Faculty:* 3 full-time, 3 part-time. *Graduates 1989-90:* 1m, 2w.

*University of Toledo. Department of Educational Technology, Toledo, OH 43606. Mary Jo Henning, Prof., Chair., Dept. of Curriculum and Educational Technology. *Program Basis:* Quarter. *Minimum Degree Requirements:* 48 credit hours including 36 in media; master's project. *Faculty:* 6 full-time. *Graduates 1989-90:* 12m, 10w.
   The school also offers a six-year specialist degree program in educational technology. *Program Basis:* Quarter. *Minimum Degree Requirements:* 45 credit hours including 5 credit-hours supervised internship. *Faculty:* 6, 5, 1. *Graduates 1989-90:* 2m, 2w.

Wright State University. 244 Millett Hall, Dayton, OH 45435. (513) 873-2509. Fax (513) 873-3301. Bonnie Mathies, Assoc. Prof., Chair, Department of Educational Technology, Vocational Education and Allied Programs, College of Education and Human Services. *Degrees Offered:* M.Ed., M.A. *Program Basis:* Quarter. *Minimum Degree Requirements:* 48 credit hours; thesis optional. *Admission Requirements:* GRE or MAT and 2.7 GPA. *Assistance:* Graduate assistantships available. *Faculty:* 2 full-time, 2 part-time, 10 adjuncts. *Students:* 1 full-time, 37 part-time, 1 foreign national. *Graduates:* 2m, 9w.

*Xavier University. Department of Education, Cincinnati, OH 45207. (513) 745-3521. John Pohlman, Asst. Prof., Dir., Graduate Programs in Educational Media, Dept. of Education. *Program Basis:* Semester. *Minimum Degree Requirements:* 30 credit hours including 18 in media; no thesis but field practicum required. *Faculty:* 1 full-time, 5 part-time. *Graduates 1989-90:* 1m, 15w.

OKLAHOMA

*Central State University. College of Education, Edmond, OK 73034-0193. Frances Alsworth, Assoc. Prof., Library Media Education, Dept. of Curriculum and Instruction, College of Education. *Program Basis:* Semester. *Minimum Degree Requirements:* 32 credit hours including 17 in media. *Faculty:* 2, 0, 1. *Graduates 1989-90:* 4w.

Oklahoma State University. Curriculum and Instruction Department, Stillwater, OK 74078. (405) 744-7124. Douglas B. Aichele, Regents, Prof., Head, Curriculum and Instruction Dept. *Program Basis:* Semester. *Minimum Degree Requirements:* 30 credit hours including 18 in media; thesis optional. *Faculty:* 3, 8 teaching assistants. *Graduates:* 4m, 5w.
  School also offers a Library/Media Specialist certificate program.

Southwestern Oklahoma State University. School of Education, Weatherford, OK 73096. (405) 772-6611. Fax (405) 772-5447. Lessley Price, Asst. Prof., Coord. of Library/Media Prog., School of Education. *Degree Offered:* M.Ed. in Library/Media Education. *Program Basis:* Semester. *Minimum Degree Requirements:* 32 credit hours including 24 in media; thesis optional. *Admission Requirements:* GPA 2.5 and GRE. *Faculty:* 2 full-time, 2 part-time. *Graduates:* 16w.

**University of Central Oklahoma. 100 N. University Dr., Edmond, OK 73060-2980. (405) 341-2980. Frances Alsworth, Library Media Education. *Program Basis:* Semester. *Minimum Degree Requirements:* 15 credits in educational communications and technology and 10 in education. *Admission Requirements:* GPA of at least 2.5, GRE score. *Faculty:* 3 full-time.

*University of Oklahoma. Area of Educational Technology, Norman, OK 73019. (405) 325-0311. Fax (405) 325-3242. Tillman J. Ragan, Prof., Area Head, Educational Technology Prog. Area, Dept. of Educational Psychology. *Program Basis:* Semester. *Minimum Degree Requirements:* 32 credit hours including 21 in educational technology; no thesis required. *Faculty:* 4 full-time, 1 part-time. *Graduates 1989-90:* 4m, 9w.

OREGON

Portland State University. School of Education, P.O. Box 751, Portland, OR 97207. (503) 725-4678. Fax (503) 725-4882. Joyce Petrie, Prof., Coord., Educational Media, School of Education. *Program Basis:* Quarter. *Minimum Degree Requirements:* 45 credit hours including 42 in media; thesis optional. *Faculty:* 2 full-time, 4 part-time. *Graduates:* 14m, 23w.

University of Oregon. Division of Teacher Education, 1787 Agate St., Eugene, OR 97403. Gary W. Ferrington, Program Head. This program has been discontinued.

Western Oregon State College. Department of Secondary Education, Monmouth, OR 97361. Richard C. Forcier, Prof., Dir., Div. of Information Technology, Dept. of Secondary Education. *Specialization:* Computer education; instructional systems. *Features:* Offers advanced courses in media management, media production, instructional systems, instructional development, and computer technology. Some specialization in "distance delivery" of instruction and computer-interactive video instruction. *Program Basis:* Quarter. *Minimum Degree Requirements:* 45 credit hours including 36 in media; thesis optional. *Admission Requirements:* Bachelor's degree, minimum of 2.75 GPA in undergraduate program, interview, satisfactory performance on GRE or MAT. *Faculty:* 6. *Graduates:* 5m, 7w, including 4 foreign nationals.

PENNSYLVANIA

*Clarion University of Pennsylvania. Department of Communication, Clarion, PA 16214. (814) 226-2541. William Lloyd, Chair, Dept. of Communication. *Program Basis:* Semester. *Minimum Degree Requirements:* 36 credit hours. Emphasis on training and development. Courses in design, production, research; electives include interactive video, multi-image. Thesis optional. *Faculty:* 9 full-time. *Graduates 1989-90:* 14m, 14w, including 12 foreign nationals.

Drexel University. College of Information Studies, Philadelphia, PA 19104. (215) 895-2474. Fax (215) 895-2494. Richard H. Lytle, Prof. and Dean, College of Information Studies. *Program Basis:* Quarter. *Minimum Degree Requirements:* M.S. program of 48 credit hours comprised primarily of 6 functional groupings: technology of information systems; principles of information systems; information organizations; collection management; information resources and services; and research. *Faculty:* 18. *Graduates:* 28m, 80w, including 2 foreign nationals.

Indiana University of Pennsylvania. Department of Communications, Indiana, PA 15701. Kurt P. Dudt, Assoc. Prof., Chair., Dept. of Communications Media. *Program Basis:* Semester. *Minimum Degree Requirements:* 36 credit hours including 21 in media; thesis optional. *Faculty:* 11. *Graduates:* 15m, 8w, including 7 foreign nationals.

*Lehigh University. Lehigh University School of Education, Bethlehem, PA 18015. (215) 758-3231. Fax (215) 758-5432. Leroy J. Tuscher, Prof., Dir. Educational Technology Center, Lehigh University School of Education. *Program Basis:* Semester. *Minimum Degree Requirements:* 30 credit hours including 15 in media; thesis optional. *Faculty:* 4 full-time, 8 part-time. *Graduates 1989-90:* 5m, 9w, including 3 foreign nationals.

Pennsylvania State University. Division of Adult Education and Instructional Systems, University Park, PA 16802. (814) 865-1500. Fax (814) 863-7602. Kyle L. Peck, contact person, Instructional Systems Prog. *Program Basis:* Semester. *Minimum Degree Requirements:* 30 credit hours including either thesis or project paper. *Faculty:* 10. *Graduates:* 4m, 10w.

*Shippensburg University. Department of Communications and Journalism, Shippensburg, PA 17257. Dr. Pat Waltermyer, Chair., Dept. of Communication, Journalism, College of Arts and Sciences. *Program Basis:* Semester. *Minimum Degree Requirements:* 30 credit hours in media/communications studies; thesis optional. Program stresses mass communications.

*Temple University. Educational Media Program, Philadelphia, PA 19122. (215) 787-7000. Fax (215) 787-6926. Elton Robertson, Prof., Chair, Educational Media Program. *Program Basis:* Semester. *Minimum Degree Requirements:* 33 credit hours including 24 in media; thesis optional. *Faculty:* 2 full-time. *Graduates 1989-90:* 11m, 9w, including 3 foreign nationals.

University of Pittsburgh. Instructional Design and Technology, School of Education, Pittsburgh, PA 15260. (412) 612-7254. Fax (412) 648-5911. Barbara Seels, Assoc. Prof., Prog. Coord., Instructional Design and Technology, Dept. of Instruction and Learning, School of Education. *Program Basis:* Trimester. *Minimum Degree Requirements:* 36 credit hours including 18 in instructional technology, 9 in core courses, and 9 in electives; comprehensive examination. *Faculty:* 3. *Students:* 61, including 12 foreign nationals. *Graduates:* 4m, 7w.

The school also offers a 45-credit specialist certification program. This instructional design and technology program offers a sequence of courses leading to Pennsylvania state certification as an instructional technologist. This option provides for study of media design and production, design of inservice programs, application of instructional technology to the curriculum, curriculum development, group processes, leadership skills, selection and utilization of materials with consideration for a multicultural society, evaluation strategies, and administration of media programs. The certification program can be taken concurrently with a master's degree sequence. *Graduates:* Data not available.

West Chester University. School of Education, West Chester, PA 19383. (215) 436-2447. Joseph Spiecker, Prof., Chair., Instructional Media Dept., School of Education. *Program Basis:* Semester. *Minimum Degree Requirements:* 34 credit hours including 28 in media; thesis optional. *Faculty:* 5 full-time. *Graduates 1989-90:* 10m, 4w, including 1 foreign national.

RHODE ISLAND

Rhode Island College. 600 Mt. Pleasant Ave., Providence, RI 02908. (410) 456-8000. James E. Davis, Assoc. Prof., Chair, Dept. of Administration, Curriculum, and Instructional Technology. *Program Basis:* Semester. *Minimum Degree Requirements:* 30 credit hours including 21 in media; thesis optional. *Faculty:* 2 full-time, 1 part-time. *Graduates 1989-90:* 5m, 5w.

The University of Rhode Island. Graduate School of Library and Information Studies, Rodman Hall, Kingston, RI 02881-0815. (401) 792-2947. Fax (401) 792-4395. Elizabeth Futas, Prof. and Dir. *Specializations:* M.L.I.S. degree. Offers accredited master's degree with specialities in archives, law, health sciences, and rare books librarianship. 42-credit program offered in Rhode Island and regionally in Boston and Amherst, MA, and Durham, NH. *Admission Requirements:* 3.0 GPA, 50th percentile or higher MAT or 1,000 combined GRE. *Program Basis:* Semester. *Faculty:* 9 full-time, 20 adjunct. *Students:* 300 plus. *Graduates:* 5m, 52w. *Assistance:* 6 half-time graduate assistantships, some scholarship aid.

SOUTH CAROLINA

University of South Carolina. Educational Psychology Department, Columbia, SC 29208. J. C. Rotter, Prof., Chair., Educational Psychology Dept. *Program Basis:* Semester. *Minimum Degree Requirements:* 33 credit hours including 3 each in administration, curriculum, and research; 9 in production; and 3 in instructional theory; no thesis required. *Faculty:* 3, 1, 2. *Graduates 1989-90:* 1m, 3w, including 1 foreign national.

Winthrop College. Division of Leadership, Counseling and Media, Rock Hill, SC 29733. (803) 323-2136. George H. Robinson, Assoc. Prof., Educational Media Coord., School of Education. *Program Basis:* Semester. *Minimum Degree Requirements:* 36-42 credit hours including 15-33 in media, depending on media courses student has had prior to this program; nonthesis. *Faculty:* 7 part-time. *Graduates 1989-90:* 13w.

TENNESSEE

East Tennessee State University. College of Education, Box 23020A, Johnson City, TN 37614. (615) 929-5848. Fax (615) 929-5770. Rudy Miller, Assoc. Prof., Dir. Media Services, Dept. of Curriculum and Instruction. *Program Basis:* Semester. *Minimum Degree Requirements:* 36 credit hours including 18 in instructional technology; thesis optional. *Faculty:* 2 full-time. *Graduates:* 5w.

Memphis State University. College of Education, Memphis, TN 38152. (901) 678-3413. Fax (901) 678-4778. Thomas A. Rakes, Professor, Chair., Dept. of Curriculum and Instruction. *Program Basis:* Semester. *Minimum Degree Requirements:* 36 credit hours including 15 in instructional design and technology; thesis optional. *Faculty:* 4. *Graduates:* 1m, 6w.

The school also offers a six-year specialist degree program in instructional technology. The program requires 66 credit hours, including 36 in the major, 3 hours in educational research, 21 hours of supportive collateral, and 2 years' teaching experience or equivalent.

*Middle Tennessee State University. Department of Youth Education, School of Education, Murfreesboro, TN 37132. (615) 898-2804. Ralph L. White, Prof. and Chair., Dept. of Youth Education and School Personnel Services. *Program Basis:* Semester. *Minimum Degree Requirements:* 33 credit hours including 15 in media; no thesis required. *Faculty:* 2 full-time. *Graduates 1989-90:* 9m, 26w.

University of Tennessee-Knoxville. College of Education, Knoxville, TN 37906-3400. (615) 974-3165. Dr. Alfred D. Grant, Coord., Graduate Media Program, Dept. of Curriculum and Instruction. *Program Basis:* Semester. *Minimum Degree Requirements:* M.S. in Education, concentration in Instructional Media and Technology; 33 semester hours, thesis optional. *Faculty:* 1. *Graduates:* 2m.

The Department of Curriculum and Instruction also offers a six-year specialist degree program in curriculum and instruction with a concentration in instructional media and technology. This new program has 24 semester hours beyond the M.S. and a seminar paper (6 semester hours) for a total of 30 hours.

TEXAS

*East Texas State University. Department of Secondary and Higher Education, Commerce, TX 75428. (903) 886-5607. Fax (903) 886-5039. Robert S. Munday, Prof., Head, Dept. of Secondary and Higher Education. *Program Basis:* Semester. *Minimum Degree Requirements:* 30 credit hours with thesis, 36 without thesis, including 18 in media. *Faculty:* 2 full-time, 2 part-time. *Graduates 1989-90:* 8m, 19w, including 12 foreign nationals.

*North Texas State University. College of Education, Denton, TX 76203-3857. J. L. Poirot, Prof., Prog. Coord., Computer Education and Cognitive Systems, College of Education. *Program Basis:* Semester. *Minimum Degree Requirements:* 36 hours including 27 hours in instructional technology and computer education; nonthesis. *Faculty:* 8. *Graduates 1989-90:* 5m, 8w, including 10 foreign nationals.

*Prairie View A&M University. Department of School Services, Prairie View, TX 77446. (409) 857-3018. Marion Henry, Prof., Dir., Educational Media and Technology Program. *Program Basis:* Semester. *Minimum Degree Requirements:* 36 credit hours, 21 in media; no thesis required. *Faculty:* 3 full-time, 1 part-time. *Graduates 1989-90:* 10w.

Texas A&M University. College of Education, College Station, TX 77843-3256. (409) 845-3211. Fax (409) 845-9663. Ronald D. Zellner, Assoc. Prof., Coord., Educational Technology Prog., College of Education. *Program Basis:* Semester. *Minimum Degree Requirements:* 37 credit hours including 19 in educational technology; nonthesis. *Faculty:* 6 full-time, 1 part-time. *Graduates:* 7m, 10w, including 6 foreign nationals.

Texas Tech University. College of Education, Box 4560, Lubbock, TX 79409. (806) 742-2011. Robert Price, Assoc. Prof., Dir., Instructional Technology Program, College of Education. *Program Basis:* Semester. *Minimum Degree Requirements:* 39 credit hours; nonthesis. *Faculty:* 2 full-time, 2 part-time. *Graduates:* 9m, 8w, including 3 foreign nationals.

University of Texas-Austin. College of Education, Austin, TX 78712. (512) 471-5211. DeLayne Hudspeth, Assoc. Prof., Coord., Area of Instructional Technology, Dept. of Curriculum and Instruction, College of Education. *Program Basis:* Semester. *Minimum Degree Requirements:* 30-36 hours minimum depending on selection of program; 18 in instructional technology plus research course; thesis optional. A six-hour minor is required outside the department. *Faculty:* 4 full-time, 1 part-time. *Graduates:* 10, including 3 foreign nationals.

*The University of Texas-Southwestern Medical Center at Dallas. Biomedical Communications Department, Dallas, TX 75235-9065. (214) 688-3691. Fax (214) 688-2645. James B. Battles, Ph.D., Chair, Media Development Progs., Biomedical Communications Dept. *Program Basis:* Semester. *Minimum Degree Requirements:* 36 credit hours including 24 in media; thesis required. *Faculty:* 1 full-time, 8 part-time. *Graduates 1989-90:* 9m, 18w, including 3 foreign nationals.

UTAH

*Brigham Young University. Department of Educational Psychology, 201 MCKB, Provo, UT 84602. (801) 378-7072. Fax (801) 378-4017. Paul F. Merrill, Prof., Chair. *Program Basis:* Semester. *Minimum Degree Requirements:* 36 credit hours including 13 in core; thesis required. *Faculty:* 7 full-time, 5 part-time. *Graduates 1989-90:* 4m, 3w.

Utah State University. Department of Instructional Technology, Logan, UT 84322-2830. (801) 750-2694. Fax (801) 750-2693. Don C. Smellie, Prof., Head, Department of Instructional Technology. *Specializations:* Master's programs include the areas of instructional development, interactive learning, educational technology, and information technology/school library media administration. Programs in information technology/school library media administration and master resource teacher/educational technology are also delivered via an electronic distance education system. *Program Basis:* Quarter. *Minimum Degree Requirements:* 60 credit hours including 45 in media; thesis or project option. *Faculty:* 7 full-time, 5 part-time. *Graduates:* 14m, 17w, including 1 foreign national.

The school also offers a six-year specialist degree program in instructional technology. Program prepares individuals in the design, development, and evaluation of learning programs and materials for use in education, industry, and government. Admission requires 3.2 GPA, 1,000 GRE or 46 MAT, master's degree, three letters of recommendation, and individual's written statement of goals and philosophy. Program includes minimum of 45 quarter hours emphasizing research, core, and electives plus either a developmental practicum project or practicum internship. *Graduates:* 0.

VIRGINIA

James Madison University. Department of Secondary Education, Library Science and Educational Leadership, Harrisonburg, VA 22807. (703) 568-6486. Fax (703) 568-6920. Alvin Pettus, Head, Dept. of Secondary Education, Library Science and Educational Leadership. *Program Basis:* Semester. *Minimum Degree Requirements:* 33 credit hours including 21 in media; thesis optional. *Faculty:* 3 full-time, 2 part-time. *Graduates:* 1.

*Radford University. Human Services Department, Radford, VA 24142. Gary Ellerman, Prof., Academic Advisor, Educational Media. *Program Basis:* Semester. *Minimum Degree Requirements:* 33 credit hours; thesis optional. *Faculty:* 1 full-time, 3 part-time. *Graduates 1989-90:* 2m, 4w.

University of Virginia. Curry School of Education, Ruffner Hall, Charlottesville, VA 22903. (804) 924-7471. Fax (804) 924-0747. John D. Bunch, Assoc. Prof., Coord., Instructional Technology Prog., Dept. of Educational Studies, Curry School of Education. *Program Basis:* Semester. *Minimum Degree Requirements:* 36 credit hours including 18 in media and computers. *Faculty:* 3 full-time. *Graduates:* 3m, 2w.

The school also offers post-master's degree programs (Ed.S, Ed.D, and Ph.D.) in instructional technology. Applicants for the Ed.S. degree must hold a master's degree; have earned a GPA of B or better; submit an application for admission and official transcripts of all undergraduate and graduate work; be recommended by two persons qualified to judge his or her potential; submit basic aptitude test scores for the GRE; and submit a statement of professional goals. To earn the degree, a minimum of 30 credit hours is required in the student's program area and a written comprehensive exam of 8-10 hours is also required. *Graduates 1990:* 2 Ph.D., 4 M.Ed.

*Virginia Commonwealth University. Division of Teacher Education, Richmond, VA 23284. (804) 367-1324. Fax (804) 367-1323. Sheary Johnson, Assist. Prof., Core Coord. of Instructional Technology, Dept. of Teacher Education. *Program Basis:* Semester. *Minimum Degree Requirements:* 36 credits, thesis or project, and comprehensive exam. *Faculty:* 2 full-time. *Graduates 1989-90:* 6w.

Virginia Polytechnic Institute and State University (Virginia Tech). College of Education, Blacksburg, VA 24061-0313. (703) 213-5598. Fax (703) 231-3717. Thomas M. Sherman, Prof., Program Area Leader, Instructional Systems Development, Curriculum and Instruction. *Program Basis:* Semester. *Minimum Degree Requirements:* 30 credit hours including 15 in instructional technology; thesis optional. *Faculty:* 9. *Graduates:* 4m, 2w.

*Virginia State University. School of Education, Petersburg, VA 23803. (804) 524-5934. Vykuntapathi Thota, Prog. Dir., Dept. of Educational Leadership. *Program Basis:* Semester. *Minimum Degree Requirements:* 30 credit hours plus thesis for M.S.; 33 semester hours plus project for the M.Ed.; comprehensive exam. *Faculty:* 1 full-time.

WASHINGTON

*Eastern Washington University. Department of Education, Cheney, WA 99004. Thomas Keith Midgley, Dept. of Education. *Program Basis:* Quarter. *Minimum Degree Requirements:* M.Ed. in Instructional Communications: 48-60 credit hours, production thesis required. *Faculty:* 2 full-time.

**Saint Martin's College. Department of Education, Lacey, WA 98503. (206) 438-4333. Dan Windisch, Dir., Dept. of Education. *Program Basis:* Semester. *Minimum Degree Requirements:* M.Ed. with emphasis on Instructional Design and Development, Hypertalk Programming, and Materials Production: 30 credits, thesis required. *Faculty:* 4 full-time.

*University of Washington. Department of Education, Seattle, WA 98195. (206) 543-1877. Fax (206) 543-8439. William D. Winn, Prof., Prog. in Educational Communication and Technology, School of Education. *Program Basis:* Quarter. *Minimum Degree Requirements:* 45 credit hours including 24 in media; thesis optional. *Faculty:* 2 full-time. *Graduates 1989-90:* 3w, including 1 foreign national.

Western Washington University. Woodring College of Education, Bellingham, WA 98225-9087. (206) 676-3381. Tony Jongejan, Assoc. Prof., Instructional Technology Program, Dept. of Educational Administration and Foundations. *Specializations*: M.Ed. for Curriculum and Instruction, with emphasis in computer education, elementary and secondary programs; Adult Education, with emphasis on instructional technology and design; Instructional Technology and Design, with emphasis on multimedia master's program for education and industry persons; and Learning Resources (Library Science) for K-12 school librarians only. *Program Basis:* Quarter. *Minimum Degree Requirements:* 52 quarter hours (15 hours in computers, 24 hours in education-related courses, 0 hours outside education); thesis required; internship and practicum possible. *Admission Requirements:* 3.0 undergraduate GPA, acceptable GRE scores, three letters of reference, written career objectives. Successful experience teaching K-12 may be waived under special circumstances. *Assistance:* Standard financial assistance for graduate students, some special assistance for minority graduate students. *Faculty:* 3.5 full-time, 8 part-time. *Students:* 5 full-time, 15 part-time, 42 off-campus. *Graduates:* 8m, 9w.

WEST VIRGINIA

*Marshall University. Department of Instructional Technology and Library Science, Huntington, WV 25701. Virginia D. Plumley, Prof., Chair., Dept. of Instructional Technology and Library Science. *Program Basis:* Semester. *Minimum Degree Requirements:* 36 credit hours including 24 in media; thesis optional. *Faculty:* 2, 5, 0. *Graduates:* 1m, 3w, including 2 foreign nationals.

*West Virginia University. Technology Education, 706 Allen Hall, Morgantown, WV 26506. (304) 293-3803. Fax (304) 293-7300. David McCrory, Prof., Chair., Technology Education Program, Communication and Information Systems, College of Human Resources and Education. *Program Basis:* Semester. *Minimum Degree Requirements:* 37 credit hours including 15 hours in communication technology; thesis or research project. *Faculty:* 4 full-time. *Graduates 1989-90:* 3m, 1w, including 1 foreign national.

WISCONSIN

University of Wisconsin-La Crosse. Educational Media Program, Rm. 109, Morris Hall, La Crosse, WI 54601. (608) 785-8000. Fax (608) 785-8909. Russ Phillips, Dir., Educational Media Program, College of Education. *Program Basis:* Semester. *Minimum Degree Requirements:* 30 credit hours including 15 in media; nonthesis. *Faculty:* 2 full-time, 2 part-time. *Students:* 27, including 5 foreign nationals. *Graduates:* 5m, 10w.

*University of Wisconsin-Madison. School of Education, Madison, WI 53706. (608) 263-4600. Fax (608) 263-9992. Ann DeVaney, Prof., Coord., Educational Communications and Technology, Dept. of Curriculum and Instruction, School of Education. *Program Basis:* Semester. *Minimum Degree Requirements:* 30 credit hours including 22 hours in media; thesis or project required. *Faculty:* 5. *Graduates 1989-90:* 40m, 33w, including 14 foreign nationals.

*University of Wisconsin-Oshkosh. 800 Algoma Blvd., Oshkosh, WI 54901. (414) 424-1490. Richard R. Hammes, Prof., Coord., Dept. of Human Services and Professional Leadership, College of Education and Human Services. *Program Basis:* Semester. *Minimum Degree Requirements:* 36 credit hours including 15-21 in library, media, and technology. *Faculty:* 6 full-time, 1 part-time. *Graduates 1989-90:* 6m, 2w.

University of Wisconsin-Stout. Menomonie, WI 54751. (715) 232-1202. Fax (715) 232-1274. Dr. Roger L. Hartz, Program Dir., Media Technology Program. *Specializations:* M.S. in Media Technology. Curricular tracks may be developed in instructional development, media production, media management, and school media. This is an educational media/instructional technology program, not a mass media or media arts program. *Program Basis:* Semester. *Minimum Degree Requirements:* 32 credit hours including 15 in media; thesis optional. Coursework is drawn from many departments across the university; internship or field study strongly recommended. *Admission Requirements:* Bachelor's degree with minimum 2.75 GPA; three letters of recommendation; maximum 11 hours acceptable credits may be transferred into the M.S. program. *Assistance:* Limited number of graduate and teaching assistantships available; on-campus employment available; out-of-state tuition waivers for some international students. *Program Trends:* Increased involvement in distance education. *Faculty:* 4 full-time. *Students:* 8 full-time, 6 part-time, including 4 foreign nationals. *Graduates:* 5m, 4w.

WYOMING

University of Wyoming. College of Education, Box 3374, Laramie, WY 82071. Dr. Patricia McClurg, Prog. Area Coord., Instructional Technology. *Program Basis:* Semester. *Minimum Degree Requirements:* Master of Science in Instructional Technology: 36 credit hours including 32 in instructional technology and 4 in thesis option, or 36 hours of coursework including project option. Two tracks are available: (a) Instructional Design, and (b) Library/Media Studies. *Faculty:* 6. *Graduates:* 4m, 11w. For additional information, contact Dr. Patricia McClurg.

Graduate Programs in Educational Computing

When the directory of graduate programs in educational computing first appeared in *EMTY 1986*, there were only 50 programs. This year's listing consists of 78 such programs in 31 states, the District of Columbia, and the U.S. Virgin Islands. The information in this section has been revised and updates the information assembled in *EMTY 1991*. Individuals who are considering graduate study in educational computing should contact the institution of their choice for current information. It should be noted that several programs that appeared in the listing of master's and six-year programs in *EMTY 1991* now appear in this list.

Copies of the entries from *EMTY 1991* were sent to the programs with a request for updated information and/or corrections, with the proviso that, if no response was received, the 1991 entry would be used again so that the program would be represented in the list. Programs from which no response was received are indicated with an asterisk. It should be noted that not all of the information is necessarily correct for the current year. Any programs that were not listed in *EMTY 1991* are indicated with two asterisks.

We would like to express our appreciation to the many program administrators who complied with our request. In some cases, we were able to provide additional information for the entries from other sources. We are particularly indebted to Jenny Johnson (*Graduate Curricula in Educational Communications and Technology: A Descriptive Directory*, 4th ed., Association for Educational Communications and Technology, February 1992) and to Mark Bugler of the University of Iowa, who shared with us the results of his recent survey of doctoral programs in the United States.

Data in this section include the name of the institution and the program, telephone and fax numbers, a contact person, the degree(s) offered and the year the program began, minimum requirements for each degree, the number of full- and part-time faculty, the number of students currently enrolled, information on the availability of summer sessions and outside funding for the department, and tuition per credit hour.

This section is arranged alphabetically by state and name of institution.

ARIZONA

*Arizona State University. Educational Media and Computers. FMC Payne 146, Tempe, AZ 85287-0111. Dr. Gary Bitter, Coord., Educational Media and Computers. (602) 965-7192. Fax (602) 967-8887. *Specializations:* M.A. and Ph.D. in Educational Media and Computers. Master's program started in 1971 and doctorate started in 1976. *Minimum Degree Requirements:* Master's—33 semester hours (21 hours in educational media and computers, 9 hours in education, 3 hours outside education); thesis not required; internship required; comprehensive exam and practicum required. Doctorate—93 semester hours (24 hours in educational media and computers, 57 hours in education, 12 hours outside education); thesis required; internship required; practicum required. *Faculty:* 9 full-time. *Students 1989-90:* 25m, 29w at the master's level; 7m, 6w at the doctoral level. *Summer Sessions:* 10 weeks. *Outside Funding for the Department:* Yes (various grants). *Tuition per Credit Hour 1989-90:* $67 residents (summer and 6 hours or less, $681 for 7 hours or more); $67 nonresidents (summer and 6 hours or less, cost varies for 7-11 hours, $2,742 for 12 hours or more).

CALIFORNIA

San Diego State University. Department of Educational Technology, San Diego, CA 92182-0311. Dr. Pat Harrison, Chair., Dept. of Educational Technology. (619) 594-6718. *Specialization:* M.A. in Education with specializations in Educational Technology and Educational Computing. *Minimum Degree Requirements:* 36 semester hours (3 hours in education, hours in computers and outside education not specified); thesis not required; internship not required; practicum required. *Faculty:* 7 full-time, 3 part-time. *Students:* 40m, 75w. *Summer Sessions:* 12 weeks. *Outside Funding for the Department:* Yes (local companies, gifts from Apple Computer, federal and state grants). *Tuition per Credit Hour:* 0 to 6 units, $361 total; 6.1 or more, $559 total resident; $246 per unit nonresident.

United States International University. School of Education, 10455 Pomerado Rd., San Diego, CA, 92131. Dr. Maria T. Fernandez, Prof. and Program Director, Computer Education Programs. (619) 693-4721. *Specializations:* M.A. in Computer Education and Ed.D. with specialization in computer education. Master's and doctoral programs started in 1983. *Minimum Degree Requirements:* Master's—45 quarter credit hours (30 hours in computers, 15 hours in education, 0 hours outside education); thesis not required; internship not required; practicum required. Doctorate—95 quarter credit hours (60 hours in computers, 35 hours in education, 0 hours outside education); thesis required; internship required; practicum required. *Faculty:* 4 full-time, 4 part-time; *Students:* 40m, 60w on master's level; 25m, 25w on doctoral level. *Summer Sessions:* 10 weeks. *Outside Funding for the Department:* No. *Tuition per Credit Hour:* $215.

COLORADO

*University of Colorado-Colorado Springs. School of Education, P.O. Box 7150, Colorado Springs, CO, 80933-7150. Dr. Doris Carey, Graduate Faculty. (719) 593-3299. *Specialization:* M.A. in Curriculum and Instruction with an emphasis in Educational Computing and Technology. Students reflect K-12 track for educators or CBT instructional design track for corporate trainers. Master's program started in 1983. *Minimum Degree Requirements:* 33 semester hours (27 hours required in educational technology; 6 hours in education; 0 hours outside education); no thesis required; no internship required; no practicum required. *Faculty:* 1 full-time, 6 part-time. *Students:* 15m, 14w. *Summer Sessions:* 4-8 weeks. *Outside Funding for the Department:* No. *Tuition per Credit Hour:* $77 residents; $227 nonresidents.

*University of Denver. School of Education, Denver, CO 80208. Dr. Raymond Kluever, Coord., Graduate Study in Education. (303) 871-2508. *Specialization:* M.A. in Curriculum and Instruction or in Educational Psychology. Master's program started in 1984. *Minimum Degree Requirements:* 45 quarter credit hours (20 hours in computers, 35 hours in education, 0-10 hours outside education); thesis not required; internship not required; practicum not required. *Faculty:* 3 full-time, 3 part-time. *Students:* 2m, 2w. *Summer Sessions:* Yes (number of weeks not specified). *Outside Funding for the Department:* No. *Tuition per Credit Hour:* $330 residents and nonresidents.

CONNECTICUT

**Fairfield University. Computers in Education, Fairfield, CT 06430. Dr. John J. Schurdak, Dir., Dept. of Computers in Education. (203) 254-4000; Dr. Ibrahim Hefzallah, Dir. of Media/Educational Technology Program. *Specializations:* Master of Arts in two tracks: (1)

computers in education, or (2) media/educational technology (for school media specialists, includes instructional development and television production, or a customized course of study). C.A.S. in media management includes instructional development, television production, or a customized course of study. *Minimum Degree Requirements:* For master's degree, 33 semester credits and comprehensive exam. *Admission Requirements*: Bachelor's degree and, for foreign students, TESOL minimum score of 550. *Faculty:* 2 full-time, number of part-time varies. *Summer Sessions:* 3, each approximately 4 weeks long.

*University of Hartford. Math Education and Educational Computing, 200 Bloomfield Ave., West Hartford, CT 06117. Dr. Marilyn Schaffer, Associate Prof. of Educational Computing. (203) 243-4277. *Specializations:* M.Ed. in Educational Computing. Master's program started in 1985. *Minimum Degree Requirements:* 30 semester hours (21 hours in computers, 9 hours in education); thesis not specified; internship not specified; practicum not specified. *Faculty:* 2 full-time, 24 part-time. *Students:* 8m, 27w. *Summer Sessions:* 7 courses/1 week per course. *Outside Funding for the Department:* Yes (NSF grant). *Tuition per Credit Hour:* $180.

DISTRICT OF COLUMBIA

The George Washington University. 2201 G Street NW, Washington, DC 20052. Mary Louise Ortenzo, Coord. of Admissions. (202) 994-6163; Dr. William Lynch. (202) 994-6862. *Specializations:* School offers M.A. in Educational Technology Leadership. Master's program started in 1988. *Minimum Degree Requirements:* 36 semester hours (15 hours in computers, 9 hours in education, 12 hours electives inside or outside education); thesis required; internship not required; practicum not required. *Features:* Beginning with the spring 1991 semester, this program will be offered nationally with the cooperation of Mind Extension University, the Education Network. Students can complete the entire degree via instructional television through cable or satellite delivery. *Faculty:* 5 full-time, 2 part-time. *Students:* 12. *Summer Sessions:* Yes, varying length sessions, normally 6-8 weeks. *Outside Funding for the Department:* No. *Off-Campus Tuition per Credit Hour:* $594/3 residents and nonresidents.

FLORIDA

Florida Institute of Technology. Computer Education Department, 150 West University Blvd., Melbourne, FL 32901-6988. Dr. Robert Fronk, Head of Computer Education Dept. (407) 768-8000, ext. 8126. Fax (407) 984-8461. *Minimum Degree Requirements:* 48 quarter hours (18 in computer, 18 in education, 12 outside education); thesis and internship not required; practicum required. *Faculty:* 5 full-time, 4 part-time. *Students:* 10m, 9w. *Summer Sessions:* 8 weeks. *Outside Funding for the Department:* No. *Tuition per Credit Hour:* $234.

*Jacksonville University. Department of Education, 2800 University Blvd. North, Jacksonville, FL 32211. Dr. Daryle C. May, Director, Teacher Education and M.A.T. Program. (904) 744-3950. *Specializations:* Master of Arts in Teaching in Computer Education. Master's program started in 1983. *Minimum Degree Requirements:* 36 semester hours (21 hours in computer, 15 hours in education, 0 hours outside education); thesis not required; internship not required; practicum not required; comprehensive exam required. *Faculty:* 5 full-time, 2 part-time. *Students:* 7m, 5w. *Summer Sessions:* 6 weeks. *Outside Funding for the Department:* No. *Tuition per Credit Hour:* $250/semester-hour.

*Nova University. Ed.D./CED Program, Ft. Lauderdale, FL 33314. Dr. John Kingsbury, Director of Marketing. (305) 475-7047; (800) 541-6682, ext. 7047. *Specializations:* M.S., Ed.D., and Ed.S. in Computer Education. Master's program started in 1985; specialist in 1984; doctoral in 1984. *Minimum Degree Requirements:* Master's—36 semester hours (24 hours in computer, 12 hours in education, 0 hours outside education); no thesis required; no internship required; practicum required. Doctorate—66 semester hours (33 hours in computer, 21 hours in education, 12 hours outside education); thesis required; internship not required; practicum required. *Faculty:* 2 full-time on master's level; 8 full-time on doctoral level. *Students:* 35m, 35w students on master's level; 2m, 3w on specialist's level; 55m, 44w on doctoral level. *Summer Sessions:* Number of weeks not specified. *Outside Funding for the Department:* No. *Tuition per Credit Hour:* Master's, $190; doctorate, $225.

*University of Florida. College of Education, G-518 Norman Hall, Gainesville, FL 32611. Dr. Roy Bolduc, Prof. (904) 392-5049. *Specializations:* Ed.S. and Ph.D. in Computers in Education. Specialist program started in 1984 and doctoral in 1984. *Minimum Degree Requirements:* Specialist—semester hours vary (dependent on student's background); a minor in computer science (not computers in education) is required; thesis not required; internship not required; practicum required. Doctorate—semester hours vary (dependent on student's background); a minor in computer science is required; thesis required; internship not required; practicum not required. *Faculty:* 2 full-time, 1 part-time. *Students:* 2m, 1w on specialist level; 3m, 2w on doctoral level. *Summer Sessions:* Two 6-week terms. *Outside Funding for the Department:* No. *Tuition per Credit Hour:* Not specified.

GEORGIA

*Georgia State University. Educational Foundations Department, Atlanta, GA 30303. Dr. Dave O'Neil, Associate Prof. (404) 651-2582. *Specializations:* Department offers M.A. and Ph.D. in Educational Psychology (emphasis option in educational computers). Master's and doctoral programs started in 1984. *Minimum Degree Requirements:* Master's—60 quarter hours (25 hours in computers, 35 hours in education); thesis required; internship not required; practicum not required. Doctorate—90 quarter hours (35 hours in computers, 40 hours in education, 15 hours outside education); thesis required; internship not required; practicum not required. *Faculty:* 2 full-time, 2 part-time. *Students:* 4m, 21w on master's level; 5m, 5w on doctoral level. *Summer Sessions:* 6 and 8 weeks. *Outside Funding for the Department:* No. *Tuition per Credit Hour:* $22 residents; $74 nonresidents.

University of Georgia. College of Education, Athens, GA 30602. Dr. C. Hugh Gardner, Associate Prof. of Instructional Technology. (404) 542-3810. *Specializations:* M.Ed. in Computer-Based Education. Master's program started in 1985. *Minimum Degree Requirements:* 60 quarter credit hours (25 hours in computers, 10 hours in education, 25 hours not specified [55 hours with applied project]); thesis not required; internship and practicum optional. *Faculty:* 3 full-time, 5 part-time. *Students:* 20. *Summer Sessions:* Variable (4-9 weeks). *Outside Funding for the Department:* No. *Tuition per Credit Hour:* $46 residents; $138 nonresidents.

HAWAII

University of Hawaii-Manoa. Educational Technology Department, 1776 University Ave., Honolulu, HI 96822. Dr. Geoffrey Z. Kucera, Prof. and Chair, Educational Technology Dept. (808) 956-7671 or 956-3910. Fax (808) 956-3905. *Specialization:* Educational Computing as an area of concentration in Educational Technology, which began in 1983. *Minimum Degree Requirements:* 39 semester credit hours (27 in computing, 6 in instructional design, 6 electives); thesis available; practicum required, internship required. *Faculty:* 4 full-time, 3 part-time. *Students:* 2m, 3w. *Summer Sessions:* 12 weeks. *Outside Funding for the Department:* No. *Tuition per Credit Hour:* $67 residents; $201 nonresidents.

ILLINOIS

*Concordia College. 7400 Augusta, River Forest, IL 60305-1499. Dr. Paul T. Kreiss, Assoc. Dean, School of Graduate Studies. (708) 209-3010. *Specialization:* M.A. in Mathematic Computer Science Education. Master's program started in 1987. *Minimum Degree Requirements:* 48 quarter hours; no thesis, internship, or practicum required. *Faculty:* 8 full-time, 3 part-time. *Students:* 11m, 19w. *Summer Sessions:* 4 weeks each. *Outside Funding for the Department:* No. *Tuition per Credit Hour:* $170 for all students.

*Governors State University. College of Education, University Park, IL 60466. Dr. John Meyer, University Prof. (312) 534-5000, ext. 2273. *Specialization:* M.A. in Education (with computer education as specialization). Master's program started in 1986. *Minimum Degree Requirements:* 36-39 semester hours (15 hours in computer, 21-24 hours in education, 0 hours outside education); thesis/project required; internship not required; practicum required. *Faculty:* 3 full-time, 5 part-time. *Students:* 16m, 30w. *Summer Sessions:* 8 weeks. *Outside Funding for the Department:* No. *Tuition per Credit Hour:* $70 residents; $210 nonresidents.

National-Louis University (formerly National College of Education). Department of Computer Education, 2840 Sheridan Rd., Evanston, IL 60201. Dr. Sandra V. Turner, Chair., Dept. of Computer Education. (708) 475-1100, ext. 2256. Fax (708) 256-1057. *Specializations:* M.Ed., M.S., C.A.S. (certificate of advanced studies) in Computer Education, and Ed.D. in Instructional Leadership with minor concentration in computer education. Master's program started in 1983, specialist in 1983, and doctoral in 1984. *Minimum Degree Requirements:* Master's—34 semester hours (18 hours in computers, 10 hours in education, and 0 hours outside education); thesis optional; internship not required, practicum not required. Specialist, C.A.S.—30 semester hours (18 hours in computers, 4 hours in education, 0 hours outside education); thesis not required; internship not required; practicum not required. Doctorate—63 semester hours (14 hours in computers, 37 hours in education, 0 hours outside education); thesis required; internship required; practicum not required. *Faculty:* 3 full-time. *Students:* 62 in master's program; 12 in specialist program; 3 in doctoral program. *Summer Sessions:* 6 weeks. *Outside Funding for the Department:* No. *Tuition per Credit Hour:* $255. *Graduates*: 28.

Northern Illinois University. College of Education, DeKalb, IL 60115. Dr. Gary L. McConeghy, Chair., Instructional Technology. (815) 753-0465. *Specialization:* M.S.Ed. in Instructional Technology with a concentration in Microcomputers or Instructional Design in Education and Training. Master's program started in 1968. *Minimum Degree Requirements:* 39 hours (27 hours in technology, 9 hours in education, 0 hours outside education); thesis not required; internship not required; practicum not required. *Faculty:* 6 full-time, 2 part-time. *Students:* 102. *Summer Sessions:* 8 weeks. *Outside Funding for the Department:* No. *Tuition per Credit Hour:* Not specified.

*Southern Illinois University-Carbondale. Department of Curriculum and Instruction, Carbondale, IL 62901. Dr. Pierre Barrette, Coord., Dept. of Curriculum and Instruction. (618) 536-2441. *Specializations:* M.S. in Curriculum and Instruction with a specialization in computer-based education and Ph.D. in Curriculum and Instruction with a specialization in instructional technology. Master's and doctoral programs started in 1983. *Minimum Degree Requirements:* Master's—32 semester hours (specialty in computer-based education: 21 hours in computers, 9 hours in education, 2-6 hours outside education); thesis optional; internship not required; practicum not required. Doctorate—64 semester hours (specialty in instructional technology: hours in computers vary, 17 hours in education, hours outside education vary); thesis required; internship not required; practicum not required. *Faculty:* 5 full-time, 5 part-time. *Students:* 11m, 14w on master's level; 5m, 4w on doctoral level. *Summer Sessions:* 8 weeks. *Outside Funding for the Department:* Over $1 million in the areas of early childhood, science education, math education, and teacher education. *Tuition per Credit Hour:* $65 residents; $195 nonresidents.

INDIANA

Purdue University. School of Education, Dept. of Curriculum and Instruction, West Lafayette, IN 47907. Dr. James Russell, Chair., Educational Computing and Instructional Development. (317) 494-5673; (317) 494-0587. *Specializations:* M.S., Ed.S., and Ph.D. in Educational Computing and Instructional Development. Master's program started in 1982 and specialist and doctoral in 1985. *Minimum Degree Requirements:* Master's—36 semester hours (15 in computer or instructional development, 9 in education, 12 unspecified); thesis optional. Specialist—60-65 semester hours (15-18 in computer or instructional development, 30-35 in education); thesis required; internship required; practicum required. Doctorate—90 semester hours (15-18 in computer or instructional development, 42-45 in education); thesis required; internship required; practicum required. *Faculty:* 6 full-time. *Students:* 40 on master's level; 32 on doctoral level. *Summer Sessions:* 8 weeks. *Outside Funding for the Department:* No. *Tuition per Credit Hour:* $77.50 residents; $222.50 nonresidents.

IOWA

Clarke College. See listing for Tri-College Department of Education.

Iowa State University. College of Education, Ames, IA 50011. Dr. Michael R. Simonson, Prof. (515) 294-6840. *Specializations*: Master's and Ph.D. in Curriculum and Instructional Technology with an emphasis in instructional computing. Master's and doctoral programs started in 1967. *Minimum Degree Requirements:* Master's—30 semester hours; thesis required; internship not required; practicum not required. Doctorate—78 semester hours, thesis required; internship not required; practicum not required. *Faculty:* 4 full-time, 5 part-time. *Students:* 10m, 24w on master's level; 10m, 10w on doctoral level. *Summer Sessions:* 4 or 8 weeks.

***Marycrest College**. Graduate and Adult Programs, 1607 W. 12th St., Davenport, IA 52804. Thomas Faquet, Dean, Graduate and Adult Programs. *Program Basis*: Semester. *Minimum Degree Requirements:* For M.A. in Education: Computer Applications, 30 hours; for M.S. in Computer Science, 33 hours with thesis, 36 hours nonthesis. *Faculty:* 4, 0, 0. *Graduates*: 9m, 6w.

Tri-College Department of Education (a consortium of Clarke College, The University of Dubuque, and Loras College). Graduate Studies, 1450 Alta Vista, Dubuque, IA 52001. (319) 588-7842. Judy Decker, Clarke College, (319) 588-6425. *Specialization:* M.A. in Education: Technology in Education. *Minimum Degree Requirements:* 22 semester hours in computer courses, 12 in education, 3 electives. Predominantly summer program. *Admission Requirements*: 2 recommendations, teacher certification, submission of scores on verbal and quantitative portions of GRE or MAT, minimal GPA of 2.5 on a 4.0 scale. *Faculty:* 3 full-time and occasional adjunct instructors. *Students:* 13 part-time. *Outside Funding for the Department:* No. *Financial Assistance*: No financial aid available except in the form of student loans. *Tuition per Credit Hour:* Not specified. *Graduate Program Trends*: Moved from program in Computers in Education to Technology in Education, encompassing a multimedia perspective for instructional development. *Graduates 1990-91:* 3m, 3w.

KANSAS

*Kansas State University. Educational Technology and Computer Education, 253 Bluemont Hall, Manhattan, KS 66506. Dr. Jackson A. Byars, Chair., Educational Technology and Computer Education. (913) 532-5556. *Specializations:* M.S. in Elementary or Secondary Education with specialization in computer-based education, Ed.D. in computer education, and Ph.D. in computer education. Master's program started in 1982; doctoral in 1984. *Minimum Degree Requirements:* Master's—30 semester hours (minimum of 9 in computer education); thesis not required; internship not required; practicum not required (but these are possible). Doctorate—90 semester hours (minimum of 18 in computer education, 12 hours outside education); thesis required; internship and practicum not required but encouraged. *Faculty:* 4 full-time, 3 part-time on master's level; 4 full-time on doctoral level. *Students:* 10m, 10w on master's level; 6m, 3w on doctoral level. *Summer Sessions:* 8 weeks. *Outside Funding for the Department:* Yes (WEEA grant, others pending). *Tuition per Credit Hour:* fall and spring—residents, part-time $37-$45, full-time $550-$600; nonresidents, part-time $118-$126, full-time $1,765-$1,885.

KENTUCKY

*Spalding University. Education Technology Program, 851 South Fourth Ave., Louisville, KY 40203. Dr. Eileen Boyle Young, Dir., Education Technology Program. (502) 585-9911, ext. 237. *Specializations:* Ed.S. in Technology in Education and M.A. in Education Technology. Master's program started in 1983; specialist in 1983. *Minimum Degree Requirements:* Master's—30-36 semester hours (21-27 in computers, 9 hours in education, 0 hours outside education); thesis not required; internship not required; practicum required (directed study and position paper). Specialist—30-36 semester hours (21-27 hours in computers, 9 hours in education, 0 hours outside education); thesis not required; internship not required; practicum required (directed study and position paper). Students may obtain Kentucky certificate endorsements (K-12) as specialist in Computerized Instruction (36 graduate semester hours) and Indiana certificate endorsement (K-12) as Computer Educator (15 graduate semester hours). *Faculty:* 1 full-time, 1 part-time. *Students:* 11 students on master's level; 8 on specialist level. *Summer Sessions:* 2 sessions of 5 weeks each. *Outside Funding for the Department:* No. *Tuition per Credit Hour:* $185 plus fees; Ed.S. $195.

*University of Kentucky. Department of Special Education, Lexington, KY 40506-0001. Dr. A. Edward Blackhurst, Prof. (606) 257-4713. *Specializations:* Ed.S. degree in Special Education Microcomputer Specialist Program. Specialist program started in 1984. *Minimum Degree Requirements:* 35 semester hours (35 hours in education [all courses offered in Special Education Department and focus on computer applications], 0 hours outside education); thesis required; internship not required; practicum required. *Faculty:* 5 part-time. *Students:* 3m, 10w. *Summer Sessions:* 8 weeks. *Outside Funding for the Department:* Yes (Office of Special Education Programs, U.S. Dept. of Education). *Tuition per Credit Hour:* Under review.

LOUISIANA

Grambling State University. College of Education, Grambling, LA 71245. Dr. Vernon Farmer, Dept. Chair. (318) 274-2656; Dr. Ben Lowery, Assistant Prof. (318) 274-2238. *Specializations:* Ed.D. and M.A. in Developmental Education with an Instructional Systems and Technology specialization. Doctoral program started in 1986. *Minimum Degree Requirements:* 90+ semester hours (6 hours CAI, 6 hours design, 6 hours educational psychology, 6 hours video, 6 hours theory, 36 hours minimum in education, 0 hours outside education [but encouraged as cognate]); dissertation required; internship required; practicum not required. *Faculty:* 9 full-time, 4-6 part-time. *Students:* 60 admitted, 120+ taking classes and applying for admission. *Summer Sessions:* Yes (number of weeks 6-12). *Outside Funding for the Department:* No. *Tuition per Credit Hour:* residents, 1-3 units, $303; 12 units $637. Nonresidents, 1-3 units, $303; 12 units, $1,312.

MARYLAND

Johns Hopkins University. Division of Education, Rm. 101 Whitehead Hall, Baltimore, MD 21218. Dr. Dianne Tobin, Assistant Prof. (410) 516-8273. Fax (410) 516-8424. *Specializations:* M.S. in Education, concentration in Technology for Educators, C.A.S.E. in Technology for Educators, and Ed.D. in Human Communication and Its Disorders—Technology and Special Education. Master's program started in 1980 and doctoral in 1984. *Minimum Degree Requirements:* Master's—33 semester hours (24 hours in computers, 9 hours in education [computer courses are all education related]); thesis not required; internship and practicum required. Specialist—30 hours (30 hours in computers and education [computer courses are all education-related]); thesis not required; internship required; practicum required. Doctorate—99 semester hours (hours in computers and education vary); thesis, internship, and practicum required. *Faculty:* 3 full-time, 25 part-time. *Students:* Not specified. *Summer Sessions:* Yes (number of weeks varies). Special summers-only master's degree offered. *Outside Funding for the Department:* Yes (for doctoral program only, sources not specified). *Tuition per Credit Hour:* $165 residents, $190 nonresidents.

MASSACHUSETTS

*Fitchburg State College. Graduate Program in Educational Technology, 160 Pearl St., Fitchburg, MA 01420. Dr. Sandy Miller-Jacobs, Chair., Graduate Program. (508) 345-2151, ext. 3308. *Specializations:* Program offers M.Ed. in Computers in Education. Master's program started in 1983. *Minimum Degree Requirements:* 39 semester hours (30 hours in educational computers, 9 hours outside education; [electives]); thesis not required; internship not required; practicum not required. *Faculty:* 9 full-time, 5 part-time. *Students:* 85 (about 50 on campus and 35 off campus). *Summer Sessions:* 4 weeks. *Outside Funding for the Department:* Yes (students pay educational services fees—$15 per lab course—used for purchasing software). *Tuition per Credit Hour:* $90 credit Massachusetts resident; $110 credit nonresident. *Other Features:* Lab has been upgraded—(networked) 2 MacPlus, 15 Apple IIgs, 5 Apple IIe.

Harvard University. Graduate School of Education, 111 Longfellow Hall, Cambridge, MA 02138. For more information contact the Office of Admissions at (617) 495-3414. *Specializations:* Ed.M. and C.A.S. with a concentration in technology in education. Master's program started in 1983. Minimum Degree Requirements: 32 semester hours (number of hours in computers, education, and outside education not specified); thesis not required; internship not required; practicum not required. *Faculty:* 8 part-time. *Students:* Data not available; students do not have to declare a concentration until the beginning of their last semester. *Summer Sessions:* No. *Outside Funding for the Department:* Not specified. *Tuition per Credit Hour:* $1,774/course (4 credit hours).

Lesley College. 29 Everett St., Cambridge, MA 02138-2790. Dr. Nancy Roberts, Prof. of Computer Education. (617) 349-8419. *Specializations:* M.A. in Computers in Education, C.A.G.S. in Computers in Education, and Ph.D in Education with a Computers in Education major. Master's program started in 1980. *Minimum Degree Requirements:* Master's—33 semester hours in computers (number of hours in education and outside education not specified); thesis not required; internship not required; practicum not required. Specialist—36 semester hours (hours in computers, in education, and outside education not specified); thesis, internship, practicum not specified. Ph.D. requirements available on request. *Faculty:* 5 full-time, 12 part-time on the master's and specialist levels. *Students:* 9m, 28w on master's level; 2m, 3w on specialist level. *Summer Sessions:* Two 4- and 5-week sessions. *Outside Funding for the Department:* Yes (NSF grants). *Tuition per Credit Hour:* $300 residents and nonresidents.

University of Massachusetts-Lowell. College of Education, One University Ave., Lowell, MA 01854. Dr. John LeBaron, Associate Prof., College of Education. (508) 934-4621. Fax (508) 934-3005. *Specializations:* M.Ed. in Curriculum and Instruction, C.A.G.S. in Curriculum and Instruction, Ed.D. in Leadership in Schooling. (Note: Program concentration in Technology and Learning Environments is offered within broader program streams at M.Ed. and C.A.G.S. levels.) Master's, specialist, and doctoral programs started in 1984. *Minimum Degree Requirements:* Master's—33 semester hours (hours in computers, education, and outside education not specified); thesis not required; internship not required; practicum required. Doctorate—60 semester hours beyond master's plus dissertation (hours in computers, education, and outside education not specified); thesis required; residency required; comprehensive exams required. *Faculty:* 1 full-time (plus courses taught by other faculty). *Students:* Not specified. *Summer Sessions:* Yes (individual courses, schedule varies). *Outside Funding for the Department:* No. *Tuition and Fees per Credit Hour:* residents, $317.59; nonresidents, $499.59.

MICHIGAN

*Eastern Michigan University. College of Education, Boone Hall, Ypsilanti, MI 48197. Dr. Bert Greene, Prof., Dept. of Teacher Education. (313) 487-3260. *Specialization:* M.A. in Educational Psychology with an Educational Technology area of concentration. Master's program started in 1983. *Minimum Degree Requirements:* 30 semester hours (22 hours in computers, 8 hours in education); thesis optional. *Faculty:* 8 full-time. *Students 1989-90:* 55m, 137w. *Summer Session:* 6 weeks. *Outside Funding for the Department:* No.

MINNESOTA

*Mankato State University. Education Technology M.S. Program, Box 20, Mankato, MN 56002. Kenneth C. Pengelly, Prof. and Coord. of Educational Technology M.S. Program. (507) 389-1965. *Specialization:* M.S. in Educational Technology (integrated interdisciplinary degree). Master's program started in 1986. *Minimum Degree Requirements:* 51 quarter credit hours (6-15 hours in computers, 12-15 hours in education, 12-18 hours [optional] outside education); internship required. *Faculty:* 3 full-time. *Students 1989-90:* 35. *Summer Sessions:* Yes. *Outside Funding for the Department:* No. *Tuition per Credit Hour:* $52.40 residents; $73.35 nonresidents.

University of Minnesota. Department of Curriculum and Instructional Systems, 130 Peik Hall, 159 Pillsbury Drive SE, Minneapolis, MN 55455. Dr. Gregory Sales, Curriculum and Instructional Systems. (612) 624-2034. *Specializations:* M.Ed., M.A., Ph.D. in Instructional Design and Technology. Master's and doctoral programs started in 1972. *Minimum Degree Requirements:* Master's—45 quarter credit hours (18 hours in technology, 45 hours in education, 0 hours outside education); M.A. thesis (4 credits) required; practicum required for M.Ed.; Doctorate—136 quarter credit hours; thesis (36 credits) required. *Faculty:* 4 full-time, 4 part-time. *Students:* 75 students in master's program; 40 students in doctoral program. *Summer Sessions:* Two 5-week sessions. *Outside Funding for the Department:* Yes (assistantships with business). *Tuition per Credit Hour:* Varies by degree program and number of credits for which student enrolls.

MISSOURI

*Central Missouri State University. Lovinger 300, Warrensburg, MO 64093. Dr. Max McCulloch, Prof. (816) 429-4235. *Specialization:* M.S.E. Curriculum and Instruction emphasis Educational Computing. Master's program started in 1986. *Minimum Degree Requirements:* 32 semester hours (15 hours in computers, 10 hours in education, 7 hours outside education). *Faculty:* 15 full-time, 2 part-time. *Students 1989-90:* 3m, 4w. *Summer Sessions:* 8-12 weeks. *Outside Funding for the Department:* Not specified. *Tuition per Credit Hour:* $75 residents; $136 nonresidents.

Fontbonne College. 6800 Wydown Blvd., St. Louis, MO 63105. Dr. Mary K. Abkemeier, Master of Science in Computer Education. (314) 862-3456, ext. 365. *Specializations:* M.S. in Computer Education. Master's program started started in 1986. *Minimum Degree Requirements:* 33 semester hours. *Students:* 110. *Summer Sessions:* 6 weeks; fall and winter sessions. *Outside Funding for the Department:* Yes. *Tuition per Credit Hour:* $246 per credit hour with 15 percent discount for full-time currently employed educators. *Graduates 1986-91:* 80 (K-junior college teachers).

Northwest Missouri State University. Department of Computer Science, Maryville, MO 64468. (816) 562-1600. Fax (816) 562-1484. Phillip J. Heeler, Prof., Dir., School Computer Studies Prog., Dept. of Computer Science. *Program Basis:* Semester. *Minimum Degree Requirements:* 32 credit hours for each of three master's degree programs: (1) M.S. in school computer studies includes 26 credit hours of core computer courses; (2) M.S.Ed. in educational uses of computers includes 14 credit hours of core computer courses and 12 hours of educational courses; and (3) M.S.Ed. in using computers in specific disciplines requires 7 hours of core computer courses, 12 hours of education courses, and 7 hours in technology-related areas. *Faculty:* 6. *Students:* 27 full-time, 8 part-time. *Graduates:* 4m, 4w, including 6 foreign nationals.

*Southwest Baptist University. School of Education, 1601 South Springfield, Bolivar, MO 65613. Dr. Fred A. Teague, Dean, School of Education. (417) 326-1710. *Specialization:* M.S. in Education with specialization in Computer Education. Master's program started in 1982. *Minimum Degree Requirements:* 36 semester hours (18 hours in computers, 18 hours in education, 0 hours outside education); thesis not required; internship not required; practicum required. *Faculty:* 2 full-time, 3 part-time. *Students:* 9m, 19w. *Summer Sessions:* Two 4-week terms. *Outside Funding for the Department:* No. *Tuition per Credit Hour:* $88.

NEBRASKA

*Kearney State College. Kearney, NE 68849. Dr. Lynn Johnson, Chair, Professional Teacher Education. (308) 234-8513. *Specializations:* M.S. in Educational Technology. Master's program started in 1984. *Minimum Degree Requirements:* 36 semester hours (18 hours in computers, 18 hours in education); internship not required; practicum not required. *Faculty 1989-90:* 3 full-time, 5 part-time. *Students:* 21m, 11w. *Summer Sessions:* 8 weeks. *Outside Funding for the Department:* No. *Tuition per Credit Hour:* $40.50 residents; $64.50 nonresidents.

NEVADA

*University of Nevada-Reno. College of Education, Reno, NV 89557. Dr. LaMont Johnson, Prof., Dept. of Curriculum and Instruction. (702) 784-4961. Fax (707) 784-4526. *Specialization:* M.Ed. in Curriculum/Instruction. Master's program started in 1986. *Minimum Degree Requirements:* 36 semester hours (12 hours in computers, 24 in education); thesis optional; practicum required. *Faculty (1989-90):* 2 full-time, 2 part-time. *Students:* 15m, 20w. *Summer Sessions:* Two 5-week sessions. *Outside Funding for the Department:* No. *Tuition per Credit Hour:* $40 residents; $1,100 nonresidents for 7 or more credits plus $40 per credit.

NEW JERSEY

*Saint Peter's College. Graduate Programs in Education, 2641 Kennedy Blvd., Jersey City, NJ 07306. Dr. Henry F. Harty, Director, Graduate Programs in Education. (201) 915-9254. *Specialization*: M.A. in Education-Computer Science/Data Processing. Master's program started in 1979. *Minimum Degree Requirements:* 39 semester hours (27 hours in computers, 12 hours in education, 0 hours outside education). *Faculty 1989-90*: 9 full-time, 8 part-time. *Students:* 12m, 47w. *Summer Sessions:* 5 weeks. *Outside Funding for the Department:* No. *Tuition per Credit Hour:* $227.

NEW YORK

*Buffalo State College. 1300 Elmwood Ave., Buffalo, NY 14222-1095. Mr. Anthony J. Nowakowski, Acting Coord. of M.S. in Education in Educational Computing. (716) 878-4923. *Specialization:* M.S. Ed. in Educational Computing. Master's program started in 1988. *Minimum Degree Requirements:* 33 semester hours (18 hours in computers, 12-15 hours in education, 0 hours outside education); thesis or project required; internship not required; practicum not required. *Faculty 1989-90:* 10 part-time. *Students:* 29m, 39w. *Summer Sessions:* Three 3-week sessions, two 6-week sessions. *Outside Funding for the Department:* No. *Tuition per Credit Hour:* $90 residents; $192 nonresidents.

*Iona College. New Rochelle, NY 10801. Dr. Catherine Ricardo, Coord. and Assoc. Prof., Computer and Information Sciences. (914) 633-2578. *Specializations*: M.S. in Educational Computing. Master's program started in 1982. *Minimum Degree Requirements:* 36 hours— trimester basis—("all hours listed in educational computing"). *Faculty 1989-90:* 5 full-time, 2 part-time. *Students:* 50m, 50w. *Summer Sessions:* Two 5-week sessions and 2-week institute. *Outside Funding for the Department:* No. *Tuition per Credit Hour:* $270.

Long Island University. C. W. Post, Brookville, NY 11548; Brooklyn Campus, Brooklyn, NY 11201; Rockland Campus, Orangeburg, NY 10962. School of Education, Advisor of Educational Technology. (516) 299-2199. *Specialization:* M.S. in Education, concentration in Computers in Education or Certificate of Advanced Studies. One of the oldest and most established programs on the East Coast. Master's program started in 1985. *Minimum Degree Requirements:* 36 semester hours for M.S.; 18 credits for C.A.S.; technology project required; evening courses. Special programs available, some on weekends. *Faculty:* 4 full-time, 15 part-time. *Students:* Approx. 507 across 3 campuses. *Summer Sessions:* Usually offered in an intensified one-week format. *Other Features:* On-campus computing facilities available to all students. 90 percent hands-on course work. No GRE required. *Outside Funding for the Department:* No. *Tuition per Credit Hour:* $310 per credit. Financial assistance available.

Pace University. Department of Educational Administration, White Plains, NY 10606. Dr. Lawrence Roder, Chair., Dept. of Educational Administration. (914) 422-4198. *Specialization:* M.S. in Curriculum and Instruction with a concentration in computers. Master's program started in 1986. *Minimum Degree Requirements:* 33 semester hours (15 hours in computers, 18 hours in educational administration); comprehensive exam required. *Faculty:* 2 full-time, 15 part-time. *Students:* 10m, 35w. *Summer Sessions:* 4 weeks. *Outside Funding for the Department:* No. *Tuition per Credit Hour:* $355.

State University College of Arts and Science at Potsdam. 204 Satterlee Hall, Potsdam, NY 13676. Dr. Norman Licht, Prof. of Education. (315) 267-2527. Fax (315) 267-2771. *Specializations:* M.S. in Education, Instructional Technology, and Media Management with educational computing concentration. Master's program started in 1981. *Minimum Degree Requirements:* 33 semester hours (15 hours in computers, 18 hours in education, 0 hours outside education); thesis not required; internship or practicum required. *Faculty:* 6 full-time, 4 part-time. *Students:* 44m, 54w, and 10 foreign students (Taiwan). *Summer Sessions:* Two 5-week sessions (early and regular). *Outside Funding for the Department:* No. *Tuition per Credit Hour:* $134 residents; $274 nonresidents.

State University of New York. Department of Educational Theory and Practice, 1400 Washington Ave., Albany, NY 12222. Dr. Audrey Champagne, Chair. *Specializations:* M.S. in Curriculum Development and Instructional Technology. *Minimum Degree Requirements:* Flexible curriculum designed by students with advisor; minimum requirement of 30 credit hours; thesis optional. *Faculty:* 23. *Students:* 111 full- and part-time. *Tuition per Credit Hour:* Not specified. *Graduates 1990-91:* 4m, 16w.

State University of New York. Department of Technology and Society, Stonybrook, NY 11794. Dr. Thomas T. Liao, Prof. and Chair. (516) 632-8767. *Specializations:* Master's in Technological Systems Management with a 15-credit concentration in educational computing. Master's program started in 1979. *Minimum Degree Requirements:* 30 semester hours (hours in computer, education, and outside education not specified); thesis required; internship or practicum not specified. *Faculty:* 5 full-time, 10 part-time. *Students:* Not specified. *Summer Sessions:* 6 weeks. *Outside Funding for the Department:* Yes (source not specified). *Tuition per Credit Hour:* $102.50 residents; $242.50 nonresidents. *Graduates 1990-91:* 29m, 21w.

NORTH CAROLINA

*Appalachian State University. Department of Library Science and Educational Foundations, Boone, NC 28608. Dr. John H. Tashner. (704) 262-2243. *Specializations:* M.A. in Educational

Media (Instructional Technology-Computers). Master's program started in 1986. *Minimum Degree Requirements:* 36 semester hours; thesis optional; internship required. *Admission Requirements*: Selective. *Faculty 1989-90:* 2 full-time, 1 part-time. *Summer Sessions:* Two 5-week terms. *Outside Funding for the Department:* No. *Tuition per Credit Hour:* $480 full-time residents (in-state, 9 hours or more).

North Carolina State University. Department of Curriculum and Instruction, P.O. Box 7801, Raleigh, NC 27695-7801. Dr. Ellen Vasu, Assoc. Prof., Dept. of Curriculum and Instruction. (919) 515-3221. *Specializations:* M.Ed. and M.S. in Instructional Technology-Computers (program track within one master's in Curriculum and Instruction). Master's program started in 1986. *Minimum Degree Requirements:* 36 semester hours; thesis optional; practicum required. *Faculty:* 3 full-time. *Students:* 18. *Summer Sessions:* Yes (number of weeks not specified). *Outside Funding for the Department:* No. *Tuition per Credit Hour:* Not specified.

*University of North Carolina-Charlotte. College of Education, Charlotte, NC 28223. Dr. Clarence Smith, Prof. of Education. (704) 547-4542. *Specialization:* M.Ed. in Curriculum and Instruction—Computer. Master's program started in 1987. *Minimum Degree Requirements:* 36 semester hours (12 hours in computers, 15 hours in education, 9 hours outside education); internship required. *Faculty 1989-90:* 6 part-time. *Students:* 2m, 18w. *Summer Sessions:* Two 5-week sessions. *Outside Funding for the Department:* No. *Tuition per Credit Hour:* $190.38 per 3-semester-hour course; nonresidents, $1,323.25 per 3-semester-hour course.

*Western Carolina University. Cullowhee, NC 28723. Dr. Don Chalker, Head, Department of Administration, Curriculum and Instruction. (704) 227-7415. *Specializations:* M.A.Ed. in Supervision, with concentration in Educational Technology—Computers. Master's program started in 1987. *Minimum Degree Requirements:* 41 semester hours (18 hours in computers, 20 hours in education, 3 hours outside education); internship required. *Faculty 1989-90:* 25 plus full-time. *Students:* 6m, 7w. *Summer Sessions:* Two 5-week sessions. *Outside Funding for the Department:* No. *Tuition per Credit Hour:* residents, $71.05 per semester hour; nonresidents, $551.05 per semester hour.

NORTH DAKOTA

Minot State University. 500 University Ave. West, Minot, ND 58701. Dr. James Croonquist, Dean, Graduate School. (701) 857-3817. *Specializations:* M.S. in Audiology, M.S. in Education of the Deaf, M.S. in Elementary Education, M.S. in Learning Disabilities, M.S. in Special Education, M.S. in Speech-Language Pathology, M.A.T. in Mathematics, M.S. in Criminal Justice, M.A.T. in Science, M.M.E. in Music. Master's program started started in 1964. *Minimum Degree Requirements:* 45 quarter hours (hours in computers, in education, and outside education vary according to program). *Faculty:* 40 full-time, 9 part-time. *Students:* 12m, 68w. *Summer Sessions:* 8 weeks. *Outside Funding for the Department:* Yes (federal grants in special education and speech-language pathology). *Tuition per Credit Hour:* full-time students: $749 residents (Minnesota Reciprocity $921); $1,905 nonresidents (contiguous states/provinces $921). *Graduates*: 4m, 42w.

OHIO

Kent State University. Educational Technology Program, 405 White Hall, Kent, OH 44242. Dr. David Dalton, Program Coord. (216) 672-2294. *Minimum Degree Requirements:* 34 semester hours, including 15-20 hours in computer studies, 12-17 hours in education. *Faculty:* 4. *Students:* Data not specified. *Summer Sessions:* Two 5-week sessions. *Tuition per Credit Hour:* $117 in-state; $209 out-of-state. *Graduates:* approx. 10 per year.

*The Ohio State University. 225 Ramseyer Hall, 29 W. Woodruff Ave., Columbus, OH 43210-1177. Dr. Marjorie A. Cambre, Associate Prof. (614) 292-4872. *Specializations:* M.A. and Ph.D. in Computers in Education in the Program Area of Instructional Design and Technology. *Minimum Degree Requirements:* M.A.—50 quarter credit hours (18 hours core, 6 hours foundations, 3 hours multicultural minimum). Ph.D.—35 hours post-bachelor's, general examination (written and oral), dissertation. *Faculty 1989-90:* 8 full-time, 4 part-time. *Students:* 34 students in master's program; 29 students in doctoral program. *Summer Sessions:* 3, 5, 8, and 10 weeks. *Outside Funding for the Department:* No. *Tuition per Credit Hour:* 1 credit Ohio resident $108, out-of-state $144; 10 or more credits Ohio resident $867, out-of-state $2,230.

Wright State University. Department of Educational Technology, Vocational Education and Allied Programs, 244 Millett Hall, Dayton, OH 45435. Dr. Bonnie K. Mathies, Chair, Department of Educational Technology, Vocational Education, and Allied Programs. (513) 873-2509. Fax (513) 873-3301. *Specializations:* M.E. Computer Education, M.E. Computer Coordinator, M.A. Computer Education. Master's programs started in 1985. *Minimum Degree Requirements:* 48 quarter hours (hours in computers, education, and outside education not specified); thesis required for M.A. degree only; internship required (for computer education); practicum required (for computer coordinator). *Faculty:* 2.5 full-time, 2.5 part-time. *Students:* 5m, 13w in computer education program; 3m, 11w in computer coordinator program. *Summer Sessions:* Two 5-week sessions. *Outside Funding for the Department:* No (not yet). Graduate assistantships available. *Tuition per Credit Hour:* residents, $106 per quarter hour to 10.5 hours, $1,114 for 11-18 hours; nonresidents, $183 per quarter hour to 10.5 hours, $1,923 for 11-18 hours.

*Xavier University. Department of Mathematics and Computer Science, 3800 Victory Parkway, Cincinnati, OH 45207. Dr. David D. Berry, Director, Computer Science. (513) 745-3462. *Specializations:* M.Ed. with concentration in computer science. Master's program started in 1981. *Minimum Degree Requirements:* 30 semester hours (12 hours in computers, 12 hours in education, 6 hours either computers or education). *Faculty 1989-90:* 4 full-time in Computer Science; 24 part-time in Education. *Students:* 11. *Summer Sessions:* 6 weeks. *Outside Funding for the Department:* No. *Tuition per Credit Hour:* $150 residents and nonresidents.

OKLAHOMA

The University of Oklahoma. Educational Technology Graduate Program, Norman, OK 73019. Dr. Tillman J. Ragan, Prof. and Area Head. (405) 325-1521. *Specialization:* M.Ed. in Educational and Technology—Computer emphasis option. Master's program started in 1982. *Minimum Degree Requirements:* 32 semester hours (12 hours in computers, 21 hours in education [including computers' 12]); internship required. *Faculty:* 3 full-time, 2 part-time. *Students:* 10m, 16w. *Summer Sessions:* 8 weeks. *Outside Funding for the Department:* Yes (Special Educational Technology grant, Office of Education). *Tuition per Credit Hour:* $61.50 as of 6/90; nonresidents, $190.40 as of 6/90.

OREGON

University of Oregon, ISTE, Eugene, OR 97403. David Moursund, Prof., ISTE. (503) 346-4414. M.S., M.A., M.Ed., and D.Ed./Ph.D. programs in Curriculum and Instruction with specialization in computers in education have been terminated because of budget cuts at the university.

PENNSYLVANIA

The Pennsylvania State University. University Park, PA 16802. Kyle L. Peck. (814) 865-0473. *Specializations:* M.S. in Instructional Systems, M.Ed. in Instructional Systems, Ph.D. in Instructional Systems, and D.Ed. in Instructional Systems. Master's program started in 1971. *Minimum Degree Requirements:* Master's—30 semester hours (15 hours in instructional design, 9 hours in education, 6 hours outside education); thesis or paper required; internship not required; practicum not required. Doctorate—90 semester hours (27 hours in instructional design, 33 hours in education, 15 hours outside education); thesis required; internship not required; practicum not required. *Faculty:* 7 full-time, 3 part-time. *Students:* 16m, 28w on master's level; 42m, 33w on doctoral level. *Summer Sessions:* 3-, 6-, and 8-week sessions. *Outside Funding for the Department:* Yes. *Tuition per Credit Hour:* $187 residents; $370 nonresidents.

*Widener University. Center for Education, Chester, PA 19013. Dr. James P. Randall, Assistant Prof. of Instructional Technology. (215) 499-4497. Fax (215) 676-9715. *Specializations:* M.Ed. in Computer Science Education. Master's program started in 1986. *Minimum Degree Requirements:* 30 semester hours (18 hours in computers, 6-12 hours in education, up to 6 hours outside education), 3.0 GPA. *Faculty:* 1 full-time, 2 part-time. *Students 1989-90:* 25m, 28w. *Summer Sessions:* Three terms. *Outside Funding for the Department:* No. *Tuition per Credit Hour:* $200 residents and nonresidents.

TEXAS

Texas A&M University. Department of Interdisciplinary Education, Educational Technology Program, College Station, TX 77843. Dr. Ronald Zellner, Coord., Educational Technology. (409) 845-7276. Fax (409) 845-9663. *Specialization:* M.Ed. in Educational Technology, emphasis in computer applications. Master's program started in 1984. *Minimum Degree Requirements:* 37 semester hours (12 hours in computers, 6 hours in education); internship or practicum required. *Faculty:* 4 full-time. *Students:* 7m, 10w. *Summer Sessions:* Two 6-week sessions. *Outside Funding for the Department:* No. *Tuition per Credit Hour:* $18 residents; $122 nonresidents.

*Texas Christian University. P.O. Box 32925, Fort Worth, TX 76129. Dr. Sherrie Reynolds, Assistant Prof. (817) 921-7660. *Specialization:* Master of General Education with specialization in computers in education. Master's program started in 1984. *Minimum Degree Requirements:* 36 semester hours (18 hours in specialization, 6 hours in professional education, 6 hours thesis, 6 hours elective); thesis required; practicum required. *Faculty 1989-90:* 1 full-time, 1 part-time. *Students:* Not specified. *Summer Sessions:* One 3-week session, two 5-week sessions. *Outside Funding for the Department:* No. *Tuition per Credit Hour:* Not specified (financial assistance is available).

Texas Tech University. College of Education, Box 41071, TTU, Lubbock, TX 79409. Dr. Robert Price, Director, Instructional Technology. (806) 742-2362. *Specializations:* M.Ed. in Instructional Technology (educational computing) and Ed.D. in Instructional Technology (educational computing). Master's program started in 1981; doctoral in 1982. *Minimum Degree Requirements:* Master's—39 hours (24 hours in computing, 15 hours in education or outside education); practicum required. Doctorate—81 hours (33 hours in computers, 24 hours in education, 24 hours in resource area or minor); practicum required. *Faculty:* 3 full-time, 2 part-time. *Students:* 28 students on master's level, 17 students on doctoral level. *Summer Sessions:* Two 6-week sessions. *Outside Funding for the Department:* No. *Tuition per Credit Hour:* $16 residents; $120 nonresidents.

*Texas Wesleyan University. School of Education, Fort Worth, TX 76105. Dr. Allen Henderson, Dean, School of Education. (817) 531-4940. *Specializations:* M.S. in Computers in Education. Master's program started in 1982. *Minimum Degree Requirements:* 36 semester hours (18 hours in computers, 18 hours in education, 0 hours outside education); thesis or practicum required. *Faculty 1989-90:* 3 full-time, 1 part-time. *Students:* 10m, 19w. *Summer Sessions:* Two 5-week sessions. *Outside Funding for the Department:* No. *Tuition per Credit Hour:* $180.

*Texas Woman's University. Denton, TX 76204. Vera T. Gershner, Prof. (817) 898-2256. *Specializations:* M.A. and M.Ed. major in elementary education. Master's program started in 1985. *Minimum Degree Requirements:* 36 semester hours (6 hours in computer science, 30 hours in education [6-9 hours in computers in education]); thesis, internship, practicum not specified. *Faculty 1989-90:* 3 full-time. *Students:* 4w. *Summer Sessions:* 12 weeks. *Outside Funding for the Department:* Not specified. *Tuition per Credit Hour:* varies for residents (minimum of $100 through 6 hours); $120 per hour for nonresidents.

*University of Houston. University Park, College of Education, Houston, TX 77204-5872. Department of Curriculum and Instruction. (713) 749-1685. *Specializations:* M.Ed. and Ed.D. in curriculum and instruction with emphasis in instructional technology, specialization in computer education. Master's and doctoral programs started in 1981. *Minimum Degree Requirements:* Master's—36 semester hours without thesis. Doctorate—60 semester hours plus dissertation beyond master's. *Faculty 1989-90:* 3 full-time, 5 part-time. *Students:* about 50 on master's level; about 12 on doctoral level. *Summer Sessions:* 12 weeks. *Outside Funding for the Department:* Yes (NSF, U.S. Dept. of Education, Texas Educational Agency, institutional grants). *Tuition per Credit Hour:* $18 residents; $122 nonresidents.

University of North Texas. Department of Computer Education and Cognitive Systems, Box 5155, Denton, TX 76203. Dr. Jon Young, Chair. (817) 369-8790. Fax (817) 369-8799. *Specializations:* M.S. in Computer Education and Cognitive Systems. Master's program started in 1987. *Minimum Degree Requirements:* 36 semester hours (33 in computers, 6 in education); thesis, internship, practicum not specified. *Faculty:* 7 full-time, 3 part-time. *Students:* 30m, 50w. *Summer Sessions:* Two 5-week terms. *Outside Funding for the Department:* Yes (computer grant for equipment). *Tuition per Credit Hour:* $16 residents; $120 nonresidents.

University of Texas-Austin. College of Education, Austin, TX 78712. Dr. DeLayne Hudspeth, Associate Prof., Area Coord. (512) 471-5211. *Specializations:* M.Ed. and M.A. in a specialization in Instructional Technology. Master's programs started in 1984. *Minimum Degree Requirements:* 12-18 semester hours in computers, 18-24 hours in education, 6 hours outside education; thesis and internship optional. *Faculty:* 4 full-time, 2 part-time. *Students:* about 40. *Summer Sessions:* Two 6-week sessions. *Outside Funding for the Department:* Yes (source not specified). *Tuition per Credit Hour:* Not specified. *Graduates 1989-90:* Master's awarded, 9.

VIRGIN ISLANDS

*University of Virgin Islands. St. Thomas, Vl 00802. Dr. Dennis O. Harper, Associate Prof. of Computer Ed. (809) 776-9200. *Specialization:* M.A. with emphasis in Computers and Technology in Education. Master's program started in 1989 (January). *Minimum Degree Requirements:* 36 semester credits (21 credits in computers and technology, 15 credits in education, 0 credits outside education); thesis optional; practicum required. *Faculty 1989-90:* 1 full-time. *Students:* Anticipated enrollment of 60. *Summer Sessions:* 6 weeks. *Outside Funding for the Department:* U.S. Dept. of Education. *Tuition per Credit Hour:* $82 residents; $164 nonresidents.

VIRGINIA

George Mason University. Center for Interactive Educational Technology, 4400 University Dr., Fairfax, VA 22030. Dr. Chris Dede, Center Director, (703) 993-2019; Dr. Charles S. White, I.A.M. Coord., (703) 993-2052; Dr. Michael M. Behrmann, S.E.T. Coord., (703) 993-2051. Fax (703) 993-2019. *Specializations:* M.Ed. in Curriculum and Instruction, specialization in Instructional Applications and Microcomputers (I.A.M.), Special Education Technology (S.E.T.) and D.A.Ed. specialization in Instructional Computing. Master's program started in 1983 and doctoral in 1984. *Minimum Degree Requirements:* Master's school-based computer coordinator—30 semester hours (12 hours in computers, 18 hours in education, 0 hours outside education); thesis, internship, and practicum optional. Master's computer science educator—30 semester hours (15 hours in computers [12 of 15 are the "outside education" hours], 15 in education, 12 outside education); thesis, internship, and practicum optional. Master's special education technology—36-42 hours. Doctorate—69 hours beyond master's (12 hours in computers, 54 hours in education—12 of these are computer courses, 15 hours outside education); thesis, internship, and practicum are required. *Faculty:* 4 full-time, 5 part-time. *Students:* 15m, 45w on master's level; 5m, 37w on doctoral level. *Summer Sessions:* Yes (three 5-week sessions, one 8-week session). *Outside Funding for the Department:* Yes (various grants and contracts, generally federal and state). *Tuition per Credit Hour:* $124.50 residents; $311 nonresidents.

Hampton University. School of Liberal Arts and Education, Hampton, VA 23668. Dr. Carlton E. Brown, Dean. (804) 727-5793. (804) 727-5400. Fax (804) 727-5084. *Specialization:* M.A. in Computer Education. Master's program started in 1983. *Minimum Degree Requirements:* 36 semester hours (21 hours in computers, 15 in education, 0 hours outside education); practicum required. *Faculty:* 4 part-time. *Students:* 8m, 20w. *Summer Sessions:* 8 weeks. *Outside Funding for the Department:* No. *Tuition per Credit Hour:* $115 residents and nonresidents.

Virginia Tech University. Instructional Systems Development, College of Education, War Memorial Hall, Blacksburg, VA 24061-0313. Thomas M. Sherman, Prof., Program Area Leader, Instructional Systems Development, Curriculum and Instruction. (703) 231-5598. Fax (703) 231-3717. *Specializations:* M.A., M.S., and Ed.D programs in instructional technology. Preparation for education, business, and industry. *Features:* Areas of emphasis are instructional design, educational computing, evaluation, and media management. Psychology is the disciplinary theory/research perspective. The Instructional Systems Development Program houses the Education Technology Lab, which contains some 70 microcomputers (Apple, IBM, and Macintosh), including interactive video and speech synthesis capabilities. The program is also affiliated with the university's Learning Resources Center, which houses production services for graphics and video as well as satellite communications. Doctoral students are expected to intern either on campus or off campus (i.e., Arthur Andersen Associates, AT&T, etc.) or both. *Admission*

Requirements: 3.3 GPA for master's degree, three letters of recommendation, all transcripts. Experience in education recommended but not required. *Faculty:* 9 full-time, 7 part-time. *Students:* 14 full-time, 18 part-time. *Assistance*: Seven graduate assistantships; three tuition waivers; 2-4 additional graduate assistantships usually available due to contracts and grants. *Doctoral Program Trends*: Increasing use of computers for most production; increasing liaison with private sector, although most doctorates still take academic positions; continued emphasis on graduate student research and publication presentation. *Graduates 1990-91:* Doctorates awarded, 3m 4w.

WASHINGTON

Eastern Washington University. Department of Mathematics and Computer Science, Cheney, WA 99004-2495. Dr. Donald R. Horner, Prof. of Computer Science. (509) 359-7092. Fax (509) 359-6927. *Specializations:* M.Ed. in Computer Education (elementary), M.Ed. in Computer Education (secondary), M.S. in Computer Education (interdisciplinary), and M.S.T. (interdisciplinary). Master's program started in 1983. *Minimum Degree Requirements:* Master of Science— 52 quarter hours (30 hours in computers, 0 hours in education, 8 hours outside education—not specifically computer science; the hours do not total to 52 because of freedom to choose where Methods of Research is taken, where 12 credits of supporting courses are taken, and where additional electives are taken); thesis not required (a research project with formal report is required, although it need not be a thesis in format); internship not required; practicum not required. M.S.T.—52 quarter hours divided between computer science and another science or mathematics; one area is primary and includes a research project; the second area generally requires fewer hours than the primary. Master of Education—48 quarter hours minimum (24 hours in computer science, 16 hours in education, 8 hours outside education). *Faculty:* 11 full-time, 2 part-time. *Students:* about 50, most active in summers only. *Summer Session*: 8 weeks. *Outside Funding for the Department:* No. *Tuition per Credit Hour:* $90 residents and nonresidents.

*Western Washington University. Woodring College of Education, Bellingham, WA 98225. Prof. Tony Jongejan, Assistant Prof. of Education. (206) 676-3090. Fax (206) 647-4856. *Specializations:* M.Ed. in Computers in Education. Master's program started in 1981. *Minimum Degree Requirements:* 52 quarter hours (15 hours in computers, 24 hours in education, 0 hours outside education); thesis required; internship and practicum possible. *Faculty 1989-90:* 4 full-time, 2 part-time. *Students:* 10m, 15w. *Summer Sessions:* 9 weeks. *Outside Funding for the Department:* No. *Tuition per Credit Hour:* $87 residents; $263 nonresidents (up to 10 credits).

WISCONSIN

Cardinal Stritch College. Department of Educational Computing, 6802 North Yates Rd., Milwaukee, WI 53217. Dr. Jim Kasum, Chair, Department of Educational Computing. (414) 351-7516. *Specializations:* M.E. in Educational Computing and M.S. in Computer Science Education. Master's program started in 1984. *Minimum Degree Requirements:* Master of Education—30-32 semester hours (15-21 hours in computer, 6-15 hours in education, 0 hours outside education). Degrees may be completed via coursework option or one of the culminating experiences: thesis, field experience, or software project. Master of Science—30-32 semester hours (24-26 hours in computer, 3-6 in education, 0 hours outside education). *Faculty:* 3 full-time, 3 part-time. *Students:* 50m, 54w. *Summer Sessions:* 6 weeks generally; although there are courses which span 1 week, 4 weeks. *Outside Funding for the Department:* No. *Tuition per Credit Hour:* $227.50 on-campus (residents and nonresidents); $175 off-campus (residents and nonresidents).

Edgewood College. Department of Education, 855 Woodrow St., Madison, WI 53711. Dr. Joseph E. Schmiedicke, Chair., Department of Education. (608) 257-4861, ext. 2293. *Specialization:* M.A. in Education with emphasis on computer-based education. Master's program started in 1987. *Minimum Degree Requirements:* 36 semester hours (18 hours in computers, 30 hours in education, 6 hours outside education). *Faculty:* 2 full-time, 6 part-time. *Students:* 40m, 68w. *Summer Session:* Yes (number of weeks not specified). *Outside Funding for the Department:* No. *Tuition per Credit Hour:* $240 residents; $240 nonresidents.

Scholarships, Fellowships, and Awards

In the instructional technology/media-related fields, various scholarships, fellowships, and awards have been established. Many of these are available to those who either are or will be pursuing advanced degrees at the Master's, six-year specialist, or doctoral levels.

Because various colleges, universities, professional organizations, and governmental agencies offer scholarships, fellowships, and awards and may wish to have them included in this section, it would be greatly appreciated if those aware of such financial awards would contact either the editors or the publisher for inclusion of such entries in the next edition of *EMTY*.

We are greatly indebted to the staff members of the Association for Educational Communications and Technology (AECT) for assisting with this section.

Information is furnished in the following sequence:

- Overview of AECT and ECT Foundation Awards

- AECT Awards

- ECT Foundation Awards

AECT AND ECT FOUNDATION AWARDS

The Association for Educational Communications and Technology recognizes and rewards the outstanding achievement of its members and associates through a program that provides for three major annual awards — Achievement, Special Service, and Distinguished Service — and through the ECT Foundation, which provides awards in the areas of leadership, scholarship, and research.

AECT encourages members and associates to apply for these awards and to disseminate information about the awards to professional colleagues. Specific information about each award is available from the AECT national office. The annual deadline for submitting most award applications is November 1.

All ECT Foundation and AECT awards are presented during the AECT National Convention and INFOCOMM International Exposition.

For additional information on all awards, please contact:

AECT Awards Program
1025 Vermont Ave. NW
Suite 820
Washington, DC 20005
(202) 347-7834

AECT Awards

The Association for Educational Communications and Technology (AECT) provides for three annual awards:

Special Service Award: Granted to a person who has shown notable service to AECT as a whole or to one of its programs or divisions (nominee must have been a member of AECT for at least 10 years and must not be currently an AECT officer, board member, or member of the Awards Committee).

Distinguished Service Award: Granted to a person who has shown outstanding leadership in advancing the theory and/or practice of educational communications and technology over a substantial period of time (nominee need not be an AECT member but must not have received this award previously).

Annual Achievement Award: Honors the individual who during the past year has made the most significant contribution to the advancement of educational communications and technology (nominee need not be a member of AECT, and the award can be given to the same person more than once).

ECT Foundation Awards

The ECT Foundation, a nonprofit organization that carries out the purposes of AECT that are charitable and educational in nature, coordinates the following awards:

AECT/SIRS Intellectual Freedom Award (in conjunction with the Social Issues Resources Services Inc.): Recognizes a media specialist at any level who has upheld the principles of intellectual freedom as set forth in AECT's publication "Media, the Learner, and Intellectual Freedom" and provides $1,000 for the individual and $1,000 for the media center of the recipient's choice (recipient must be a personal member of AECT).

AECT Annual Conference and Earl F. Strobehn Internship Award: Provides complimentary registration and housing at the annual conference plus a cash award for four full-time graduate students (applicant must be a member of AECT and enrolled in a recognized program in educational communications and technology).

Richard B. Lewis Memorial Award: Presented to the outstanding school district media utilization program along with a cash award (awarded to either a public or private school having media utilization programs in place).

AECT Leadership Development Grants: Supports innovative leadership development activities undertaken by affiliates, divisions, or regions with cash grants (special consideration will be given to proposals that demonstrate a commitment to leadership development, that propose programs unique to the applicant's organization, and that include activities of potential benefit to other AECT programs).

AECT Memorial Scholarship Award: Donations given in memory of specific past leaders of the field provide a scholarship fund that gives annual cash grants to AECT members enrolled in educational technology graduate studies (three letters of recommendation are required).

Dean and Sybil McClusky Research Award: Recognizes the year's outstanding doctoral thesis proposal that has been approved by the student's university and offers a cash reward to defray the research expenses (the winner must agree to complete the proposed study).

Carl F. & Viola V. Mahnke Film Production Award: Honors excellence in message design for film and video products created by undergraduate students who are members of AECT (products must have been completed within a two-year period prior to the competition).

Robert M. Gagné Instructional Development Research Award: Recognizes the most significant contribution by a graduate student to the body of knowledge on which instructional development is based with a plaque and a cash prize (the research must have been done in past three years while the candidate was enrolled as a graduate student).

James W. Brown Publication Award: Recognizes the outstanding publication in the field of educational technology in any media format during the past year with a cash award (excluded from consideration are doctoral, master's, or other types of dissertations prepared in fulfillment of degree program requirements).

ETR&D Young Scholar Award: Recognizes fresh, creative approach to research and theory in educational technology by a young scholar (applicant must be an individual who does not hold a doctorate degree or who has received a doctorate degree within the past three years).

Young Researcher Award: Recognizes an outstanding unpublished report of research of an experimental, descriptive, or historical nature by a researcher who has not yet attained the doctorate or is less than three years beyond the degree (jointly published papers are not accepted).

Jerry R. Coltharp Award: Recognizes innovative media management practices which enhance the provision of instructional media services or advance media applications.

DOT-AECT Crystal Award: Recognizes the most innovative and outstanding instructional telecommunications project.

AECT Special Service Award

Qualifications

- Award is granted to a person who has shown notable service to AECT. This service may be to the organization as a whole, one of its programs, or one of its divisions.

- Nominee currently must be a member of AECT and have at least 10 years of service to AECT.

Disqualifications

- Recipient may not now be serving as an elected officer of AECT nor as a member of the board of directors.

- Nominee must not be currently serving as a member of the AECT Awards Committee.

Nomination

Nominations are judged and selected on the basis of an outstanding contribution to a division, committee, commission, or program of AECT but not to an affiliate organization. Please provide as much information as you can.

- Write in 100 words or less why you think nominee should receive this award. Include a description of nominee's contribution.

- What year did nominee join AECT?

AECT Distinguished Service Award

Qualifications

- Award is granted to a person who has shown outstanding leadership in advancing the theory and/or practice of educational communications and technology over a substantial period of time.

- The nominee need not be a member of AECT.

- Award may be given posthumously.

Disqualifications

- Nominee must not have received this award previously.

- Nominee must not be currently serving as a member of the AECT Awards Committee.

Nomination

Nominations are judged primarily on the distinction or magnitude of the nominee's leadership in advancing the field rather than the association.

Categories

- The following categories suggest areas in which the nominee may have rendered distinguished service to the field. The nominee may not be represented in these areas. Use those that apply or add others.

  - Leadership • Research/Theory • Development/Production • Writing
  - Major Contribution to Education Outside the United States

AECT Annual Achievement Award

Qualifications

- Recipient may be an individual or a group.

- The AAA honors the individual who during the past year has made the most significant contribution to the advancement of educational communications and technology.

- The nominee need not be a member of AECT.

- The contribution being honored should be publicly visible — a specific thing or event.

- It must be timely — taking place within approximately the past year.

- Award can be given to the same person more than once.

Nomination

The nature of this award precludes the use of a single checklist or set of categories for nomination. The nomination and selection are inherently subjective. You are asked simply to present a succinct argument in favor of your nominee. Your statement ought to answer the following questions:

- What is the specific achievement being honored?

- What impact has this achievement had, or is likely to have, on the field?

- How is the nominee connected with the achievement?

ECT Foundation
1992 AECT/SIRS Intellectual Freedom Award

Purpose: To recognize, annually, a media professional at any level who has upheld the principles of intellectual freedom as set forth in *Media, the Learner, and Intellectual Freedom: A Handbook,* published by AECT.

The Award: The award shall consist of:

1. a plaque and $1,000 for the winning media professional, to be presented at the AECT National Convention and INFOCOMM International Exposition;

2. a plaque plus $1,000 for the media center designated by the recipient;

3. the opportunity for the recipient to present a session on intellectual freedom at the AECT National Convention and INFOCOMM International Exposition.

Selection: The following criteria will be used in the selection process:

1. the recipient will be a media specialist at any level.

2. the recipient will be a member of AECT.

3. the recipient shall not have received another intellectual freedom award in the same year if that award was sponsored by SIRS, Inc.

4. the recipient will meet at least one of the following criteria:

   • has developed and implemented an exemplary selection policy/ challenge procedure for educational nonprint material.

   • has developed an innovative information program on intellectual freedom for nonprint media.

   • has upheld intellectual freedom principles in the face of a challenge to educational nonprint media.

   • has been active in the establishment and/or continuation of a coalition relating to intellectual freedom.

   • has been active in the development of a legal base for the continued enjoyment of intellectual freedom.

Selection
Committee: A subcommittee of the AECT Intellectual Freedom committee is responsible for the selection of the winner.

ECT Foundation
1992 AECT National Convention—
Earl F. Strobehn Internship Program

Awards:
Six students will be chosen as convention interns. The winners will receive complimentary convention registration, complimentary housing, and a $100 cash award. The interns will be expected to arrive at the convention on the day before the convention and to stay until the close of the convention. (Applicants are encouraged to request financial support for transportation and on-site expenses from their institutions or state affiliate organizations.)

Program
Activities:
Each intern will be expected to participate fully in a coordinated program of activities. These activities include private seminars with selected association and professional leaders in the field, observation of the AECT governance and program committees, and behind-the-scenes views of the convention itself. Each intern will also be responsible for specific convention-related assignments, which will require approximately 15 hours of time during the convention. A former intern, who is now a member of the AECT Leadership Development Committee, will serve as the program coordinator.

Eligibility:
To qualify for consideration, an applicant must be a full-time student throughout the current academic year in a recognized graduate program in educational communications and technology, and must be a member of AECT. (Applicant may join AECT when applying for the award.)

Application
Process:
To apply for the internship program, qualified graduate students must complete and return an application form and must submit two letters of recommendation.

ECT Foundation
1992 Richard B. Lewis Memorial Award

Award: $750, provided by the Richard B. Lewis Memorial Fund for "Outstanding School District Media Utilization," is awarded to the winner.

Selection
Process: The winner will be selected by a unified committee appointed from the divisions of Educational Media Management (DEMM) and School Media Specialists (DSMS) of the Association for Educational Communications and Technology, and the National Association of Regional Media Centers (NARMC).

Selection
Criteria: • Evidence of strong media utilization as gathered from:

  1. special utilization studies conducted by or for the school district;

  2. specific instances of good utilization as described in writing by school district or other personnel.

• Evidence of having provided in the school district budget means of implementing good utilization programs in its schools and of the degree to which AECT/ALA media standards are met for services, equipment, and personnel.

• Assessment of applicant's statements as to how the $750 (if awarded) would be spent, such as for:

  1. attending national, regional, or state conferences or workshops related to media utilization;

  2. selecting media specialist(s) to attend advanced training programs;

  3. buying software or hardware needed to improve media utilization programs;

  4. other purposes (indicating especially creative approaches).

• Recognition by an AECT state, regional, or national affiliate organization or representative, or from a National Association of Regional Media Centers state or regional representative:

  1. through prior recognition or awards;

  2. through a recommendation.

Eligibility: All school districts, public and private, having media utilization programs in place, and conforming to the preceding criteria, are eligible.

Other: The winning district will receive a plaque as part of this award.

ECT Foundation
1992 Leadership Development Grants

Grants: Grants of up to $500 are provided by the ECT Foundation and administered by the AECT Leadership Development Committee. The grants are awarded to assist AECT affiliates, AECT divisions, and AECT regional organizations to undertake leadership development activities that will improve participants' skills as leaders in the professional organization or in educational technology.

Selection: Grant awards will be recommended by the Leadership Committee's Subcommittee on Leadership Development Grants.

Criteria
for
Selection: All AECT state affiliates, divisions, and regional organizations are eligible for these competitive grants. An application from a previous grant recipient will not be considered unless a summary report has been submitted to the Leadership Development Committee and the AECT national office. Organizations that have not received a grant in the past are particularly invited to apply. Funds must be intended for some unique aspect or function not previously undertaken. Proposals that demonstrate a commitment to leadership development, that propose programs that are unique to the applicant's organization, and that include activities or products of potential benefit to other AECT programs will be given special consideration.

Awards: The awards will be presented during the AECT National Convention and INFOCOMM International Exposition.

ECT Foundation
1992 AECT Memorial Scholarships

Awards:

One scholarship of $1,000 and one scholarship of $750 are awarded to graduate students in educational communications/technology to carry out a research project in the field. The scholarships may be used to assist the recipients to further their education in a summer session or academic year of graduate study at any accredited college or university in the United States or Canada. Programs of study may be at the master's or doctoral level.

Eligibility:

All recipients must be members of AECT and accepted in or enrolled in a graduate-level degree program as outlined above.

Selection
Criteria:

Selections will be based on the following:

1. scholarship;

2. experience related to the field of educational media, communications, or technology, such as employment, field experience, course work, assistantships, publications, etc.;

3. service to the field through AECT activities and membership in other related professional organizations;

4. three letters of recommendation from persons familiar with the candidate's professional qualifications and leadership potential;

5. the candidate's own knowledge of key issues and opportunities facing the educational communications/technology field today, with respect to the candidate's own goals.

ECT Foundation
1992 Dean and Sybil McClusky
Research Award

Award: $1,000 is available to honor two outstanding doctoral research proposals in educational technology, as selected by a jury of researchers from AECT's Research and Theory Division. Each winner will be awarded $500.

Guidelines
for Preparing
and Submitting
Papers: Submitted proposals may follow acceptable formats of individual schools but must include at least:

1. The definition of the problem including a statement of significance.

2. A review of pertinent literature.

3. Research hypothesis to be examined.

4. Research design and procedures including statistical techniques.

Applicants are encouraged to review pages 157-61 of Stephen Isaac and William B. Michaels, *Handbook in Research and Evaluation*, Robert R. Knapp, San Diego, CA, 1971.

Eligibility: Applicants must be presently enrolled in a doctoral program in educational technology and have obtained committee acceptance of their proposal. The winner will be expected to sign a statement that the proposed doctoral study will be completed in accordance with the sponsoring university's graduate school policies (including any time limitations) or be required to return the funds received.

ECT Foundation
1992 Carl F. and Viola V. Mahnke
Film Production Award

Award: $500 will be awarded to honor a film or video product that demonstrates excellence in message design and production for educational purposes. In addition, certificates of merit will be awarded to entries with outstanding qualities worthy of recognition. In the event that no entry demonstrates excellence, in the opinion of the judges, no award will be given.

Eligibility: Eligibility is limited to film and video products that are educational in nature and produced by undergraduate or graduate students. The winners must be members of AECT. Only entries completed within a two-year period prior to the competition will qualify.

Formats: All entries must be either on film or videotape. Film entries are limited to 16mm. Video entries can either be ½-inch VHS or ¾-inch U-matic.

Judging: All entries will be judged during the AECT National Convention by a panel of judges from the AECT Media Design and Production Division.

Entry Fee: Entrants must include an entry fee of $10 per program, made payable to MDPD-AECT. For programs consisting of more than one film or videocassette, each must be submitted separately. An entry form must be completed for each entry. The entry form may be duplicated if necessary.

ECT Foundation
1992 Robert M. Gagné Award for Graduate Student
Research in Instructional Technology

Purpose:
To provide recognition and financial assistance for outstanding research by a graduate student in the field of instructional development.

Description:
The Robert M. Gagné Award Fund is coordinated by the ECT Foundation, a nonprofit organization sponsored and controlled by the Association for Educational Communications and Technology (AECT). The Division of Instructional Development will solicit nominations for the Gagné Award and will select the winner. The ECT Foundation is responsible for the administration of the award fund and will issue the cash award to the recipient.

Award:
$500 is awarded for the most significant contribution to the body of knowledge upon which instructional development is based. The Gagné Award competition is sponsored by the Association for Educational Communications and Technology (AECT) and its Division of Instructional Development. A jury of scholars will select the winning contribution. The award will be presented to the recipient during the AECT National Convention.

Eligibility:
The work must have been completed after December 31, 1988, while the award candidate was enrolled as a graduate student.

Nomination
Procedure:
You may nominate any individual (including yourself) for the Gagné Award.

ECT Foundation
1992 James W. Brown Publication Award

Award: $300 will be given to the author or authors of an outstanding publication in the field of educational technology.

Eligibility: Nominated items are not restricted to books or print; they may be in any media format (film, video, broadcast program, book, etc.). Any nonperiodic publication in the field of educational technology is eligible if it bears a publication date of 1990 or 1991.

Guidelines
for
Nominations: Nominations are solicited from all possible sources: AECT members, media-related publishers and producers, authors themselves, the AECT nonperiodic publications committee, and others.

Criteria: Nominated publications shall be judged on the basis of:

1. Significance of the item's content for the field of media/instructional technology, as defined in the *Definition of Educational Technology*, published by AECT in 1977, or in any subset of the publication.

2. Professional quality of the item.

3. Potential impact of the item's content on the field of media/instructional technology, as defined in the *Definition of Educational Technology*.

4. Technical quality of the item.

ECT Foundation
1992 ETR&D Young Scholar Award

Award: $500 will be presented to the winner. Additionally, the winning paper will be published in *ETR&D*, the refereed scholarly research journal published by the Association for Educational Communications and Technology (AECT).

For: The best paper discussing a theoretical construct that could guide research in educational technology, considered worthy by a panel of judges.

Eligibility: An individual who does not hold a doctorate degree or who received a doctorate not more than three years ago as of September 1, 1991.

Guidelines
for Preparing
and Submitting
Papers:

1. Papers must deal with research and theory in educational technology and must include:

   • A problem area stated within a well-explicated theoretical construct;

   • Supporting citations and analyses of related research;

   • A concluding discussion centering on what directions future research might take, with specific regard to variables, subjects, settings, etc., and, if appropriate, suggestions concerning other theoretical constructs that should be taken into consideration;

2. The paper should not be a report of a specific study;

3. A fresh, imaginative approach — which may go beyond the data — is encouraged;

4. The paper must be an original unpublished work;

5. The paper should be a maximum of 35 double-spaced typewritten pages;

6. The paper must be submitted in publishable journal format and must conform to the *American Psychological Association Style Manual*, 3d ed.

Selection
of
Winner: The selection of the winning paper will be the responsibility of the editor and editorial board of *ETR&D*. Only the best paper judged worthy of the award will win. (There may not be a recipient of this award every year.)

ECT Foundation
1992 Young Researcher Award

Award:
$500 for the best report of an experimental, descriptive, or historical study in educational technology. The Young Researcher Award competition is sponsored by the Research and Theory Division of the Association for Educational Communications and Technology (AECT). A jury of scholars will select the best contribution for presentation at the AECT National Convention and INFOCOMM International Exposition. The winner will receive the cash award plus a certificate suitable for framing.

Eligibility:
Anyone who is not more than three years beyond a doctorate as of December 31, 1991. A doctorate is *not* required. Jointly published papers are not acceptable.

Guidelines
for Preparing
and Submitting
Papers:
Papers must report an original, unpublished research effort of experimental, descriptive, or historical nature and must include the following:

1. problem area stated within a well-explicated theoretical construct(s);

2. supporting citations and analyses of related research;

3. exemplary reporting of research design or procedures and full description of statistical procedures where applicable;

4. concluding discussion that centers on directions for future research and implications for future directions in the field.

Other:
Manuscripts may be a maximum of 35 double-spaced typewritten pages. The manuscript must be submitted in publishable journal format and must conform to the *American Psychological Association Style Manual*, 3d ed. The author's name should be included *only* on the cover sheet. All manuscripts will be coded and reviewed "blind."

ECT Foundation
1992 Jerry R. Coltharp Memorial
Innovative Media Management Award

Award: This award is funded and coordinated by DEMM. One $400 award is presented annually, in recognition of innovative media management practices that enhance the provision of instructional media services or advance media applications.

Eligibility: Media service programs in schools, school districts, colleges and universities, regional media centers, government/military, allied health, and business and industry are eligible for the award.

Submission: Projects that demonstrate exemplary management practices and a potential for enhancing associated media services are to be described in an article format not to exceed 10 double-spaced typed pages. Supporting photographs and graphic materials are encouraged. Article organization may be determined by the author but must include a definition of the specific need to be addressed, a review of the management approach applied, and an evaluation of the effectiveness of the project. Project categories are unrestricted and may encompass such areas as staff development, client training, public relations, service assessment, facilities design, etc.

Selection: Submissions are reviewed and the recipient is determined by a selection committee appointed by the president of the AECT Division of Educational Media Management.

Criteria: Criteria for evaluating submissions are as follows:

Originality: Did the project demonstrate a unique approach to addressing specific needs?

Need: Did the need to be addressed relate to the enhancement of media services or the advancement of media utilization?

Design: Was the structure of the project appropriate to the need?

Impact: Was the project successful in meeting the defined needs?

Reporting: Articles detailing project parameters shall be considered for publication in an AECT publication. Publication rights will be assumed by AECT.

Other: Manuscripts may be a maximum of 35 double-spaced typewritten pages. The manuscript must be submitted in publishable journal format and must conform to the *American Psychological Association Style Manual*, 3d ed. The author's name should be included *only* on the cover sheet. All manuscripts will be coded and reviewed "blind."

1992 DOT-AECT Crystal Award

Purpose:	To recognize the most innovative and outstanding instructional telecommunications project.
Sponsor:	The Division of Telecommunications of the Association for Educational Communications and Technology (AECT).
Eligibility:	Limited to telecommunications projects that include a video component, that are instructional in nature and are designed for any age level, and that have been completed since September 30, 1990. Awards will be presented to the producing agency.
Entry Fee:	A $25 fee must accompany each entry. Make checks payable to DOT-AECT.
Judging:	Entries will be judged by a "blue ribbon" panel chosen by the president of DOT.
Criteria:	Entries will be judged using the following criteria:

- Instructional value and relevance

- Quality of production

- Evidence of successful utilization and implementation

- Evidence of achievement of goals and objectives

Entry
Information: The following information must be provided for each entry. Please provide the essential information only. This information may not exceed four pages.

1. Contact person's name, title, address, and telephone number

2. Official name of submitting agency

3. Name of individual to accept award for producing agency, if selected as winner

4. Intended audience(s)

5. Goals and objectives of project

6. Design and production process, including names of principal project staff

7. Time line for project

8. Budget and sources of funding

9. Evidence of successful utilization and implementation

10. Samples of all project components

11. Return address for all items sent.

Part Eight
Mediagraphy
Print and Nonprint Resources

Introduction

Nancy R. Preston
User Services Coordinator
ERIC Clearinghouse on Information Resources
Syracuse University
Syracuse, New York

CONTENTS

This resource list includes media-related journals, books, ERIC documents, and journal articles of interest to practitioners, researchers, students, and others concerned with educational technology and educational media. Emphasis in this section is on *currency*; the vast majority of books, ERIC documents, and journal articles cited here were published in 1991. Media-related journals include those listed in past issues of *EMTY* and new entries in the field.

SELECTION

Items were selected for the mediagraphy in several ways. The ERIC (Educational Resources Information Center) Database was the source for ERIC document and journal article citations. Most of these entries are from a subset of the database selected by the directors of the ERIC Clearinghouse on Information Resources as being the year's most important database entries for this field. Media-related journals were either retained on the list or added to the list when they met one or more of the following criteria: were from a reputable publisher; had a broad circulation; were covered by indexing services; were peer reviewed; filled a gap in the literature. Journal data were verified using *Ulrich's International Periodicals Directory 1991-92*. Finally, the complete contents of the mediagraphy were reviewed by the editors of *EMTY 1992*.

OBTAINING RESOURCES

Media-Related Periodicals and Books: Publisher, price, and ordering/subscription address are listed whenever available.

ERIC Documents. ERIC documents can be read in microfiche at any library holding an ERIC microfiche collection. The identification number beginning with ED (for example, ED 332 677) is used to find the document in the collection. ERIC documents can also be ordered from the ERIC Document Reproduction Service. Prices charged depend upon format chosen (microfiche or paper copy), length of the document, and method of shipping. Online orders, fax orders, and expedited delivery are available.

To find the closest library with an ERIC microfiche collection, contact:

ACCESS ERIC
1600 Research Blvd.
Rockville, MD 20850-3172
1-800-LET-ERIC (538-3742)

To order ERIC documents, contact:

ERIC Document Reproduction Service (EDRS)
7420 Fullerton Rd., Suite 110
Springfield, VA 22153-2852
1-800-443-ERIC (3742)

Journal Articles. Journal articles can be obtained in one of the following ways: (1) from a library subscribing to the title; (2) through interlibrary loan; (3) through the purchase of a back issue from the journal publisher; or (4) from an article reprint service. Articles noted as being available from the UMI (University Microfilms International) reprint service can be ordered using their ERIC identification numbers (numbers beginning with EJ, such as EJ 421 772).

University Microfilms International (UMI)
Article Clearinghouse
300 North Zeeb Rd.
Ann Arbor, MI 48106
1-800-732-0616

ARRANGEMENT

Mediagraphy entries are classified according to major subject emphasis under the following headings:

- Artificial Intelligence and Robotics

- CD-ROM

- Computer-Assisted Instruction

- Copyright Issues for Schools and Libraries

- Databases and Online Searching

- Distance Education

- Educational Research

- Educational Technology

- Electronic Publishing

- Information Science and Technology

- Instructional Design and Training

- Libraries and Media Centers

- Telecommunication Systems

- Television and Children

- Video Communication Technologies

Mediagraphy

ARTIFICIAL INTELLIGENCE AND ROBOTICS

Media-Related Periodicals

Artificial Intelligence Abstracts. Bowker A & I Publishing, Box 31, New Providence, NJ 07974. mo.; $495. Primarily for the specialist, the abstracts are of journal articles, reports, research documents, and other sources about artificial intelligence.

International Journal of Robotics Research. MIT Press, 55 Hayward St., Cambridge, MA 02142. bi-mo.; $80 indiv., $155 inst., $50 students and retired. Interdisciplinary approach to the study of robotics for researchers, scientists, and students.

Knowledge-Based Systems. Butterworth-Heinemann Ltd., Turpin Transactions, Ltd., Distribution Centre, Blackhorse Rd., Letchworth, Herts SG6 1HM, England. q.; £118. Interdisciplinary and applications-oriented journal on fifth-generation computing, expert systems, and knowledge-based methods in system design.

Mind and Machines. Kluwer Academic Publishers, Box 358, Accord Station, Hingham Station, MA 02018-0358. q.; $157. Discusses issues concerning machines and mentality, artificial intelligence, epistemology, simulation, and modeling.

Books

Davies, Peter. (1991). **Artificial intelligence: Its role in the information industry**. Learned Information, Inc., 143 Old Marlton Pike, Medford, NJ 08055-8750. 114pp. $39.50 plus $3.50 shipping and handling. Discusses what artificial intelligence is, how it might be applied to information users' needs, and near-term and future possibilities for application from the point of view of decision makers in the information industry and other information providers.

Yazdani, Masoud, ed. (1991). **Artificial intelligence and education, volume two: Principles and case studies**. Ablex Publishing Corp., 355 Chestnut St., Norwood, NJ 07648. 352pp. $65 cloth, $29.50 paper, prepaid. A collection of papers documenting the application of artificial intelligence in education. Reflects a convergence of interests between advocates of intelligent tutoring systems and those of more exploratory learning environments.

ERIC Documents

Baker, Eva L., and Butler, Frances A. (1991, February). **Artificial intelligence measurement system, overview and lessons learned: Final project report**. Los Angeles, CA: California University, Center for the Study of Evaluation. 31pp. ED 332 677. Summarizes an exploration of methodology to consider how the effects of artificial intelligence systems could be compared to human performance.

Gozzi, Raymond, Jr. (1991, March). **The metaphor of the mind-as-computer: Some considerations for teachers**. Paper presented at the Annual Meeting of the Conference on College Composition and Communication, Boston, MA, March 21-23, 1991. 10pp. ED 329 997. Discusses the ongoing debate of the information age that the mind is a computer or that, conversely, the computer has a mind, and the implications of such metaphors for the future of computers and teaching.

Journal Articles

Khawam, Yves J. (1991, June). Epistemological grounds for cybernetic models. **Journal of the American Society for Information Science, 42**(5), 372-77. EJ 428 891. (Available UMI.) Addresses philosophical grounds for artificial intelligence and cybernetic models by investigating realism, a priorism, and phenomenology, to determine the problems in information transfer between a model and the real world.

Tamashiro, Roy, and Bechtelheimer, Lynne. (1991, February). Expert systems in the elementary grades: Developing thinking skills and independent learning. **Computing Teacher, 18**(5), 21-26. EJ 421 772. (Available UMI.) Discusses expert systems as tools, tutors, and tutees; differences in learning styles; problem-solving skills; and uses of expert systems in science and social studies.

CD-ROM

Media-Related Periodicals

CD-ROM Librarian. Meckler Publishing Corp., 11 Ferry Ln. W., Westport, CT 06880-5808. 11/yr.; $75. Information about optical technologies relevant to libraries and information centers.

CD-ROM Professional. (Formerly **Laserdisk Professional**.) Pemberton Press, Inc., 11 Tannery Ln., Weston, CT 06883. bi-mo.; $86. Assists publishers, librarians, and other information professionals in the selection, evaluation, purchase, and operation of CD-ROM systems.

Books

Chen, Ching-Chih. (1991). **Optical discs in libraries: Use and trends**. Learned Information, Inc., 143 Old Marlton Pike, Medford, NJ 08055-8750. 240pp. $79.50 plus $3.00 shipping and handling. Provides several study-generated components offering the most comprehensive information on library use of optical discs in the United States and Canada, with comparative information for Western Europe.

Jacso, Peter. (1991). **CD-ROM software, dataware, and hardware: Evaluation, selection, and installation**. Libraries Unlimited, Inc., P.O. Box 6633, Englewood, CO 80155-6633. 256pp. $35 prepaid. Explains the criteria by which CD-ROM databases, their search software, and CD-ROM drives may be assessed. Comparative charts, tables, templates, and screen samples illustrate features such as search and display options and help and error-handling features.

Shelton, James, and Webb, Joseph, eds. (1991). **Optical publishing directory. 4th ed. 1991/1992**. Learned Information, Inc., 143 Old Marlton Pike, Medford, NJ 08055-8750. 393pp. $59 plus $3.50 shipping and handling. Full description of over 700 CD-ROM titles, including product content, hardware/software requirements, and market data. Indexed by product features and by subject.

Journal Articles

Akeroyd, John. (1991, February). CD-ROM networks. **Electronic Library, 9**(1), 21-25. EJ 427 504. Provides an overview of CD-ROM networking technology in libraries and evaluates six systems currently in operation.

Arps, Mark. (1991, July). Hardware and media options for CD-ROM publishing. **CD-ROM Professional, 4**(4), 66-68. EJ 430 291. Explains the basic hardware, software, and media options for changing from a CD-ROM user to a CD-ROM publisher.

Becker, Henry Jay. (1991, February). Encyclopedias on CD-ROM: Two orders of magnitude more than any other educational software has ever delivered before. **Educational Technology, 31**(2), 7-20. EJ 423 362. (Available UMI.) Describes Grolier's *Electronic Encyclopedia*, World Book's *Information Finder*, and Compton's *Multimedia Encyclopedia*, and offers suggestions for classroom use.

Jensen, Mary Brandt. (1991, March). CD-ROM licenses: What's in the fine or nonexistent print may surprise you. **CD-ROM Professional, 4**(2), 13-16. Licensing terms and agreements of 12 CD-ROM producers are examined, and downloading, multiple-use restrictions, and the making of backup copies of support software are discussed.

LaGuardia, Cheryl, et al. (1991, March). CD-ROM networking in ARL academic libraries: A survey. **CD-ROM Professional, 4**(2), 36, 38-39. EJ 423 399. A study of academic libraries' CD-ROM use shows diversity in numbers of databases owned, number of workstations, staffing patterns, and network participation.

Nicholls, Paul Travis. (1991, March). A survey of commercially available CD-ROM database titles. **CD-ROM Professional, 4**(2), 23-28. EJ 423 397. Summarizes trends in growth of CD-ROM titles, types and subjects of products produced, update options, and hardware requirements.

COMPUTER-ASSISTED INSTRUCTION

Media-Related Periodicals

Apple Library Users Group Newsletter. c/o Monica Ertel, Apple Computer, 10381 Bandley Dr., Cupertino, CA 95014. 4/yr.; free. For people interested in using Apple and Macintosh computers in libraries and information centers.

BYTE. Box 550, Hightstown, NJ 08520-9886. mo.; $29.95. Current articles on computer hardware, software, and applications, and reviews of computer products.

CALICO Journal. Brigham Young University Press, 3078 JKHB, Brigham Young University, Provo, UT 84602. q.; $35 indiv., $65 inst. Provides information on the applications of technology in teaching and learning languages.

Collegiate Microcomputer. Rose-Hulman Institute of Technology, Department of Mathematics, Terre Haute, IN 47803. q.; $34. Features articles about instructional uses of microcomputers in college and university courses.

Compute! Compute Publications, Inc., 324 W. Wendover Ave., Suite 200, Greensboro, NC 27408. mo.; $19.97. Specifically designed for users of IBM PC, Tandy, and compatible machines at home, at work, and in the school.

Computer Book Review. Maeventec, 735 Ekekela Place, Honolulu, HI 96817. mo.; $25. Reviews books on computers and computer-related subjects.

Computers & Education. Pergamon Press, Journals Division, Maxwell House, Fairview Park, Elmsford, NY 10523. 8/yr.; $510. A theoretical, refereed journal that emphasizes research project reports.

Computers and People. Berkeley Enterprises, Inc., 815 Washington St., Newtonville, MA 02160. bi-mo.; $24.50. Covers all aspects of information processing systems through articles, reviews, and games.

Computers and the Humanities. Kluwer Academic Publishers, Box 358, Accord Station, Hingham, MA 02018-0358. bi-mo.; $66 indiv., $189.50 inst. Contains scholarly articles on computer applications in the humanities.

Computing Teacher. International Society for Technology in Education, University of Oregon, 1787 Agate St., Eugene, OR 97403-9905. 8/yr.; $28.50. For persons interested in the instructional use of computers with an emphasis on teaching about computers, using computers in teaching, teacher education, and the computer's impact on curricula.

Datapro Reports. Datapro Research Corp., 1805 Underwood Blvd., Delran, NJ 08075. Base volumes and monthly updates range from $385 to $950 depending on the topic (such as microcomputers, software, or minicomputers). The updates provide evaluations as well as descriptions of new products. Includes directories to vendors and companies.

Digest of Software Reviews: Education. School & Home Courseware, Inc., 3999 N. Chestnut Diag., Suite 333, Fresno, CA 93726-4797. mo.; $147.50. Compiles software reviews from over 60 journals and magazines that emphasize critical features of the instructional software for grades K-12.

Dr. Dobb's Journal. M & T Publishing, Inc., 501 Galveston Dr., Redwood City, CA 94063-4728. mo.; $29.97. Articles on the latest in operating systems, programming languages, hardware design and architecture, data structures, and telecommunications; in-depth hardware and software reviews.

Education & Computing. Elsevier Science Publishers, B.V., Postbus 211, 1000 AE Amsterdam, Netherlands. q. (price not available). For educators, computer scientists, and decision makers in government, education, and industry, with emphasis on the technical developments in information technology.

Education Computer News. Business Publishers, Inc., 951 Pershing Dr., Silver Spring, MD 20910-4464. bi-w.; $213. Summarizes federal, state, and district programs involved with uses of technology in the classroom. Also provides contact information and brief descriptions about resources, grants, and foundations.

Electronic Learning. Scholastic, Inc., Box 3024, Southeast, PA 19398. 8/yr.; $19.95. Professional magazine for media specialists, teachers, and administrators that stresses nontechnical information about uses of computers, video equipment, and other electronic devices.

Family Computing. Scholastic, Inc., Box 3024, Southeast, PA 19398. mo.; $19.95. Explains to parents what their children are doing with microcomputers and gives suggestions for additional activities.

Home Office Computing. Scholastic, Inc., Box 53561, Boulder, CO 80321-1346. mo.; $19.97. For professionals who use computers and do business at home.

InCider-A Plus. IDG Communications, Box 58618, Boulder, CO 80322-8616. mo.; $27.97. A magazine for all levels of users of any Apple product. Reviews new developments in software and hardware and provides how-to articles.

InfoWorld. IDG Communications, 1060 Marsh Rd., Menlo Park, CA 94025. w.; $110. News of the information and microcomputer field, including software reviews.

Interactive Learning International. John Wiley & Sons, Baffins Ln., Chichester, Sussex, PO19 1UD, England. q.; $195. International journal that covers applications of computer-based training, analyzes strengths and weaknesses of interactive learning that uses computer technology, examines state-of-the-art technologies, and reports research findings.

Journal of Computer Assisted Learning. Blackwell Scientific Publications Ltd., Osney Mead, Oxford OX2 0EL, England. q.; $38 indiv., $155 inst. Articles and research on the use of computer-assisted learning.

Journal of Computer-Based Instruction. Association for the Development of Computer Based Instructional Systems, International Headquarters, 1601 West Fifth Ave., Suite 111, Columbus, OH 43212. q.; $36 nonmembers, single copy $10. Contains both scholarly research and descriptions of practical CBI techniques.

Journal of Educational Computing Research. Baywood Publishing Co., 26 Austin Ave., Box 337, Amityville, NY 11701. q.; $75 indiv., $109 inst. Publishes new research in the theory and applications of educational computing in a variety of content areas and with various ages.

Journal of Research on Computing in Education. International Society for Technology in Education, 2700 Bay Area Blvd., Box 509, Houston, TX 77058. q.; $38 nonmembers. A technical publication emphasizing current computer research and advances as they apply to all levels of education.

MacWorld. MacWorld Communications, Inc., Box 54515, Boulder, CO 80322-4515. mo.; $30. Describes software, tutorials, and applications for users of the Macintosh microcomputer.

Microcomputer Index. Learned Information, Inc., 143 Old Marlton Pike, Medford, NJ 08055-8750. bi-mo.; $149. A guide to articles and reviews in 23 popular microcomputer magazines.

Microcomputer Industry Update. Industry Market Reports, Inc., Box 681, Los Altos, CA 94022. mo.; $295. Briefly summarizes articles and new products announcements from eight microcomputer publications.

Nibble. Mindcraft Publishing Corp., 52 Domino Dr., Concord, MA 01742. mo.; $26.95. Reviews Apple software and has how-to articles on using and enhancing the software.

Observer. (Formerly **Word Processing News**.) Automated Office Resources, 812 Via Tornasol, Aptos, CA 95003-5624. 6/yr., $95. Contains information on office systems technology and educational computer use.

PC Magazine: The Independent Guide to IBM-Standard Personal Computing. Ziff-Davis Publishing Co., Box 2445, Boulder, CO 80322. bi-w.; $34.97. Objective product reviews for IBM personal computer users, including user reports.

PC Week. Ziff-Davis Publishing Co., 800 Boylston St., Boston, MA 02199-8102. w.; $160, free to qualified personnel. Provides current information on and analyses of hardware, software, and peripherals for the IBM PC, as well as buyers' guides and news of the industry.

PC World. PC World Communications, Inc., Box 55029, Boulder, CO 80322-5029. mo.; $29.90. Contains new reports on hardware, software, and applications of the IBM PC.

School Tech News. Business Publishers, Inc., 951 Pershing Dr., Silver Spring, MD 20910-4464. mo.; $41. Reports on current developments in computer-based instruction.

Social Science Computer Review. (Formerly **Computers and the Social Sciences**.) Duke University Press, 6697 College Station, Durham, NC 27708. q.; $32 indiv., $64 inst. Features include software reviews, new product announcements, and tutorials for beginners.

Software Digest Ratings Report. National Software Testing Laboratories, Plymouth Corporate Center, Box 1000, Plymouth Meeting, PA 19462. 15/yr.; $445. For IBM personal computer users. Each issue reports the ratings for one category of IBM PC software, based on multiple-user tests.

Software Magazine. Sentry Publishing Co., 1900 W. Park Dr., Westborough, MA 01581. 15/yr.; $48. Focuses on selecting and using business software. Gives addresses of vendors and features of new products.

Software Reviews on File. Facts on File, 460 Park Ave. S., New York, NY 10016. mo.; $175. Condensed software reviews from a variety of computer publications are provided monthly for software ranging from business to games to educational. At least two abstracts with bibliographic information are given for each software package.

Teaching and Computers. Scholastic, Inc., 730 Broadway, New York, NY 10003-9538. 6/yr.; $23.95. For the elementary/junior high school teacher with articles that clearly explain software, hardware, and the mechanics of a computer. Includes reviews.

Technology and Learning. (Formerly **Classroom Computer Learning**.) Peter Li, Inc., 2451 East River Rd., Dayton, OH 45439. 8/yr.; $24. Features reviews, news, and announcements of educational activities and opportunities in programming, software development, and hardware configurations.

T.H.E. Journal (Technological Horizons in Education). Information Synergy, Inc., 150 El Camino Real, Suite 112, Tustin, CA 92680-3670. 10/yr.; free to administrators and trainers, $29 others. Describes the application and administration of technology in education and training. Reviews use of new or alternative learning delivery systems and research studies on applicability.

Whole Earth Review. Point Foundation, Box 15187, Santa Ana, CA 92705-0187. q.; $18. Guides personal computer users through software, hardware, books, and online services.

Books

Directory of computer and high technology grants. (1991). Research Grant Guides, Box 3A, P.O. Box 1214, Loxahatchee, FL 33470. $44.50 plus $4.00 shipping and handling. Lists 640 funding sources for computers, software, and high-tech related grants, and gives advice on securing a grant.

Neill, George W., and Neill, Shirley Boes. (1991). **Only the best: Annual guide to highest-rated education software/multimedia, preschool-grade 12. 1992 edition**. Education News Service, Box 1789, Carmichael, CA 95609. $27.95. Information from 31 respected evaluation services is examined to identify the top courseware programs produced each year. The 1992 edition describes 183 programs judged to be excellent.

Price, Robert V. (1991). **Computer-aided instruction: A guide for authors**. Brooks/Cole Publishing Co., 511 Forest Lodge Rd., Pacific Grove, CA 93950. $37.50 prepaid. A hands-on book that takes readers step-by-step through the entire lifespan of development, implementation, and documentation.

ERIC Documents

Computer courseware. Advisory list. (1991, April). Raleigh, NC: North Carolina State Department of Public Instruction, Division of Media Evaluation Service. 10pp. ED 332 692. Classified listing of courseware appropriate for instruction in grades K-12, with assessment and recommended uses.

Coorough, Randall P. (1991, February). **The effects of program control, learner control, and learner control with advisement lesson control strategies on anxiety and learning from computer-assisted instruction**. Paper presented at the Annual Convention of the Association for Educational Communications and Technology, Orlando, FL, February 13-17, 1991. 20pp. ED 334 979. Reports on a study examining the effects of three computer-assisted instruction locus-of-instruction control strategies – learner control, learner control with advisement, and program control – on posttest performance anxiety.

Kubota, Kenichi. (1991, February). **Applying a collaborative learning model to a course development project**. Paper presented at the Annual Convention of the Association for Educational Communications and Technology, Orlando, FL, February 13-17, 1991. 26pp. ED 331 490. Presents the results of a qualitative study of the interaction between computer-assisted instruction and cooperative learning.

Mattoon, Joseph S., et al. (1991, February). **Learner control versus computer control in instructional simulation**. Paper presented at the Annual Convention of the Association for Educational Communications and Technology, Orlando, FL, February 13-17, 1991. 19pp. ED 334 995. Reports an experiment designed to assess the effects of learner control over the level of challenge in computer-assisted instruction.

Morse, Ronald H. (1991, April). **Computer uses in secondary science education. ERIC digest**. Syracuse, N.Y.: ERIC Clearinghouse on Information Resources, 4pp. ED 331 489. Provides an overview of uses of computers in science classrooms, which has been linked with improved achievement and increased scientific reasoning skills.

Poage, Julie A. (1991, April). **Computer confidence: A factorial model for the prediction of success in an introductory computer class for preservice teachers**. Paper presented at the Annual Conference of the American Educational Research Association, Chicago, IL, April 3-7, 1991. 10pp. ED 333 859. Describes a research project examining lack of confidence as an obstacle to succes in classroom computer use.

Ross, Steven M., et al. (1991, February). **The development of writing skills in a computer-intensive environment**. Paper presented at the Annual Convention of the Association for Educational Communications and Technology, Orlando, FL, February 13-17, 1991. 18pp. ED 335 010. Reports on a study of uses of the computer to support the development of writing skills in an Apple Classroom of Tomorrow setting.

Troutman, Andria P. (1991, February). **Attitudes toward personal and school use of computers**. Paper presented at the Annual Conference of the Eastern Educational Research Association, Boston, MA, February 13-16, 1991. 11pp. ED 331 480. Presents the findings of a survey of 292 preservice teachers concerning their attitudes toward the personal and school use of microcomputers.

Yeaman, Andrew R. J. (1991, February). **Sociocultural aspects of computers in education**. Paper presented at the Annual Convention of the Association for Educational Communications and Technology, Orlando, FL, February 13-17, 1991. 6pp. ED 335 025. Presents research findings about the status of computers in education, including price, ease of use, acceptance, and utilization.

Journal Articles

Borne, Isabelle, and Girardot, Colette. (1991). Object-oriented programming in the primary classroom. **Computers and Education, 16**(1), 93-98. EJ 421 747. Describes the use of Smalltalk-80, a French programming language, to teach young children to program effectively using object-oriented concepts.

Collis, Betty A., and De Diana, Italo. (1990, Winter). The portability of computer-related educational resources: An overview of issues and directions. **Journal of Research on Computing in Education, 23**(2), 147-59. EJ 421 749. (Available UMI.) Introductory article in a special issue dealing with the portability, or transferability, of educational computer software.

Cordell, Barbara J. (1991). A study of learning styles and computer-assisted instruction. **Computers and Education, 16**(2), 175-83. EJ 423 426. Describes a study of health care employees that was designed to determine whether learning styles affect outcomes of learning with two computer-assisted instruction design strategies, linear and branching.

Espinosa, Leonard J. (1991, May-June). Ten commandments for microcomputer facility planners. **Media and Methods, 27**(5), 32-34. EJ 430 220. (Available UMI.) Presents factors involved in designing a microcomputer facility, including educational specifications, workstation design, local area networks, security, and communication with architects and suppliers.

Gray, Elaine. (1991, February). The mobile math lab project. **Computing Teacher, 18**(5), 16-19. EJ 421 771. (Available UMI.) Describes the use of a mobile computer lab for a fourth-grade math program emphasizing problem solving and spatial visualization.

Held, Chris, et al. (1991, March). The integrated technology classroom: An experiment in restructuring elementary school instruction. **Computer Teacher, 18**(6), 21-23. EJ 423 420. (Available UMI.) Describes the development of an integrated approach to using computer technology in a multiage classroom with grades four and five that emphasizes the role of the teacher.

Hopkins, Michael. (1991, April). Technologies as tools for transforming learning environments. **Computing Teacher, 18**(7), 27-30. EJ 424 859. (Available UMI.) Describes the Saturn School of Tomorrow, which was developed in the St. Paul public schools to incorporate current technology into instruction for grades four through eight.

Lieberman, Debra A., and Linn, Marcia C. (1991, Spring). Learning to learn revisited: Computers and the development of self-directed learning skills. **Journal of Research on Computing in Education, 23**(3), 373-95. EJ 424 862. (Available UMI.) Considers three main components of self-directed learning: topics knowledge, procedural skills, and self-monitoring.

McCormick, Theresa E., and McCoy, Sue Boney. (1990). Computer-assisted instruction and multicultural nonsexist education: A caveat for those who select and design software. **Computers in the Schools, 7**(4), 105-24. EJ 427 491. Forty software programs for K-12 social studies are reviewed in terms of six forms of bias. Suggestions for integrating CAI with multicultural nonsexist education concepts are offered.

Mizokawa, Donald T. (1991, January). Computer-managed testing in schools. **Educational Technology, 31**(1), 21-25. EJ 421 739. (Available UMI.) Describes a study of elementary school students that compared computerized and paper-and-pencil testing. Offers guidelines for hardware and software decisions.

Olson, Beth, and Krendl, Kathy A. (1991). At-risk students and microcomputers: What do we know and how do we know it? **Journal of Educational Technology Systems, 19**(2), 166-75, 199. EJ 421 730. Provides an overview of research on the effectiveness of microcomputer applications with at-risk students and suggests that many findings in the literature are questionable because of flaws in research methodology.

Sales, Gregory C., et al. (1991, Spring). The evolution of K-12 instructional software: An analysis of leading microcomputer-based programs from 1981-1988. **Journal of Computer-Based Instruction, 18**(2), 41-47. EJ 430 238. (Available UMI.) Describes a study that analyzed the evolution of instructional software to develop a chronology and identify trends.

Thomas, Rex, and Hooper, Elizabeth. (1991, Summer). Simulations: An opportunity we are missing. **Journal of Research on Computing Education, 23**(4), 497-513. EJ 430 249. (Available UMI.) Discusses and defines computer-based instructional simulations based on a review and analysis of computer-based simulation studies in the literature.

Watson, Jim. (1991, December-January). Cooperative learning and computers: One way to address student differences. **Computing Teacher, 18**(4), 9-10, 12, 14-15. EJ 420 355. (Available UMI.) Discusses research exploring benefits of group versus individual computer use and factors such as group size and individual differences.

Woodrow, Janice E. J. (1991). A comparison of four computer attitude scales. **Journal of Educational Computing Research, 7**(2), 165-87. EJ 430 222. Examines and compares the characteristics of computer attitude scales by Stevens, Reece and Gable, Gressard and Loyd, and Griswold.

COPYRIGHT ISSUES FOR SCHOOLS
AND LIBRARIES*

ERIC Documents

Mulligan, Stuart. (1988, September). **What does copyright have to do with my teaching activities? What is fair use? What is an anthology?** Paper presented at the Western New York/Ontario Chapter of the Association of College and Research Libraries Workshop, Buffalo, NY, September 1988. 8pp. ED 329 258. This paper examines the third fair use standard in section 107 of the 1976 Copyright Act — "the amount and substantiality of the portion used in relation to the copyrighted work as a whole" — as it applies to copying for extended classroom uses such as library reserve. The guidelines are interpreted in terms of amount, substantiality, public use, and multiples of single copies. The connection of this standard with the "anthologizing" principles outlined in the fair use guidelines and with the "systemic reproduction" provision in section 108, which deals with library and archive exemptions, is also discussed.

Talab, R. S. (1989). **Copyright and instructional technologies: A guide to fair use and permissions procedures. 2d ed.** 51pp. ED 322 893. (Available from EDRS in microfiche only. Available in paper from Association for Educational Communications and Technology, 1025 Vermont Ave. NW, Washington, DC 20005.) This document examines some of the questions concerning copyright law and the educational use of equipment that can easily duplicate, store, and transmit instructional materials. The discussion covers copyright law; videotaping, video rental, and closed-circuit television; library reproduction; computer software, database downloading, and telefacsimile; licensing agreements; and copyright policy development. Guidelines for using copyrighted materials for educational purposes are included.

Journal Articles

Barron, Daniel D. (1991, January). Ethics, the school library media specialist, and copyright. **School Library Media Activities Monthly,** 7(5), 48-50. EJ 420 386. Discussion of professional ethics for school library media specialists highlights issues involving copyright. Ethics and the school curriculum are discussed and the librarian's code of ethics reviewed. Educating teachers as well as students about copyright law is suggested and resources dealing with copyright issues are listed.

Dratler, Jay, Jr. (1990, Winter). To copy or not to copy: The educator's dilemma. **Journal of Law and Education,** 19(1), 1-49. EJ 405 174. Argues for a balance of copyright incentives more favorable to education: (1) introduces the dilemma of choice between infringing others' copyrights and observing legal procedure; (2) discusses Congress's accommodation of education under the Copyright Act of 1976; (3) describes a legislative solution; and (4) suggests statutory language for an amendment.

*This section is based on a minibibliography prepared by Nancy Preston, User Services Coordinator, ERIC Clearinghouse on Information Resources, Syracuse University, 030 Huntington Hall, Syracuse, NY 13244-2340. (315) 443-3640. December 1991.

This publication was prepared with funding from the Office of Educational Research and Improvement, U.S. Department of Education, under contract no. R188062008. The opinions expressed in this bibliography do not necessarily reflect the positions or policies of OERI or ED.

Gamble, Lanny R., and Anderson, Larry S. (1989, September). Nine easy steps to avoiding software copyright infringement. **NASSP Bulletin, 73**(518), 90-93. EJ 396 509. (Available UMI.) To avoid microcomputer software copyright infringement, administrators must be aware of the law, read the software agreements, maintain good records, submit all software registration cards, provide secure storage, post warnings, be consistent when establishing and enforcing policies, consider a site license, and ensure the legality of currently owned software.

Gilbert, Steven W. (1990, Spring). Information technology, intellectual property, and education. **EDUCOM Review, 25**(1), 14-20. EJ 410 623. Discusses issues affecting the fields of information technology, intellectual property, and education. Four main needs are addressed: (1) new economic mechanisms beyond copyright and patent; (2) new codes of ethics for education; (3) effective representation for creator/producers and users of information; and (4) a forum for the voice of education.

Goldsmith, Kory. (1989, Summer). Copyright for public schools. **School Law Bulletin, 20**(3), 10-17. EJ 396 531. (Available UMI.) Provides guidelines intended to help teachers, librarians, and administrators recognize when they must obtain permission to copy, perform, or display a work. Reviews the exceptions to the copyright law and its application to photocopying, reproduction by libraries and archives, videotaping, live and transmitted performances, and computer programs.

Jackson, Mary E. (1992, January-February). Copyright, libraries and media centers. **Media and Methods, 27**(3), 34, 36. EJ 421 706. (Available UMI.) Discusses the interpretation of copyright law that affects libraries and media centers that provide videotapes to patrons. Topics discussed include the concept of fair use; conditions that permit copyrighted materials to be used in the classroom; patrons' use of copyrighted videotapes within the library; and licensing and duplication rights.

Jensen, Mary Brandt. (1991, March). CD-ROM licenses: What's in the fine or nonexistent print may surprise you. **CD-ROM Professional, 4**(2), 13-16. EJ 423 396. Points out that purchasers of CD-ROM products do not acquire the same rights as they do when purchasing print products. Licensing terms and agreements of 12 CD-ROM producers are examined, and the making of backup copies of support software, downloading, multiple use and other restrictions, and negotiating different licensing terms are discussed.

Wilkins, Marilyn. (1990, April). Teach your students how to use scanners legally. **Business Education Forum, 44**(7), 14-15. EJ 406 414. (Available UMI.) Image scanning technology permits the desktop publisher wide latitude in graphic representations. Care must be taken not to use creative material belonging to others. Teachers can have a positive impact on this problem by including instruction on the legal and ethical issues of image scanning.

Wynbrandt, Robert A. (1990, Summer). Musical performances in libraries: Is a license from ASCAP required? **School Library Media Quarterly, 18**(4), 245-46. EJ 413 692. (Available UMI.) Prepared at the request of the American Library Association by its attorneys, this article discusses federal copyright law as it pertains to musical performances in libraries. Guidelines are presented for determining whether a license from the American Society of Composers, Authors, and Publishers or any other performing rights organization is required.

DATABASES AND ONLINE SEARCHING

Media-Related Periodicals

Data Sources. Ziff-Davis Publishing Co., One Park Ave., New York, NY 10016. 2/yr.; $440. A guide to the information processing industry. Covers equipment, software, services, companies, and systems.

Database. Online, Inc., 11 Tannery Ln., Weston, CT 06883. bi-mo.; $89. Includes articles on new databases and techniques for searching online databases as well as new products information and news updates.

Database Searcher. Meckler Publishing, 11 Ferry Ln. W., Westport, CT 06880-5808. mo.; $95. Includes techniques, new products, conferences, and news items related to database uses.

Directory of Online Databases. Cuadra Associates, Inc., Box 872, Madison Square Station, New York, NY 10159. q.; $190. Identifies over 4,500 databases that are publicly available to online service users. Includes information on database selection and vendors.

Information Today. Learned Information, Inc., Old Marlton Pike, Medford, NJ 08055. 11/yr.; $34.95. Covers news and trends, reviews of hardware, software, and database, job listings. Has online service buyer's guide and a calendar of events.

Infotecture. Espial Productions, Box 624, Station K, Toronto, Ontario M4P 2H1, Canada. fortn.; $295 in the United States. A news publication covering the online information industry in Canada.

Journal of Database Administration. Idea Group Publishing, 4751 Lindle Rd., Suite 116, Harrisburg, PA 17111. q.; $55 indiv., $95 inst. Provides state-of-the-art research to those who design, develop, and administer DBMS-based information systems.

Link-Up. Learned Information, Inc., 143 Old Marlton Pike, Medford, NJ 08055. bi-mo.; $25. Focuses on current online and videotex news, new products, and features for business, personal, and educational uses. Reviews software, books, hardware, and databases related to small computer communications.

Online Review. Learned Information, Inc., 143 Old Marlton Pike, Medford, NJ 08055. bi-mo.; $95. An international journal of online information systems featuring articles on using and managing online systems, training and educating online users, developing search aids, and creating and marketing databases.

Online Today. 5000 Arlington Centre Blvd., Columbus, OH 43220. mo.; $30. A CompuServe publication. Gives current news about computer communication and information retrieval, in-depth articles on issues and techniques, and software and book reviews.

Resource Sharing and Information Networks. Haworth Press, 10 Alice St., Binghamton, NY 13904. semi-ann.; $32 indiv., $75 inst. Practical aspects of using various types of network services, training, cost-effectiveness, and user access to public terminals.

Books

Davis, Charles H., ed. (1991). **Database management: How much power is enough? Issues for librarians and information scientists**. Graduate School of Library and Information Science, University of Illinois at Urbana-Champaign, 249 Armory Building, 505 East Armory St., Champaign, IL 61820. 68pp. $20 plus $2 shipping ($.50 for each additional copy). Orders must be prepaid. A collection of papers originally produced for the 26th Annual Clinic on Library Applications of Data Processing.

Journal Articles

Civale, Cosmo M., Jr. (1991, March-April). Connecting library and classroom environments via networking. **Media and Methods, 27**(4), 32-34. EJ 423 428. (Available UMI.) Discusses the benefits for students and teachers in implementing computer networks in libraries and/or classrooms. Offers guidelines for selecting hardware and software, and planning guidelines.

Duggan, Mary Kay. (1991, May). Copyright of electronic information: Issues and questions. **Online, 15**(3), 20-26. EJ 426 057. (Available UMI.) Discusses changes in the electronic information environment and copyright issues that have arisen for librarians because of technological advances.

DISTANCE EDUCATION

Media-Related Periodicals

American Journal of Distance Education. Pennsylvania State University, School of Education, 403 S. Allen St., Suite 206, University Park, PA 16801-5202. 3/yr.; $50. Focuses on the professional trainer, adult educator, college teacher, and others interested in the latest developments in methods and systems for delivering education to adults.

Appropriate Technology. Intermediate Technology Publications, Ltd., 103-105 Southampton Row, London, WC1B 4HH, England. q.; $23 indiv., $30 inst. Articles are on low-cost, small-scale technology, particularly for developing countries.

Development Communication Report. Clearinghouse on Development Communication, 1815 N. Ft. Myer Dr., Suite 600, Arlington, VA 22209. q.; free to readers in developing countries, $10 to others. Applications of communications technology to international development problems such as agriculture, health, and nutrition are covered.

Distance Education. USQ Publications, Darling Heights, Toowoomba, Queensland 4350, Australia. semi-ann.; $40. Papers on the history, politics, and administration of distance education.

International Council for Distance Education Bulletin. Open University, Regional Academic Services, Walton Hall, Milton Keynes, MK7 6AA7, England. 3/yr.; $45. A publication of ICDE, this quarterly journal reports on activities and programs of its membership.

Journal of Distance Education. Canadian Association for Distance Education, 151 Slater St., Ottawa, Ontario K1P 5N1, Canada. 2/yr.; $40. A forum for the dissemination of current theory, research, and practice related to teaching and learning at a distance. A peer-reviewed international journal.

Research in Distance Education. Centre for Distance Education, Athabasca University, Box 10,000, Athabasca, Alberta T0G 2R0, Canada. q.; price not available. A forum for the discussion of issues surrounding the process of conducting research within the field of distance education.

Books

Bradshaw, Dean H., and Desser, Karen. (1991). **Audiographics distance learning: A resource handbook**. Far West Laboratory for Educational Research and Development, 730 Harrison St., San Francisco, CA 94107. 68pp. Order No. FW-890-RD. $13.50 prepaid. This step-by-step guide for developing an audiographics program describes the basic workings, installation, hardware and software, and effective teaching strategies.

Funding distance education projects. (1991). Virginia Ostendorf, Inc., P.O. Box 2896, Littleton, CO 80161-2896. $150. Developed in conjunction with the Public Service Satellite Consortium, this book identifies and describes sources of funding available to any type of organization in the United States wishing to start or continue distance education projects.

Moore, Michael G., Thompson, Melody M., Quigley, B. Allan, Clark, G. Christopher, and Goff, Gerald G. (1991). **The effects of distance education: A summary of literature**. American Center for the Study of Distance Education, College of Education, The Pennsylvania State University, 403 South Allen St., Suite 206, University Park, PA 16801-5202. 74pp. $12.50. Reports, through a review of the literature, the research of the 1980s on issues in teaching, learning, educational planning, organization, and policy making with regard to the use of telecommunications technology in contemporary distance education.

ERIC Documents

Barker, Bruce O. (1991, April). **K-12 distance education in the United States: Technology strengths, weaknesses, and issues**. Paper presented at the Annual International Conference on Distance Learning, United States Distance Learning Association, Washington, DC. 10pp. ED 332 687. Identifies seven distance education case study projects completed for the Office of Technology Assessment as part of the November 1989 report, "Linking for Learning: A New Course for Education" (ED 310 765).

Phelps, Malcom. (1991, March). **Planning guidelines for the implementation of wide area educational telecommunication systems**. Paper presented to the Learning by Satellite VI Conference, Dallas, TX, March 29, 1991. 12pp. ED 331 486. Describes the role of a consortium in delivering cost-effective distance education and the need to address the curriculum development, technical assistance, organizational, and financial components of the educational infrastructure.

Journal Articles

Cyrs, Thomas E., and Smith, Frank A. (1991). Designing interactive study guides with word pictures for teleclass teaching. **TechTrends, 36**(1), 37-39. EJ 423 405. (Available UMI.) Discusses college student note-taking behavior in teleclasses and describes the development and use of interactive study guides to improve note-taking accuracy.

Sachs, Steven G. (1991). Teaching thinking skills to distant learners. **TechTrends, 36**(1), 28-32. EJ 423 403. (Available UMI.) Describes strategies that can be used to teach thinking skills in distance education courses and criteria and methods for teaching thinking skills.

Wilkes, C. Wynn, and Burnham, Byron R. (1991). Adult learner motivations and electronic distance education. **American Journal of Distance Education, 5**(1), 43-50. EJ 430 246. Describes a study at Utah State University that compared students using an audio/graphic system with students taught by traditional methods.

Zvacek, Susan M. (1991). Effective affective design for distance education. **TechTrends, 36**(1), 40-43. EJ 423 406. (Available UMI.) Discusses learner motivation based on Keller's ARCS model, communication patterns that facilitate interaction between students, and other topics related to affective aspects of distance education.

EDUCATIONAL RESEARCH

Media-Related Periodicals

American Educational Research Journal. American Educational Research Association, 1230 17th St. NW, Washington, DC 20036. q.; $33 indiv., $41 inst. Reports original research, both empirical and theoretical, and brief synopses of research.

Current Index to Journals in Education (CIJE). Oryx Press, 4041 N. Central at Indian School Rd., Phoenix, AZ 85012-3399. mo.; $238. A guide to articles published in some 780 education and education-related journals. Includes complete bibliographic information, annotations, and indexes. Semiannual cumulations available. Contents are produced by the ERIC (Educational Resources Information Center) system, Office of Educational Research and Improvement, U.S. Department of Education.

Education Index. H. W. Wilson, 950 University Ave., Bronx, NY 10452. mo. (except July and August); variable costs. Provides easy access to information in 319 educational periodicals, yearbooks, monographs, and other publications. Offers quarterly cumulations and bound annual cumulations.

Educational Research. NFER Publishing, Darville House, 20 Oxford Road E., Windsor Berkshire SL2 1DF, England. 3/yr.; $90. A journal of educational research reporting on current research, evaluation, and applications.

Educational Researcher. American Educational Research Association, 1230 17th St. NW, Washington, DC 20036. 9/yr.; $33. Contains news and features of general significance in educational research.

Research in Science and Technological Education. Carfax Publishing Co., P.O. Box 25, Abington, Oxfordshire OX14 3VE England. 2/yr.; $228. Publication of original research in the science and technological fields. Includes articles on psychological, sociological, economic, and organizational aspects.

Resources in Education (RIE). Superintendent of Documents, U.S. Government Printing Office, Washington, DC 20402. mo.; $66. Announcement of research reports and other documents in education, including abstracts and indexes by subject, author, and institution. Cumulative semiannual indexes available. Contents produced by the ERIC (Educational Resources Information Center) system, Office of Educational Research and Improvement, U.S. Department of Education.

Books

Krathwohl, David R. (1991). **How to prepare a research proposal. 3d ed.** Syracuse University Press, 1600 Jamesville Ave., Syracuse, NY 13244-5160. 305pp. $14.95 plus $2.50 shipping and handling. A complete guide to preparing a proposal and securing funding for dissertations and research in the social and behavioral sciences.

Thompson, Ann D., Simonson, Michael R., and Hargrave, Constance P. (1991). **Educational technology: A review of the research**. Association for Educational Communications and Technology, 1025 Vermont Ave. NW, Washington, DC 20005. $15 AECT members, $22 others, plus $3 shipping and handling. Summarizes five types of educational media research and discusses the influence of behaviorism, cognitive theory, communications theory, and systems theory.

ERIC Documents

Berry, Louis S. (1991, February). **Visual complexity and pictorial memory: A fifteen year research perspective**. Paper presented at the Annual Convention of the Association for Educational Communications and Technology, Orlando, FL, February 13-17, 1991. 13pp. ED 334 975. Reports on an ongoing research project focusing on the effects of variations in visual complexity and color on the storage and retrieval of visual information by learners.

Dempsey, John V., and Tucker, Susan A. (1991, February). **Using photo-interviewing as a tool for research and evaluation**. Paper presented at the Annual Convention of the Association for Educational Communications and Technology, Orlando, FL, February 13-17, 1991. 24pp. ED 334 980. Describes a nine-step strategy for carrying out photo-interviewing as a research technique.

Jesky, Romaine R., and Berry, Louis H. (1991, February). **The effects of pictorial complexity and cognitive style on visual recall memory**. Paper presented at the Annual Convention of the Association for Educational Communications and Technology, Orlando, FL, February 13-17, 1991. 9pp. ED 334 987. Describes a research project using three sets of visuals in different formats to study the effect of the interaction between cognitive style and various degrees of visual complexity on pictorial recall memory.

Spencer, Ken. (1991, January). Models, media and methods: The search for educational effectiveness. **British Journal of Educational Technology, 22**(1), 12-22. EJ 423 369. Discusses the instructional effectiveness of illustrations, visual-based instructional media, programmed learning, computer-assisted learning, and other educational media.

EDUCATIONAL TECHNOLOGY

Media-Related Periodicals

British Journal of Educational Technology. Council for Educational Technology, 3 Devonshire St., London W1N 2BA, England. 3/yr.; $62. Published by the National Council for Educational Technology, this journal includes articles on education and training, especially theory, applications, and development of educational technology and communications.

Canadian Journal of Educational Communication. Association of Media and Technology in Education in Canada, AMTEC-CJEC Subscription, 3-1750 The Queensway, No. 1318, Etobicoke, Ontario, M9C 5H5, Canada. 3/yr.; $40. Articles, research reports, and literature reviews on all areas of educational communication and technology.

Education and Training Technology International. (Formerly **Programmed Learning and Educational Technology**.) Kogan Page Ltd., 120 Pentonville Rd., London N1 9JN, England. q.; $74. Journal of the Association for Educational and Training Technology, emphasizing developing trends in and the efficient employment of educational technology.

Educational Technology. Educational Technology Publications, Inc., 720 Palisade Ave., Englewood Cliffs, NJ 07632. mo.; $119, single copy $12. Covers telecommunications, computer-aided instruction, information retrieval, educational television, and electronic media in the classroom.

Educational Technology Abstracts. Carfax Publishing Co., P.O. Box 25, Abington, Oxfordshire OX14 3VE, England. 6/yr.; $302. An international publication of abstracts of recently published material in the field of educational and training technology.

Educational Technology Research and Development. Association for Educational Communications and Technology, 1025 Vermont Ave. NW, Suite 820, Washington, DC 20005-3516. q.; $45, single copy $12. Focuses on research and instructional development in the ever-changing field of educational technology.

Knowledge: Creation, Diffusion, Utilization. Sage Publications, Inc., 2455 Teller Rd., Newbury Park, CA 91320. q.; $45 indiv., $115 inst., $14 single issue. An international, interdisciplinary journal examining the nature of expertise and the translation of knowledge into practice and policy.

TechTrends. Association for Educational Communications and Technology, 1025 Vermont Ave. NW, Suite 820, Washington, DC 20005-3516. 6/yr.; $30, single copy $4. Features authoritative, practical articles about technology and its integration into the learning environment.

Books

Anglin, Gary. (1991). **Instructional technology: Past, present, and future**. Libraries Unlimited, Dept. 920, P.O. Box 6633, Englewood, CO 80155-6633. 399pp. $35 plus shipping and handling. A state-of-the-art overview of educational technology today, including current issues, instructional design, computer applications, research and evaluation, and future prospects.

Saettler, Paul. (1990). **The evolution of American educational technology**. Libraries Unlimited, Dept. 920, P.O. Box 6633, Englewood, CO 80155-6633. 570pp. $46 plus shipping and handling. Provides the historical foundations for the theoretical and methodological approaches to educational technology used today.

ERIC Documents

Images in action. Learning tomorrow: Linking technology and restructuring. (1991). Washington, D.C.: National Foundation for the Improvement of Education. 40pp. ED 332 672. Contains descriptions of the most promising educational practices submitted by teachers in response to two nationwide calls for Innovation in Practice.

Koetting, J. Randall, and Januszewski, Alan. (1991). **Theory building and educational technology: Foundations for reconceptualization**. Paper presented at the Annual Convention of the Association for Educational Communications and Technology, Orlando, FL, February 13-17, 1991. 16pp. ED 334 991. Arguing that the notions of contested/problematic suggest debate, reinterpretation, and the need for dialogue with others to establish meaning, this paper suggests that through the diversity of understandings of this concept, new language can be used to talk about the work of educational technologists.

Pedras, Melvin J., and Jackson, Christi. (1991). **Elementary school technology education: A modular resource package**. Washington, D.C.: Education and Human Services Consortium. 32pp. ED 330 301. Three learning modules designed to provide elementary school teachers with exploratory level learning activities to encourage students to become technologically literate.

Journal Articles

Boston, Jane, et al. (1991, January-February). Classroom technology and its global connections. **Media and Methods, 27**(3), 18, 48-49, 54. EJ 421 705. (Available UMI.) Describes three projects using technology to add global interest to a curriculum: a videotape of a Japanese child, a hypermedia presentation on community issues, and a telecommunications system to create an economics simulation.

Ray, Doris. (1991, March). Technology and restructuring part I: New educational directions. **Computing Teacher, 18**(6), 9-16, 18-20. EJ 423 419. (Available UMI.) Discusses the relationship of technology to school restructuring and describes new educational directions that incorporate technology and support restructuring.

Wiburg, Karin M. (1991). Teaching teachers about technology. **Computers in the Schools, 8**(1-3), 115-29. EJ 428 870. Discusses issues in teaching teachers about technology, including what students need to know, the changing role of teachers, and the need for new forms of student evaluation.

Woodrow, Janice E. J. (1991). Determinants of student teacher computer literacy achievement. **Computers and Education, 16**(3), 247-56. EJ 427 493. Describes a study of student teachers' computer literacy, focusing on computer attitudes, perceived locus of control, gender, age, and prior experience.

ELECTRONIC PUBLISHING

Media-Related Periodicals

Desktop Communications. International Desktop Communications, Ltd., 48 E. 43rd St., New York, NY 10017. bi-mo.; $24. Helps small businesses, corporate, and individual computer users design and implement innovative and effective newsletters, reports, presentations, and other business communications.

Publish. PCW Communications, Inc., Box 55415, Boulder, CO 80322-5415. mo.; $39.90. A how-to magazine for desktop publishing.

Books

Joan N. Bursyn, ed. (1991). **Desktop publishing in the university**. Syracuse University Press, 1600 Jamesville Ave., Syracuse, NY 13244-5160. 137pp. $12.95 plus $2.50 shipping and handling. For university faculty and administrators, this book includes nine essays examining the effects of desktop publishing on professors and students, librarians, and those who work at university presses and in publication departments.

Misanchuk, Earl R. (1992). **Preparing instructional text: Document design using desktop publishing**. Educational Technology Publications, 700 Palisade Ave., Englewood Cliffs, NJ 07632. $32.95 prepaid. A guide to producing professional-looking instructional materials with desktop publishing. Emphasizes ways in which designing documents for instruction differs from other publishing.

ERIC Documents

Knupfer, Nancy Nelson, and McIsaac, Marina Stock. (1991, February). **A fine-tuned look at white space variation in desktop publishing**. Paper presented at the Annual Convention of the Association for Educational Communications and Technology, Orlando, FL, February 13-17, 1991. 16pp. ED 334 989. An investigation of the use of white space in print-based, computer-generated text, focusing on the point at which the white space interferes with reading speed and comprehension.

Journal Articles

Arnold, Stephen E. (1991, July). Storage technology: A review of options and their implications for electronic publishing. **Online, 15**(4), 39-51. EJ 428 879. (Available UMI.) Describes magnetic storage media, high-capacity magnetic drives, and optical storage technologies and their implications for electronic publishing.

Bailey, Charles W., Jr. (1991, January). Electronic (online) publishing in action: The Public-Access Computer Systems Review and other electronic serials. **Online, 15**(1), 28-35. EJ 420 368. (Available UMI.) Describes the development and operation of an electronic serial, "The Public Access Computer Systems Review," which evolved from a computer conference, and other electronic serials available on BITNET.

Basch, Reva. (1991, July). Books online: Visions, plans, and perspectives for electronic text. **Online, 15**(4), 13-23. EJ 428 877. (Available UMI.) This discussion of applications of electronic text in higher education covers input technology, standardization, copyright issues, networked access, user interfaces, and future possibilities.

Hernon, Peter, et al. (1991). Discussion forum: The Bureau of the Census, the Depository Library Program, information retrieval systems, and electronic publishing. **Government Information Quarterly, 8**(1), 1-76. EJ 424 855. Four articles discuss the role of the Bureau of the Census depository library program, the history of the Federal Information Locator System, design criteria for creating a government-wide information locator system, and the potential for electronic census products.

INFORMATION SCIENCE AND TECHNOLOGY

Media-Related Periodicals

Datamation. Reed Publishing, 275 Washington St., Newton, MA 02158-1630. 24/yr.; $69. Covers semitechnical news and views on hardware, software, and databases, for data and information processing professionals.

Information Retrieval and Library Automation. Lomond Publications, Inc., Box 88, Mt. Airy, MD 21771. mo.; $66. Topics include new techniques, equipment, software, and publications. Also covers events, meetings, international developments, networks and communications, media innovation, technology transfer, and federal policies.

Information Services & Use. Elsevier Science Publishing Co., Box 882, Madison Square Station, New York, NY 10159. bi-mo.; $104. An international journal for those in the information management field. Includes online and offline systems, library automation, micrographics, videotex, and telecommunications.

The Information Society. Taylor and Francis, 1900 Frost Rd., Suite 101, Bristol, PA 19007. q.; $80. Provides a forum for discussion of the world of information, including transborder data flow, regulatory issues, and the impact of the information industry.

Information Technology and Libraries. American Library Association, Library and Information Technology Association, 50 E. Huron St., Chicago, IL 60611-2795. q.; $45. Articles on library automation, communication technology, cable systems, computerized information processing, and video technologies.

Journal of Documentation. ASLIB, Association for Information Management, Publications Department, Information House, 20-24 Old St., London EC1V 9AP, England. q.; $87. Describes how technical, scientific, and other specialized knowledge is recorded, organized, and disseminated.

Journal of the American Society for Information Science. John Wiley and Sons, Inc., Journals, 605 3rd Ave., New York, NY 10158-0012. 10/yr.; $295. Publishes research articles in the area of information science.

Books

Cone, Robert J. (1991). **How the new technology works: A guide to high-tech concepts.** Oryx Press, 4041 N. Central, Phoenix, AZ 85012-3397. 136pp. $26.50 prepaid. Makes complex technical concepts and industries easily comprehensible. Each entry contains a basic description of the topic, real-world applications, historical background, and future applications.

Williams, Martha E., ed. (1991). **ARIST 26: Annual review of information science and technology.** Learned Information, Inc., 143 Old Marlton Pike, Medford, NJ 08055-8750. 515pp. $69.90 plus $3.50 shipping and handling. A literary source of ideas, trends, and references that offers a comprehensive view of information science technology. Nine chapters cover planning information systems and services, basic techniques and technologies, and the profession.

Journal Articles

Kuhlthau, Carol C. (1991, June). Inside the search process: Information seeking from the user's perspective. **Journal of the American Society for Information Science, 42**(5), 361-71. EJ 428 890. (Available UMI.) Discussion of the information search process, focusing on a model derived from longitudinal studies of high school and college students.

Lange, Holley R. (1991, February). The voice as computer interface: A look at tomorrow's technologies. **Electronic Library, 9**(1), 7-11. EJ 427 502. Discussion of voice as the communication device for computer-human interaction, focusing on voice recognition systems for use in libraries.

Mitchell, Maurice, and Saunders, Laverna M. (1991, April). The virtual library: An agenda for the 1990s. **Computers in Libraries, 11**(4), 10-11. EJ 428 850. (Available UMI.) Discusses issues related to the idea of a virtual library in an academic setting, including human and technological issues and administration.

Ranade, Sanjay, and Schraeder, Jeff. (1991, January-February). Mass storage systems. **Optical Information Systems, 11**(1), 29-38. EJ 423 356. (Available UMI.) Presents an overview of the mass storage market and discusses mass storage systems as part of computer networks.

Telem, Moshe. (1991, Summer). A knowledge base for information technology in educational administration. **Journal of Research on Computing in Education, 23**(4), 594-610. EJ 430 252. (Available UMI.) Highlights a five-part sociotechnical conceptual framework for including information technology in an educational administration knowledge base.

INSTRUCTIONAL DESIGN AND TRAINING

Media-Related Periodicals

AVC Presentation Development & Delivery. PTN Publishing Co., 445 Broad Hollow Rd., Melville, NY 11747. mo.; $60, single issue $6. Industry news and applications for those who manage audiovisual, video, or computer presentation.

Data Training: The Monthly Newspaper for Information Trainers. Weingarten Publications, Inc., 38 Chauncy St., Boston, MA 02111. mo.; $24. Articles from consultants and in-house trainers describe how to train computer users and design computer-based training. Software and hardware are reviewed, trends discussed, and training techniques described.

Instructional Developments. School of Education, Syracuse University, 364 Huntington Hall, Syracuse, NY 13244-2340. 3/yr.; free. Feature articles, research reviews, innovations, and job aids.

Instructional Science. Kluwer Academic Publishers, Box 358, Accord Station, Hingham, MA 02018-0358. 6/yr.; $217. Aimed at promoting a deeper understanding of the nature, theory, and practice of the instructional process and the learning resulting from this process.

Journal of Educational Multimedia and Hypermedia. Association for the Advancement of Computing in Education, Box 2966, Charlottesville, VA 22902. q.; $40 indiv., $68 inst. A multidisciplinary information source presenting research and applications on multimedia and hypermedia tools that allow the integration of images, sounds, text, and data in learning and teaching.

Journal of Educational Technology Systems. Baywood Publishing Co., 26 Austin Ave., Box 337, Amityville, NY 11701. q.; $96. In-depth articles on completed and ongoing research in all phases of educational technology and its application and future within the teaching profession.

Journal of Interactive Instruction Development. Communicative Technology Corp., Society for Applied Learning Technology, 50 Culpeper St., Warrenton, VA 22186. q.; $30 members, $50 nonmembers. A showcase of successful programs that introduce innovative, creative, and effective approaches to courseware development for interactive technology.

Journal of Technical Writing and Communication. Baywood Publishing Co., 26 Austin Ave., Box 337, Amityville, NY 11701. q.; $36 indiv., $75 inst. Expresses the views of communicators, records their problems and successes, promotes their research, and acts as a forum.

Machine-Mediated Learning. Taylor and Francis, 1900 Frost Rd., Suite 101, Bristol, PA 19007. 4/yr.; $110. Focuses on the scientific, technological, and management aspects of the application of machines to instruction and training. Analyzes computer, telecommunication, videodisc, and other technological developments.

Multimedia Review. Meckler Publishing Corp., 11 Ferry Ln. W., Westport, CT 06880. 4/yr.; $97. Dedicated to analysis of trends, paradigms, and strategies affecting the creation and production, design and development, and implementation and use of multimedia programs and configurations.

Performance and Instruction. National Society for Performance and Instruction, 1300 L St. NW, Suite 1250, Washington, DC 20005. 10/yr.; $50. Journal of NSPI, intended to promote the advantage of performance science and technology. Contains articles, research, and case studies relating to improving human performance.

Training. Lakewood Publications, Inc., 50 S. Ninth, Minneapolis, MN 55402. mo.; $54. News, how-to features, case studies, and opinions on managing training and human resources development activities.

Books

Banathy, Bela H. (1991). **Systems design of education: A journey to create the future**. Educational Technology Publications, 700 Palisade Ave., Englewood Cliffs, NJ 07632. $29.95 prepaid. Argument for a new design of education that proposes the notion of "user designers," the involvement in systems design of all those in the community and beyond who have a stake in education and human development.

Fantzreb, Richard B., ed. (1991). **Training and development yearbook — 1991**. Advanced Personnel Systems, P.O. Box 1438, Roseville, CA 95661. 640pp. $79.50 plus $7.50 shipping and handling. A collection of 70 articles and over 300 abstracts covering every aspect of HRD, from training administration to computer-based training.

Gagné, Robert M., Briggs, Leslie J., and Wager, Walter W. (1992). **Principles of instructional design**. 4th ed. Harcourt Brace Jovanovich College Publishers, 7555 Caldwell Ave., Chicago, IL 60648. 384pp. Price not available. Drawing on a strong base in cognitive psychology and information processing theory, this comprehensive text describes a rationally consistent basis for instructional design that will prepare teachers to design and develop a course, unit, and module of instruction.

Greer, Michael. (1991). **ID project management**. Educational Technology Publications, 700 Palisade Ave., Englewood Cliffs, NJ 07632. $34.95 prepaid. Presents a management model and 37 different tools to help ID managers plan and complete projects.

Harel, Idit, and Papert, Seymour, eds. (1991). **Constructionism**. Ablex Publishing Corp., 355 Chestnut St., Norwood, NJ 07648. 460pp. Cloth $75.50, paper $37.50, prepaid. A collection of papers on constructionism, the paradigm for learning research followed by the Epistemology and Learning Group at the MIT Media Lab.

Leshin, Cynthia B., Pollock, Joellyn, and Reigeluth, Charles M. (1992). **Instructional design strategies and tactics**. Educational Technology Publications, 700 Palisade Ave., Englewood Cliffs, NJ 07632. $34.95 prepaid. This book extends the traditional instructional systems development models by emphasizing guidance for the selection and use of instructional strategies and tactics.

Reynolds, Angus, and Anderson, Ronald H. (1992). **Selecting and developing media for instruction. 3d ed.** Van Nostrand Reinhold, 115 Fifth Ave., New York, NY 10003. 270pp. Paper, $34.95. Includes decision charts providing a thorough and systematic process for the selection of media, suggesting optimum delivery systems while allowing for situational variables.

ERIC Documents

Anglin, Gary J., and Towers, Robert L. (1991, February). **Citation networks of selected instructional design and technology journals, 1985-1990**. Paper presented at the Annual Convention of the Association for Educational Communications and Technology, Orlando, FL, February 13-17, 1991. 20pp. ED 334 970. A study of the patterns of communication in the field of instructional technology based on the reference lists for each article or review in three journals over a five-year period.

Cafarella, Edward P., and Sachs, Steven G. (1991, February). **Doctoral dissertation research in instructional design and technology from 1976 through 1988**. Paper presented at the Annual Convention of the Association for Educational Communications and Technology, Orlando, FL, February 13-17, 1991. 13pp. ED 334 977. Presents several analyses of doctoral dissertation research in instruction design and technology, including a historical analysis and a comparison of prolific ID&T programs.

Gustafson, Kent L., and Powell, Gary C. (1991). **A survey of instructional development models with an annotated ERIC bibliography. 2d ed.** Syracuse, N.Y.: ERIC Clearinghouse on Information Resources. 77pp. ED 335 027. (Also available from Information Resources Publications, 030 Huntington Hall, Syracuse University, Syracuse, NY 13244-2340. $7.50 plus $2 shipping and handling.) Presents a definition of instructional development (ID), a taxonomy for classifying ID models, and descriptions of 11 specific models.

Orey, Michael A., et al. (1991, February). **Integrating cognitive theory into Gagné's instructional events**. Paper presented at the Annual Convention of the Association for Educational Communications and Technology, Orlando, FL, February 13-17, 1991. 10pp. ED 335 004. This paper explores the possibility of integrating cognitive theory into an established instructional development model, i.e., Gagné's nine events of instruction.

Russell, Daniel M., and Kelley, Loretta. (1991, April). **Using IDE in instructional design through automated design tools**. Paper presented at the Annual Conference of the American Educational Research Association, Chicago, IL, April 3-7, 1991. 10pp. ED 332 688. Evaluates the incorporation of a computer-assisted instruction tool for instructional design into mathematics instruction in the Stanford Teacher Education Program.

Schlenk, George W., and Shrock, Sharon A. (1991, February). **The use of instructional development procedures to create exhibits: A survey of major American museums.** Paper presented at the Annual Convention of the Association for Educational Communications and Technology, Orlando, FL, February 13-17, 1991. 16pp. ED 335 012. Reports on the nature of instructional development at museums, including findings on the exhibit development process and the role of instructional developers.

Seels, Barbara, and Glasgow, Z. (1991, February). **Survey of instruction design needs and competencies.** Paper presented at the Annual Convention of the Association for Educational Communications and Technology, Orlando, FL, February 13-17, 1991. 11pp. ED 335 026. A survey designed to obtain information on jobs and task requirements for instructional design professionals and relate positions in the field to academic programs.

Spector, J. Michael, et al. (1991, April). **Modeling user interactions with instructional design software.** Paper presented at the Annual Meeting of the American Educational Research Association, Chicago, IL April 3-7, 1991. 22pp. ED 332 695. Reports on a software evaluation study as one of a series of studies being conducted to develop a predictive model of the instructional design process that is appropriate to military technical training settings.

Journal Articles

Beck, Charles R. (1991, March). Strategies for cueing visual information: Research findings and instructional design implications. **Educational Technology, 31**(3), 16-20. EJ 423 417. (Available UMI.) Describes a series of studies of fourth graders that investigated the cueing effectiveness of seven variables for use with visual information.

Brinkley, Robert, et al. (1991). Designing and producing courseware for distance learning instruction in higher education. **TechTrends, 36**(1), 50-54. EJ 423 407. (Available UMI.) Describes a nine-step method for the design and production of instructional television courses used for distance learning instruction in higher education.

Hlynka, Denis. (1991, June). Postmodern excursions into educational technology. **Educational Technology, 31**(6), 27-30. EJ 430 237. (Available UMI.) Explains postmodernism, the systems approach to instructional design, and the relationship between the psychological paradigm of constructivism and the aesthetic paradigm of poststructuralism.

Hudspeth, DeLayne R. (1991). Interactivity and design of case materials. **Performance Improvement Quarterly, 4**(1), 63-72. EJ 427 481. Discusses the functions of case materials, the potential for interaction, instructional needs, elements of interaction, and levels and formats of case materials.

Keeps, Erica J. (1991). Selecting and writing case studies for improving human performance. **Performance Improvement Quarterly, 4**(1), 43-54. EJ 427 480. Describes critical and variable attributes of case studies, suggests guidelines for creating a case, and presents criteria for evaluating a case study.

Knirk, Frederick G. (1991). Case materials: Research and practice. **Performance Improvement Quarterly, 4**(1), 73-81. EJ 427 482. Identifies sources of information and research about the effectiveness of case studies, examples of their use, and design considerations.

Okey, James R., and Santiago, Rowena S. (1991). Integrating instructional motivational design. **Performance Improvement Quarterly, 4**(2), 11-21. EJ 430 260. Describes Keller's ARCS model of motivational design and Gagné's instructional design theory. Explains how they can be integrated and used by instructional developers and designers.

Stepich, Don. (1991, July). From novice to expert: Implications for instructional design. **Performance and Instruction, 30**(6), 13-17. EJ 430 280. (Available UMI.) Discusses instructional strategies that can be used in any skill domain and uses Gagné's conditions of learning as a model to suggest internal and external conditions of expertise.

LIBRARIES AND MEDIA CENTERS

Media-Related Periodicals

Braille Book Review. Library of Congress, National Library Service for the Blind and Physically Handicapped, Washington, DC 20542. bi-mo.; free to qualified persons. In braille or in print. Announces braille books and magazines available to readers and includes information about developments and activities in library services to the handicapped.

Collection Building. Neal-Schuman, 23 Leonard St., New York, NY 10013. q.; $55. Focuses on all aspects of collection building, ranging from microcomputers to business collections to popular topics and censorship.

Computers in Libraries. Meckler Publishing, 11 Ferry Ln. W., Westport, CT 06880-5808. mo.; $65. Practical applications of microcomputers to library situations are covered, as are recent news items, in this newsletter-type journal.

Electronic Library. Learned Information, Inc., 143 Old Marlton Pike, Medford, NJ 08055. bi-mo.; $95. For librarians and information center managers interested in microcomputer and library automation. Features industry news and product announcements.

Emergency Librarian. Dyad Services, P.O. Box C34069, Dept. 284, Seattle WA 98124-1069; or P.O. Box 46258, Station G, Vancouver, BC V6R 4G6, Canada. bi-mo. (except July-August); $45. Articles, review columns, and critical analyses of management and programming issues for children's and young adult librarians.

Journal of Academic Librarianship. Mountainside Publishing, 321 S. Main St., Box 8330, Ann Arbor, MI 48107. bi-mo.; $27 indiv., $49 inst. Results of significant research, issues and problems facing academic libraries, book reviews, and innovations in academic libraries.

Journal of Librarianship and Information Science. Bailey Bros. and Swinfen, Ltd., Warner House, Boules Well Gardens, Folkestone, Kent CT19 6PH, England. q.; $99. Deals with all aspects of library and information work in the United Kingdom and reviews literature from international sources.

Library and Information Science Abstracts. Library Association Publishing, Bailey Bros. and Swinfen Ltd., Warner House, Boules Well Gardens, Folkestone, Kent CT19 6PH, England. mo.; $499. Over 500 abstracts per issue from over 500 periodicals, reports, books, and conference proceedings.

Library and Information Science Research. Ablex Publishing Corp., 355 Chestnut St., Norwood, NJ 07648. q.; $75. Research articles, dissertation reviews, and book reviews on issues concerning information resources management.

Library Computer Systems & Equipment Review. Meckler Publishing, 11 Ferry Ln. W., Westport, CT 06880-5808. semi-ann.; $195. Features articles on automated systems for library and applications. Each issue focuses on one topic.

Library Hi Tech Journal. Pierian Press, Box 1808, Ann Arbor, MI 48106. q.; $40 indiv., $65 inst. Concentrates on reporting on the selection, installation, maintenance, and integration of systems and hardware.

Library Hi Tech News. Pierian Press, Box 1808, Ann Arbor, MI 48106. 10/yr.; $70 indiv., $95 inst. News and ideas about technology related to library operations, database developments, and annotated bibliographies.

Library Journal. R. R. Bowker, Box 1977, Marion, OH 43305-1977. 20/yr.; $69. A professional periodical for librarians with current issues and news, professional reading, lengthy book review section, and classifieds.

Library Quarterly. University of Chicago Press, Box 37005, Chicago, IL 60637. q.; $23 indiv., $35 inst. Scholarly articles of interest to librarians.

Library Software Review. Meckler Publishing Corp., 11 Ferry Ln. W., Westport, CT 06880. bi-mo.; $115. Articles on software evaluation, procurement, applications, and installation decisions.

Library Trends. University of Illinois, Graduate School of Library and Information Science, 249 Armory Bldg., 505 E. Armory St., Champaign, IL 61820. q.; $60. Each issue is concerned with one aspect of library and information science, analyzing current thought and practice and examining ideas that hold the greatest potential for the field.

Microcomputers for Information Management. Ablex Publishing Corp., 355 Chestnut St., Norwood, NJ 07648. q.; $34.50 indiv., $85 inst. Focuses on new developments with microcomputer technology in libraries and in information science in the United States and abroad.

Public Libraries. Public Library Association, American Library Association, 50 E. Huron St., Chicago, IL 60611. 6/yr.; $45. News and articles of interest to public librarians.

Public Library Quarterly. Haworth Press, 10 Alice St., Binghamton, NY 13904. q.; $36 indiv., $80 inst. Serves as a forum for discussion of issues relating to public library administration, research, and practice.

School Library Journal. Box 1978, Marion, OH 43305-1978. mo.; $59. For school and youth service librarians. Contains about 2,500 critical book reviews annually.

School Library Media Activities Monthly. LMS Associates, 17 E. Henrietta St., Baltimore, MD 21230. mo.; $44. A vehicle for distributing ideas for teaching library media skills and for the development and implementation of library media skills programs.

School Library Media Quarterly. American Association of School Librarians, American Library Association, 50 E. Huron St., Chicago, IL 60611. q.; $40. For library media specialists, district supervisors, and others concerned with the selection and purchase of print and nonprint media and with the development of programs and services for preschool through high school libraries.

The Unabashed Librarian. Box 2631, New York, NY 10116. q.; $20. Down-to-earth library items: procedures, forms, programs, cataloging, booklists, software reviews.

Wilson Library Bulletin. H. W. Wilson Co., 950 University Ave., Bronx, NY 10452. mo. (except July and August); $46. Significant articles on librarianship, news, and reviews of films, books, and professional literature.

Books

Costa, Betty, and Costa, Marie. (1991). **A micro handbook for small libraries and media centers. 3d ed.** Libraries Unlimited, P.O. Box 6633, Englewood, CO 80155-6633. 444pp., $27. A complete guide for small libraries beginning the automation process or adding new features to their systems. Covers planning, hardware and software choices, applications, networking, and computer ethics.

Smith, Jane Bandy, and Coleman, J. Gordon, eds. (1991). **School library media annual 1991**. Libraries Unlimited, P.O. Box 6633, Englewood, CO 80155-6633. 301pp. $34.50. A tool for every school media specialist, this volume contains essays on topics in continuing education and the challenge of change, as well as information on the events of the year, professional association activities, award-winning publications, and an index to 1990 journal literature.

Weihs, Jean. **The integrated library: Encouraging access to multimedia materials. 2d ed.** Oryx Press, 4041 N. Central, Phoenix, AZ 85012. $27.50 prepaid. Explores the procedure for integrating book and nonbook materials together in a browsing collection to make the best and most useful materials available to the largest number of patrons.

Video

Information 2000: Library and information services for the 21st century. (1991). Superintendent of Documents, U.S. Government Printing Office, Washington, DC 20402. (202) 783-3238. $6 plus shipping and handling. Also available from Encyclopaedia Brittanica Educational Corp., 310 S. Michigan Ave., Chicago, IL. (800) 554-9862. $20 plus $4 shipping and handling. This 20-minute production is the official video of the 1991 White House Conference on Library and Information Services.

ERIC Documents

Eisenberg, Michael B., et al. (1990). **Trends and issues in library and information science 1990**. Syracuse, N.Y.: ERIC Clearinghouse on Information Resources. 75pp. ED 335 061. Also available from Information Resources Publications, 030 Huntington Hall, Syracuse University, Syracuse, NY 13244-2340. $7.50 plus $2 shipping and handling. This synthesis paper provides a state-of-the-art analysis of the field of library and information science based on a content analysis of the literature for 1990.

Federal Pre-White House Conference on Library and Information Services proceedings. (1991, February). Conference held in Bethesda, MD, November 26-27, 1990. Washington, D.C.: Federal Library and Information Center Committee. 134pp. ED 331 515. Presents the recommendations and proceedings of the Federal Pre-Conference, including a discussion of 13 issues of high national priority and a directory of national delegates.

Information 2000: Library and information services for the 21st century. Summary report of the 1991 White House Conference on Library and Information Services. (1991). Washington, D.C.: National Commission on Library and Information Science. 78pp. ED 341 399. Also available from U.S. Government Printing Office, Superintendent of Documents, Washington, DC 20402. This report contains the 95 policy recommendations adopted by the conference as well as the delegation's 15 priority proposals.

White, Charles S. (1991, May). **Information technology and the informed citizen: New challenges for government and libraries. ERIC digest.** Syracuse, N.Y.: ERIC Clearinghouse on Information Resources; and Bloomington, Ind.: ERIC Clearinghouse for Social Studies/Social Science Education. 4pp. ED 331 528. Arguing that the foundation of a free civilization is an informed citizenry, this digest discusses the new challenges faced by the government and libraries in the Information Age.

Journal Articles

Barron, Daniel D. (1991, January). Ethics, the school library media specialist, and copyright. **School Library Media Activities Monthly,** 7(5), 48-50. EJ 420 386. Discusses ethics and the school curriculum, the librarian's code of ethics, and the need to educate teachers as well as students about copyright law.

Boykin, Joseph. (1991, Winter). Library automation, 1970-1990: From the few to the many. **Library Administration and Management,** 5(1), 10-15. EJ 421 764. (Available UMI.) Discusses key developments in library automation in such areas as bibliographic utilities, local online systems, commercial integrated systems, CD-ROM, and facsimile.

Dennis, Nancy, and Stadthaus, Alice. (1991, January). Teaching information technologies in a classroom setting. **Computers in Libraries,** 11(1), 17-19. EJ 423 390. (Available UMI.) Describes an undergraduate course that was developed at Salem State College to provide students with an overview of information technologies, including online databases, online catalogs, CD-ROM, hypertext, interactive video, electronic bulletin boards, and computer networks.

Forsslund, Titti. (1991). Factors that influence the use and impact of educational television in school. **Journal of Educational Television, 17**(1), 15-30. EJ 427 483. Discusses access to video recorders, program series, support materials, relation of ETV to the curriculum, attitudes toward ETV, cultural differences, and strategies for using ETV.

Jackson, Mary E. (1991, January-February). Copyright, libraries and media centers. **Media and Methods, 27**(3), 34, 36. EJ 421 706. (Available UMI.) Discusses the concept of fair use, conditions that permit copyrighted materials to be used in the classroom, and licensing and duplication rights.

Neuman, Delia. (1991, March). Designing library instruction for undergraduates: Combing instructional systems design and naturalistic inquiry. **College and Research Libraries, 52**(2), 165-76. EJ 424 841. (Available UMI.) Reports on the formative evaluation of MAJIK/1, a HyperCard program delivering basic, individualized library instruction to college students.

Smith, Eldred. (1991, May). Resolving the acquisitions dilemma: Into the electronic information environment. **College and Research Libraries, 52**(3), 231-40. EJ 427 506. (Available UMI.) Discusses electronic communication as a possible solution to the serials pricing crisis in academic libraries.

TELECOMMUNICATION SYSTEMS

Media-Related Periodicals

Canadian Journal of Educational Communication. Association for Media and Technology in Education in Canada, 3-1750 The Queensway, Suite 1318, Etobicoke, Ontario, M9C 5H5, Canada. 3/yr.; $55 nonmembers.

Computer Communications. Butterworth-Heinemann, Ltd., Turpin Transactions, Ltd., Distribution Centre, Blackhorse Rd., Letchworth, Herts SG6 1HM, England. 10/yr.; £178. Focuses on networking and distributed computing techniques, communications hardware and software, and standardization.

Data Communications. McGraw-Hill, Inc., 1221 Ave. of the Americas, New York, NY 10020. mo.; $33. Provides users with news and analysis of changing technology for the networking of computers.

EDUCOM Review. EDUCOM, 1112 16th St. NW, Suite 600, Washington, DC 20036-4823. q.; $40. Features articles on current issues and applications of computing and communications technology in higher education. Reports of EDUCOM consortium activities.

Electronic Networking: Research, Applications, and Policy. Meckler Corp., 11 Ferry Ln. W., Westport, CT 06880. q.; $95. A cross-disciplinary journal presenting research findings related to electronic networks, analyses of policy issues related to networking, and descriptions of current and potential applications of electronic networking for communication, computation, and provision of information services.

EMMS: Electronic Mail & Micro Systems. International Resource Development, Inc., Box 1716, New Canaan, CT 06840. semi-mo.; $535. Up-to-the-minute coverage of new technological products and market trends in facsimile, office communications, and record and graphic communications.

Networking Management. Penn Well Publishing Co., Box 2417, Tulsa, OK 74101-2417. mo.; $39, free to qualified individuals. Covers issues and applications for planning, support, and management of voice data networks.

Telecommunications. Horizon House Publications, Inc., 685 Canton St., Norwood, MA 02062. mo.; $60, single copies $7.50, free to qualified individuals. Feature articles and news for the field of telecommunications.

Books

McClure, Charles R., Bishop, Ann P., Doty, Philip, and Rosenbaum, Howard. (1991). **The National Research and Education Network (NREN): Research and policy perspectives**. Ablex Publishing Corp., 355 Chestnut St., Norwood, NJ 07648. 743pp. $45 indiv., $95 inst. Provides an overview and status report on the progress made in developing a national research and education network; reports on a number of investigations that provide a research and policy perspective on the NREN and computer-mediated communication; brings together key source documents that have directed the development of the NREN.

Okerson, Ann, ed. (1991). **Directory of electronic journals, newsletters and academic discussion lists**. Office of Scientific and Academic Publishing, Association of Research Libraries, 1527 New Hampshire Ave. NW, Washington, DC 20036. (202) 232-2466. 173pp. This publication celebrates the coming of age of the electronic network as a medium used vigorously and enthusiastically by scholars, researchers, academics, and others connected to the scholarly process.

Waggoner, Michael D. (1992). **Empowering networks: Computer conferencing in education**. Educational Technology Publications, 700 Palisade Ave., Englewood Cliffs, NJ 07632. $34.95 prepaid. Highlights various examples of computer-based telecommunications employed in education, including teacher training, continuing education to rural and special populations, and research collaborations.

ERIC Documents

Johnson, Dell. (1991, May). **The future of electronic educational networks: Some ethical issues**. 15pp. ED 332 689. Discusses privacy, equal access, security, and ethical issues surrounding growing use of educational communication networks such as the Internet.

Sheekey, Arthur D., ed. (1991, May). **Education policy and telecommunications technologies**. Washington, D.C.: Department of Education, Office of Educational Research and Improvement. 92pp. ED 331 497. A collection of papers focusing on the critical issues associated with the application of new telecommunications technologies for improving elementary and secondary education.

Wishnietsky, Dan H. (1991). **Using electronic mail in an educational setting. Fastback 316.** Bloomington, Ind.: Phi Delta Kappa Educational Foundation. 39pp. ED 333 865. Discusses the growing use of electronic mail/message systems among administrators, teachers, staff, and students in K-12 schools.

Journal Articles

Hall, Stephen C. (1991, Spring). The four stages of National Research and Education Network growth. **EDUCOM Review, 26**(1), 18-25. EJ 426 067. Describes stages in the growth of NREN from 1970 to 2015 and discusses finances, prospects for management and users, and suggestions for future growth.

Katz, James E., and Graveman, Richard F. (1991). Privacy issues of a National Research and Education Network. **Telematics and Informatics, 8**(1-2), 71-120. Discussion of privacy needs in scientific and education communications, network security, and protection strategies.

Updegrove, Daniel. (1991, April). Electronic mail in education. **Educational Technology, 31**(4), 37-40. EJ 427 486. (Available UMI.) National and international academic networks are described and uses of electronic mail for faculty, administrators, and students are examined.

Weingarten, Fred. (1991, Spring). Five steps to NREN enlightenment. **EDUCOM Review, 26**(1), 26-30. EJ 426 068. A discussion of NREN, focusing on balancing the needs of a wider user constituency with those of the more technical scientific community.

TELEVISION AND CHILDREN*

ERIC Documents

Comstock, George, and Paik, Hae-Jung. (1987). **Television and children: A review of recent research.** Syracuse, N.Y.: ERIC Clearinghouse on Information Resources. 71pp. ED 292 466. (Available from Information Resources Publications, 030 Huntington Hall, Syracuse University, Syracuse, NY 13244-2340. $6.50 plus $2 shipping and handling.) This review of recent empirical research on the effects of television on children and teenagers finds that experts generally agree that television harms formal scholastic achievement while providing general knowledge; that it has contributed to misperceptions about sex roles, ethnic groups, and politics; that it has increased aggressive behavior; and that it has increased the degree to which children behave as consumers.

*This section is based on a minibibliography prepared by Nancy Preston, User Services Coordinator, ERIC Clearinghouse on Information Resources, Syracuse University, 030 Huntington Hall, Syracuse, NY 13244-2340. (315) 443-3640. January 1992.

This publication was prepared with funding from the Office of Educational Research and Improvement, U.S. Department of Education, under contract no. R188062008. The opinions expressed in this bibliography do not necessarily reflect the positions or policies of OERI or ED.

Kunkel, Dale. (1988, October). **Children and television advertising: Can the marketplace protect the public interest?** Paper presented at the Telecommunications Policy Research Conference, Warrenton, VA, October 30-November 1, 1988. 30pp. ED 305 040. This report surveys the basic research on how children understand and respond to television advertising messages in order to determine whether regulation is necessary. The implications of the research findings for likely marketplace developments in an unregulated environment are discussed; it is concluded that there is no sound basis to expect that unregulated marketplace mechanisms will effectively limit the amount of advertising aimed at children.

St. Peters, Michelle, et al. (1989, April). **Television and families: Parental coviewing and young children's language development, social behavior, and television processing**. Paper presented at the Biennial Meeting of the Society for Research in Child Development, Kansas City, MO, April 27-30, 1989. 26pp. ED 312 040. A study investigated several questions concerning the amount of viewing and types of programs children and parents watched alone and together and the relation of viewing patterns to children's development. The paucity of findings favoring positive developmental outcomes from coviewing suggests that family viewing time is not used as an occasion for beneficial or instructional interactions.

TV tips for parents: Using television to help your child learn. (1988). Washington, D.C.: Corporation for Public Broadcasting. 24pp. ED 299 948. This booklet is designed to help parents redirect their children's television viewing to higher quality programs. Tips include: (1) set your child's television schedule; (2) get involved; (3) do not be concerned if children of differing ages will be watching at the same time; (4) make public television a "special friend" for children who are at home alone; (5) consult your child's teacher and other available resources; (6) use television to spur an interest in reading; (7) use television to promote writing; (8) help your child to explore the world, on-screen and off; (9) help children see math as fun and practical; and (10) set your own pace for family involvement.

Journal Articles

Cecil, Nancy Lee. (1988, April). Help children become more critical TV watchers. **PTA Today, 13**(6), 12-14. EJ 372 807. (Available UMI.) Watching television is not necessarily a bad habit, and when parents monitor their children's viewing habits, it can prove educational. Ways parents might teach their children to view television programs and commercials critically are suggested.

Christopher, F. Scott, et al. (1989, April). Family television viewing: Implications for family life education. **Family Relations, 38**(2), 210-14. EJ 396 313. (Available UMI.) Parents were interviewed to investigate the interrelationship of family television viewing and family interaction, and to explore the different approaches families take towards television. Parental attitudes about children's viewing were found to be moderately related to family interaction. Results suggest that educators need to attend to families' attitudes about television.

Huston, Aletha, C., et al. (1990, May). Development of television viewing patterns in early childhood: A longitudinal investigation. **Developmental Psychology, 26**(3), 409-20. EJ 412 179. (Available UMI.) A two-year study concludes that cognitive and developmental changes are less important determinants of children's television use than are family patterns and external variables affecting the opportunity to view.

NAEYC Position Statement on media violence in children's lives. (1990, July). **Young Children, 45**(5), 18-21. EJ 415 397. (Available UMI.) States the position of the National Association for the Education of Young Children on violence in children's programming. Presents research upon which the statement is based, as well as recommendations for policymakers, teachers, and parents.

Neuman, Susan B. (1988, Fall). The displacement effect: Assessing the relation between television viewing and reading performance. **Reading Research Quarterly, 23**(4), 414-40. EJ 378 640. (Available UMI.) Examines television's impact on reading and school achievement in terms of the displacement hypothesis (watching television displaces developmental reading activities). Indicates small differences in reading scores for children watching two to four hours a day, but beyond four hours effects are negative and increasingly deleterious.

Notar, Ellen. (1989, Winter). Children and TV commercials: "Wave after wave of exploitation." **Childhood Education, 66**(2), 66-67. EJ 401 261. (Available UMI.) Maintains that parents and educators should watch what children watch on television, especially commercials. Parents and educators should teach children to critically observe and analyze the messages and assumptions of television commercials.

Reinking, David, and Wu, Jen-Huey. (1990, Winter). Reexamining the research on television and reading. **Reading Research and Instruction, 29**(2), 30-43. EJ 406 700. (Available UMI.) Updates earlier reviews of the research investigating how television viewing and reading might be related. Points out new directions in the research, focusing on research after 1980. Discusses implications for professionals in the field of reading.

VIDEO COMMUNICATION TECHNOLOGIES

Media-Related Periodicals

Broadcasting. Broadcasting Publications, 1705 DeSales St. NW, Washington, DC 20036. w.; $70. All-inclusive newsweekly for radio, television, cable, and allied business.

CableVision. Cable Publishing Group, 600 S. Cherry St., Suite 400, Denver, CO 80222. 26/yr.; $55. A newsmagazine for the cable television industry. Covers programming, marketing, advertising, business, and other topics.

Communication Abstracts. Sage Publications, Inc., 2455 Teller Rd., Newbury Park, CA 91320. bi-mo.; $98 indiv., $295 inst. Abstracts communication-related articles, reports, books; cumulative annual index.

Communication Booknotes. Center for Advanced Study in Telecommunications (CAST), Ohio State University, 210 Baker Systems, 1971 Neil Ave., Columbus, OH. bi-mo.; $45. Newsletter that reviews books and periodicals about mass media, telecommunications, and information policy.

Communication News. Nelson Publishing, 2504 N. Tamiami Trail, Nokomis, FL 34275. mo.; $27. Up-to-date information from around the world regarding voice, video, and data communications.

Federal Communications Commission Reports. Superintendent of Documents, Government Printing Office, Washington, DC 20402. w.; price varies. Decisions, public notices, and other documents pertaining to FCC activities.

Historical Journal of Film, Radio, and Television. Carfax Publishing Co., P.O. Box 25, Abington, Oxfordshire OX14 3VE, England. 3/yr.; $270. Articles by international experts in the field, news and notices, and book reviews.

Journal of Broadcasting and Electronic Media. Broadcast Education Association, 1771 N St. NW, Washington, DC 20036. q.; $40. Includes articles, book reviews, research reports, and analyses. Provides a forum for research relating to telecommunications and related fields.

Journal of Educational Television. Carfax Publishing Co., P.O. Box 25, Abingdon, Oxfordshire OX14 3VE, England. 3/yr.; $270. This journal of the Educational Television Association serves as an international forum for discussions and reports on developments in the field of television and related media in teaching, learning, and training.

Journal of Popular Film and Television. Heldref Publications, 4000 Albemarle St. NW, Washington, DC 20016. q.; $24. Articles on film and television, book reviews, and theory.

Journal of Visual Literacy. (Formerly **Journal of Visual/Verbal Languaging**). International Visual Literacy Association, c/o Ann DeVaney, ed., University of Wisconsin, 225 N. Mills St., Madison, WI 53706. semi-ann.; $10 members, $25 nonmembers. Concerned with the study of visual language and visual literacy and their interaction with verbal communication.

Media International. Reed Publishing Services, 7-11 St. John's Hill, London SW11 1TR, England. mo.; $95. Contains features on the world's major media developments and regional news reports from the international media scene.

Optical Information Systems Magazine. Meckler Publishing, 11 Ferry Ln. W., Westport, CT 06880-5808. bi-mo.; $115. Features articles on the applications of videodisc, optical disc, and teletext systems; future implications; system and software compatibilities; and cost comparisons. Also tracks videodisc projects and covers world news.

Optical Information Systems Update. Meckler Publishing, 11 Ferry Ln. W., Westport, CT 06880-5808. 12/yr.; $277. A newsletter with news and facts about technology, software, courseware developments, calendar, conference reports, and job listings.

Telematics and Informatics. Pergamon Press, Inc., Journals Division, Maxwell House, Fairview Park, Elmsford, NY 10523. q.; $280. Intended for the specialist in telecommunications and information science. Covers the merging of computer and telecommunications technologies worldwide.

Video-Tronics. (Formerly **Video**.) Video Publishing Co. Pty. Ltd., 762 Victoria Rd., Ryde, N.S.W. 2112, Australia. q.; $18. Devoted to video equipment, videotapes, video recordings, and the video environment.

Video Review. Viare Publishing Corp., Box 57751, Boulder, CO 80322-7751. mo.; $15.97. Emphasizes how-to articles. Also reviews news items and equipment test reviews.

Video Systems. Intertec Publishing Corp., 9221 Quivera Rd., Box 12901, Overland Park, KS 66212-9981. mo.; $45. Edited for video professionals. Contains articles such as state-of-the-art audio and video technology reports, how-to ideas on equipment and facilities, and production techniques.

The Videodisc Monitor. Future Systems, Inc., Box 26, Falls Church, VA 22040. mo.; $277. Current events in the videodisc marketplace and in training and development are described in this journal.

Videography. United Newspapers Publications, Inc., 2 Park Ave., 4th floor, New York, NY 10016. mo.; $25. For the video professional; covers techniques, applications, equipment, technology, and video art.

Books

Bergman, Robert E., and Moore, Thomas V. (1991). **Managing interactive video/multimedia projects**. Educational Technology Publications, 700 Palisade Ave., Englewood Cliffs, NJ 07632. $39.95 prepaid. A guide to the management of interactive video/multimedia projects, covering topics such as estimating times and costs, evaluating deliverables, understanding development documentation, and working with vendors.

Comstock, George, and Paik, Haejung. (1991). **Television and the American child**. Academic Press, Inc., 465 S. Lincoln Dr., Troy, MO 63379. 386pp. $39.95 prepaid. A comprehensive examination of the research conducted by behavioral scientists over the last 40 years on the influence of television on the lives of American children and adolescents.

McAleese, Ray, ed. **Hypertext: Theory into practice**. (1989). Ablex Publishing Corp., 355 Chestnut St., Norwood, NJ 07648. 192pp. $32.50 prepaid. An introduction to hypertext practice covering practical aspects as well as a wide variety of interpretations of hypertext theory.

McAleese, Ray, and Green, Catherine, eds. (1990). **Hypertext: State of the art**. Ablex Publishing Corp., 355 Chestnut St., Norwood, NJ 07648. 280pp. $39.50 prepaid. A sequel to *Hypertext: Theory into practice*, this volume covers applications of hypertext, usability, interfaces, knowledge representation, and authoring.

Videodisc Compedium 1991-92. Emerging Technology Consultants, Inc., P.O. Box 120444, St. Paul, MN 55112. $30 plus shipping and handling. Descriptions of over 1,800 videodiscs, related software, and CD titles in the field of education and training.

ERIC Documents

Arnone, Marilyn Plavocos, and Grabowski, Barbara L. (1991, February). **Effects of variations in learner control on children's curiosity and learning from interactive video**. Paper presented at the Annual Convention of the Association for Educational Communications and Technology, Orlando, FL, February 13-17, 1991. 24pp. ED 334 972. Reports on the use of a videodisc program in art education to measure learner outcomes among groups in three experimental conditions: designer control, learner control, and learner control with advisement.

Lowry, William H., and Thorkildsen, Ron. (1991, February). **Implementation levels of a videodisc-based mathematics program and achievement**. Paper presented at the Annual Convention of the Association for Educational Communications and Technology, Orlando, FL, February 13-17, 1991. 20pp. ED 334 994. This study addressed the question of whether the level of student achievement differs across levels of implementation of a mediated program that is based on a well-defined instructional model.

Misanchuk, Earl R., and Schwier, Richard. (1991, February). **Interactive media audit trails: Approaches and issues**. Paper presented at the Annual Convention of the Association for Educational Communications and Technology, Orlando, FL, February 13-17, 1991. 26pp. ED 334 996. A discussion of uses for audit trails in instructional research, focusing on the determination of the effects of taking different paths through instruction.

Journal Articles

Burwell, Lawrence B. (1991, March). The interaction of learning styles with learner control treatments in an interactive videodisc lesson. **Educational Technology, 31**(3), 37-43. EJ 423 418. (Available UMI.) This discussion of learning styles and learner control focuses on a study of college students that paired field-dependent and field-independent learning styles with different instructional control treatments.

Cockayne, Susan. (1991, February). Effects of small group sizes on learning with interactive videodisc. **Educational Technology, 31**(2), 43-45. EJ 423 364. (Available UMI.) Describes a study of undergraduates that compared the effects of different small group sizes on learner achievement using computer-controlled interactive videodisc.

Jensen, Eric. (1991, March). HyperCard and AppleShare help at-risk students. **Computing Teacher, 18**(6), 26-29. EJ 423 421. (Available UMI.) Describes the Knowledge Gateway Project, a program that emphasizes intensive use of computer technology to help at-risk high school students.

Louie, Ray, et al. (1991, May-June). Interactive video: Disseminating vital science and math information. **Media and Methods, 27**(5), 22-23. EJ 430 219. (Available UMI.) Describes the use of interactive videodiscs for science and math instruction, and discusses student attitudes, facility planning, time management, and accommodating individual needs.

Mathisen, Ralph W. (1991, May). Interactive multimedia and education: Specifications, standards, and applications. **Collegiate Microcomputer, 9**(2), 93-102. EJ 430 242. (Available UMI.) Provides a general overview of multimedia and its significance in educational applications.

McNeil, Barbara J., and Nelson, Karyn R. (1991, Winter). Meta-analysis of interactive video instruction: A 10 year review of achievement effects. **Journal of Computer-Based Instruction, 18**(1), 1-6. EJ 427 477. (Available UMI.) Describes a quantitative study that examined the effectiveness of interactive video instruction by using a meta-analytic research review of the literature.

Schiller, Scott S. (1991, March-April). Educational applications of instructional television and cable programming. **Media and Methods, 27**(4), 20-21, 52. EJ 423 427. (Available UMI.) Describes the use of instructional television and cable programming in Prince George's County public schools and discusses operation of and programming for an educational access channel.

Index

This index gives page locations of names of associations and organizations, authors, titles, and subjects (bold entries indicate subjects). In addition, acronyms for all organizations and associations are cross-referenced to the full name. Please note that a classified list of U.S. organizations and associations appears on pages 163 to 169.

A&E (television), 114
A&E Classroom (television program), 16
AACJC. *See* American Association of Community and Junior Colleges
AAP. *See* Association of American Publishers
AASA. *See* American Association of School Administrators
AASL. *See* American Association of School Librarians
AAVT. *See* Association of Audio-Visual Technicians
Academy of Motion Picture Arts and Sciences , 170
ACCESS ERIC, 190
ACCESS NETWORK (Canada), 215
ACE. *See* Association for Computer Educators
ACEI. *See* Association for Childhood Education International
ACHE. *See* Association for Continuing Higher Education
ACRL. *See* Association of College and Research Libraries
ADCIS. *See* Association for the Development of Computer-Based Instructional Systems
Addison, Roger, 49
ADJ/AR. *See* Adjunct ERIC Clearinghouse for Art Education
ADJ/CN. *See* Adjunct ERIC Clearinghouse for United States-Japan Studies
ADJ/Chapter 1. *See* Adjunct ERIC Clearinghouse on Chapter 1
ADJ/JS. *See* Adjunct ERIC Clearinghouse on Consumer Education
ADJ/LE. *See* Adjunct ERIC Clearinghouse on Literacy Education for Limited-English- Proficient Adults
Adjunct ERIC Clearinghouse for Art Education, 191
Adjunct ERIC Clearinghouse for United States-Japan Studies, 191
Adjunct ERIC Clearinghouse on Chapter 1, 191
Adjunct ERIC Clearinghouse on Consumer Education, 191
Adjunct ERIC Clearinghouse on Literacy Education for Limited English-Proficient Adults, 191

"Adult Learner Motivations and Electronic Distance Education," 327
AECT. *See* Association for Educational Communications and Technology
AECT Annual Conference and Earl F. Strobehn Internship Award, 293, 298
AECT Leadership Development Grants, 293, 300
AECT Memorial Scholarship Award, 294, 301
AECT/SIRS Intellectual Freedom Award, 293, 297
AERA. *See* American Educational Research Association
AFA. *See* American Federation of Arts, The
AFC. *See* Anthropology Film Center
AFE. *See* Association for Experiential Education
AFVA. *See* American Film and Video Association
Agency for Instructional Technology, 170
Ainkins, Herbert Austin, 119
AIR. *See* American Institutes for Research
AIT. *See* Agency for Instructional Technology
Akeroyd, John, 314
ALA. *See* American Library Association
Alabama, professional education, 218, 240
Alabama State University, 240
ALCTS. *See* Association for Library Collections and Technical Services
ALSC. *See* Association for Library Service to Children
ALTA. *See* American Library Trustee Association
AMA. *See* American Management Association
America 2000, 7, 33
American Association of Community and Junior Colleges, 170
American Association of School Administrators, 170
American Association of School Librarians, 171
American Association of State Colleges and Universities, 170
American Educational Research Association, 8, 171
American Educational Research Journal, 327
American Federation of Arts, The, 171
American Film and Video Association, 171
American Institutes for Research, 150
American Journal of Distance Education, 325
American Library Association, 171